EUI — Series A — 2.2
Cappelletti/Seccombe/Weiler (Gen. Eds.)
Integration Through Law
Vol. 2: Rehbinder/Stewart, Environmental Protection Policy

European University Institute
Institut Universitaire Européen
Europäisches Hochschulinstitut
Istituto Universitario Europeo

Series A

Law/Droit/Recht/Diritto

2.2

Badia Fiesolana — Firenze

Integration Through Law

Europe and the American Federal Experience

A Series under the General Editorship of

Mauro Cappelletti · Monica Seccombe · Joseph Weiler

Volume 2

Environmental Protection Policy

by

Eckard Rehbinder and Richard Stewart

Associate Editor

Patrick Del Duca

1985

Walter de Gruyter · Berlin · New York

Library of Congress Cataloging-in-Publication Data

Main entry under title:

Integration through law.
(Series A, Law / European University Institute = Series A, Droit / Institute Universitaire Européen ; 2.1.-)
Includes index.
Contents: v. 1. Methods, tools, and institutions. bk. 1. A political, legal, and economic overview. bk. 2. Political organs, integration techniques, and judicial process. bk. 3. Forces and potential for a European identity--v. 2. Environmental protection policy / E. Rehbinder and R. Stewart.
1. Law--European Economic Community countries.
2. Law--United States. 3. Federal government.
I. Cappelletti, Mauro. II. Seccombe, Monica. III. Weiler, Joseph, 1951- . IV. Series: Series A--Law ; 2.1, etc.
KJE5075.I58 1985 340'.2 85-16320
ISBN 0-89925-112-9 (U.S. : v. 2) 342

CIP-Kurztitelaufnahme der Deutschen Bibliothek

Integration through law : Europe and the American federal experience a ser. under the general editorship of Mauro Cappelletti ... — Berlin; New York : de Gruyter
(European University Institute : Ser. A, Law; 2)
NE: Cappelletti, Mauro [Hrsg.]; Istituto Universitario Europeo (Fiesole): European University Institute / A
Vol. 2. Environmental protection policy / by Eckard Rehbinder and Richard Stewart. Assoc. ed Patrick Del Duca. — 1985.
ISBN 3-11-010200-5
NE: Rehbinder, Eckard [Mitverf.]

Dust Cover Design: Rudolf Hübler, Berlin. — Setting: Satz-Rechen-Zentrum, Berlin.
Printing: H. Heenemann GmbH & Co., Berlin.
Binding: Verlagsbuchbinderei Dieter Mikolai, Berlin.
Printed in Germany.

General Editors' Foreword

The Florence Integration Through Law Series is the product of a research project centered in the Law Department of the European University Institute, and as such it reflects the research interests of the Department: it is a contextual examination of European legal developments in comparative perspective. In the general introduction to the Series (published in Book One of Volume I), we explained fully the philosophy, methodology and scope of the Project. Here we wish merely to recapitulate some of the principal themes of special relevance to this Volume on Environmental Protection.

The European Legal Integration Project set out to examine the role of law in, and the legal impact of, integration in Europe, using the United States federal system as a comparative point of reference. The Project was conceived and executed in two parts. In Part One (published in Volume I entitled "Methods, Tools and Institutions") a number of teams of American and European scholars examined a wide range of legal techniques and mechanisms for integration and undertook an overall general analysis of law and integration. The first book of Volume I ("A Political, Legal, and Economic Overview") establishes the comparative and interdisciplinary context, providing background studies on the political, legal and economic implications of integration in Europe and America and including studies on other federal systems (Australia, Canada, Germany and Switzerland) to add comparative perspective. The second book ("Political Organs, Integration Techniques, and Judicial Process") analyzes the pre- and post-normative stages, examining the decision-making and implementation problems, and the role of political and judicial organs therein, and describing the various forms of normative techniques available in a federal or supranational context.

The third and final book of Volume I ("Forces and Potential for a European Identity") focusses on how the law can be harnessed to promote the governmental or integrational objectives of union. It isolates for consideration some substantive goals (foreign policy, free movement of goods and persons, human rights protection and legal education), in order to elucidate the ways in which law has been or can be used to promote substantive objectives. This approach is more fully developed in the studies in Part Two of the Project which deals in greater detail with substantive areas of federal/transnational policy an is open-ended. To date, in addition to the present volume on environmental policy, monographs have been planned in the following four areas: consumer protection, harmonization of corporation law and capital markets, energy policy, and regional policy. It is hoped that further studies may be undertaken in the future.

One may ask how our choices were made. Why should environmental protection be selected as the first substantive study in a project dealing with European integration in a comparative context? There is more than one explanation.

In the first place we tried to concentrate on areas which may be regarded as second or even third generation Community policies. Environmental policy is not explicitly envisaged in the Treaties; indeed there existed a serious legal problem as regards the competence of the Communities to enter this field. But it is a typical example of the kind of policy which has emerged on the foundations of the classical common market and which is a result of, and a condition for, the market's successful operation and evolution. More specifically, it is a policy which represents the operation of the "positive state" in the mixed economy. It is thus far more representative of current exigencies than the first generation policies — of the "negative" kind which simply required the states to eliminate certain practices. It typifies the kind of challenge which the process of European integration will increasingly face.

The inclusion of environmental protection as the first of the substantive studies had another attraction. It represents, alongside consumer protection which is the subject of another study in this part of the Project, the need for the Community to spread into new areas of social relevance. In some ways these areas could be seen as policies enhancing the Common Market: equalizing competition, harmonizing regulations so as to remove barriers to trade and so forth. But they also represent a social challenge in their own right. It is fashionable today to dismiss the protection of the consumer or the environment as a luxury, or indeed a fad, of the 1960's, a characteristic of economic growth and ample resources (though the steady destruction of European age-old forests by "transnational" acid rain has provided a new urgency to the environmental issue). But in our view, this, and similar social activity by the Community, is essential if Europe is really to progress into a social rather than merely legal and economic reality.

Finally, there is another, less "rational," reason for presenting this study first. It is common today to feel gloomy about the future of European integration. Much in this Project highlights the reasons, frequently justified, for such gloom. But European environmental protection is a story of some success and future hope. The ecological challenge in many of its dimensions does not recognize national boundaries. It is a classical area for transnational cooperation. Measured against the challenge it might seem that very little has been done; the limited success is dwarfed by the environmental hazards. But, nonetheless, the study illustrates that given even a limited amount of political will, the European transnational level offers possibilities for tackling problems which could not otherwise be easily confronted.

Environmental law as a topic for legal analysis has, of course, already elicited a substantial amount of scholarly attention. Why then present this new examination? First and foremost is the value of a fresh analysis by the distinguished authors of this volume. But in addition, it is our belief that the Integration Project provided a special context for specific and unique insights. Most obvious is the comparative context: this study presents a tight comparative analysis of the European and American experiences. Through this comparative analysis we gain a better understanding of the problems associated with, for example, cross-frontier control of environmental hazards; we also gain a better understanding of the workings of the transnational/federal system of governance. There is as much to be learnt from this volume on the process of integration and its problems as there is to be learnt on the legal dimensions of environmental protection.

The Project has invited, however, more than the comparative contribution. The Florence Integration Through Law Series is dedicated to the concept of Law in Context: the examination of legal problems in their political, economic and social setting. There has been much pontification in recent years about the value of interdisciplinarity. Implementation of this value, however, often falls short of much hallowed theoretical expectations. In this regard our claims were modest; we did not ask our contributors to bring the full scientific paraphernalia of, say economics or political science to bear on their subject. We simply asked that the legal analysis be situated in, and be sensitive to, the implications of the socio-economic and political context. The present volume is, in our view, an extraordinarily successful example of this approach.

The European Integration Project follows on from an earlier wide-ranging research project which was carried out at the European University Institute — the Florence Access-to-Justice Project. Access to Justice was not only concerned with an examination and, indeed, extension of the procedural and institutional mechanisms for the vindication of rights in contemporary society. It was an approach which sought to emphasize that in legal study, an analysis of the normative content of legal rules and policies — while still central — can give only a partial picture of the function and shortcomings of the law in its societal context. Normative analysis is but one layer of analysis: the effective (or otherwise) reach of the law, its implementation and enforcement, its accessibility to subjects to whom it is addressed as a source of rights and duties, is a second no less important layer. This approach has been a constant guideline to all contributions to the European Integration Project.

Problems of implementation and enforcement are notorious in the field of environmental protection. They are aggravated in the European transnational system which has its own inherent difficulties of supervision and compliance. This study deals in depth with this dimension, and is one of the first of its kind in the European context. Moreover, it is not only in highlighting implementation problems existent at the time of writing that the study makes a contribution. Its overriding value in this connection is in providing an analytical framework for examining the problem in general, a framework which will have a value well beyond the identification of concrete issues at any given point in time.

If the Access-to-Justice philosophy postulated the addition of this post-normative layer in the analysis of law, the institutional and procedural character of the Integration Project postulated the addition of yet another layer — a pre-normative layer. Both in the first general methodological part of the Project and in its second substantive part we have given considerable attention to the decision-making process by and through which norms emerge. The necessity of this addition is so clear as to obviate any lengthy explanation. Not only is decision-making an essential component in the analysis of the system as a whole, but it also gives, particularly in the context of the European transnational concordance of interests, an insight into the normative outcome and, as explained throughout the Project, into the very problems of implementation, application and enforcement. The study on the environment, as well as other studies in Part Two of the Project, has adopted what one may call a "total" approach to legal analysis. Certainly the normative, "black letter" dimension of the law is explored; but this normative analysis is sandwiched between the pre- and post-normative phase. The volume explores fully the process of policy-making, the difficulty it encounters and the political context against which normative compromises are reached.

The Integration Through Law Series represents a collective effort over a long period of time. At its inception we believed that the first methodological part of the Project would be the setting against which the subsequent substantive parts, such as this study on environmental protection policy, would be written. Things often do not turn out as they were planned. The two parts of the Project in fact evolved simultaneously, and while the Part Two studies undoubtedly did rely on the general methodological background studies of Part One, the studies in Part One equally drew upon the analysis contained in the concrete substantive studies of Part Two. In this process of cross-fertilization Professors Rehbinder and Stewart played a key role. Their insight into the evolution and problems of federalism and integration informed and enhanced much of the rest of our work. Their level of dedication and scholarship set a standard for the entire Project. Their collegiality and cooperation with the editors significantly facilitated our tasks. We are truly grateful to them.

Florence, December 1984

Mauro Cappelletti
Monica Seccombe
Joseph Weiler

Acknowledgements

This is one of several volumes on "Integration Through Law: Europe and the American Federal Experience" being published under the joint sponsorship of the European University Institute and the Ford Foundation, which together funded an international research project on "Methods, Tools and Potential for European Legal Integration in Light of the American Federal Experience" co-directed by Professors Mauro Cappelletti and Joseph Weiler. The Project, headquartered at the European University Institute in Florence, involved the participation of over forty scholars mostly from Europe and America. In addition to thanking the European University Institute and the Ford Foundation which were the principal sponsors, the Project Directors would like to express their gratitude to the Institutions of the European Communities, particularly the Commission, whose contribution has been most encouraging. A special acknowledgement is due to Professor Martin Shapiro of the University of California at Berkeley, who coordinated the American contributions to the Project.

Table of Contents

Table of Cases

Austria

Belgium

European Community

France

Germany, Federal Republic of

Italy

The Netherlands

United Kingdom

United States

I. Environmental Policy, Integration and the Law: Introduction

This introduction identifies the areas of environmental law to be considered and briefly describes the different kinds of legal tools which have been employed to deal with environmental problems. After listing some of the basic incentives and obstacles to harmonization of policy within federal/community systems, it discusses mechanisms of complete and partial integration. Finally, a set of working hypotheses about the logic of integration are presented. This simple model will be revised in the concluding chapter in light of the intervening empirical chapters.

A. Scope

This study examines the following fields of European Community (EC) and United States (US) environmental law:

1. Water Pollution
   Regulation and litigation concerning discharges into surface waters (including streams, rivers, and lakes) and marine pollution.
2. Air Pollution
   Regulation and litigation concerning air pollution from stationary sources (primarily industrial plants) and motor vehicles.
3. Noise Pollution
   Regulation of noise pollution from stationary sources, motor vehicles, construction equipment, and products.
4. Waste Disposal
   Regulation and litigation concerning the disposal of various categories of wastes, including toxic, solid, and used oil wastes.
5. Hazardous Chemicals
   Regulatory requirements, including testing for toxic and other effects, governing the production and sale of chemicals.
6. Radioactivity
   Regulation dealing with radioactive emissions from industrial and commercial sources, including nuclear power plants.
7. Land Use Planning and Protection of Nature, Landscape, Flora, and Fauna
   This topic is less fully developed because of the great disparity between the EC and the US in the extent of community/federal activity. In the US, the

federal government owns one third of the nation's lands and an even larger share of mineral and other valuable natural resources. It also affects land use and natural resource decisions through grants, development programs, and licensing approvals. The extent of EC activity in the realm of land use and natural resources is quite modest. The topic is included primarily to establish this contrast and to identify some of the factors that explain it.

8. Environmental Impact Assessment
Procedures to promote assessment by the responsible government agencies of environmental impacts associated with government development, planning, and licensing decisions.

B. Tools for Environmental Control and Mechanisms of Integration

This section lists and briefly discusses the variety of tools or incentives government may use to promote environmental quality.

Private or public litigation against polluters and other activities that degrade the environment suffers from substantial limitations. These include the limited capacity of the courts to deal with technical and scientific issues; the multiplicity of sources and interests involved and the polycentric character of the problems presented; the patchwork, decentralized character of litigation and the need for coordination and consistency in the control of different facilities, particularly those of firms that compete directly against one another; the need for prophylactic measures and for ongoing monitoring and supervision; and the perception that the policy choices involved are political in character. Private litigation is also impaired because the costs of litigation are typically large in relation to the stake of any particular litigant, and because of the difficulties in establishing causation and quantifying harm when damages are sought. However, litigation may have an important role in directing attention to neglected problems, including activities not yet regulated, injuries not yet compensated, and the problem of transboundary spillovers.

Command and control regulation, through which government authorities specify the conduct required of each firm or individual subject to control, is the dominant approach to environmental protection today. There are two basic strategies that may be followed within the broad category of command and control regulation.

One strategy is case by case screening. Particular products, such as new chemicals, or proposals to locate a major industrial facility at a given site are reviewed on a case by case basis in accordance with general criteria, such as prohibition of "unreasonable risk" or undue harm to the environment. A particularized decision is then made whether to permit the marketing of the chemical or the use of the site.

An alternative strategy is to adopt general uniform standards applicable to many regions and to entire categories of facilities or products. One technique is to establish environmental quality standards, such as a standard specifying the maximum concentration of a pollutant anywhere in the air at ground level.

In order to enforce such standards, appropriate controls on emissions from sources in the region must be developed and implemented. A second technique is to adopt regulatory standards that directly govern the operation or design of industrial products or facilities. Such regulations may take the form of performance standards which designate the level of environmental performance to be achieved. An example is a regulation requiring each new automobile to emit no more than a specified amount of certain air pollutants. Alternatively, such regulations may consist of specification standards requiring the use of particular control technologies or processes. The degree of control required is linked only loosely with overall environmental quality objectives.

Subsidies provide both an incentive for and a means of financing environmental quality improvement. They may take the form of tax credits or outright revenue grants to private firms or public authorities.

Economic Incentives. Economists criticize both command and control regulation and subsidies because they tend to impose uniform solutions. Such solutions are excessively costly because they ignore differences in abatement costs among different firms; are biased in favor of certain forms of control, such as end of pipe technologies; and provide inadequate incentives for the development of environmentally superior products and technologies. Economists favor economic incentives, such as pollution taxes or transferable pollution rights, that would promote cost minimizing abatement strategies and provide product and technology incentives, but political and practical objections have limited the use of such incentives.

Environmental impact assessment procedures. These procedures require decisionmakers to inventory, gather information on, analyze, and take into account environmental impacts in connection with their decisions. They are designed to correct the uninformed or inadequate consideration given to environmental impacts in government decisions concerning land use, natural resource management, and development projects.

C. Incentives and Obstacles to Integration in Environmental Policy

Integration of environmental law in a federal system occurs through two basic mechanisms: central determination by a federal/community authority (legislature, executive authority or court), or coordination of law and policy by member states through negotiated agreement, development of common working understandings, conscious parallelism in judge-made law, and so on. The degree of integration achieved in particular areas reflects institutional arrangements and the following incentives and disincentives to integration:

1. Incentives to Integration

Removal of trade barriers with respect to products and resources. The adoption by different states of different environmental regulations with respect to products impedes free commerce among states, thus reducing producer revenues and economic welfare, and may impose cumulative and potentially inconsistent regulatory burdens on producers seeking to sell their products or services in more than one state. Adoption by a state of stringent controls or taxes on the use of its resources (for example, extraction of oil shale or use of a site for toxic waste disposal) may also impede commerce and reduce the welfare of persons in other states. Removal or harmonization of such measures can increase producer and consumer welfare.

Removal of the "competitive distortions" and relocation incentives caused by differing controls on industrial processes and natural resource development. Different regulatory requirements governing industrial processes and resource development do not threaten free trade as directly as differential product regulations. But adoption by one state of more stringent controls will increase the costs of producers located within that state, creating a competitive advantage for producers in states with less stringent controls.[1] This advantage may cause firms to locate new facilities in states with less stringent controls or even relocate existing facilities to such states. Competition among states to attract or retain industry may encourage laxity in controls everywhere. Those states and interests in favor of more stringent environmental controls will accordingly favor measures to achieve equivalent (and relatively high) levels of control in all states.

Transboundary spillovers. Transboundary spillovers are unlikely to be adequately dealt with by resort to the municipal law of either the originating or receiving state, which may often have a municipal bias. In addition, the receiving state may face serious difficulties in enforcing remedial measures against activities in originating states.

Economies of scale in research, analysis, and decisionmaking. To the extent that environmental regulatory problems in different states present common scientific, technological, and analytical issues, there may be economies of scale in acquiring and processing the necessary information once on a centralized basis, rather than many times on a decentralized basis. In addition, adequate resources to perform the necessary work may not be available in some states.

Achievement of more stringent and effective controls through centralized direction. As noted above, "competitive distortions" may hinder the adoption by states of effective environmental controls. Centralized decisions may also favor more stringent environmental controls because central bureaucracies and political actors are less subject to short term political accountability and more attuned to the achievement of longer term objectives.

Need for common front in international negotiation. In order to achieve greater bargaining power in international negotiation, a common environmental policy may be desirable. This has, for example, been a strong incentive for EC regulation of chemical manufacture and sale.

[1] In theory, with perfect information and perfect labor markets, and no interjurisdictional spillovers, industries in a state with strict environmental standards might not be competitively disadvantaged because workers in that state would accept lower wages in return for the environmental benefits produced by regulation; lower wages could offset the higher costs to industry of complying with strict environmental standards. In practice, however, markets are imperfect and spillovers exist.

2. Disincentives to Integration

Variations in preferences. Citizens in different states often have different preferences for enhanced environmental quality versus economic and industrial development and higher money incomes. Because of political and administrative factors, integrated environmental policies often tend to be uniform. Uniformity can result in insufficient environmental quality in states with a high preference for environmental quality, and excessive environmental quality in those states with low preferences. These discrepancies will generate opposition to integrated environmental policies.

Differences in geographic, ecological, and industrial conditions. Quite apart from differences in preferences, integrated, uniform environmental policies may be inappropriate because of geographic and ecological differences that can significantly alter the consequences of a given amount of pollution. For example, welfare losses attributable to reduced visibility are much greater in scenic than industrialized areas. Organic waste discharges that can cause serious damage to a stream or river may have little effect if discharged into deep ocean sites. Uniform environmental quality standards and uniform technology-based source controls fail to deal fully with these variations, resulting in overcontrol in some areas and undercontrol in others.

Resentment at centralized direction. Common environmental policies, particularly if formulated and enforced by central authority, cause resentment at the resulting interference with member state autonomy. This resentment is likely to be especially severe when it infringes on industrial policies and land use and development decisions.

Differences among legal and administrative systems in member states. As developed below, considerable reliance must be placed on state and local authorities to implement and enforce common environmental policies, particularly in the case of industrial process regulation and land use and natural resource management. Differences in legal and administrative systems will often translate into differences in implementation and enforcement, hindering effective harmonization.

Diseconomies of scale and information processing. To the extent that decisions on environmental policy are centrally made, information must be gathered and processed centrally. In addition, central authorities will have to monitor state and local implementation and enforcement. This will introduce substantial information processing costs, and tend to introduce multiple and redundant layers of decisionmaking and review.

Functional interconnection between environmental regulation and local functions. Many forms of environmental regulation involve traditional local functions such as zoning and other forms of land use control and traffic regulation. So long as these controls are exercised by local officials in response to local circumstances and pressures, the effective degree of integration in environmental policy is substantially reduced. On the other hand, to centralize the exercise of such functions would create very substantial diseconomies and seriously intrude upon local autonomy.

Industrial and commercial oppositon to integrated policies. Particularly in the area of industrial process regulation, integrated environmental policies are more likely to be protective of the environment than decentralized policies, imposing costs upon and restricting development by industry and commercial interests. They will accordingly tend to oppose integration. Transboundary polluters will oppose such measures for similar reasons.

D. Mechanisms of Complete Integration

Centralized determination of environmental law and policy. Centralized legislative or executive determination of environmental law is the most direct and obvious method of insuring integrated environmental policies. However, it can also be the most destructive of state autonomy, and may result in uniformities that exhibit various diseconomies. Central adoption of regulatory standards and screening programs has been the dominant mechanism for integration of environmental laws and policies in the US and the EC. Federal/ community court creation of law governing public or private litigation against environmental degradation is an alternative mechanism that is more likely to be responsive to variations in state conditions. But this alternative, for reasons noted above, is also far less likely to be effective. Very little law has developed by this route, the most notable effort being that by federal courts in the US to develop a law of transboundary spillovers.

Implementation of federal/community law. Once established, centrally determined law and policy must be implemented and enforced. The most reliable means of insuring that such implementation and enforcement occurs in an effective and uniform way is through federal/community administrative agencies and courts charged with responsibility for issuing regulations and permits, monitoring, initiating enforcement actions, and adjudicating controversies.

An alternative route is for central authorities to determine environmental measures and laws but leave their implementation and enforcement in the first instance to member states while retaining powers of supervision and review. These powers include that of a central authority to institute litigation against member states seeking to require them to undertake implementation/enforcement; imposition of sanctions for implementation failure, such as cut-offs of funds; assumption by federal/community authorities of implementation/enforcement responsibilities when member states have failed to do an adequate job; or development of federal/community law that would allow environmental advocates to challenge and remedy deficient implementation/enforcement by member state authorities through litigation in member state or federal/ community courts.

Federal/community encouragement of state environmental measures. In lieu of adopting regulatory standards and programs (whether implemented centrally or by member states), central authorities could seek to encourage state adoption of programs through research and information programs, subsidies to underwrite the administrative costs of such programs, or waiver of federal law that would otherwise displace such programs. The central authority may impose criteria which state programs must meet in order to qualify for subsidy or waiver. Alternatively the central authority may urge states to adopt standards to deal with certain environmental problems, with the threat of more intensive central intervention if state action is not forthcoming.

Judicial invalidation of state environmental measures that impede trade. The methods of integration discussed above are positive efforts to obtain a minimum level of environmental protection in all states, as well as to eliminate the barriers to trade created by nonharmonized state measures. In contrast, courts applying the "negative commerce clause" doctrine, or its equivalent,[2] may act to invalidate state product standards that are more restrictive than those adopted by neighboring states. In so doing, they eliminate barriers to trade (including the threat posed by multiple and potentially inconsistent state regulations to manufacturers' ability to realize economies of scale) without regard for achieving minimal levels of environmental protection.

E. Mechanisms of Partial Integration

Total harmonization is achieved when all states enforce the same standards or measures. Total harmonization may be achieved by central adoption of uniform measures to preempt state measures of varing stringency or by judicial application of the negative commerce clause doctrine to invalidate state product standards that restrict trade. The latter technique of total harmonization leads to the lowest common denominator of environmental protection. There are a variety of institutional strategies other than total harmonization which can mediate the competing claims of integration and local autonomy.[3]

With the technique of *minimum harmonization*, member states are permitted to adopt measures controlling products, processes, or natural resource development that are more stringent than those adopted by central authorities or by agreement among member states. However, they may not adopt less stringent

[2] *See generally* Kommers & Waelbroeck, *Legal Integration and the Free Movement of Goods: The American and European Experience*, at §§ II.B-C & III.C-D.1, in INTEGRATION THROUGH LAW, Vol. 1, Book 3.

[3] For a discussion of harmonization techniques in the EEC *see* P. J. SLOT, TECHNICAL AND ADMINISTRATIVE OBSTACLES TO TRADE IN THE EEC 80 *et seq.* (Sijthoff, Leyden 1975); W. SCHMEDER, DIE RECHTSANGLEICHUNG ALS INTEGRATIONSMITTEL DER EUROPÄISCHEN GEMEINSCHAFT 71 *et seq.* (Carl Heymanns Verlag, Köln 1978); Europäisches Parlament, Bericht über den Vorschlag der Kommission der Europäischen Gemeinschaften an den Rat für ein Allgemeines Programm zur Beseitigung der technischen Hemmnisse im inner-gemeinschaftlichen Warenverkehr, die sich aus der Unterschiedlichkeit der einzelstaatlichen Vorschriften ergeben, EP Doc. 15/1968–69; WEINSTOCK, *Nur eine Umwelt? Europäische Umweltpolitik im Spannungsfeld zwischen ökologischer Vielfalt und ökonomischer Einheit*, 6 ZEITSCHRIFT FÜR UMWELTPOLITIK 1, 29, 33, 34 *et seq.* (1983).

measures. The minimum "floor" provided by this method limits state competition for industrial development through weaker environmental measures, while allowing those states with stronger preferences for environmental quality to give them effect. This approach, however, allows barriers to trade to persist.

Partial harmonization. Under this approach federal/community law governs only interstate product transactions – for example, the sale in state A of automobiles or chemicals manufactured in state B. This technique allows a state to impose stricter or laxer controls on domestic products, but forbids imposition of stricter standards on imports.[4]

Optional harmonization. Under this strategy, states may adopt their own standards, but, if a state adopts a standard different from the federal/community standard for interstate transactions, a domestic or foreign manufacturer selling products in that state may elect to comply either with the community standard or the state standard.[5]

The advantages of partial and optional harmonization in eliminating trade barriers while partially accommodating differences in states' preferences for environmental quality are limited by the fact that manufacturers wishing to export to other states must meet two standards, one for instrastate transactions and another for interstate transactions. Manufacturing different products to meet different standards may increase costs by reducing scale economies and thus provide firms with financial incentives to follow the more stringent standard in order to reach the widest possible market with a standardized product. This undercuts the economic advantage to a state of a less stringent standard for intrastate transactions.

[4] In order to illustrate the implications of partial harmonization, consider the example of controls on automobile emissions of air pollutants.

State A, in order to achieve higher environmental quality, could adopt stricter standards for cars manufactured and sold within A, but its manufacturers would be vulnerable to import competition from State B manufacturers, who would have the right to sell their cars in A upon compliance with the less stringent and costly federal/community standard.

Alternatively, State A could adopt laxer standards for cars manufactured and sold within A, resulting in lower environmental quality and giving A manufacturers a cost advantage over imports (so long as the state can bar imported cars that do not comply with the federal/community standard). On the other hand, if A manufacturers wished to sell their cars in B, they would have to tool up to meet the more demanding federal/community standard.

[5] Optional harmonization is similar to partial harmonization, but there are important differences. First, a state must affirmatively "opt out" of federal/community standards. Second, when State A adopts laxer standards, State B manufacturers who sell within State A need only comply with State A's standards rather than the stricter federal/community standards, undercutting the competitive advantage that State A manufacturers would otherwise enjoy. Third, when State A adopts such standards, whether higher or lower, State A manufacturers can "opt out" of those standards in favor of federal/community standards.

Alternative harmonization. Under this approach, federal/community law establishes two or more alternative standards or means of compliance which a member state may elect. For example, to control water pollution a state may be allowed to choose between an ambient standards approach or an approach based on uniform technology-based source controls. Alternative techniques for measuring ambient standards may be authorized.[6]

Recognition of other states' product certification is a harmonization technique designed to eliminate repetitive licensing or testing procedures. Certification by the state of manufacture that a new chemical has met standardized EC testing protocols is an example. As the example indicates, the recognition technique is most appropriate when the underlying regulatory requirements have been harmonized. But even where they are not, the technique could be applied to limit review and testing by the importing state to that necessary to ascertain compliance with those of its requirements that go beyond those of the manufacturing state's.

Strategies that allow the states considerable discretion in implementing and enforcing centrally determined standards are also partial integration techniques. Still greater decentralization can be achieved under a regime that *allows states to set environmental quality standards or product or process controls in the first instance*, subject to centralized review under general criteria.

Centralized research, analysis, and recommendation present a still more modest approach towards integration. Economies of scale in research and analysis, reinforced by the tendency of centralized decisionmaking to favor strong environmental protective measures, are realized through central generation of information and dissemination. But basic policy determinations, implementation, and enforcement are left to the member states.

F. The Logic of Integration in the Federal System

How are the considerations for and against integration likely to operate in a federal system, and what form of harmonization is likely to result? We here offer some working hypotheses to be tested by the evidence canvassed in later chapters. We evaluate and refine these hypotheses in Chapter X.

Let us assume, for purposes of initial analysis, that the only relevant actors are states. All states want both environmental quality and economic growth; there is, however, a tradeoff between these two goals, at least in the short to medium term. Different states, for a variety of reasons, make this tradeoff differently. Some states give greater weight to environmental quality, and therefore favor more stringent environmental controls (environmental states) while other states favor economic development with less stringent environmental controls (polluter states). When products, capital, and labor cross state bound-

[6] The federal/community authorities will ordinarily have a clear preference for one set of standards or means of compliance. Selection of the alternative will ordinarily be allowed only under narrowly defined criteria, and it may be subject to later review.

aries, each state's tradeoff between environmental quality and economic performance is affected by other states' environmental policies. This interdependency, explained in greater detail below, creates two basic incentives for harmonization: the removal of trade barriers and competitive distortions, and the desire to increase the stringency of environmental controls. Our working hypotheses on integration require a distinction between two basic categories of regulation: product regulation and regulation of industrial processes. The relations between these two categories of regulation and incentives for harmonization are depicted visually by the following matrix:

	Eliminate Trade Barriers and Competitive Distortions	Promote Environmental Quality
Product regulation	1	2
Process regulation	3	4

For each element of the matrix one must examine the incentives for harmonization on the part of both polluter states and environmental states.

First, consider the question of trade barriers in connection with product regulation (element 1 of the matrix). If environmental states can exclude heavily polluting or risky products from polluter states, polluter states will be denied access to markets in environmental states. They will accordingly have an interest in harmonization. Assume initially that we are dealing only with total harmonization. In a system requiring unanimous consent of all states, the level of control at which harmonization will occur will depend on how polluter states evaluate the tradeoff between the costs associated with more stringent controls and the benefits of expanded markets. More precisely, the level of control to which polluter states will assent is the lowest level at which the marginal costs and benefits of increased control are equal for any polluter state. However, this incentive for harmonization disappears if polluter states can successfully challenge the exclusion by environmental states of polluter states' products as an undue restraint on trade. Such litigation would have little success in the US under prevailing interpretations of the commerce clause, but might have greater success in the EC in light of *Cassis de Dijon* and its interpretation by the Commission.[7]

Now consider the incentives for product harmonization from the perspective of states wanting to promote environmental quality (element 2 of the ma-

[7] For discussion of the *Cassis de Dijon* decision (European Court of Justice, case 120/78, Rewe-Zentral-AG v. Bundesmonopolverwaltung für Branntwein, [1979] ECR 649) and "negative commerce clause" doctrine in the EC, *see* Kommers & Waelbroeck, *supra* note 2, at § III.C.3, especially notes 188–197 and accompanying text; Heller & Pelkmans, *The Federal Economy: Law and Economic Integration and the Positive State – The U.S.A. and Europe Compared*, at § III.C.2.b(i) (by Pelkmans), in INTEGRATION THROUGH LAW, Vol. 1, Book 1. *See also infra* Ch. II, at pp.28–31.

trix). Such environmental states will be undercut in product competition by polluter states. If a negative commerce clause doctrine prevents them from excluding the products of polluter states, they will suffer this competitive disadvantage in all markets. But even if exclusion is possible, the environmental states will have to compete in polluter state markets, and economies of scale may preclude the development of a less controlled product for those markets. In order to avoid the competitive disadvantages of differential standards, environmental states will support harmonization, preferably at a level close to what they would adopt for themselves in the absence of trade.

Now consider regulation of processes from the perspective of trade barriers (element 3 of the matrix). Environmental states can not exclude products from polluting states on the ground that manufacturing processes in those states are less well controlled. Nothing in the US or EC negative commerce clause doctrine would permit this. Accordingly, products from polluter states have free access to markets in environmental states, and polluter states have no interest in harmonization.

Those states desiring to promote environmental quality (element 4 of the matrix) still have an incentive to support harmonization in order to avoid the competitive disadvantages that they will suffer by reason of higher process costs. These disadvantages are likely to be greater than in the case of product regulation because there is no hope of excluding products from polluter states. The resulting cost disadvantage can give rise to a flight of capital and labor to polluting states.

Now consider the case of another category of states, those that import products but do not manufacture them. In the absence of transboundary spillovers, they would oppose any process controls at all, since their citizens would bear the cost of controls but enjoy none of the benefits. In this respect, they may be more opposed to integration than polluter states, which would presumably not oppose a community standard at the lowest common denominator level. On the other hand, in the case of product controls, an importer state would not only bear all or most of the costs of control, but would also enjoy the benefits of control. Thus, the control level it would favor would depend upon its relative preference for environmental quality. Transboundary spillovers will create support for harmonization on the part of receptor states.

In a federal system requiring unanimous consent, there will, in the case of product regulation, be support from both polluter and environmental states for harmonization through mutual adoption of uniform standards. To the extent that a *Cassis de Dijon* principle restricts the ability of environmental states from excluding polluter state products, the support of environmental states for harmonization will be increased and the support of polluter states will be decreased. Since, however, there is a rule of unanimous agreement, the net impact of such a rule will be to significantly reduce the stringency of harmonized measures. In the case of process regulation it is difficult to see why there would be any harmonization at all above the lowest common denominator level, since it would never be in the interests of polluter or importer states to agree to more stringent controls.

In a federal system allowing harmonization on the basis of some form of majority vote, the incentives are similar in direction, but deleting the requirement of unanimity will mean uniform product regulation at a more stringent level. In addition, some uniform process regulation is likely to occur, depending on the voting power of environmental states and the intensity of their preferences for environmental quality. The implications of transboundary spillovers are more complex, and depend upon the pattern of spillovers and the configuration of net importing and net exporting states.

What is the relevance of the number of states and their size relative to that of the federation? Where states' internal markets are small relative to that of the federation, the support of both environmental and polluter states for harmonization of product regulation is likely to be strengthened. Such a configuration would also increase the support of environmental states for harmonized process regulation, and strengthen the opposition of polluter states to such harmonization.

Given the possibility of less than total harmonization, what form would harmonization be likely to take? In the case of product regulation, polluter states would want total harmonization at the lowest possible level, but would favor minimal harmonization for process regulation. Environmental states would, in the case of both product and process regulation, favor either total or minimal harmonization, depending on the level at which the two forms of harmonization would likely occur.

Partial and optional harmonization apply only to product regulation. They allow polluter states access to environmental states, but only at the price of controls more stringent than they would otherwise prefer. Environmental states are protected against competition from polluter states' products in their own domestic markets, but must either suffer a price disadvantage or develop an alternative line of products in order to compete in polluter state markets.

Alternative harmonization is another compromise technique that narrows but does not eliminate the competitive disadvantages suffered by environmental states.

The above analysis would indicate that in the US there would be a very high degree of uniform product regulation through federal legislation, and a considerable but lesser degree of federal process regulation, much of which might take the form of minimum harmonization. In the case of the EC for product regulation before *Cassis de Dijon* it would predict considerable uniform harmonization (at an intermediate level) or optional or partial harmonization. It would predict no harmonization at all in process regulation. Yet there is some harmonization of process regulation in the EC, and perhaps more harmonization of product regulation than might be expected. What might account for this? The following factors might be considered:

Unanimity on a variety of issues may be achieved through a process of reciprocal concession over time, even though there would not be unanimity on any single issue considered in isolation. Polluter states may go along with proposals for harmonization that are intensely supported by environmental states, in exchange for later concessions on other issues. This process of "logrolling" need not be explicit. Implicit norms of reciprocating may develop, allowing sequential concessions without explicit agreement. In the case of product regulation the ability of an environmental state in the absence of harmonization to adopt and enforce regulations that will restrain trade is also an incentive for polluter states to acquiesce in harmonized initiatives.

Environmental states tend to be the most industrially developed and economically and politically powerful states. Despite the rule of unanimity, these states may have a disproportionate influence on EC decisionmaking. Process harmonization will be a strong objective for such states, because it will impose costs on less developed states that will restrict economic and political competition from them.

Multinational firms with manufacturing plants in both polluter and environmental states may find it to their net advantage to have harmonized regulation at levels higher than polluter states would prefer, and will therefore lobby polluter states in which they have plants to support such harmonization.

There may be a Community-wide environmental sentiment favoring stronger process controls that finds expression in all states.

Government officials of polluter states, particularly those in environmental ministries, may personally tend to favor higher environmental controls but would face strong local opposition if they attempted to adopt such controls unilaterally. By acquiescing in Commission initiatives, they can secure their objectives through the back door.

Polluter states may believe that the EC as an institution is on balance quite favorable to their interests. Psychologically and otherwise, it may be difficult to oppose otherwise plausible Commission proposals unless the economic disadvantage imposed on industries in polluting states is severe.

These factors, which may explain why significant EC harmonization has occurred, would tend to predict an even greater level of harmonization through federal legislation in the US. Most large industrial enterprises operate in many states and would therefore strongly oppose significant barriers to trade arising from differential standards, particularly given the small size of most domestic state markets. Moreover, the existence of national media and national politics tends to favor the development of a national environmental constituency.

G. Order of Presentation

The succeeding chapters alternate between consideration of the EC and the US. First the legislative competence of each of the two systems in environmental matters is described. Then the substantive law of each system is presented. Subsequent chapters discuss implementation and enforcement of the substantive law and the policy process by which such law is determined.

The concluding chapter returns to the working hypotheses advanced in this introduction. Based on comparative analysis of the empirical material presented in the intervening chapters, a fuller understanding of policymaking and implementation becomes possible.

II. Legislative Competences and Instruments in the Community

A. Community Competences for Environmental Protection

Unlike the US, environmental policy did not develop at the Community level after far-reaching economic, political, and legal integration had already occurred. Its development and implementation have depended upon and reflected the progress and extent of European integration (particularly the Community's institutional development and the state of legal integration). At the same time, environmental policy has itself been a factor influencing the direction and degree of the Community integration process.[1]

1. EEC Treaty

The European treaties, and particularly the Treaty of Rome which established the European Economic Community (the EEC Treaty), do not expressly permit Community institutions to act in the field of environmental protection. The ultimate purpose of the EEC Treaty is to create an economic community by establishment of a common market. This purpose is to be achieved through implementation of the four freedoms (free circulation of goods, services, persons, and capital), a customs union, a system of free competition, and certain common or coordinated policies. Environmental policy is not directly linked with the establishment and functioning of the Common Market as an economic institution. It is not contained in the Treaty chapter concerning common or coordinated policies. The Treaty does not even contain the words "environment" and "pollution."

Nevertheless, environmental policy is now undeniably well established as a distinct area of Community policy. Given that many of the institutional and economic goals of the Treaty have not been achieved, and given that the pace of integration has in some respects slowed, the development of a common environmental policy,[2] although still fragmentary, is a rather remarkable step that has contributed substantially to the continued growth of the Community as a political system. This contribution, however, is primarily in the area of substantive policy rather than in new forms of institutional or legal integration.

[1] *See, e.g.*, J. Weiler's recent treatment of the matter (Supranationalism Revisited — Retrospective and Prospective, EUI Working Paper No. 2, at 27, 43).

[2] ZULEEG, *EG-Richtlinien auf dem Gebiet des Wasserrechts und ihre innerstaatliche Auswirkung*, 14 ZEITSCHRIFT FÜR WASSERRECHT 133, 137 (1975).

Uncertainty about the jurisdictional basis for Community environmental policy was an initial impediment to establishment of such policy. Art. 36 of the EEC Treaty, which authorizes member states to limit exports and imports to protect health and life of persons, animals, and plants, implies that the basic competence for environmental protection is vested in member states. To counter this implication, the Community institutions have, in developing a common environmental policy, relied primarily on Art. 100 and secondarily on Art. 235 of the EEC Treaty.

Art. 100 authorizes Community directives "for the approximation" of member state laws, regulations, and administrative actions that "directly affect the establishment or functioning of the common market." Art. 235 provides that the Council, by unanimous action, may take "appropriate measures" to "attain, in the course of the operation of the common market, one of the objectives of the Community" when the Treaty has not provided the necessary powers to do so.

Both of these provisions were designed to give Community institutions powers to ensure the establishment and functioning of the Common Market as an economic institution and were not aimed at environmental protection as such. But actual EEC environmental policy has transcended the purely economic objective of removing trade barriers, and frankly seeks to promote environmental quality as a Community goal. This emancipation of the EEC's environmental policy from the constraints implied by Articles 100 and 235 marks its institutionalization as a common policy.

a. Developmental Phases of EEC Environmental Policy

The historical development of an institutionalized environmental policy can be separated into two distinct phases.

In the first phase, environmental policy was incidental to measures to harmonize national environmental laws in order to abolish obstacles to trade between member states.[3] Examples include: the Community initiatives dating from 1964 to 1975 under Articles 30, 92, 93 and 95 of the EEC Treaty to prevent excessive subsidization of the regeneration or incineration of used oils; the directive of 1967[4] which established a uniform system of classification, labeling, and packaging for hazardous substances; and the directives 70/157/EEC[5] regulating noise levels and exhaust systems of vehicles and 70/220/

[3] General Program for Elimination of Technical Obstacles to Trade of 28 May 1969, JO No. C 76, 17 June 1969, p. 1, as updated on 17 Dec. 1973, OJ No. C 117, 31 Dec. 1973, p. 1. *See* F. Behrens, Rechtsgrundlagen der Umweltpolitik der Europäischen Gemeinschaften 25 *et seq.* (Erich Schmidt Verlag, Berlin 1976); J. P. Hannequart, La Mise en place d'une politique communautaire de l'environnement (Université Catholique, Centre d'Études Européennes, Louvain-la-Neuve 1978).

[4] Directive 67/548/EEC of 27 June 1967 on classification, packaging and labelling of dangerous substances, JO No. 196, 16 Aug. 1967, p. 1 ([1967] OJ (special English ed.) at 234).

[5] Directive 70/157/EEC of 6 Feb. 1970 on the approximation of the laws of the Member States relating to the permissible sound level and the exhaust system of motor vehicles, JO No. L 42, 23 Feb. 1970, p. 16 ([1970] OJ (special English ed.) at 111).

EEC[6] limiting vehicle emissions. These directives were all part of the Community's general harmonization program.[7] The motor vehicle emission directive illustrates particularly well the focus of EEC environmental policy at the time on elimination or prevention of trade barriers. It was issued by the Community in reaction to legislative proposals in West Germany and France aiming at increased protection from the health and environmental risks of motor vehicle emissions. The proposed national regulations threatened the uniform European system of type approval of motor vehicles; thus, the Community acted to preserve the existing system.

Many of these initiatives did result in improved environmental protection. Strongly environmentalist member states were more or less able to set the pace and direction for Community action by unilaterally proposing strong national environmental legislation, which forced the Community to react with measures of its own. But Community policy initiatives were not based on a comprehensive political program. They were patchwork responses to member state initiatives and were prompted by the need for harmonization to preserve or improve the functioning of the Common Market as an economic institution. Consequently, product standards were emphasized because differing national product requirements had a direct impact on interstate trade.

The second phase of Community environmental policy[8] is marked by the development and implementation of a true common environmental policy. Although environmental policy still primarily relies on the lawmaking instruments of the first phase, i.e., harmonization of national laws under Art. 100 of the EEC Treaty, it has been largely freed from the objective of economic and commercial harmonization and primarily pursues environmental protection goals for their own sake. The second phase began in 1971 when the Community institutions made several cautious steps towards recognizing the need for Community commitment to environmental protection. Then at the Paris Summit Conference of October 1972 the heads of state or government of the original Community members and of the new members (United Kingdom, Denmark, and Ireland) endorsed a Commission initiative to expressly formulate a common Community environmental policy. Pursuant to that endorsement, the Commission drafted a "Programme of environmental action of the European Communities," which was forwarded to the Council on 17 April 1973 and formally approved by the Council and the representatives of the member states on 22 November 1973.[9] The environmental program of 1973 set objectives, stated principles, established priorities, and described the measures to be taken for the following two years. It opened a field for Community action not

[6] Directive 70/220/EEC of 20 March 1970 on the approximation of the laws of the Member States relating to the emissions of positive ignition engines of motor vehicles, JO No. L 76, 6 April 1970, p. 1 ([1970] OJ (special English ed.) at 171).

[7] *Supra* note 3.

[8] *See also* H. Bungarten, Umweltpolitik in Westeuropa 128 *et seq.* (Europa Union Verlag, Bonn 1978).

[9] OJ No. C 112, 20 Dec. 1973, p. 3. *See also* Seventh General Report of the European Communities (Brussels 1973), point 258; Bull. EC 11–1974, at pp. 11–12, point 1203.

originally provided for in the treaties and "added a new dimension to the construction of Europe."[10] In addition, the Community's harmonization program was amended to increase its responsiveness to environmental concerns.[11]

The environmental program of 1973, which marks the beginning of a true common environmental policy, was followed in 1976 by a second, more comprehensive environmental program covering the period from 1977 to 1981. Prior to the recent adoption in 1983 of the third environmental program, the second program was prolonged by one and a half years to provide more time for thorough discussion. More time was needed due to problems of institutional transition brought about by the accession of Greece and the "promotion" of the Environment and Consumer Protection Service to a Directorate-General for Environment, Consumer Protection and Nuclear Safety.

Since 1973, the Community institutions have been increasingly active in implementing environmental policy. Between 1973 and mid-1983 over seventy legislative texts were adopted, and the sections on environmental protection in the monthly Bulletin of the Community give an impressive picture of the density of activities in this new field of Community commitment, although in the last two years a certain slowing can not be overlooked.

Legal writers generally agree that the legal basis for a far-reaching common environmental policy is relatively weak.[12] Because environmental degradation

[10] Seventh General Report, *supra* note 9, point 258.

[11] Council Resolution of 17 Dec. 1973, OJ No. C 117, 31 Dec. 1973, p. 1.

[12] *See* Bericht im Namen des Rechtsausschusses (Berichterstatter Armengaud) über die im Rahmen der Gemeinschaftsverträge gegebenen Möglichkeiten für den Umweltschutz und die gegebenenfalls hierzu vorzuschlagenden Änderungen, EP Doc. 15/72; F. BEHRENS, *supra* note 3, *passim; id., Die Umweltpolitik der Europäischen Gemeinschaften und Art. 235 EWGV*, 93 DEUTSCHES VERWALTUNGSBLATT 460 (1978); BÉRAUD, *Fondements juridiques du droit de l'environnement dans le Traité de Rome*, 1979 REVUE DU MARCHÉ COMMUN 35; BURHENNE & SCHOENBAUM, *The European Community and Management of the Environment: A Dilemma*, 13 NAT. RESOURCES J. 494 (1973); CARPENTIER, *L'action de la Communauté en matière d'environnement*, 1972 REVUE DU MARCHÉ COMMUN 381; CLOSE, *Harmonisation of Laws: Use or Abuse of the Powers under the EEC Treaty?*, 3 EUROPEAN L. REV. 461 (1978); GERARD, *Les limites et les moyens juridiques de l'intervention des Communautés Européennes en matière de protection de l'environnement*, 1975 CAHIERS DE DROIT EUROP. 14; E. GRABITZ & C. SASSE, COMPETENCE OF THE EUROPEAN COMMUNITIES FOR ENVIRONMENTAL POLICY 24 *et seq.*, 39 *et seq.* (Erich Schmidt-Verlag, Berlin 1977); House of Lords, Debates, Hansard vol. 394, No. 207 (4 July 1978); House of Lords, Select Committee on the European Communities, Session 1977–78, Approximation of Laws under Article 100 of the EEC Treaty, 22ND REPORT, H. L. 131 (HMSO, London 1978), partly *reprinted in* 4 ENVT'L POL'Y & L. 193 (1978); *id.*, 35TH REPORT, H. L. 199 (HMSO, London 1978); KAISER, *Grenzen der EG-Zuständigkeit*, 15 EUROPARECHT 97 (1980); Lukes, *Umweltschutz und Rechtsangleichung in den Europäischen Gemeinschaften*, in UMWELTSCHUTZ UND INTERNATIONALE WIRTSCHAFT 160 *et seq.* (V. Götz, D. Rauschning & G. Zieger eds., Carl Heymanns Verlag, Köln 1975); VON MOLTKE, *The Legal Basis for Environmental Policy*, 3 ENVT'L POL'Y & L. 136 (1977); OFFERMANN-CLAS, *Das Abfallrecht der Europäischen Gemeinschaften*, 96 DEUTSCHES VERWALTUNGSBLATT 1125, 1126 *et seq.* (1981); RIEGEL, *Für eine umfassende Kompetenz der Gemeinschaftsorgane auf dem Gebiet des*

was not yet perceived as a problem when the Treaty was concluded, it was not included among the express competences of the Community. The Community's expansion into this policy area is a considerable extension of Community law and policy at the expense of member states without any express authority.[13]

b. Specific Treaty Provisions

There are some specific provisions in the EEC Treaty, particularly Art. 43(2) regarding the common agricultural policy and Articles 75(1)(c) and 84(2) regarding the common transportation policy, which give the Community some competence for environmental protection. However, these provisions are too narrow to serve as the foundation of a comprehensive environmental policy, and their scope of application and relationship to Art. 100 of the EEC Treaty were the subject of much controversy.[14] Under the narrow view taken by West Germany, these provisions only justify Community action with eco-

Umweltschutzes, 12 EUROPARECHT 74 (1977); E. RÖHLING, ÜBERBETRIEBLICHE TECHNISCHE NORMEN ALS NICHTTARIFÄRE HANDELSHEMMNISSE IM GEMEINSAMEN MARKT 55 *et seq.* (Carl Heymanns Verlag, Köln 1972); W. SCHMEDER, DIE RECHTSANGLEICHUNG ALS INTEGRATIONSINSTRUMENT IN DER EUROPÄISCHEN GEMEINSCHAFT 38 *et seq.* (Carl Heymanns Verlag, Köln 1978); SEIDEL, *Ziele und Ausmaß der Rechtsangleichung in der EWG - Zur britischen Auffassung -*, 14 EUROPARECHT 171 (1979); *id., Regeln der Technik und Europäisches Gemeinschaftsrecht*, 34 NEUE JURISTISCHE WOCHENSCHRIFT 1120 (1981); TOUSCOZ, *L'action des Communautés Européennes en matière d'environnement*, 1973 REVUE TRIMESTRIELLE DE DROIT EUROP. 29; VYGEN, *Ergänzung des EWG-Vertrages im Hinblick auf eine europäische Umweltpolitik*, 6 ZEITSCHRIFT FÜR RECHTSPOLITIK 58 (1974); ZULEEG, *EG-Richtlinien auf dem Gebiet des Wasserrechts und ihre innerstaatlichen Auswirkungen*, 14 ZEITSCHRIFT FÜR WASSERRECHT 133 (1975).

[13] Everling, *Vom Zweckverband zur Europäischen Union - Überlegungen zur Struktur der Europäischen Gemeinschaft*, in HAMBURG, DEUTSCHLAND, EUROPA, FESTSCHRIFT FÜR H. P. IPSEN 595, 611 (R. Stödter & W. Thieme eds., Mohr Siebeck, Tübingen 1977); KAISER, *supra* note 12, at 105; TEITGEN & MÉGRET, *La fumée de la cigarette dans la zone "grise" des competences de la C.E.E.*, 1981 REVUE TRIMESTRIELLE DE DROIT EUROP. 68, 69.

[14] *See* CATALANO, *Limiti delle competenze communitarie in materia di ecologia*, 1974 RIVISTA DI DIRITTO EUROPEO 60, 66–67; C.-D. EHLERMANN, AGRARRECHT DER EUROPÄISCHEN WIRTSCHAFTSGEMEINSCHAFT, KÖLNER SCHRIFTEN ZUM EUROPARECHT, vol. 10, at 57, 82 *et seq.* (Carl Heymanns Verlag, Köln 1969); F. BEHRENS, *supra* note 3, at 107 *et seq.*, 114 *et seq.*; E. GRABITZ & C. SASSE, *supra* note 12, at 25–26; F. MARX, FUNKTION UND GRENZEN DER RECHTSANGLEICHUNG NACH ART. 100 EWG-VERTRAG 113 *et seq.*, 162 *et seq.* (Carl Heymanns Verlag, Köln 1976); RIEGEL, *supra* note 12, at 76–77; Vignes, in LE DROIT DE LA COMMUNAUTÉ ÉCONOMIQUE EUROPÉENNE, vol. 5, *Art. 100 annot. 25*, at 167 *et seq.* (J. Mégret, J. Louis, D. Vignes & M. Waelbroeck, Presses Universitaires, Brussels 1973); Verloren van Themaat, *Die Rechtsangleichung als Integrationsinstrument*, in ZUR INTEGRATION EUROPAS, FESTSCHRIFT FÜR C. F. OPHÜLS 243, 249 (W. Hallstein & H.-J. Schlochauer eds., C. F. Müller, Karlsruhe 1965); W. SCHMEDER, *supra* note 12, at 56 *et seq.*; VYGEN, *supra* note 12, at 61. For arguments favoring narrow interpretation of the powers under Articles 43(2) and 75(1) of the EEC Trea-

nomic objectives. In contrast, under the liberal view taken by the Commission, all other member states, and legal writers, all environmental problems related to agriculture or transportation activities, including, for example, limitations on pesticide residues in human and animal food, and vehicle emission limitations, are covered by Articles 43(2), 75(1)(c), and 84(2) of the EEC Treaty.[15] Since this controversy could not be resolved, the first directives harmonizing environmental requirements for vehicles were issued under the 1969 program for the elimination of technical barriers to trade, i.e. under Art. 100 rather than under Art. 75(1)(c) of the EEC Treaty. Directives concerning pesticides were based either on Art. 100 or on both Articles 100 and 43 of the EEC Treaty. By the same token, the directive concerning water quality for shellfish harvesting relied on Art. 100. Recently, however, the directive on limitation of aircraft noise and some directives on marine pollution have been based on Art. 84(2); and some directives concerning the protection of fish resources and whales have been based on Art. 43(2). Thus, it seems that West Germany now accepts that Articles 43(2), 75(1)(c), and 84(2) of the EEC Treaty authorize regulation of direct environmental effects of agricultural and transportation activities. This new consensus does not, however, remedy the fundamental weakness of these provisions, namely that their scope is too narrow to allow them to be the foundation of a comprehensive environmental policy.

c. The Preamble and Art. 2 of the EEC Treaty

EEC environmental legislation is usually based on the harmonization powers granted to the Community by Art. 100 of the EEC Treaty, and to a lesser extent on the powers granted by Art. 235 of the EEC Treaty, a catch-all provision for cases where Community action is necessary to attain a Community objective and the Treaty has not otherwise provided the necessary powers. The Community institutions have interpreted these powers broadly.[16] The justification for using these two Articles as the foundation of a common environmental policy depends ultimately on basic Community goals. Art. 3 of the EEC Treaty directs that harmonization under Art. 100 is to promote the proper functioning of the Common Market and the Community objectives set out in Art. 2. Art. 235 of the EEC Treaty also directs that the measures taken pursuant to it be necessary to attain a Community objective. Consequently, understanding the goals of the Community is necessary to appreciate the nature of Community powers for environmental protection.

The Preamble and Art. 2 of the EEC Treaty declare that the "constant improvement of ... living and working conditions" and "the harmonious devel-

ty, *see* E. RÖHLING, *supra* note 12, at 72–73; HOLCH, *Der deutsche Bundesrat zur Rechtssetzung der EWG*, 2 EUROPARECHT 217, 227 (1967).

[15] *See* C.-D. EHLERMANN, *supra* note 14.

[16] *See* Resolution of the Heads of State and Government at the Paris Summit Conference of 19–20 Oct. 1972, BULL. EC. 10–1972, p. 20, at point 8; European Parliament, Resolution of 18 April 1972, OJ No. C 46, 9 May 1972, p. 13; CLOSE, *supra* note 12, at 465–466.

opment of economic activities" are Community goals. This mandate is interpreted by the Community institutions to include "an improved quality as well as an improved standard of life." This interpretation, which implies that environmental protection is included within the Community's objectives,[17] is widely shared but not uncontroversial.[18] Pollution can be considered as a part of economic activity, and it has economic consequences. Thus it is reasonable to interpret the Preamble and Art. 2 of the EEC Treaty as including economic concepts of environmental pollution, such as those of external cost and of the environment as a common good. Also, it is true that when the EEC Treaty was concluded, environmental problems were not yet recognized as important enough to mandate an explicit Community commitment to solving them. A new factor affecting or arising out of economic activities, such as environmental pollution, can arguably be considered within the notion of harmonious development of economic activities under Art. 2 of the EEC Treaty. Such a dynamic perspective is required by the constitutional character of the EEC Treaty. Thus, it would seem that the insistence on a narrow economic and static concept of Community goals by critics of Community environmental policy, among whom the British House of Lords figures prominently,[19] is no longer warranted in light of the Community's development and the societal factors shaping its operation.

d. Art. 100 of the EEC Treaty

A generous reading of the Preamble and Art. 2 does not mean that the application of Art. 100 is without complications. It has been asserted that Art. 100 can not support a comprehensive environmental policy because environmental concerns are only indirect or incidental to its primary purpose of abolishing obstacles to trade between member states.[20] While environmental concerns may, in light of the Treaty's legislative history, be regarded as "incidental," the argument overlooks the necessarily dual function of any harmoni-

[17] *See, e.g.*, CARPENTIER, *supra* note 12, at 382–393; CLOSE, *supra* note 12, at 475–476; BÉRAUD, *supra* note 12, at 37.

[18] In favor of a broad interpretation *see* F. BEHRENS, *supra* note 3, at 71 *et seq.*; GERARD, *supra* note 12, at 21, 27; E. GRABITZ & C. SASSE, *supra* note 12, at 24, 30; Lukes, *supra* note 12, at 160; Ipsen, in UMWELTSCHUTZ UND INTERNATIONALE WIRTSCHAFT 187 (V. Götz, D. Rauschning & G. Zieger eds., Carl Heymanns Verlag, Köln 1975); RIEGEL, *supra* note 12, at 77–78, 82; ZULEEG, *supra* note 12, at 136. *Contra*, House of Lords, Select Committee, 22ND REPORT, *supra* note 12, No. 9; VYGEN, *supra* note 12, at 60.

[19] *Supra* note 12.

[20] European Parliament, Resolution of 18 April 1972, *supra* note 16; Bericht im Namen des Rechtsausschusses, *supra* note 12, at 15 *et seq.*; CARPENTIER, *supra* note 12, at 391–392; F. BEHRENS, *supra* note 3, at 258; E. GRABITZ & C. SASSE, *supra* note 12, at 27; VON MOLTKE, *supra* note 12, at 137.

zation measure under Art. 100.[21] One function is to coordinate the laws and regulations of member states as such. But Art. 100 measures must also determine substantive policies in the process of establishing new harmonized substantive rules applicable throughout the Community. Such rules may be quite different from those existing in member states. The problem with using Art. 100 as a basis for a common environmental policy is not so much that environmental concerns are only incidental to harmonization but rather that it does not provide substantive standards to guide the environmental policies that harmonizing measures must necessarily establish.

This problem reflects the two alternative strategies on which the Treaty is based. The Treaty presumes that "apolitical" market mechanisms — established through implementation of the four freedoms, competition policy, and harmonization measures — will achieve most Treaty objectives. For subjects where the signatory states thought the market mechanism was inappropriate, the Treaty enunciates substantive standards for the development of common policies. This design of the Treaty limited and therefore made acceptable transfer of sovereignty from member states to the Community. The problem with Community environmental policy is that harmonization may be needed and justified on the economic, market-oriented ground of restoring allocative efficiency by removing trade barriers, but such harmonization requires that the Community adopt its own "positive," interventionist environmental policy[22] for which substantive standards agreed upon by the member states are lacking. Community environmental policy thus straddles the two Treaty strategies described above. This helps explain the fact that the common environmental policy has been developed by a process of bargaining between governments and bureaucracies not subject to the rules of political democracy governing the political processes in the member states.

Other objections are frequently voiced to the use of Art. 100 to justify comprehensive Community environmental initiatives. One thesis is that Art. 100 can only justify reactive measures to deal with economic problems created by

[21] *See* F. BEHRENS, *supra* note 3, at 249–250; CLOSE, *supra* note 12, at 467; VON DER GROEBEN, *Die Politik der Europäischen Kommission auf dem Gebiet der Rechtsangleichung*, 23 NEUE JURISTISCHE WOCHENSCHRIFT 359, 361 (1970); H. P. IPSEN, EUROPÄISCHES GEMEINSCHAFTSRECHT 687, 694 (Mohr Siebeck, Tübingen 1972); F. MARX, *supra* note 14, at 48; W. SCHMEDER, *supra* note 12, at 10, 21 *et seq.*; Schwartz, *Zur Konzeption der Rechtsangleichung in der Europäischen Wirtschaftsgemeinschaft*, in PROBLEME DES EUROPÄISCHEN RECHTS, FESTSCHRIFT FÜR W. HALLSTEIN 474, 483, 495–496; (E. von Caemmerer, H. J. Schlochauer & E. Steindorff eds., Vittorio Klostermann, Frankfurt 1966); SEIDEL, *supra* note 12, at 175; ZULEEG, *supra* note 12, at 134–135.

[22] F. MARX, *supra* note 14, at 145 *et seq.*, particularly at 159; H. VON DER GROEBEN & H. MÖLLER, MÖGLICHKEITEN UND GRENZEN EINER EUROPÄISCHEN UNION, VOL. 1: DIE EUROPÄISCHE UNION ALS PROZESS 391 (Nomos Verlag, Baden-Baden 1980).

In theory, economic analysis could determine the level of environmental regulations that would secure allocational efficiency. In practice, however, the guidance which it provides is highly indeterminate. *See* R. STEWART & J. KRIER, ENVIRONMENTAL LAW AND POLICY 350–366 (Bobbs-Merrill, Indianapolis, 2d ed. 1978).

the existence of different environmental laws in member states, or at least of a single environmental law in one member state.[23] It has also been argued that existing national legislation bounds the framework for harmonization so that innovative action is not possible.[24]

These views are unduly narrow. They are belied by the information/standstill agreement of 1973 (as amended in 1974),[25] which obliges member states to inform the Commission about *draft* legislation which may either directly affect the functioning of the Common Market or affect the implementation of the Community's environmental program. It may be conceded that this agreement does not, as a legal matter, clarify the scope of Art. 100 of the EEC Treaty. Indeed, by couching the agreement in the form of a mere "gentlemen's agreement," the member states have avoided formally acknowledging that draft legislation as well as existing environmental laws are arguably, via Art. 5 of the EEC Treaty, covered by Art. 100. Nonetheless, the agreement's practical result is to broaden the scope of Art. 100.

More importantly, the reactive view of Art. 100 neglects the fact that, although a particular subject may not be covered by a specific environmental regulation, it is often governed by general environmental law which in most cases differs among member states.[26] Such differences make the specific problem area in question a suitable object of harmonization under Art. 100. That the non-existence of specific, conflicting national provisions is no real jurisdictional barrier to Community legislation is demonstrated by the PCB waste directive,[27] which established common rules for disposal of PCB waste although no member state previously had such specific legislation. The justification for this kind of harmonization is simply that the various national rules of general ap-

[23] F. Behrens, *supra* note 3, at 243–244, 282–283, 295; Carpentier, *supra* note 12, at 390; E. Grabitz & C. Sasse, *supra* note 12, at 27; C.-D. Ehlermann, *supra* note 14, at 101; Gerard, *supra* note 12, at 24; Lukes, *supra* note 12, at 161; House of Lords, Select Committee, 22nd Report, *supra* note 12, No. 13(4); Kaiser, *supra* note 12, at 114; F. Marx, *supra* note 14, at 38, 156; E. Röhling, *supra* note 12, at 58 *et seq.*; Riegel, *supra* note 12, at 79; Touscoz, *supra* note 12, at 40; Vygen, *supra* note 12, at 61; Zuleeg, *supra* note 12, at 134–135. *Contra*, H. P. Ipsen, *supra* note 21, at 694; Taschner, *Art. 100 annot. 22-23*, in Kommentar zum EWG-Vertrag (H. von der Groeben, H. von Boekh, J. Thiesing & C.-D. Ehlermann eds., Nomos Verlag, Baden-Baden, 3rd ed. 1983); Offermann-Clas, *supra* note 12, at 1127; W. Schmeder, *supra* note 12, at 10; Vignes, *supra* note 14, *Art. 100 annot. 4*, at 154.

[24] C.-D. Ehlermann, *supra* note 14, at 101; Seidl-Hohenveldern, *Rechtsakte der Organe der EWG als Mittel der Rechtsangleichung*, in Angleichung des Rechts der Wirtschaft in Europa 170, 192 (Carl Heymanns Verlag, Köln 1969).

[25] Agreement of the representatives of the Governments of the Member States meeting in Council of 5 March 1973 on information for the Commission and for the Member States with a view to possible harmonization throughout the Communities of urgent measures concerning the protection of the environment, OJ No. C 9, 15 March 1973, p. 1, as amended by the agreement of 15 July 1974, OJ No. C 86, 20 July 1974, p. 2.

[26] F. Behrens, *supra* note 3, at 244; Vignes, *supra* note 14, at 244.

[27] Directive 76/403/EEC of 6 April 1976 on the disposal of polychlorinated biphenyls and polychlorinated terphenyls, OJ No. L 108, 26 April 1976, p. 41.

plicability (in this case the laws covering waste disposal in general) were different. Finally, the view that existing national legislation sets the legal bounds for the content of harmonized solutions is rejected by the great majority of legal writers.[28]

The most serious challenge to the use of Art. 100 as a basis for the development of common environmental policy is perhaps the requirement in Art. 100 itself that directives for the approximation of the laws of the member states are only justified if these laws "directly affect the establishment or functioning of the common market." This requirement is designed to prevent a limitless expansion of Community legislation and must therefore be taken seriously. A direct effect can easily be found in the case of product related requirements. Different national provisions concerning the design or composition of cars, fuels, or detergents are technical barriers to trade and clearly affect the Common Market directly. However, it is controversial whether the same is true of emission standards,[29] ambient quality standards,[30] the regulation of waste disposal,[31] the prohibition or restriction of the use of products,[32] the protection of flora, fauna, and landscape, or the regulation of land use.[33] National differences in such standards or regulations do not directly affect the exchange of goods between member states; they are at best a production cost factor like other production cost factors, which vary due to differing natural conditions, such as location in population centers, or governmental policies, such as tax levels. It is certainly not reasonable to conclude that the harmonization program estab-

[28] *See* the authors cited *supra* note 21. *See also* Taschner, *supra* note 23, at annot. 13; B. BEUTLER, R. BIEBER, F. PIPKORN & J. STREIL, DIE EUROPÄISCHE GEMEINSCHAFT – RECHTSORDNUNG UND POLITIK 308 (Nomos Verlag, Baden-Baden 1979); LELEUX, *Le rapprochement des législations nationales dans la CEE,* 1968 CAHIERS DE DROIT EUROP. 129, 143; E. RÖHLING, *supra* note 12, at 59; SEIDEL, *The Harmonization of Laws Relating to Pharmaceuticals in the EEC,* 6 COMMON MKT. L. REV. 309, 312–313 (1968–1969). *Cf.* House of Lords, Select Committee, 22ND REPORT, *supra* note 12, No. 13(3).

[29] Denying legislative competence *see* Lukes, *supra* note 12, at 167 *et seq.*; House of Lords, Select Committee, 22ND REPORT, *supra* note 12, No. 13(1). Affirming legislative competence *see* ZULEEG, *supra* note 12, at 135; F. BEHRENS, *supra* note 3, at 241.

[30] Denying legislative competence *see* House of Lords, Select Committee, 22ND REPORT, *supra* note 12, No. 13(1); Lukes, *supra* note 12, at 167 *et seq.* Affirming legislative competence *see* F. BEHRENS, *supra* note 3, at 241; BÉRAUD, *supra* note 12, at 37; ZULEEG, *supra* note 12, at 135.

[31] Affirming legislative competence *see* G. NICOLAYSEN, EUROPÄISCHES GEMEINSCHAFTSRECHT 169 (Kohlhammer, Stuttgart 1979); OFFERMANN-CLAS, *supra* note 12, at 1127.

[32] Affirming legislative competence where related to product quality norms *see* SEIDEL, *supra* note 12, at 179. *See also* OFFERMANN-CLAS, *Die Kompetenzen der Europäischen Gemeinschaften im Umweltschutz,* 6 ZEITSCHRIFT FÜR UMWELTPOLITIK 47, 52 (1983) (skeptical).

[33] Denying legislative competence *see* House of Lords, Select Committee, 22ND REPORT, *supra* note 12, No. 10; BOTHE, *The Trends in Both National and International Politics for Achieving a Unification of Standards in Pollution Matters,* 2 ZEITSCHRIFT FÜR UMWELTPOLITIK 293, 303 (1979); KAISER, *supra* note 12, at 116.

lished under Art. 99 of the EEC Treaty for turnover taxes, excise duties, and other forms of indirect taxation implies that all production cost factors must be harmonized. Such a conclusion would require a depth and density of legal integration hardly achieved even in fully developed federal states.

But the concept of directness must be interpreted in light of the objective which it is to serve, namely the functioning of the Common Market. Therefore, the requirement of direct impact has to be interpreted dynamically: It covers any effect on competitive conditions in the Common Market (e.g., production cost, location conditions) that has a sufficiently close connection with, and is liable to substantially affect the functioning of the Common Market in its present state of development.[34]

This view is taken by the majority of recent legal literature and apparently shared by the European Court of Justice. In two recent decisions concerning the consistency with the Treaty of the directive on detergents[35] and the directive on the sulfur content of gas oil,[36] the European Court of Justice[37] pointed out that both directives were covered by the environmental program of 1973 as well as the general program of 1969 for the elimination of technical barriers to trade. Since both directives established product requirements, the Court could have rested with the argument that different national requirements on products clearly have a direct effect on the Common Market. However, it proceeded in dictum to approach the general problem: "Furthermore, it is by no means ruled out that provisions on the environment may be based upon Art. 100 of the Treaty. Provisions which are made necessary by considerations relating to the environment and health may be a burden upon the undertakings to which they apply and if there is no harmonization of the national provisions on the matter, competition may be appreciably distorted." This decision can be interpreted as confirming the Court's dynamic view of the Treaty[38] and

[34] Ehlermann, *Community Policy with Regard to Approximation of Laws*, in House of Lords, Select Committee, 22ND REPORT, *supra* note 12, Annex, at 14; BÉRAUD, *supra* note 12, at 37–38; CLOSE, *supra* note 12, at 470 *et seq.*; F. BEHRENS, *supra* note 3, at 238 *et. seq.*; LELEUX, *supra* note 28, at 140; Schwartz, *supra* note 21, at 489, 491; RIEGEL, *supra* note 12, at 78; SEIDEL, *supra* note 12, at 180 *et. seq.*; B. GOLDMANN, DROIT COMMERCIAL EUROPÉEN 480 (Dalloz, Paris, 3d ed. 1975); E. RÖHLING, *supra* note 12, at 68; Verloren van Themaat, *supra* note 14, at 249–250; Vignes, *supra* note 14, at 155; ZULEEG, *supra* note 12, at 135; probably also KAISER, *supra* note 12, at 114–115. *Contra*, German Bundesrat, Bundesrats-Drucksache 502/68; House of Lords, Select Committee, 22ND REPORT, *supra* note 12, No. 13(1); E. GRABITZ & C. SASSE, *supra* note 12, at 27; Lukes, *supra* note 12, at 167 *et seq.*; F. MARX, *supra* note 14, at 161.

[35] Directive 73/404/EEC of 22 Nov. 1973 on the approximation of the laws of the Member States relating to detergents, OJ No. L 347, 17 Dec. 1973, p. 51.

[36] Directive 75/716/EEC of 24 Nov. 1975 on the approximation of the laws of the Member States relating to the sulphur content of certain liquid fuels, OJ No. L 307, 27 Nov. 1975, p. 22.

[37] Case 91/79, Commission v. Italy, [1980] ECR 1099, 1106; case 92/79, Commission v. Italy, [1980] ECR 1115, 1122.

[38] European Court of Justice, case 148/77, H. Hansen jun. & O. C. Balle GmbH & Co. v. Hauptzollamt Flensburg, [1978] ECR 1787, 1806.

consequently as announcing a judicial attitude favorable to the development of a common environmental policy.

It was anticipated that the Court would have the chance to resolve the question of Community competence for environmental policy in two pending cases[39] which challenged the legality of the titanium waste directive.[40] However, these cases at present are dormant because the Commission anticipated reversal of its decision on other grounds and has taken steps to reconsider its decision.

The Court's dictum would not validate any and all Community environmental initiatives. The Court's dictum implies that, in addition to product related requirements, certain producer related requirements such as emission standards are also covered by Art. 100. Whether the same is true of ambient quality standards is an open question,[41] and regulating non-industrial pollution,[42] protecting flora and fauna, or regulating land use would normally seem to be beyond the scope of Art. 100. To this extent Art. 100's origin as a vehicle for harmonizing competitive conditions imposes limitations on the legislative competence of the Community. The regulation of an environmental problem under Art. 100 must be substantially related to industrial or commercial activities.[43]

e. Art. 235 of the EEC Treaty

Where Art. 100 fails to apply, Art. 235 may fill the gap. Interpreting the Preamble and Art. 2 of the EEC Treaty to include environmental protection as a Community goal means that Art. 235 can also be used as the foundation of an environmental policy. Art. 235 goes beyond Art. 100 because it is not limited by the catalog of instruments made available in Art. 3 of the EEC Treaty for the achievement of Community goals. Under Art. 235, the Community can take on new functions where necessary to achieve the goals set forth in the Preamble and Art. 2.

The limits of Art. 235 are unclear. The legal literature agrees that Art. 235's reference to the "common market" can no longer be understood in exclusively economic terms. Rather, the Article is to be understood as a flexible instrument

[39] Case 78/79, BTP Tioxide Ltd. v. Commission, and case 79/79, Laporte Industries Ltd. v. Commission, OJ No. C 153, 20 June 1979, p. 5.

[40] Directive 78/176/EEC of 20 Feb. 1978 on waste from the titanium dioxide industry, OJ No. L 54, 25 Feb. 1978, p. 19.

[41] *See* authors cited *supra* note 30.

[42] ZULEEG, *supra* note 12, at 135 (municipal sewage).

[43] Besides Art. 100 of the EEC Treaty, Articles 101 and 102 of the EEC Treaty could also theoretically be used as a basis for Community environmental legislation. However, the requirement of a "specific distortion," i.e. a distortion within a single member state which does not have a parallel in other member states, is normally not present in the field of environmental protection. *See* F. BEHRENS, *supra* note 3, at 260 *et seq.* On the limited scope of Articles 117 and 118 of the EEC Treaty *see id.*, at 199 *et seq.*

for dynamic development of integration in the framework of the Preamble and Articles 2 and 3 of the EEC Treaty. Under this view, utilization of Art. 235 is limited only by the institutional framework established by the Treaty.[44] Such a limit is not insignificant. The principle of limited Community competences and the fundamental distinction which the Treaty makes between common policy, coordinated policy, and approximation of laws would preclude the Community from developing, wholly independently of member states' measures, a common environmental policy comparable to the agriculture, transportation, and foreign trade policies.[45] However, Art. 235 can be used in appropriate cases and together with Art. 100 may therefore serve as the framework for something like a common policy.

The European Court of Justice seems to favor a broad interpretation of Art. 235.[46] Others take a much narrower view. For them Art. 235 is a "residual" grant of power whose function is to fill gaps within the framework of existing policies, rather than to extend that framework.[47] Under this view initiatives can not be justified as directly based on the objectives of the Community as set forth in the Preamble and Art. 2. Also, many who favor a broader interpretation believe that some economic relationship to the Common Market, however tenuous, is necessary.[48]

The consequences of requiring an economic relationship to the Common Market are unclear. Certainly, Art. 235 can be used to regulate environmental problems which are related to economic activities but whose direct effect on competitive conditions within the Common Market can not be established, rendering Art. 100 inapplicable. Moreover, Art. 235 also encompasses situations where exclusive reliance on the logic of Art. 100 would lead to fragmentary and hence ineffective regulation of an environmental problem. But Com-

[44] F. Behrens, *supra* note 3, at 271 *et seq.*; *id., supra* note 12, at 466–467; Carpentier, *supra* note 12, at 393; Close, *supra* note 12, at 476 *et seq.*; Bericht im Namen des Rechtsausschusses, *supra* note 12, at 18 *et seq.*; Riegel, *supra* note 12, at 80 *et. seq. See generally* B. Beutler, R. Bieber, J. Pipkorn & J. Streil, *supra* note 28, at 313; G. Nicolaysen, *supra* note 31, at 46; H. P. Ipsen, *supra* note 21, at 687; Tomuschat, *Die Rechtsetzungsbefugnisse der EWG in Generalermächtigungen, insbesondere in Art. 235 EWGV,* 11 Europarecht, Supplement 45, 60 (1976) (with further references).

[45] F. Behrens, *supra* note 3, at 276–277, 290–291.

[46] *See* case 8/73, Hauptzollamt Bremerhaven v. Massey-Ferguson GmbH, [1973] ECR 897.

[47] Burhenne & Schoenbaum, *supra* note 12, at 498–499; Catalano, *supra* note 14, at 63–64; Gerard, *supra* note 12, at 28–29; E. Grabitz & C. Sasse, *supra* note 12, at 30–31; Kaiser, *supra* note 12, at 115 *et seq.*; von Moltke, *supra* note 12, at 136; Zuleeg, *supra* note 12, at 136 *et seq.*; Vygen, *supra* note 12, at 60; Touscoz, *supra* note 12, at 43–44.

[48] F. Behrens, *supra* note 3, at 277, 466; Close, *supra* note 12, at 477, 479; Offermann-Clas, *supra* note 12, at 1128; *id., supra* note 32, at 53. In the same sense *see generally* Lauwaars, *Art. 235 als Grundlage für die flankierenden Politiken im Rahmen der Wirtschafts- und Währungsunion,* 11 Europarecht 100 (1976).

munity action not involving products, or pollution that is not at least tenuously tied to economic activities, clearly remains on unsafe jurisdictional ground.[49]

In the political practice of the Community, Art. 235 is used wherever different national regulations of an activity potentially harmful to the environment do not have a clear or exclusive financial impact on trade or industry. This is the case with respect to ambient quality standards, emission standards for non-industrial sources, the regulation of non-industrial waste, information exchange, and research and development. Moreover, the Community has relied on Art. 235 to expand its activities, although sporadically, into noneconomic environmental problems, such as protection of wild birds and endangered species. Finally, adherence to conventions for the prevention of marine and long range air pollution is based on Art. 235.[50] Accordingly, Art. 235, although less frequently invoked than Art. 100, is an important foundation for Community environmental policy.

Apart from product regulation, environmental directives are normally based on both Articles 100 and 235; unique reliance on Art. 235 is very rare. Some directives are based on both articles because Art. 100 was not thought sufficient for legal reasons. In many other cases, this happened because agreement on the correct jurisdictional base could not be reached for political reasons.[51]

More important than the choice between the two articles is the fact that there is an undisputed core of general Community legislative competence for environmental protection. It is only the outer limits of this competence that remain unclear and may give rise to controversy.

f. Limits of Member State Competences (Articles 30, 34, and 36 of the EEC Treaty)

Apart from the "positive" legislative competences established by Articles 100 and 235, the "negative" legislative competences of the Community have become an important factor in the development of European legal integration. Art. 30 prohibits member states from imposing "quantitative restrictions on imports" or "measures having an equivalent effect" unless justified as consistent with the Treaty. This prohibition is understood to encompass any measure liable to directly or indirectly, actually or potentially, hinder trade within the Community. It includes not only measures which discriminate facially against foreign producers, but also measures that, although formally equally applicable to domestic and foreign producers, in fact erect barriers to

[49] BOTHE, *supra* note 33; House of Lords, Select Committee, 22ND REPORT, *supra* note 12, No. 10; KAISER, *supra* note 12, at 116.

[50] On the question of the extent to which recourse to Art. 235 of the EEC Treaty is necessary, *see* MASTELLONE, *The External Relations of the E.E.C. in the Field of Environmental Protection*, 30 INT'L & COMP. L. Q. 104, 110 (1981); *infra* pp. 70–74, 84.

[51] *See* OFFERMANN-CLAS, *supra* note 32, at 55 *et seq.*; VIGNES, *43-100 et 100-235*, 1976 CAHIERS DE DROIT EUROP. 810; F. BEHRENS, *supra* note 3, at 293. For an explanation of these conflicts *see infra* at pp. 245–251.

interstate trade.[52] However, Art. 36 provides that Art. 30 "shall not preclude prohibitions or restrictions on imports . . . on grounds of public morality, public policy, or public security [or] the protection of health and life of humans, animals, or plants," provided that such prohibitions or restrictions may not "constitute a means of arbitrary discrimination or a disguised restriction on trade" among member states.

The European Court of Justice has developed a series of cases, beginning with its decision in *Cassis de Dijon*, extensively interpreting Articles 30 and 36, defining the notion of "measures having an equivalent effect,"[53] and clarifying the applicable standard of justification under Art. 36 in the environmental and public health contexts. The national measure must be designed for the protection of public health or the environment. Although the burden of proof is not on member states, the Court rejects an abstract justification and scrutinizes the concrete purpose of the measure in question.[54] On the other hand, the relevant member state has a certain margin of discretion in assessing the relevant

[52] European Court of Justice, case 8/74, Procureur du Roi v. Dassonville, [1974] ECR 837; case 41/76, Criel and Schou v. Procureur de la République and Directeur général des douanes et droits indirects, [1976] ECR 1921; case 120/78, Rewe-Zentral-AG v. Bundesmonopolverwaltung für Branntwein (Cassis de Dijon), [1979] ECR 649. On the notion of measures having equivalent effect *cf.* W. H. ROTH, FREIER WARENVERKEHR UND STAATLICHE REGELUNGSGEWALT IN EINEM GEMEINSAMEN MARKT 24 *et seq.* (C. H. Beck, München 1977) (with further references).

[53] Cassis de Dijon, *supra* note 52; case 244/78, Union Laitière Normande v. French Dairy Farmers Limited, [1979] ECR 2633; case 153/78, Commission v. Germany (Meat preparations), [1979] ECR 2555; case 788/79, Gilli, [1980] ECR 2071; case 152/78, Commission v. France (Advertising for alcoholic beverages), [1980] ECR 2299; case 27/80, Fietje, [1980] ECR 3839; case 53/80, Officier van Justitie v. Koninklijke Kaasfabriek Eyssen BV (Nisin), [1981] ECR 409; case 130/80, Kelderman BV (Brioches), [1981] ECR 527; case 272/80, Biologische Producten BV (Pesticides), [1981] ECR 3277; case 220/81, Robertson, [1982] ECR 2349; case 40/82, Commission v. United Kingdom (Protection of animal health), [1982] ECR 2793; case 124/81, Commission v. United Kingdom (UHT milk), [1983] ECR 203; case 174/82, Sandoz, [1983] ECR 2445. *See also* Ehlermann, *Das Verbot der Maßnahmen gleicher Wirkungen in der Rechtsprechung des Gerichtshofs*, in HAMBURG, DEUTSCHLAND, EUROPA, FESTSCHRIFT FÜR H. P. IPSEN 579 (R. Stödter & W. Thieme eds., Mohr Siebeck, Tübingen 1977); MASCLET, *Les articles 30, 36 et 100 du Traité C.E.E. à la lumière de l'arrêt "Cassis de Dijon,"* 1980 REVUE TRIMESTRIELLE DE DROIT EUROP. 23; MATTERA, *L'Arrêt "Cassis de Dijon": Une nouvelle approche pour la réalisation du bon fonctionnement du marché intérieur*, 1980 REVUE DU MARCHÉ COMMUN 505; DERINGER & SEDEMUND, *Europäisches Gemeinschaftsrecht*, 34 NEUE JURISTISCHE WOCHENSCHRIFT 1199 (1981); A. WEBER, SCHUTZNORMEN UND WIRTSCHAFTSINTEGRATION 102 *et seq.*, 247 *et seq.* (Nomos Verlag, Baden-Baden 1982); P. OLIVER, FREE MOVEMENT OF GOODS IN THE E.E.C., parts VII and VIII (European Law Centre, London 1982); DAUSES, *Dogmatik des Freien Warenverkehrs in der Europäischen Gemeinschaft*, 1984 RECHT DER INTERNATIONALEN WIRTSCHAFT 197.

[54] European Court of Justice, Nisin case, *supra* note 53; Biologische Producten, *supra* note 53.

effects, especially in setting tolerances.[55] Furthermore, the measure must be necessary for the protection of health or the environment, i.e. a measure less burdensome to interstate trade must not be available. The measure must also not place an excessive burden on interstate trade.[56] The standards are somewhat different according to whether the relevant state measure is on its face discriminatory or equally applicable to all producers.[57]

The new jurisprudence of the European Court of Justice is designed to cope with abuses of national regulatory powers ("false" public health or environmental policy); its purpose is not to compel "secondary" harmonization at the lowest common denominator in cases where the Community has not been able to agree on harmonization or has even expressly left the member states freedom to regulate. However, the principles developed by the Court are capable of some extension,[58] and they could, in the long run, have considerable impact on national environmental law. The Commission in its communication of 3 October 1980[59] has already adopted the view that products from member states must in principle be admitted to the national market when they comply with the standards of the state of origin. A member state rejecting a foreign product must prove that its stricter standards are justified. Even if there is no obligation to recognize foreign standards or foreign approvals of products, the importing state may, under the Court's opinion, be required to recognize tests made under foreign law if they are equivalent to those required under domestic law.[60]

In addition to Art. 30 of the EEC Treaty, Art. 34's prohibition on measures having an effect equivalent to quantitative export restrictions may also be applicable. The recent decision of the European Court of Justice on the German prohibition against baking at night[61] shows that producer related require-

[55] European Court of Justice, Nisin case, *supra* note 53; Sandoz case, *supra* note 53; *see* Kommers & Waelbroeck, *Legal Integration and the Free Movement of Goods: The American and European Experience*, at § III.C.1, in INTEGRATION THROUGH LAW, Vol. 1, Book 3.

[56] European Court of Justice, Meat preparations case, *supra* note 53; case 104/75, De Peijper, managing director of Centrafarm, [1976] ECR 613; Robertson, *supra* note 53; Commission v. United Kingdom, *supra* note 53. *See* W. H. ROTH, *supra* note 52, at 339.

[57] European Court of Justice, case 113/80, Commission v. Ireland (Irish Souvenirs), [1981] ECR 1625; case 59/82, Schutzverband gegen Unwesen in der Wirtschaft v. Weinvertriebs GmbH (Vermouth wine), [1983] ECR 1217 (consumer protection not recognized as public policy where measure was discriminatory); case 124/81, Commission v. United Kingdom (UHT milk), *supra* note 53 (facially discriminatory measure can be justified under Art. 36 as protection of public health).

[58] W. H. ROTH, *supra* note 52, at 339; SLOT, *Handelsbarrières, Nationaal recht en Europees recht*, 28 SOCIAAL-ECONOMISCHE WETGEVING 233, 258–259 (1980).

[59] OJ No. C 256, 3 Oct. 1980, p. 2.

[60] Biologische Producten, *supra* note 53.

[61] Case 155/80, Oebel (Prohibition on baking bread at night), [1981] ECR 1993. *See also* cases 141–143/81, Holdijk (Protection of fatted calves), [1982] ECR 1299.

ments having direct effect on intrastate distribution of products are also not immune from judicial scrutiny. However, the Court still limits the scope of Art. 34 by requiring a specific danger of restriction on export transactions.

All told, the *Cassis de Dijon* doctrine has an as yet untested potential for Community control over, and intervention into, national environmental law.[62] Since Community regulation of widely marketed products is already fairly comprehensive and major gaps exist only with respect to existing products, the *Cassis de Dijon* doctrine in the long run will be more important in the field of producer related requirements than that of product requirements. However, there would have to be considerable extension of the doctrine in order to threaten seriously existing member state competences in this area.

2. The Other Treaties

While the Treaty for the Establishment of the European Coal and Steel Community covers only limited research aspects of pollution from the coal and steel industry, the Euratom Treaty is a true second, although much more restricted, foundation of Community environmental policy because of its concern with health and safety problems arising from operation of nuclear power plants. One of the tasks of the Euratom Treaty is to "establish uniform safety standards to protect the health and safety of workers and the general public" (Art. 2(b)). For these purposes, Articles 30 and 31 empower the Council to establish basic health standards (i.e. maximum permissible doses, maximum permissible levels of exposure and contamination, and fundamental principles for monitoring worker health). Under Art. 37 of the Euratom Treaty, member states must inform the Commission of any plan for discharge of radioactive substances, in order to enable the Commission to determine whether the discharge may contaminate the water, air, or soil of other member states. The Commission may then comment on the discharge. In case of emergency, the Commission may issue a directive to require the member states to prevent infringements of the basic standards (Art. 38).

The powers of Articles 30 and 31 were used as early as 1959. The directive of 1959 establishing basic health standards[63] and the superseding directive of 1976 establishing revised basic safety standards[64] represented a system of rather detailed health and safety standards for protection from radiation. To this extent, Community policy on radiation exposure is a forerunner of the common environmental policy.

[62] *See* W. H. ROTH, *supra* note 52, at 28–29, 336 *et seq.*

[63] Directive (Euratom) of 2 Feb. 1959 laying down the basic standards for the protection of the health of workers and the general public against the dangers arising from ionising radiations [*sic*], 1959 JO No. 221, 20 Feb. 1959, p. 59 ([1959–62] OJ (special English ed.) at 7).

[64] Directive 76/579/Euratom of 1 June 1976 laying down the revised basic safety standards for the health protection of the general public and the workers against the dangers of ionizing radiation, OJ No. L 187, 12 July 1976, p. 1.

Despite the seeming breadth of Articles 2(b) and 30, the Community's power to deal with health and environmental problems presented by the peaceful use of nuclear energy is limited. In particular, the Euratom Treaty does not provide specific powers for the Community to regulate the design and location of nuclear power plants. Moreover, the Treaty provides no Community competences to regulate nuclear waste, apart from establishment of a joint enterprise, application of basic health standards, and the consultation procedure under Art. 37. The fact that the Community is and remains the owner of all nuclear material, including waste (Art. 86 Euratom Treaty), does not accord additional regulatory powers to Community institutions (Art. 87 Euratom Treaty). An extension of Community powers into these areas could only be based on a broad interpretation of the Preamble of the Treaty and the Community objectives listed in Art. 2(c), namely protecting human life and health and ensuring establishment of the facilities necessary to the development of nuclear energy in the Community. If the function of the Community is understood to encompass all health and environmental effects of the peaceful use of nuclear energy, the "residual" powers provision of Art. 203 of the Euratom Treaty could be invoked for further Community action in this field. Such a broad interpretation would raise questions similar to those already examined in the case of Art. 235 of the EEC Treaty.

3. Conclusions

Environmental policy is now firmly established as a separate policy area within the institutional framework of the Community. The original EEC Treaty provisions are, from a strictly legal point of view, too narrow to provide firm support for this development. Although they have been used to support Community environmental directives, Articles 100 and 235 of the EEC Treaty are not specifically concerned with environmental protection. It is clearly the political will of the Community institutions as expressed by the environmental programs and numerous legislative texts rather than the mandate of the Treaty itself that has established environmental protection as a new quasi-common policy. This policy differs from the common policies established under the Treaty (such as agriculture, transportation, and foreign trade) because it overlaps with the remaining legislative competence of the member states. Hence, the resolutions of the Paris summit meeting of 1972 and the adoption of the first environmental program in 1973, together with later efforts to implement and extend this program, mark a qualitative step forward in the process of European integration.[65] They amount to an informal extension of the Community into a new area and therefore have "constitutional" importance for the European Community. This conclusion is supported by the fact that the initial "official" decision to go forward with formulating an environmental program was made not by a Community body, but rather by

[65] P. Mathijsen, A Guide to European Community Law 161 (Sweet & Maxwell, London, New York, 2d ed. 1975).

the heads of state and government and only later endorsed by the Council. Together with the information/standstill agreement of 1973 between the member states,[66] this initiative represents an interesting institutional development in the Community, namely, integration through "soft law."[67] Soft law consists of programs and declarations of a non-binding nature, and series of consecutive legislative steps which are of little importance when analyzed in isolation but whose aggregate weight marks a qualitative shift. This process of "incrementalism" represents a new type of policy developed through political consensus of the member states.

B. Legislative Instruments: The Directive as a Tool of Community Environmental Policy

Besides the lack of a clear legal basis in the Treaty for a common environmental policy, another institutional deficiency regarding Community implementation of environmental policy is that — unlike developed federal systems — the Community can not make laws binding upon individuals throughout the Common Market. The Treaty, in Art. 189, makes two kinds of legislative instruments available to the Community — regulations and directives. It states that a regulation "shall be binding in its entirety and directly applicable" to member states, whereas a directive "shall be binding as to the result to be achieved" but shall leave to member states "the choice of form and methods." Art. 100, which is the principal basis of Community environmental policy, provides that it may only be implemented by directive. Accordingly, the Community has relied upon the directive as the lawmaking instrument for environmental policy. In theory, Art. 235 of the EEC Treaty would allow resort to any of the instruments enumerated in Art. 189 of the EEC Treaty, but has never been so broadly used as the foundation of Community environmental law.

Coordinated national legislation has not as yet played any role in environmental protection. The mandate of Art. 220 of the EEC Treaty to conclude conventions for the further promotion of European integration does not include environmental protection. However, at least one of the conventions concluded under Art. 220, namely the 1968 Convention on jurisdiction and the enforcement of civil and commercial judgments, in conjunction with the protocol of 1971 concerning the Court of Justice's interpretation of this convention, covers private litigation over transboundary pollution. The *Rhinewater* (Alsatian Alkali) case[68] demonstrates the potential of the Convention. Furthermore, the Commission has attempted to coordinate the negotiation and ratifi-

[66] *Supra* note 25.

[67] *See generally* Bothe, *"Soft Law" im Recht der Europäischen Gemeinschaften*, in STAATSRECHT – VÖLKERRECHT – EUROPARECHT, FESTSCHRIFT FÜR H. J. SCHLOCHAUER 761 *et seq.* (I. von Münch ed., Walter de Gruyter, Berlin, New York 1981). *Cf.* KAISER, *supra* note 12, at 110.

[68] European Court of Justice, case 21/76, Handelskwekerij G. J. Beir B. V. v. Mines de Potasse d'Alsace, [1976] ECR 1735.

cation by member states of international conventions for the prevention of marine pollution[69] and of long distance air pollution, problems which concern the Community as a whole or at least several member states.

Beyond legislation, the Community institutions, as well as the European Council (a quasi-Community institution), use a variety of informal forms of action, such as decisions, resolutions, recommendations, communications, and agreements. The binding force on member states of these different forms of action varies. But all share the attribute of not being directly applicable to individuals. They are used for making fundamental policy declarations; implementing organizational and administrative measures establishing research programs and systems of information exchange; creating special funds; and acceding to international conventions. The recommendation serves as an alternative to the directive when member states do not desire a strict obligation.

Overall, the directive is by far the most important form of action in environmental policy. Its problems will accordingly be discussed in more detail.

1. Specificity of Directives

According to Art. 189(3) of the EEC Treaty, Community environmental directives are binding only on the member states. Accordingly, the directive must be incorporated into national law in order to have any legal effect in the domestic legal order of member states. Moreover, directives are binding only "as to the results to be achieved" leaving national authorities "the choice of form and methods." Consequently, Community environmental law, limited to use of the directive form, can in theory only set broad policy goals and establish a regulatory framework to be implemented by member states. This allows for flexibility in their implementation and adjustment to existing national law and administrative practice. The price is that the directive may be implemented in a quite varied manner, which may run counter to goals of consistency in environmental policy. An even more important threat to the effectuation of Community environmental policy is the problem of lax implementation and noncompliance, which grows as the number of directives increases.

Because it may be implemented only by directives, Community environmental law might seem "inferior" to the Community law of agriculture, transportation, and competition, which may be implemented by regulation. However, the already extensive legal integration of the Community, fostered in part by the jurisprudence of the European Court of Justice, has narrowed the practical distinction between directives and regulations in the environmental context.[70]

In environmental protection, there are still many directives which more or less correspond to the "result" model presumed in Art. 189. But the Community has also issued a great number of directives whose substantive provisions

[69] For that purpose, a consultation procedure has been established under Art. 84(2) of the EEC Treaty (Decision 77/587/EEC of 13 Sept. 1977, OJ No. L 239, 17 Sept. 1977, p. 23).

[70] P. Mathijsen, *supra* note 65.

are so detailed that member states have little choice as to their implementation under national law. In practice, there are three types of directives in terms of specificity and legal effect on member states:

1. *"Typical" directives* which closely follow the "result" model of Art. 189 of the EEC Treaty.
2. *Regulation-type directives*: The directive itself or an annex to it (which forms an integral part of the directive but can normally be amended by a simplified procedure) contains detailed substantive provisions, such as prohibitions, standards and tolerances, and provisions for implementation, such as testing and measurement methods.
3. *Framework directives*: The framework directive sets out the objectives and basic principles applicable to a broad area of environmental protection. Normally, this directive is binding on the member states and, while leaving them much discretion in implementing it, must be incorporated into state law. One or more special directives, which may be "typical" or regulation-type and contain more detailed substantive rules, may fill out the framework directive. It is also possible that the framework directive need not be incorporated into state law before it is made operable by special directives. For example, the aquatic environment directive of 1976[71] provides for establishment of Community-wide uniform effluent standards, enumerates a priority list of substances to be regulated, and establishes the criteria for fixing standards. The standards themselves will be fixed in a series of special directives, which may be of the regulation type.

It must be noted, however, that directives of the second and third types are seldom found in pure form. They often contain substantial components corresponding to the legislative model of Art. 189(3).

In principle, such directives cover only substantive law. When they do address questions of procedure, Community environmental directives normally allow member states great flexibility. For example, the procedural provision of a pollution control directive might in general terms require a member state to establish appropriate authorities to deal with the problem, institute a licensing system for the activity, or establish implementation plans, leaving the choice of specific mechanisms to the member states. Several recent and partly controversial Community measures seek to go further in harmonization of procedures and implementation measures. These include the proposal for environmental impact assessment and the titanium dioxide directive,[72] which provides that a member state may not exclude an existing source from an implementation plan without the Commission's agreement. The latter directive

[71] Directive 76/464/EEC of 4 May 1976 on pollution caused by certain dangerous substances discharged into the aquatic environment of the Community, OJ No. L 129, 18 May 1976, p. 23.

[72] Directive 78/176/EEC of 20 Feb. 1978 on waste from the titanium dioxide industry, OJ No. L 54, 25 Feb. 1978, p. 19; as amended by the Directive 83/29/EEC of 24 Jan. 1983, OJ No. L 32, 3 Feb. 1983, p. 28.

may even be considered a first step in making the Commission an executive authority.

On the whole, it can be safely said that with respect to substantive law the distinction between regulation and directive has blurred, although it has retained most of its validity in the field of procedure. Legal literature tends to uphold this development on the grounds that the distinction between goals and measures as drawn by Art. 189(3) is impractical and that the only test can be the need for harmonization pursuant to Art. 100.[73] Community institutions accordingly enjoy considerable flexibility to decide on a case by case basis the degree of specificity needed to address a particular environmental problem. In the few environmental cases so far decided, the European Court of Justice implicitly confirmed the legality of specific product standards and ambient quality standards.[74] However, the parties in those cases did not challenge the relevant directives on the ground that they were overly specific and therefore inconsistent with Art. 189(3). Such a challenge has been made only in the two pending titanium dioxide cases,[75] which are presently dormant.

It seems probable that the European Court of Justice will endorse the principle that the need for harmonization is the appropriate test for the degree of specificity an environmental directive can take. But it is unclear how closely the Court will scrutinize the discretion granted to Community lawmakers in assessing the need for harmonization. The answer to this question will ultimately determine the extent to which the Community's lack of authority to issue environmental regulations can be remedied by using directives to specify member state measures and to control implementation.

2. Direct Effect, Supremacy, and Preemption

Degree of specificity is only one feature distinguishing regulations and directives. According to the concept underlying Art. 189, a regulation is directly ap-

[73] *See* A. Bleckmann, Europarecht 53 *et seq.* (Carl Heymanns Verlag, Köln, 3d ed. 1978); H. P. Ipsen, *supra* note 21, at 696; *id.*, in Zur Integration Europas, Festschrift für C. F. Ophüls 67, 71 *et seq.* (W. Hallstein & H. J. Schlochauer eds., C. F. Müller, Karlsruhe 1965); P. Kapteyn & P. Verloren van Themaat, Introduction to the Law of the European Communities 113–114 (Sweet & Maxwell, Kluwer, London, Deventer, 1973); Mégret, *La technique communautaire d'harmonisation des législations*, 1967 Revue du Marché Commun 181, 186; de Ripainsel-Landy & Gerard, *La notion juridique de la directive utilisée comme instrument de rapprochement des législations dans la C.E.E.*, in Les Instruments de rapprochement des législations dans la Communauté Économique Européenne 47 *et seq.* (D. de Ripainsel-Landy, *et al.*, Université de Bruxelles, Brussels 1975); E. Röhling, *supra* note 12, at 77 *et seq.*, with further references at 82; W. Schmeder, *supra* note 12, at 53; Taschner, *supra* note 23, at annot. 11; *critical* M. Zuleeg, Das Recht der Europäischen Gemeinschaft im Innerstaatlichen Bereich 283 (Carl Heymanns Verlag, Köln 1969); *id.*, *supra* note 12, at 141.

[74] *See* cases cited *supra* note 37; case 148/78, Pubblico Ministero v. Ratti, [1979] ECR 1629.

[75] *See* cases cited *supra* note 39.

plicable in member states whereas a directive must be incorporated into national law in order to be internally binding, directly applicable and enforceable. The Treaty thus establishes a two-tier lawmaking procedure with respect to directives, similar to the "Rahmengesetz" (framework law) in West Germany. However, this two-tier concept has in practice been eroded by a growing recognition of the principles of direct effect and supremacy for directives. It is now well established in the jurisprudence of the European Court of Justice[76] and accepted by most national courts (with major qualifications by the French Conseil d'Etat[77] and recently the German Supreme Tax Court[78]) that directives (like the Treaty provisions themselves), although addressed to member states, may confer individual rights on citizens against member states which can be enforced and are to be protected by national courts (direct effect). These directives supersede all conflicting national law, even if it is enacted later or is of a constitutional nature (supremacy). Although the concepts of direct effect and supremacy have been developed independently, they are interrelated because supremacy follows from direct effect.[79]

a. Direct Effect of Directives[80]

The EEC Treaty, Art. 169, provides an infringement procedure, initiated by Community authorities, to enforce the obligations imposed upon member states to incorporate and implement the relevant directives. Recognizing direct effect for directives provides an additional mechanism, using private initiative, to enforce such obligations.

However, a member state is not absolved from its duty to incorporate and implement the relevant directive by claiming that it automatically has direct ef-

[76] *See* J. Weiler, *supra* note 1, at 44 with further references.

[77] Conseil d'Etat, 1 March 1968, Syndicat général de fabricants de semoules, [1970] COMMON MKT. L. REP. 395, 6 COMMON MKT. L. REV. 419 (1968–1969); 22 Dec. 1978, Cohn-Bendit, 1978 Receuil 524, [1980] 1 COMMON MKT. L. REP. 543, 16 COMMON MKT. L. REV. 701 (1979).

[78] Bundesfinanzhof, 16 July 1981, 27 RECHT DER INTERNATIONALEN WIRTSCHAFT 691 (1981), [1982] 1 COMMON MKT. L. REP. 527; critical annotation: MEIER, 37 DER BETRIEBS-BERATER 1883 (1981).

[79] J. Weiler, *supra* note 1, at 19.

[80] *See* PESCATORE, *L'effet des directives communautaires: une tentative de démythification*, 1980 DALLOZ CHRONIQUE 171; TIMMERMAN, *Directives: Their Effect Within the National Legal System*, 16 COMMON MKT. L. REV. 533 (1979); USHER, *The Direct Effect of Directives*, 4 EUROPEAN L. REV. 268 (1979); *id.*, EUROPEAN COMMUNITY LAW AND NATIONAL LAW: THE IRREVERSIBLE TRANSFER? 19 *et seq.*, 70 *et seq.* (UACES, London 1981); WINTER, *Direct Applicability and Direct Effect – Two Distinct and Different Concepts in Community Law*, 9 COMMON MKT. L. REV. 428 (1972); ZULEEG, *Die Rechtswirkung europäischer Richtlinien*, 11 ZEITSCHRIFT FÜR UNTERNEHMENS- UND GESELLSCHAFTSRECHT 466, 474 *et seq.* (1980); Kovar, *L'integrité de l'effet direct des directives communautaires selon la jurisprudence de la Cour de Justice de la Communauté*, in DAS EUROPA DER ZWEITEN GENERATION, GEDÄCHTNISSCHRIFT FÜR C. SASSE, vol. 1, at 115 *et seq.* (R. Bieber, A. Bleckmann & F. Capotorti eds., Nomos Verlag, Baden-Baden 1981); F. CAPELLI, LE DIRETTIVE COMUNITARIE 261 *et seq.* (Giuffrè, Milano 1983).

fect.[81] It is also doubtful whether the individual has a personal or subjective right, in the strict sense, to enforce a directive. The justification given by the European Court of Justice for recognition of direct effect is that such direct effect is a logical corollary of the obligation of the member state to incorporate and implement the relevant directive.[82] Moreover, direct effect primarily concerns the relationship of the state and individual (vertical direct effect). Consequently, a directive can not create rights and duties among individuals (horizontal direct effect).[83]

The European Court of Justice in its more recent decisions seems to endorse these principles because it no longer refers to the notion of "direct effect" of a directive; rather, it describes direct effect as the right of individuals to invoke provisions of a directive against a member state which has not fulfilled its obligation of incorporating and implementing the directive.[84]

The conditions for direct effect are that (a) the member state has not, or has not appropriately, fulfilled its obligation to implement the directive; (b) that the relevant provision is sufficiently clear and unconditional not to leave the national authority discretion in implementing it;[85] and (c) that the directive by its nature is capable of conferring rights on individuals.[86] Accordingly, specific and detailed provisions of directives normally have a direct effect and supersede conflicting national law. For example, the European Court of Justice held in the *Ratti* case[87] that the specific provisions of the directive of 1973 concerning classification, packaging, and labeling of solvents could be invoked by a citizen before a national court and that the provisions of a national law establishing stricter, more detailed, or even merely different requirements were not enforceable against him. This is an important development in view of the increasing number of regulation-type directives in the field of environment policy.

[81] European Court of Justice, case 102/79, Commission v. Belgium, [1980] ECR 1473.

[82] *See* European Court of Justice, case 158/80, Rewe v. Hauptzollamt Kiel (Butterfahrten), [1981] ECR 1805.

[83] PESCATORE, *supra* note 80, at 171 *et seq.*; TIMMERMAN, *supra* note 80, at 544; EASSON, *Can Directives Impose Obligations on Individuals?*, 4 EUROPEAN L. REV. 67, 70 *et seq.* (1979) with further references; ZULEEG, *supra* note 80, 474–475.

[84] *But see* case 106/77, Amministrazione delle Finanze dello Stato v. Simmenthal S.p.A., [1978] ECR 629 [hereinafter cited as Simmenthal II].

[85] European Court of Justice, case 33/70, SpA SACE v. Ministry for Finance of the Italian Republic, [1970] ECR 1213; case 38/77, Enka BV v. Inspecteur der Invoerrechten en Accijnzen, Arnhem, [1977] ECR 2203; case 41/74, Van Duyn v. Home Office, [1974] ECR 1337; case 148/78, Pubblico Ministero v. Ratti, [1979] ECR 1629; case 88/79, Ministère Public v. Grunert, [1980] ECR 1827; case 108/80, Ministère Public v. Kugelmann, [1981] ECR 433.

[86] European Court of Justice, case 45/75, Rewe, [1976] ECR 181, 196; Van Duyn, *supra* note 85, at 1356 (per Mayras Advocate-General). In case 8/81, Becker v. Finanzamt Münster, [1982] ECR 53, 71, the European Court of Justice indicates that these tests are mutually exclusive. *See also* USHER, *Direct Effect of Directives: Dotting the i's*, 5 EUROPEAN L. REV. 470, 472–473 (1980).

[87] *Supra* note 85.

Recent case law (although not in environmental law) has also established that even if directives are not sufficiently specific to have direct effect, they may nonetheless serve as a standard for national judicial review of the actions of national authorities.[88] Individuals may invoke provisions of a directive before a national court for a ruling "whether the competent national authorities, in exercising the choice which is left to them as to the form and methods for implementing the directive, have kept within the limits as to their discretion set out in the directive."[89] By virtue of the principle of supremacy, this rule can probably be generalized to include any national legislation, even that which does not purport to implement a directive but is inconsistent with it.

There is an important difference between direct effect and invocation of a directive as a standard for judicial review of national law. In the latter case — as in the case of unconstitutionality of legislation — national law inconsistent with the directive will merely be set aside (negative direct effect). It is then up to the national legislature to enact new implementing legislation. The directive itself has no positive effect because, for lack of specificity, it must by necessity be implemented by national authorities in order to be applicable.

b. Supremacy of Directives

Under the principle of supremacy, Community law has precedence over existing or subsequent state law.[90] Community directives bind not only the legislature but also the administrative authorities and courts. To the extent a directive has no direct effect, the state administrative authorities and courts have to apply it as a standard in interpreting vague statutory terms or in implementing the discretion which is left to them. Beyond that, incorporation must be awaited. To the extent a directive has a direct effect, it supersedes conflicting national law. It also follows from the principle of supremacy that when the Community has used its powers to regulate a matter by issuing an environmental directive, the member states are barred from enacting or at least applying new rules inconsistent with the directive.[91] To this extent, harmonization of state envi-

[88] *See* TIMMERMAN, *supra* note 80, at 544 *et seq.*; Bleckmann, *L'applicabilité directe du droit communautaire*, in LES RECOURS DES INDIVIDUS DEVANT LES INSTITUTIONS NATIONALES EN CAS DE VIOLATION DU DROIT EUROPÉEN 102, 125 (Maison F. Larcier, Brussels 1978).

[89] European Court of Justice, case 51/76, Verbond Nederlandse Ondernemingen v. Inspecteur der Invoerrechten en Accijnzen (VNO), [1977] ECR 113, 127; case 21/78, Delkvist v. Anklagemyndigheden, [1978] ECR 2327, 2339.

[90] European Court of Justice, case 6/64, Costa v. E.N.E.L., [1964] ECR 585; case 14/68, Walt Wilhelm and Others v. Bundeskartellamt, [1969] ECR 1; Simmenthal II, *supra* note 84. *See, e.g.*, Jacobs & Karst, *The "Federal" Legal Order: The U.S.A. and Europe Compared - A Juridical Perspective*, at § III.B.2.a, in INTEGRATION THROUGH LAW, Vol. 1, Book 1; J. Weiler, *supra* note 1, at 16 *et seq.*, with further references.

[91] Favoring a "transfer" of competence *see* European Court of Justice, Simmenthal II, *supra* note 84, at 644; E. W. Fuß, *Die Verantwortung der nationalen Gerichte für die Wahrung des europäischen Gemeinschaftsrechts*, in DAS EUROPA DER ZWEITEN GENERATION, *supra* note 80, at 171, 187 *et seq.*; Taschner, *supra* note 23, at annot. 16. Favoring

ronmental legislation causes a transfer of legislative power from the member states to the Community. Provided that harmonization at the Community level had the objective of protecting health or the environment, Art. 36 of the EEC Treaty is no longer available to justify subsequent state legislation inconsistent with the directive. Whether protection of health or the environment was a primary or secondary objective or whether the Community measures are adequate seems to be irrelevant.[92] Any modifications of a directive to secure the particular interests of a member state must be sought within the procedural framework of the Community.[93]

c. Preemption

It is doubtful whether the Community, by issuing a directive for the harmonization of an area, can also claim exclusive legislative jurisdiction over the area and therefore preempt member states from legislating in the area irrespective of whether or not their action is consistent with the directive.[94] In the context of environmental law, this problem has arisen in connection with the 1979 sixth amendment to the dangerous substances directive of 1967[95] and has even become a political issue in West Germany and the Netherlands. The problem here is whether the introduction of a common reporting and testing procedure for new toxic substances and of a common system of classification, packaging, and labeling of all toxic substances has preempted all national legislation on toxic substances.

The question of preemption is relatively easy to answer when Community law harmonizes a particular area of environmental protection but deliberately leaves member states the power to enact either stricter or more lenient national requirements or grants them discretion in implementing a regulatory framework. Here, the national legislature is in principle free to select the rules it considers to be in the best interest of the nation, provided it keeps within the boundaries of the discretion left to it.[96]

simple non-applicability of inconsistent national law *see* IPSEN, annotation, 14 EUROPARECHT 223, 236 (1979).

[92] European Court of Justice, Ratti, *supra* note 85, at 1644; case 35/76, Simmenthal, [1976] ECR 1871; case 5/77, Carlo Tedeschi v. Denkavit Commerciale s.r.l., [1977] ECR 1555; case 251/78, Firma Denkavit Futtermittel GmbH v. Minister für Ernährung, Landwirtschaft und Forsten des Landes Nordrhein-Westfalen (Animal feedstuffs), [1979] ECR 3369.

[93] *See infra* at pp. 279–282.

[94] *See generally* Jacobs & Karst, *supra* note 90, at § III.B.2.c.; J. Weiler, *supra* note 1, at 20 *et seq.*

[95] Directive 79/831/EEC of 18 Sept. 1979, OJ No. L 259, 15 Oct. 1979, p. 10.

[96] Product related requirements present a further complexity: unless the producers have an option between harmonized and national requirements, some additional Community controls over the reasonableness of the exercise of discretion left to the national legislature may be exercised by virtue of Articles 30 and 36 of the EEC Treaty. *See* European Court of Justice, Nisin, *supra* note 53, relating to Art. 6 of Directive 64/54/EEC of 5 Nov. 1963, 1964 JO p. 161 ([1963–1964] OJ (special English ed.) at

Apart from these cases of incomplete harmonization, the relevant question is to what extent an environmental directive regulates a particular area or subject or, in other words, to what extent the "field" is occupied. In its more recent case law, the European Court of Justice, using a pragmatic approach,[97] has been cautious in finding that Community law has occupied the field and is therefore exclusive, even in the absence of direct conflict. This is even true in areas where the Treaty itself — and not the fiat of a summit conference, as in the case of environmental protection — has established common policies.[98] The doctrine of preemption is still developing. Given the variety of solutions offered in developed federal systems, there is no reason to assume that broad preemption is really necessary to maintain the Community's ability to develop comprehensive policies. The principle of supremacy, together with recognition of the concurrent competence of the member states, will as a rule suffice to achieve this legitimate goal. The Court appears to preserve concurrent jurisdiction until the full development of a common policy and clear occupation of the field by the Community.

It would seem that such a comprehensive occupation of the field by the Community is hardly conceivable in the case of environmental policy, based on Articles 100 and 235 of the EEC Treaty. In any case, exclusiveness of Community environmental regulation by a directive can not be presumed. Finding preemption would require careful interpretation of the relevant directive, taking into account its wording, context, and legislative history and purpose. Caution is all the more warranted because there are only a few Court decisions relevant to the issue of preemption in Community environmental law.

99), which allows member states to authorize or prohibit the addition of nisin to food; case 172/82, Syndicat national des fabricants raffineurs d'huile de graissage v. Groupement d'intérêt économique "Inter-Huiles," [1983] ECR 555 (where it remains unclear whether Articles 30 and 36 limit the member states' discretion or provide guidelines for the interpretation of the directive as to the extent of their discretion).

[97] *See* Waelbroeck, *The Emergent Doctrine of Community Pre-Emption — Consent and Re-Delegation*, in COURTS AND FREE MARKETS 548 *et seq.* (T. Sandalow & E. Stein eds., Clarendon Press, Oxford 1982).

[98] *See* European Court of Justice, case 50/76, Amsterdam Bulb BV v. Produktschap voor Siergewassen, [1977] ECR 137; case 232/78, Commission v. France (Mutton and lamb), [1979] ECR 2729; cases 3, 4 and 6/76, Kramer (Biological resources of the sea), [1976] ECR 1279; case 32/79, Commission v. United Kingdom, [1980] ECR 2403; case 804/79, Commission v. United Kingdom, [1981] ECR 1045. In the earlier cases, preemption was more easily affirmed. *See, e.g.*, case 40/69, Hauptzollamt Hamburg v. Bollmann (Turkey rumps), [1970] ECR 69; case 39/70, Fleischkontor GmbH v. Hauptzollamt Hamburg (Reliable importer), [1971] ECR 49; case 94/71, Schlüter & Maack v. Hauptzollamt Hamburg, [1972] ECR 307. *See also* J. USHER, EUROPEAN COMMUNITY LAW AND NATIONAL LAW, *supra* note 80, at 43 *et seq.*; *id.*, *The Effects of Common Organization and Policy on the Power of a Member State*, 1 EUROPEAN L. REV. 428 (1977).

The *Ratti* decision[99] concerned a case in which the relevant provisions of Italian law were in direct contradiction to the provisions concerning labeling and packaging of the 1973 directive on solvents. But the Court basically relied on a textual interpretation of the relevant directive itself. The holding in *Ratti* only means that to the extent a particular field is actually occupied by Community law, the national legislature may not make different rules in the field so occupied.

The more recent *Grunert* case,[100] which concerned the closely related law of consumer protection (food), shows that the Court does not easily accept preemption. In *Grunert* the relevant directive prohibited member states from completely banning the use of listed preservatives. The list of preservatives was established by directives regulating the use of preservatives in food. As far as the marketing of such substances is concerned, the directives merely impose an obligation on member states to take all measures necessary to ensure that the substances are placed on the market only if their packaging bears certain information. The Court concluded from these provisions that a general prohibition against the marketing of such substances would hinder the application of the Community rules and must therefore be considered contrary to the objectives of the directives. Since the emphasis of the holding is on the inconsistency with the relevant directives of a general prohibition on the marketing of such substances, it can not be maintained that the Court derived its conclusion merely from the fact that the Community had also legislated in the field of marketing by subjecting marketing to certain packaging and labeling requirements. Rather, the argument seems to be that since the use of a particular substance can not be prohibited entirely, a general prohibition against the marketing of such substance can not be used to achieve the same result. The *Grunert* case, therefore, is likewise an expression of the principle of supremacy rather than of the principle of preemption.

All told, there is little warrant, in the present state of development of Community environmental policy, for a broad presumption of preemption. The common idea that directives cause an irreversible transfer of legislative competence from the member states to the Community is an expression of the principle of supremacy; it does not follow from the principle of supremacy that a directive must preempt all member state measures related to the subject of the directive.[101]

[99] *Supra* note 85.

[100] *Id.*

[101] *See* LELEUX, *supra* note 28, at 219. *Contra,* Jacobs & Karst, *supra* note 90, at § III.B.2.c, note 291 and accompanying text.

III. US Legislative Competences and Instruments

A. Federal Competence in the Field of Environmental Protection

The US Constitution does not mention environmental protection, and environmental advocates have failed to persuade the federal courts to read a right to environmental quality into the Constitution. However, the Constitution grants the Congress several lawmaking powers which allow it broad authority to legislate in the environmental area.

The most significant is the power to "regulate Commerce with foreign nations, [and] among the several States."[1] The Supreme Court has broadly construed this power to authorize Congress to regulate any commercial or industrial activity, even if it occurs wholly within one state. The commerce power extends to regulation of land use and natural resources. For example, *Hodel v. Virginia Surface Mining Association*[2] held that the commerce power authorizes Congress to regulate the reclamation of local stripmined coal lands in Virginia. Most federal environmental statutes are based upon and sustainable under the commerce power.

In addition, Congress is granted the power to "dispose of and make all needful Rules and Regulations respecting the Territory or other Property belonging to the United States."[3] The federal government owns about one third of the land in the United States, including resource-rich land in the West and Alaska, and the outer continental shelf. The property power provides authority for Congress to enact laws governing the development and protection of these lands and their resources. In addition, Congress has the power to levy taxes and spend the proceeds for the "general Welfare."[4] This power would authorize taxes on pollution and subsidies for environmental protection measures. It also enables Congress to condition the receipt of federal funds by state and local governments or private persons on compliance by the recipient with environmentally protective conditions. The power of the President, with the advice and consent of the Senate, to enter into treaties, and the power of Congress to enact legislation implementing treaties is also of potential significance.[5] For example, the Supreme Court invoked these powers to uphold legis-

[1] U.S. Const. art. I, § 8, cl. 3.

[2] 452 U.S. 264 (1981).

[3] U.S. Const. art. IV, § 3, cl. 2. Congress also enjoys legislative power over lands acquired by the federal government. *Id.* art. I, § 8, cl. 17.

[4] *Id.* art. I, § 8, cl. 1.

[5] *Id.* art. II, § 2, cl. 2.

lation, enacted pursuant to a treaty with Canada, which limits the local taking of migratory birds.[6]

Article III of the Constitution grants the Supreme Court original jurisdiction over controversies involving states, and also gives Congress power to invest the federal courts with jurisdiction over controversies arising under the "laws" of the United States. The courts have invoked these sources of jurisdiction to develop federal common law to reduce disputes over the apportionment of interstate waters,[7] interstate pollution,[8] and other interstate resource controversies.[9] It has been held that Congress has authority to enact statutes creating or modifying the law governing such controversies. Article III also grants the federal courts admiralty and maritime jurisdiction. This grant has likewise been held to support congressional authority to enact statutes governing admiralty and maritime matters, such as oil spills from ships.

Given this battery of lawmaking powers, Congress as a practical matter has virtually unlimited authority to enact measures regulating, taxing, or subsidizing the use and development of environmental and natural resources within the United States.

By virtue of the Supremacy Clause,[10] Congress also has the authority to preempt, totally or partially, state environmental and natural resource taxes and regulation. Where Congress has not regulated some aspect of commerce, the federal courts have exercised authority, assertedly derived from the commerce clause grant of power to Congress, to invalidate state measures that unduly burden or restrict such commerce.[11] This "negative commerce clause" doctrine is also a potential threat to state and local environmental regulation.

The provision in the Fifth Amendment (made applicable to the states through the Fourteenth Amendment) that "private property" shall not "be taken for public use without just compensation" may limit both federal and state government measures to protect the environment. Regulation of pollution or toxic substances posing a substantial threat to health or the natural environment would not be held a "taking," but measures barring development of private lands, such as wetlands, might be limited.[12]

[6] Missouri v. Holland, 252 U.S. 416 (1920). An earlier, similar act of Congress not based on treaty, had been invalidated as beyond its powers.

[7] *E.g.*, Arizona v. California, 373 U.S. 546 (1963).

[8] *E.g.*, Illinois v. City of Milwaukee, 406 U.S. 91 (1972).

[9] *E.g.*, City of Philadelphia v. New Jersey, 437 U.S. 617 (1978).

[10] U.S. Const. art. VI, § 2.

[11] Freeman v. Hewit, 329 U.S. 249, 252 (1946) ("the Commerce Clause ... by its own force created an area of trade free from interference by the states ... [T]he Commerce Clause even without implementing legislation by Congress is a limitation upon the power of the States"). For discussion, *see* Kommers & Waelbroeck, ***Legal Integration and the Free Movement of Goods: The American and European Experiences***, especially at § II.B.1, in INTEGRATION THROUGH LAW, Vol. 1, Book 3.

[12] *See, e.g.*, State v. Johnson, 265 A.2d 711 (Maine 1970) (state Wetlands Act's restrictions on filling held to constitute a deprivation of reasonable use, thus an unreasonable exercise of police power). ***But see*** Just v. Marinette County, 56 Wis. 2d 7, 201 N.W.2d 761 (1972), upholding a similar statute.

Another potential limitation on Congressional authority is suggested by *National League of Cities v. Usery.*[13] That decision invalidated the application of federal minimum wage legislation to state employees, on the ground that the Tenth Amendment and the federal structure preclude Congress from exercising the commerce power in ways that impair the states' exercise of governmental functions "essential to [their] separate and independent existence."[14] In the context of environmental regulation, this ruling may limit Congress' authority to require state governments or state officials to implement federal environmental measures. Several lower federal courts have invoked principles of state sovereignty to deny or limit claims by the federal Environmental Protection Agency of statutory authority under the Clean Air Act to mandate state controls on motor vehicle use in order to ensure achievement for federal air quality standards.[15] But in *Federal Energy Regulatory Commission v. Mississippi*[16] the Supreme Court recently sustained the validity of a federal statute requiring states to follow federal energy conservation objectives in state regulation of electric utilities. The potential constitutional limitations on Congress' power to conscript the states in implementing and enforcing federal programs — and to enjoin or punish state officials who refuse to undertake such enforcement — is accordingly unclear.

In any event, the Supreme Court made clear in its *Hodel* decision that *National League of Cities* imposes no limitations on the power of Congress directly to regulate private commercial and industrial acitivity, or the power to preempt state regulation of such activity. Moreover, it is widely accepted that Congress may induce the states to implement federal environmental programs by conditioning relevant federal grants of aid to the states on their cooperation in implementation and enforcement; several lower courts have rejected claims that such conditions are unconstitutional infringements of state sovereignty.[17]

[13] 426 U.S. 833 (1976).

[14] *Id.* at 845.

[15] *See* STEWART, *Pyramids of Sacrifice? Problems of Federalism in Mandating State Implementation of National Environmental Policy,* 86 YALE L.J. 1196 (1977) (discussing cases). *But cf.* United States v. Ohio Department of Highway Safety, 635 F.2d 1195 (6th Cir. 1980), *cert. denied,* 451 U.S. 949 (1981) (EPA may require Ohio to refuse registration to motor vehicles that have not passed federally-mandated inspection of pollution control devices.)

[16] 456 U.S. 742 (1982).

[17] For discussion, *see* STEWART, *supra* note 15, (discussing potential implications of *National League of Cities* for conditional grants); KADEN, *Politics, Money, and State Sovereignty: The Judicial Role,* 79 COLUM. L. REV. 847 (1979); Note, *Taking Federalism Seriously: Limiting State Acceptance of National Grants,* 90 YALE L.J. 1694 (1981). For a collection of decisions, *see id.* at 1698 n. 32. In *Hodel, supra* note 2, the Court rejected the State of Virginia claims that a statute mandating federal enforcement of strip mine controls unless the state itself enforced federal standards was an unconstitutional coercion of the states, pressuring them to undertake such enforcement.

The Constitution empowers states, with Congressional consent, to enter into federally enforceable interstate compacts. A number of such compacts have been formed to deal with the management and apportionment of interstate waters.[18]

B. Legislative Instruments

Two basic areas of federal environmental legislation may be distinguished: regulation of private conduct, and management of public resources.[19]

1. Regulation of Private Conduct

Three basic strategies of federal integration can be identified in Congressional legislation regulating private conduct: federal standards federally enforced; federal standards implemented and enforced by the states; and federal requirements or incentives for state adoption and enforcement of environmental protection measures. All of these strategies have been pursued in a variety of federal environmental regulatory statutes, most of them enacted since 1965. Some recent innovative variations on these strategies include market type systems of transferable pollution rights and federal cleanup and compensation funds.

a. Federal Standards, Federal Implementation and Enforcement

This approach is most frequently followed in the regulation of nationally marketed products. Examples include control of air pollution from new motor vehicles, regulation of motor vehicle fuel additives, control of noise pollution by new products, and the manufacture and sale of pesticides and toxic chemicals. In all of these areas the adoption of standards, implementation, and enforcement is the responsibility of the federal Environmental Protection Agency. The regulation of hazards from nuclear power plants and oil tanker operations is, with certain qualifications, also a federal responsibility exercised, respectively, by the Nuclear Regulatory Commission and the Department of Transportation. The Department of Transportation also regulates the transport of hazardous materials.[20]

These regulatory schemes often, but not invariably, preempt more rigorous or different state regulation on the rationale that divergent and possibly in-

[18] *See generally* MUYS, *Allocation and Management of Interstate Water Resources: The Emergence of the Federal-State Compact*, 6 DENVER J. INT'L L. & POL. 307, 308 (1976) (as of 1976, Congress had approved thirty-five compacts dealing primarily with interstate water resources).

[19] Conceptually, it may be difficult to distinguish regulation of private air and water pollution from management of public lands and other resources because the ultimate objective of pollution control is protection and management of public air and water resources. But, there are important political, organizational, and legal differences between the two forms of environmental programs.

[20] Hazardous Materials Transportation Act, 49 U.S.C. §§ 1801–1812.

consistent state regulations would disrupt national product markets, deny manufacturers the ability to realize scale economies in production, or otherwise subvert national interests.[21]

b. Federal Standards, State Implementation and Enforcement

This strategy is typically employed in the regulation of industrial processes.

Under one approach, the federal government adopts environmental quality standards, and the states are given responsibility to adopt and enforce controls on pollution from particular facilities in order to ensure that the federal environmental quality standards are achieved. This approach is exemplified by Title I of the Clean Air Act,[22] which requires the Environmental Protection Agency to adopt nationally uniform air quality standards,[23] and places responsibility on the states to devise state implementation plans (SIPs) through which source controls are to be imposed to achieve standards.[24] If a state is derelict in carrying out its responsibilities, (a) state measures may be enforced by the federal government or by citizens pursuant to federal citizen suit provisions,[25] or (b) the federal EPA may rewrite inadequate state plans or take over implementation and enforcement entirely.[26]

A second approach involves federal adoption of emission or effluent limitations or design standards for particular types of facilities. Federal administrators are generally given responsibility for implementation and enforcement in the first instance, but they may (and in practice often do) delegate that responsibility to a state if it meets federal requirements designed to ensure adequate implementation by state authorities. Delegated program requirements are in most cases federally enforceable by federal officials or through federally authorized citizen suits, and the delegation may be revoked if a state fails to carry out its responsibilities properly.

[21] There is no preemption of more stringent state regulation of hazardous pesticides or chemicals. Under Section 209 of the Clean Air Act, EPA may approve a more stringent state standard for motor vehicle emissions control. States have a limited but potentially significant role in the regulation of nuclear power generation. Under the Hazardous Materials Transportation Act, however, the Department of Transportation is authorized to declare that a state or local law is inconsistent with the Act and thus preempted. 49 U.S.C. § 1811 (1976). Because inconsistency is a question of statutory interpretation, an inconsistency ruling by the Department is evidence of inconsistency, but a court is not bound by that assessment. *See* National Tank Truck Carriers v. Burke, 608 F.2d 819 (1st Cir. 1979).

[22] 42 U.S.C. §§ 7401–7642. For a detailed treatment of the Clean Air Act, *see* D. Currie, Air Pollution: Federal Law & Analysis (Callaghan & Co., Wilmette, Ill. 1981).

[23] 42 U.S.C. § 7409.

[24] *Id.* § 7410.

[25] *Id.* § 7604.

[26] *Id.* § 7410, 7413.

Examples of this approach include new source performance standards under the Clean Air Act,[27] effluent limitations under the Clean Water Act,[28] strip-mine regulation under the Surface Mining Control and Reclamation Act,[29] and controls on toxic waste disposal under the Resource Conservation and Recovery Act.[30] Federal regulators have an incentive to delegate implementation and enforcement responsibility to states because of limited federal budgets and resources, the difficulties of centralized information collection and processing, the greater familiarity of state and local officials with regulated facilities, and the existence of varying local conditions that should receive consideration in implementation and enforcement. State and local authorities are usually willing to undertake implementation and enforcement in order to maintain a degree of autonomy and flexibility, and to qualify for federal funds that underwrite administrative expenses. Recent budget cutbacks at the Environmental Protection Agency and the ideological preference of the Reagan administration for state and local control have accelerated the reliance upon state and local implementation of federal environmental programs, but simultaneous cutbacks in federal financial assistance for states' environmental programs have hampered the ability of states to discharge these added responsibilities.

Regulatory programs involving federal standards and state implementation and enforcement almost never preempt more stringent state standards. The relevant statute typically provides explicitly that states may adopt and enforce standards and controls more stringent than those required by federal statute.[31]

c. *Federal Requirements or Incentives for State Adoption and Implementation of Environmental Measures*

Federal statutes sometimes call upon or provide incentives to the states to adopt and implement regulatory standards or engage in resource planning and control. This was the basic approach to air and water pollution control during

[27] *Id.* § 7411.

[28] 33 U.S.C. §§ 1251–1376. The effluent limitations are authorized by § 1311. For discussion of these and other provisions of the Clean Water Act, *see* generally 1 F. GRAD, TREATISE ON ENVIRONMENTAL LAW § 3.03 (Matthew Bender & Co., New York, NY, Loose-leaf service, 1973–).

[29] 30 U.S.C. §§ 1201–1328. *See generally* SKILLERN, *Environmental Law Issues in the Development of Energy Resources*, 29 BAYLOR L. REV. 739 (1977).

[30] 42 U.S.C. §§ 6901–6987 (1976 & Supp. IV 1980). For an overview of RCRA and its implementing regulations, *see generally* FRIEDLAND, *The New Hazardous Waste Management System: Regulation of Wastes or Wasted Regulation?*, 5 HARV. ENVT'L L. REV. 89 (1981).

Federal delegation to states of implementation and enforcement responsibility is also provided in the prevention of significant deterioration provisions of the Clean Air Act, and in certain aspects of regulation of nuclear power plants under the Atomic Energy Act.

[31] *E.g.*, § 3009 of RCRA, 42 U.S.C. § 6929. This provision was added as part of the 1980 amendments to RCRA.

the late 1960s, when federal statutes required states to adopt and implement air and water quality standards. The federal government had authority to deal with transboundary spillovers and take emergency abatement measures, but was otherwise limited to supervision and review of state programs.

This approach was adopted because of state and industry opposition to more centralized control and the apparent advantages of decentralized flexibility. Congress, however, eventually concluded that this approach generated weak standards and inadequate enforcement, and adopted far more centralized systems in the 1970 Clean Air Act and the 1972 Federal Water Pollution Control Act Amendments. But primary reliance upon state measures remains the norm in areas of environmental policy that involve land use control, water supply, sewage, and solid waste disposal — functions that have traditionally been the responsibility of local or state government.

For example, section 208 of the Clean Water Act calls upon states and localities to engage in land and water resource planning in order to control "non-point" sources of water pollution and to coordinate water supply, effluent treatment, and development policies;[32] the solid waste provisions of the Resource Conservation and Recovery Act seek to stimulate improved landfill practices by states and localities;[33] and the Coastal Zone Management Act calls upon states to plan development and land use in the coastal zone.[34] These programs generally do not preempt state and local measures more stringent than those sought by the federal government.[35]

The incentives for states and localities to participate in these programs are several. Federal grants are typically provided to underwrite a substantial portion of the expenses of state and local planning, administration, and facility construction conforming to federal conditions and requirements. Since activities of this sort would in most cases have to be undertaken in any event and paid for through local revenues, conditional federal grants can provide as substantial incentive for state and local governments to subscribe to federal programs.

In some cases, federal regulatory permission for industrial and commercial development may be withheld if related state programs do not conform to federal standards. For example, federal permits for facilities generating substantial water pollution can not be obtained unless the facility complies with appli-

[32] 33 U.S.C. § 1281.

[33] 42 U.S.C. § 6942–6949.

[34] 16 U.S.C. §§ 1451–1464 (1976 & Supp. IV 1980). For a general discussion of this statute, *see* 2 F. Grad, *supra* note 28, § 10.04[2].

[35] By and large, states are the cornerstone of federal environmental strategies; little effort has been made to develop regional authorities for pollution control to deal with environmental problems involving several states. The Delaware River Commission, established by interstate compact, is one notable exception. Another is the system of federal fisheries management, which divided coastal areas into a number of regions, and rests planning and management authority in regional councils composed of representatives of the states involved and the fishing industry.

cable regional plans.[36] The Clean Air Act empowers the federal government to withhold approval for construction of industrial plants generating automotive-type pollutants in states that have failed to adopt inspection and maintenance plans to control pollutants from automobiles in use.[37]

Another incentive for state compliance with federal standards is enhanced regulatory authority. Under the Coastal Zone Management Act, for example, states with approved Coastal Zone Management programs are granted limited regulatory authority over federally controlled developments, such as offshore oil exploitation, that they would otherwise lack.[38] There is also the threat that the federal government may adopt more centralized and intrusive controls if states do not cooperate in existing programs.

d. Market-Type Systems of Transferable Pollution Rights

An innovative approach to allocation of national and state authority, relying on market incentives rather than regulatory commands, is reflected in the "tradeoff" and "bubble" policies developed under the Clean Air Act. Under the tradeoff approach, statutorily codified in the 1977 Clean Air Act Amendments, a new source of pollution in a nonattainment area must negotiate or purchase reductions of emissions from existing sources in an amount greater than the additional emissions attributable to the new source.[39] Under the bubble approach, the existing allocation of abatement responsibilities under state implementation plans can be adjusted by agreement among the sources in question, provided that the total emissions from the sources involved do not increase. Alternatively, a plant that expands its facilities may be able to avoid full compliance with the stringent pollution controls applicable to the new facility by imposing additional, compensatory controls on existing facilities within the same plant, whose emissions may be cheaper to control.[40]

The aim of tradeoff and bubble strategies is to facilitate economic growth and maintain environmental quality by providing economic incentives for existing firms to reduce emissions in order to reuse or "sell" the reductions in a bubble or tradeoff arrangement.

Under traditional SIP regulatory practices, any change in environmental control requirements must be approved both by state and federal regulatory authorities. The EPA has adopted regulations that establish general requirements for bubble trades.[41] If a state follows such requirements in the design of

[36] 33 U.S.C. § 1288(e).

[37] 42 U.S.C. § 7503.

[38] 16 U.S.C. § 1456(c)(1). Specifically, this provision requires that certain federal actions within or affecting the coastal zone be consistent with that state's management program. *See generally* GREENBERG, *Federal Consistency under the Coastal Zone Management Act: An Emerging Focus of Environmental Controversy in the 1980's*, 11 ENVT'L L. REP. (ELI) 50,001 (1981).

[39] 42 U.S.C. § 7503.

[40] *See generally* R. STEWART & J. KRIER, ENVIRONMENTAL LAW AND POLICY Ch. 5 (2d ed. 1978 & 1982 Supp. at 90–92.) (Michie Co.-Bobbs-Merrill, Charlottesville Va.).

[41] 40 CFR § 50.

its regulatory program, it may approve particular trades without their being subject to a second tier of federal review. Elimination of dual state/federal review reduces the delay and uncertainties involved in regulatory approval and helps promote development of a market in pollution rights. The ultimate objective is to ensure federal objectives are met with minimum intrusion on the autonomy of states and enterprises.

e. Federal Cleanup and Compensation Funds

A few federal statutes establish revolving funds to clean up or provide limited compensation for damage caused by improper toxic waste disposal and certain oil spills. These measures represent a departure from the typical federal approach to pollution and toxic substances, which relies on preventive regulatory controls and does not provide for compensation.

The Comprehensive Environmental Response, Compensation and Liability Act of 1980 (CERCLA) creates a $1.6 billion revolving fund to underwrite the costs of cleaning up existing hazardous waste dump sites or to compensate for damages to public resources caused by such waste when private liability can not be established or enforced.[42] The fund is financed 87.5% from taxes on petrochemical feed stocks and basic chemicals and 12.5% from general federal revenues.[43] Federal cleanup measures are authorized in accordance with the national contingency plan[44] that requires states which wish to be eligible for federal cleanup assistance for sites within their borders to adopt qualifying programs for identification and control of hazardous dump sites and contribute 10% of cleanup costs. In appropriate cases, the cleanup efforts may be initiated by state authorities and reimbursed 90% from the federal fund. Implementation of the Act is barely underway. An important issue, currently the subject of litigation, is the extent to which the federal act preempts states from establishing supplementary liability funds through taxes on industry.[45]

The Outer Continental Shelf Lands Act Amendments of 1978 establish a fund, financed by assessments on oil extracted from the outer continental shelf, to compensate for cleanup costs and damages attributable to spills from outer continental shelf facilities or vessels serving those facilities.[46] Similar funds have been statutorily established in connection with deepwater ports and the Trans-Alaskan pipeline.[47] A number of states have similar compensation funds for marine oil spills from vessels. These measures have been held not to

[42] 42 U.S.C. §§ 9601–9657 (Supp. IV 1980). The statute is popularly referred to as "Superfund."

[43] The tax, enacted as title II of CERCLA, amends the Internal Revenue Code, 26 U.S.C. §§ 4611, 4612, 4661, 4662, and will be collected only until September 30, 1985.

[44] EPA issued a national contingency plan on July 16, 1982, 47 Fed. Reg. 31,180.

[45] Exxon v. Hunt, 4 N.J. Tax 294 (1982), 12 ENVT'L L. REP. 20,734; *cf.* Exxon v. Hunt, 683 F.2d 69 (3d Cir. 1982), *cert. denied,* 103 S. Ct. 727 (1983).

[46] 43 U.S.C. §§ 1331–1356 (1976 & Supp. III 1979).

[47] Deep Water Port Act of 1974, 33 U.S.C. §§ 1501–1524; Trans-Alaska Pipeline Authorization Act, 43 U.S.C. §§ 1651–1655.

be preempted by the federal regulatory system for controlling marine oil pollution.[48]

f. Transboundary Spillovers

Spillovers of pollution across state lines were an important justification for the adoption of centralized systems of air and water pollution control in the early 1970s. However, the performance of the federal air and water pollution control programs in dealing with such spillovers has been disappointing. In general, the Clean Air Act and the Clean Water Act do not focus on transboundary spillovers as such. The effort is rather to deal with such problems indirectly by a general system of pollution control, on the premise that if pollution controls are implemented everywhere, transboundary problems are likely to be resolved. In practice, however, this approach has had serious limitations, particularly in the air pollution context.

Under the Clean Air Act, air quality standards and enforcement measures have been geared to local concentrations of air pollutants, such as sulfur dioxide, in the immediate vicinity of emission sources. States are required to control sources within their borders in order to ensure compliance with federal air quality standards within the state. But such controls may not be adequate to prevent substantial amounts of air pollution (often, due to chemical and atmospheric interactions, in a form different than the initial emissions) from crossing state boundaries. Serious problems of transboundary pollution have therefore arisen.

2. Management of Public Resources

a. Management of Federally-Owned Resources

The management of federally-owned land and other natural resources rests primarily with the Interior Department and the Forest Service in the Agriculture Department under statutes granting them broad discretion. Among the more environmentally significant issues involved in public land management are the development of federally-owned outer continental shelf and on-shore petroleum, natural gas, coal and other mineral resources through lease to private enterprise or otherwise, the use of federal lands for grazing and timber harvesting, and the prevention of development in order to protect national parks and preserve wilderness areas. In addition to organic acts providing a general legal and administrative framework for management of various categories of public lands, there are specific statutes dealing with such matters as off-shore leasing; leasing of coal and other mineral resources; and acquisition of property interests by private discoverers of valuable minerals on public lands. Most of these statutes require, in very general terms, that responsible federal officials balance economic development and environmental and preservationist objectives in resource management decisions.

[48] Askew v. American Waterways Operators, Inc., 411 U.S. 325 (1973).

A number of more specific statutes aimed at particular environmental objectives impose sharper constraints on administrative officials. The Wilderness and Wild and Scenic Rivers Acts prohibit any substantial development of resources covered by those statutes; it is Congress that specifies which resources are covered by the Acts.[49] The Endangered Species Act (which applies to federally financed or licensed projects as well as the development of federally owned resources) prohibits any developments that would wipe out a "critical habitat" for a species listed by the Interior Department as endangered.[50] The Surface Mining Control and Reclamation Act imposes stringent limitations and controls on the surface mining of coal on federal lands.[51]

Federal water supply and navigation projects have considerable environmental significance. Water projects undertaken by the Interior Department and navigation projects built by the Army Corps of Engineers have been largely financed out of federal tax revenues. Relevant statutes grant considerable discretion to federal administrators undertaking and managing such projects. Environmentalists complain that such projects are politically motivated "pork barrels" whose environmental harms (destruction of wetlands, damming of free-running rivers, and so on) and economic costs far outweigh their benefits. They also argue that such projects encourage inefficient resource use because they fail to charge users the full economic costs of the services provided by the project.

Federal resource management policies have great economic and political importance in western states where the federal government owns a large percentage of the land. Federal decisions to develop federal resources may be opposed by a state because of the adverse environmental consequences, including pollution and "boom town" developments. On the other hand, federal decisions to restrict development of federal resources may be opposed by a state that would benefit economically from development.

An important legal issue, particularly in the context of water use in the arid west, is the extent to which federal resource management is limited by state law. Must the use of water from a federal dam or from a river flowing through federal land comply with state law regarding apportionment and use of water, or are federal resource land managers free to ignore state restrictions? In recent years, the Supreme Court has made clear that Congress has essentially unlimited power to preempt the application of state law to federal projects and resources. The Court, however, requires that such preemption be explicit; state law is presumed to govern federal projects and resources unless a contrary conclusion is plainly required by federal statute.[52]

[49] Wilderness Act, 16 U.S.C. § 1133, Wild and Scenic Rivers Act, 16 U.S.C. §§ 1271–1287. For an overview of these statutes, *see generally* 3 F. Grad, *supra* note 28, § 12.04.

[50] 16 U.S.C. §§ 1531–1543. *See generally* Note, *Federal Protection Unique Environmental Interests: Endangered and Threatened Species*, 58 N.C.L. Rev. 491 (1980).

[51] 30 U.S.C. §§ 1201-1328. *See generally* Note, *The Regulation of Coal Surface Mining in a Federal System*, 21 Nat. Resources J. 245 (1981).

[52] *See* California v. U.S., 438 U.S. 645 (1978).

b. Environmental Impact Assessment and the National Environmental Policy Act

Congress in 1969 adopted the National Environmental Policy Act (NEPA) in order to promote greater consideration of environmental values in the management of public resources.[53] The Act requires the preparation of environmental impact statements (EIS) in conjunction with "major federal actions significantly affecting the quality of the human environment."[54] It also, in very general terms, requires federal administrators to develop means to assure that environmental values are given appropriate consideration in decisionmaking, use interdisciplinary methods of analysis and planning, study and develop less environmentally damaging alternatives to proposed actions, and acquire and use ecological information in planning. The policies, regulations and public laws of the United States are to be interpreted and administered in accordance with these policies. A Council on Environmental Quality in the executive office of the President was established to oversee implementation of the Act.[55]

Implementation of NEPA has centered on the environmental impact statement process.[56] Courts have taken the lead in requiring the preparation of detailed and comprehensive impact statements in conjunction with federal projects. The courts have interpreted "major federal actions" to include not only the development of federally-owned land and other natural resources, but also federal, state or local projects (such as airports, highways, and urban redevelopment projects) that are federally funded, and private developments (such as energy projects) that must receive federal licensing approval.

The impact statement process[57] includes a procedure for determining whether the environmental consequences of a proposed project are sufficiently serious to warrant preparation of an impact statement; preparation and public circulation of a draft statement that includes a description of the environmental consequences of the proposal and a discussion of the alternatives; procedures for receiving public comments on the draft EIS, and preparation of a final EIS that responds to the comments and criticisms made of the draft. The courts have interpreted the requirements of the Act as "procedural" and have almost consistently declined to set aside a federal administrator's decision to proceed with a project involving serious environmental harms so long as the examination of those harms in the impact statement is full and accurate.[58]

[53] 42 U.S.C. §§ 4321–4347. *See generally* N. ORLOFF & G. BROOKS, THE NATIONAL ENVIRONMENTAL POLICY ACT: CASES AND MATERIALS (Bureau of National Affairs, Washington, DC 1980).

[54] 42 U.S.C. § 4332 (2) (c).

[55] *Id.* § 202. The Council, which is part of the Executive Office of the President, consists of three members appointed by the President. The Council is assisted by a professional staff; the Reagan administration has sharply reduced the size of the Council's staff budget.

[56] *See generally* LIROFF, *NEPA Litigation in the 1970s*, 21 NAT. RESOURCES J. 315 (1981).

[57] Regulations governing the preparation of impact statements were revised by CEQ in 1978 and appear at 40 C.F.R. §§ 1500–1508.

[58] *See* Strycker's Bay Neighborhood Council, Inc. v. Karlen, 444 U.S. 223 (1980).

Many states have adopted similar environmental impact assessment requirements for state funded or approved projects.[59] The federal act does not contain any preemptive provisions. Some administrative efforts are made to coordinate state and federal impact assessment procedures.

[59] *See generally* PEARLMAN, *State Environmental Policy Acts: Local Decisionmaking and Land Use Planning*, 43 J. AM. INST. PLANNERS 42 (1977).

IV. Overview of EC Substantive Environmental Law

A key factor in understanding the environmental and health issues that have been selected for Community action is that most of the early Community environmental legislation was made as trade and competition policy rather than environmental policy. The extent to which differences in national environmental laws operated as barriers to trade and distorted competition within the Common Market was a crucial factor in identifying candidates for harmonization, although once the selection had been made an attempt was also made to offer solutions to the relevant environmental problem as such. The subsequent establishment of a separate Community environmental policy has led to selection of candidates for harmonization according to environmental priorities, but the former preoccupation with trade and competition still has meaning. The focus of Community environmental policy is clearly on problems related to trade and competition, i. e. industrial pollution and environmental and health risks presented by products. Problems such as land use planning, protection of nature and landscape, and protection of flora and fauna are of minor significance. The reasons for this are the narrowness of the principal Treaty provisions on which the Community institutions rely for environmental policy-making (Articles 100 and 235) and the stronger political support enjoyed by Commission initiatives when trade and competition are at stake.

Moreover, Community environmental policy normally does not comprehensively regulate a particular environmental sector. Many directives address only selected high priority problems within a broadly defined field. Sometimes there are framework directives that set forth basic principles applicable to a broad environmental field. They may be implemented with respect to a particular problem by special directives; otherwise, they leave the member states much leeway in implementation. On the whole, the Community's legislative activity is characterized by a pragmatic and incrementalist approach which has no parallel in developed federal systems.

A. The Community's Environmental Programs

The objectives of Community environmental policy, principles to guide its implementation, priorities for action, and implementation measures are set forth in the environmental programs of the Communtiy.[1] The first environmental

[1] *See* H. Bungarten, Umweltpolitik in Westeuropa 150 *et seq.* (Europa Union Verlag, Bonn 1978); Brusasco-Mackenzie & Kiss, *Quelques réflexions sur l'action des Com-*

program[2] covers the period from 1973 to 1975. The second environmental program[3] covers the period from 1976 to 1981. The third environmental program covers the period from 1982 to 1986.[4]

A fundamental feature of all the programs is the tendency to view environmental protection as more than just pollution control. Their notion of environmental protection includes the maintenance of ecological balance, rational use of natural resources, improvement of working and living conditions, and consideration of environmental concerns in land use and infrastructure planning. However, with respect to the practical measures envisaged, the first environmental program clearly focuses on pollution control. This may be explained by the urgency of some pollution problems. The second and third environmental programs place greater emphasis on the preventive aspect of environmental policy, especially rational use of land and natural resources; in practice, however, regulatory action to control pollution still clearly prevails.[5]

The first environmental program listed a series of political principles to guide Community environmental policy; the six essential ones are:

- prevention is a more effective environmental policy than *ex post facto* cure of pollution
- polluters are to be financially responsible for the costs of prevention and control of pollution (the polluter-pays principle)
- the most appropriate geographic decisionmaking level must be sought for each type of action, meaning that the Community will only act where na-

munautés Européennes en matière de protection de l'environnement, 1978 REVUE DU MARCHÉ COMMUN 310; S. JOHNSON, THE POLLUTION CONTROL POLICY OF THE EUROPEAN COMMUNITIES (Graham & Trotman, London 1979); R. CATHALA, J. M. ROCHE & J. A. TREGOUET, LE DROIT EUROPÉEN DE L'ENVIRONNEMENT (FONNE, Paris 1979); Krämer, *Umweltpolitik*, in KOMMENTAR ZUM EWG-VERTRAG 1609 *et seq.* (vol. 2, H. von der Groeben, H. von Boekh, J. Thiesing & C. D. Ehlermann eds., Nomos Verlag, Baden-Baden, 3d ed. 1983).

[2] Declaration of the Council of the European Communities and of the Representatives of the Governments of the Member States Meeting in Council of 22 Nov. 1973 on the Programme of Action of the European Communities on the Environment, OJ No. C 112, 20 Dec. 1973, p. 1.

[3] Resolution of the Council of the European Communities and of the Governments of the Member States Meeting within the Council of 17 May 1977, OJ No. C 139, 13 June 1977, p. 1.

[4] Action Programme of the European Communities on the Environment (1982 to 1986), OJ No. C 46, 17 Feb. 1983, p. 1. *See also* European Parliament Resolution of 20 Nov. 1981 on the state of the Community Environment, OJ No. C 327, 14 Dec. 1981, p. 83; THE ENVIRONMENT IN EUROPE, BULLETIN OF THE INSTITUTE FOR EUROPEAN ENVIRONMENTAL POLICY No. 16, at 1 (Dec. 1981).

[5] *See* Commission of the European Communities, Progress Made in Connection with the Environment Action Programme and Assessment of the Work Done to Implement It, Communication from the Commission to the Council, DOC COM(80)222 final (7 May 1980), p. 2 [hereinafter cited as Progress Report 1980]. For emphasis on the preventive approach to be used in the future, *see id.* at 7.

tional action would be ineffective, there is a common interest, or divergent national action would cause major economic or social problems
- assessment of environmental impacts of official action
- prevention of transboundary pollution
- the power of member states to enact more stringent national measures.[6]

The effectiveness of these principles as guidelines for subsequent political action was weakened by their vagueness and by conflicts among the various principles. For example, there was no agreement as to how much the polluter-pays principle could be mitigated by exceptions. Only in a later document was this question resolved.[7] The principle that harmonization at the Community level should not prevent more stringent national measures was weakened by the qualification that national progress may not endanger the functioning of the Common Market. This formulation illustrates the conflict between environmental protection and trade concerns inherent in Community environmental policy; the program in itself does not solve them.

After defining the objectives and principles of Community environmental policy, the first environmental program sets out an action program for implementation of Community environmental policy. The program calls for adoption of quality objectives and standards for the more important air and water pollutants. It also announces specific actions for control of water pollution by particular industries, i. e., pulp and paper, iron and steel, titanium dioxide, petrochemicals, leather, and foodstuffs. There is a chapter on improvement of the environment which provides for promotion of agriculture and forestry with a view to protecting the landscape and for rational land use decisions. Finally, the action program contains measures in the field of international organization.

The second environmental program essentially repeats the first program's policy objectives and principles and calls for continuation of the common environmental policy as implemented pursuant to the first program. As already noted, it lays more emphasis on the preventive approach.[8] The chapter on pollution control, which had contained thirty-four pages in the first program, was restricted to eighteen pages. New sections on waste management, noise control, and nuclear energy were added. The most prominent concrete measures to be instituted are environmental impact assessment, the ecological mapping of the Community, and establishment of a resource economy, especially by recycling of wastes. Furthermore, the program proposes to redirect Community industrial policy according to environmental considerations. The emphasis on prevention fails, however, to remedy a weakness of the first environmental program; namely, major parts of the preventive program are set forth in general terms without describing specific measures.

[6] The Commission considers the first three of these principles the most important. Progress Report 1980, *supra* note 5, at 2.

[7] Council Recommendation 75/436/Euratom, ECSC, EEC of 3 March 1975 regarding cost allocation and action by public authorities on environmental matters, OJ No. L 194, 25 July 1975, p. 1.

[8] *See also* Brusasco-Mackenzie & Kiss, *supra* note 1, at 311.

The third environmental program places even greater stress on the preventive approach. In contrast to the previous two programs, it also calls for more integration of environmental policy into regulation of other sectors, such as agriculture and transport, and into regional policies. It also suggests, although rather vaguely, assessment of environmental impacts of agricultural programs. With respect to concrete measures, emphasis is laid on implementing the measures already initiated under, or proposed in, the second program, such as the aquatic environment directive and the sixth amendment of the hazardous substances directive. Few new legislative actions are envisaged. Without indicating concrete actions, the third program calls for adoption of additional air quality standards as well as limitation of emissions at the source. Automobile emissions, a priority of West Germany and the United Kingdom, are also mentioned. In the field of noise control, particular attention is to be given to economic impacts of new measures. Regulation of transboundary transport of hazardous waste is anticipated. All told, the program represents a consolidation, but not a retardation, of Community environmental policy – more or less in parallel with recent developments in most member states.

The novelty of the third action program is the changed role of the Council. Previously, the Council had endorsed the environmental programs in their entirety. In the case of the third program, the Council merely approved the "general orientation" of the program and a list of priorities for Community action, namely integration of environmental concerns into other policies, environmental impact assessment, information exchange between member states about clean technologies, cooperation with developing states, and implementation of five priority directives (the aquatic environment, titanium dioxide, sulfur dioxide limit values, toxic waste, and dangerous substances directives). This approach may at first glance appear to be a retrenchment. However, it is clear that in the past the Council did not feel obliged to act on any proposal solely on account of an environmental program. The new approach seems to give the priority areas, however broadly defined, significantly more binding force, while possibly weakening the Commission's role as initiator of policy proposals.

The following analysis attempts to describe the essentials and, if information is available, the legislative history of Community measures, including those adopted prior to the first environmental program as well as those adopted pursuant to the first and second environmental programs. Non-legislative measures, such as research, information exchange, funding programs established within the framework of the common agricultural policy, and the general impact of the common agricultural and transport policies on the environment, are not included in the analysis. The presentation is divided into sections on water pollution, air pollution, noise, waste disposal, chemicals, nuclear safety, flora and fauna and land use, and environmental impact assessment.[9]

[9] *See also* OFFERMAN-CLAS, *Das Abfallrecht der Europäischen Gemeinschaften*, 96 DEUTSCHES VERWALTUNGSBLATT 1125 (1981); MASTELLONE, *The External Relations of the E.E.C. in the Field of Environmental Protection*, 30 INT'L & COMP. L. Q. 104, 109–110 (1981); S. JOHNSON, *supra* note 1, at 11, 50, 77, 90, 99.

B. Water Pollution

Water pollution is a priority of Community environmental policy; it is the field of environmental protection in which the Community has been most actively engaged and has most comprehensively legislated.[10] The major reason appears to be that the heavy pollution of most Community rivers and seas has obvious transboundary and international implications; the Community was thus considered the most suitable decision level for addressing these problems. There is also a certain political spillover effect that has allowed expansion of Community regulation from "international" into "internal" water pollution problems; the relative success of the Community environmental policy in the former area presented a suggestive argument in favor of Community regulation in the latter areas. Four different strategies have been adopted according to the type of pollutant and receiving environment: water quality standards, effluent standards for dangerous substances, product standards for detergents that limit inputs, and design specification standards for vessels for the prevention of oil pollution. These regulatory strategies are supplemented by monitoring and information exchange.[11]

1. Surface Fresh Water Pollution

a. Specific Water Uses

The Community has established a system of water quality objectives or standards for surface waters based on their use as drinking water, bathing water, or water for harvesting fish and shellfish. [12] The Community objectives and standards must be implemented by member states through implementation plans. However, determination of the relevant end uses of particular bodies of water, and hence of the standard applicable to such waters, remains the member states' responsibility. This system of regulation is primarily designed to control pollution by degradable pollutants from scattered sources.

The most important directive in this system is the drinking water directive of 1975.[13] It establishes three categories of mandatory quality standards (A 1,

[10] *See* P. Barella, Normes et objectifs de qualité de l'eau dans la Communauté économique européenne 31 *et seq.* (Unpublished Thesis, Université des Sciences Sociales, Toulouse 1980); for a survey of Community policy in this area *see also* BRUSASCO-MACKENZIE & KISS, *supra* note 1, at 312 *et seq.*; Pleinevaux, *European Policy of Protection of Rivers and Water against Pollution*, in THE EUROPEAN ALTERNATIVES 397 *et seq.* (G. Ionescu ed., Sijthoff & Noordhoff, Alphen a. d. Rijn 1977); SCHEUER, *Aktuelle Probleme der Durchführung der EG-Gewässerschutzrichtlinie in den Mitgliedstaaten der Gemeinschaft*, 5 ZEITSCHRIFT FÜR UMWELTPOLITIK 65 (1982).

[11] *See* Council Decision 77/795/EEC of 12 Dec. 1977 establishing a common procedure for the exchange of information on the quality of surface fresh water in the Community, OJ No. L 334, 24 Dec. 1977, p. 29.

[12] *See* S. JOHNSON, *supra* note 1, at 12 *et seq.*

[13] Directive 75/440/EEC of 16 June 1975 concerning the quality required of surface water intended for the abstraction of drinking water in the Member States, OJ No. L 194, 25 July 1975, p. 26.

A 2 and A 3) for surface water used for abstraction of drinking water, as well as stricter quality goals ("guidelines") and associated standardized methods of treatment. The relevant measurement methods are established partly by the directive itself and partly by a further special directive.[14] Surface water not conforming with the least stringent of these mandatory standards (A 3) may not, subject to some exceptions, be used for abstracting drinking water.[15] However, the directive, probably unintentionally, does not cover all methods used for abstracting drinking water in the member states.

The directive relies on coordination of member state policies for the implementation of the quality standards and guidelines. It obliges member states to establish, especially for A 3 water, water quality improvement plans which are to include timetables for attaining water quality goals in relation to economic and technological conditions. The member states are expected to substantially improve water quality within ten years with the ultimate goal of meeting the quality guidelines set by the directive. However, the directive does not fix deadlines for attainment of the standards or guidelines. It is the Commission's task to examine the implementation plans as well as the grounds claimed for exceptions to the mandatory requirements of the directive and, if necessary, submit appropriate proposals to the Council for further harmonization. Finally, the directive requires that its implementation not degrade existing water quality. It also allows member states to set stricter quality standards.

The directive of 1980 on water intended for human consumption[16] establishes additional water quality standards and guidelines for water used for human consumption, especially drinking water and water used in the food industry. Concentration levels are specified for a variety of parameters including heavy metals, chlorides, fluorides, phenols, pesticides, and bacteria. Strictly speaking, the directive must be classified as a consumer (food and beverages law) rather than as an environmental protection directive.

The bathing water directive of 1975[17] establishes mandatory quality standards and stricter quality guidelines for water in bathing areas as well as associated measurement methods, while leaving the designation of bathing areas to the discretion of member states. The main purpose of the directive is protection of public health; however, the criteria established by the directive are also

[14] Directive 79/869/EEC of 9 Oct. 1979 concerning the methods of measurement and frequencies of sampling and analysis of surface water intended for the abstraction of drinking water in the Member States, OJ No. L 271, 29 Oct. 1979, p. 44.

[15] Some critics have opposed the use of A3 quality water for drinking. *See* European Parliament, EP Doc. 87/74, at 10; EUREAU, *Erfahrungen mit der EG-Richtlinie 75/440 über die Qualität von Oberflächenwasser für die Trinkwassergewinnung in den Mitgliedstaaten*, 122 GAS- UND WASSERFACH – WASSER/ABWASSER 555, 559 (1981).

[16] Directive 80/778/EEC of 15 July 1980 relating to the quality of water intended for human consumption, OJ No. L 229, 30 Aug. 1980, p. 11; *see also* SMEETS & AMAVIS, *European Communities' Directive Relating to the Quality of Water Intended for Human Consumption*, 15 WATER, AIR & SOIL POLLUTION No. 4 (1981).

[17] Directive 76/160/EEC of 8 Dec. 1975 concerning the quality of bathing water, OJ No. L 31, 5 Feb. 1976, p. 1.

designed to satisfy the interest in public amenities, aesthetic attractiveness, and the general improvement of environmental quality. Most of the standards concern microbiological, physical, and chemical aspects of water quality. The directive also covers other pollutants such as mineral oil, detergents, phenols, heavy metals, cyanides, nitrates, and phosphates. Member states are required to ensure that the quality of bathing water conforms to the standards within ten years.

Finally, there are two directives concerning water quality for aquatic life, namely the fish water and the shellfish water directives.[18]

b. Dangerous Substances: The Aquatic Environment Directive

The aquatic environment directive of 1976[19] is perhaps the most important piece of Community legislation in the field of water pollution. It is designed to generally eliminate, within a prescribed period of time, water pollution caused by the discharge of especially hazardous substances, and to reduce water pollution caused by the discharge of other somewhat less hazardous substances. It covers the inland surface and internal coastal waters of the Community. There is a separate directive[20] for ground water which follows the same system as the main directive but, due to the greater vulnerability of ground water, is even stricter.

The directive contains some obligations directly binding on member states, but it is essentially a framework directive requiring further Community implementation. It establishes two lists of hazardous substances: list I (the "black" list) and list II (the "grey" list). The regulatory strategy follows that set forth in the Council of Europe project for a European convention on international waters.[21] The lists of pollutants established under the directive parallel, to a considerable extent, those established under the convention for prevention of chemical pollution of the Rhine as well as several conventions on marine pollution to which several member states and in some cases the Community are parties. Such coordination was considered necessary to prevent member states from undertaking non-uniform or contradictory international commitments and to ensure that the conventions are implemented consistently throughout the Community. West Germany was especially interested in Community harmonization in view of the proposed convention of the International Commission for the Protection of the Rhine on prevention of chemical pollution of the

[18] Directive 78/659/EEC of 18 July 1978 on the quality requirements for water capable of supporting fresh water fish, OJ No. L 222, 14 Aug. 1978, p. 1; Directive 79/923/EEC of 30 Oct. 1979 concerning the quality required of shellfish waters, OJ No. L 281, 10 Nov. 1979, p. 47.

[19] Directive 76/464/EEC of 4 May 1976 on pollution caused by certain dangerous substances discharged into the aquatic environment of the Community, OJ No. L 129, 18 May 1976, p. 23; *see also*, S. Johnson, *supra* note 1, at 23 *et seq.*

[20] Directive 80/68/EEC of 17 Dec. 1979 on the protection of ground water against pollution caused by certain dangerous substances, OJ No. L 20, 26 Jan. 1980, p. 43.

[21] *See* Brusasco-Mackenzie & Kiss, *supra* note 1, at 314.

Rhine. German industry stiffly opposed a special regime for the Rhine because it wanted to avoid locational disadvantages and deterioration of its competitive position vis-à-vis countries such as France and the United Kingdom.[22]

List I includes mercury, cadmium, and various categories of hazardous substances such as persistent organic chemicals, carcinogenic substances, and non-biodegradable oils. It is not definitive, but requires further specification. The main strategy for eliminating pollution by list I substances is a system of uniform effluent standards; the mandate to "eliminate" pollution does not require zero emission. The directive anticipates establishment of effluent standards for these substances by implementing directives, and sets forth in general language the factors to be considered in setting such standards, to wit, concentrations; effluent per product unit where appropriate; and differentiation by industry or product. It also sets forth the risk and economic criteria to be considered: toxicity, persistence, bio-accumulation, and technical availability.

The directive also provides, in the alternative, for establishment of water quality objectives and sets forth criteria for setting them. The water quality standards apply only when a member state opts for them instead of the effluent standards. This example of alternative harmonization represents a concession to the United Kingdom. All member states except the United Kingdom believed that uniform effluent standards should be established throughout the Community. The United Kingdom, which enjoys a system of short, free-running rivers, maintained that even for highly hazardous substances the absorptive capacity of the receiving waters should be considered and therefore a system of water quality standards was appropriate. Since an agreement could not be reached, a compromise was found allowing the two strategies to coexist as alternatives.[23]

The member states are obliged to control discharges of list I substances by subjecting dischargers to a system of prior authorization. Permits must specify effluent limitations reflecting translation of the Community effluent or water quality standards into individual effluent limitations. The directive contains provisions regarding the necessary contents of the permit. Where existing water quality requires, member states may impose more stringent effluent limitations.

For list II substances, all member states agreed on the appropriateness of geographically varying water quality standards and, consequently, of varying effluent limitations. The directive relies on coordination of member state policies rather than central regulation to establish water quality standards. The member states are obliged to establish implementation programs for reduction of water pollution. These programs must contain water quality standards. Existing Community quality standards (drinking water, etc.) must be observed. The Community may also set guidelines (containing principles and criteria) upon which the quality standards are to be based. Discharges must be con-

[22] Rat von Sachverständigen für Umweltfragen, Umweltgutachten 1978, at No. 1679 (Kohlhammer, Stuttgart 1978).

[23] *See infra* pp. 216–219.

trolled by subjecting them to the requirement of a prior authorization which reflects translation of the quality objectives into individual effluent limitations. The implementation program may also regulate the composition and use of dangerous substances. It is to set deadlines for compliance. Summaries of the programs and the results of their implementation must be communicated to the Commission which, together with the member states, is to arrange for regular comparisons to ensure sufficient coordination in implementation of the programs.

The directive also provides for nondegradation, i. e. measures taken in implementing the directive may not cause deterioration of existing water quality. Finally, member states may prescribe more stringent requirements.

The requirements of subjecting discharges to prior authorization, of setting individual effluent limitations, and of establishing water quality improvement programs for list II substances are directly binding on member states (although this has sometimes been forgotten). However, to be fully operable the directive requires that the Community determine the effluent and quality standards for list I substances. This task has for several reasons proven extremely difficult.[24]

First, the directive gives no qualitative or quantitative guidance as to the application of the criteria established in the directive for selection of list I substances and determination of standards. It is unsettled whether the three criteria of toxicity, persistence, and bio-accumulation must be fulfilled jointly, to what degree they must be present, and to what extent quantitative factors, such as production volume as an indicator of exposure, are relevant. In the absence of guidance, member states' divergent philosophies on assessment of ecological risk can not be easily reconciled. The Commission has acted pragmaticly by initially selecting for priority regulation from a list of 1 500 substances twenty-one substances which all member state experts agreed were most hazardous. Later, another 122 priority substances were selected; fourteen of these substances were later excluded because of their small quantitative risk potential.[25]

[24] *See* Progress Report 1980, *supra* note 5, Annex I, at 7; RAT VON SACHVERSTÄNDIGEN FÜR UMWELTFRAGEN, *supra* note 22, at No. 1681; Fotheringham & Birnie, *Regulation of North Sea Pollution*, in THE EFFECTIVE MANAGEMENT OF RESOURCES: THE INTERNATIONAL POLITICS OF THE NORTH SEA 208 *et seq.* (C. P. Mason ed., Pinter, Nichols, London, New York 1979); Salzwedel, *Auswirkungen der EG-Richtlinien mit wasserwirtschaftlichem Bezug auf den Vollzug des deutschen Wasserrechts*, in GESELLSCHAFT FÜR UMWELTRECHT, DOKUMENTATION ZUR WISSENSCHAFTLICHEN FACHTAGUNG 1979, at 139, 147 *et seq.* (Erich Schmidt Verlag, Berlin 1980); KEUNE, *Kollidierende rechtliche, politische und wirtschaftspsychologische Gesichtspunkte bei der Auswahl der Stoffe für die Liste I der EG-Gewässerschutzrichtlinie*, 17 ZEITSCHRIFT FÜR WASSERRECHT 193 (1978); MÖBS, *Die Richtlinienpolitik der Europäischen Gemeinschaften im Gewässerschutz*, 21 RECHT DER WASSERWIRTSCHAFT 13, 24 *et seq.* (1978).

[25] *See* Progress Report 1980, *supra* note 5, Annex I, at 3; Fifteenth General Report of the European Communities (Brussels 1981), No. 330; KRISOR, *Neue Arbeiten zur Definierung der schwarzen Liste umweltgefährlicher Stoffe*, 1982 UMWELT 234 (Verein Deutscher Ingenieure, Düsseldorf 1982).

The final list of dangerous substances was thus composed of 129 substances.[26] Such a pragmatic approach runs the risk of omitting substances deserving priority treatment and becomes more difficult as the area of non-controversial substances is exhausted. Moreover, it does not solve the problems of setting standards for the substances selected, a task which is complicated by the fact that the relevance of economic and technological feasibility is unclear. Thus, difficulties arise when factors such as differences in the size of the industries concerned, age of plant, processes used, and their profitability are brought into play. So far, the Commission has submitted proposals for standards for mercury, organohalogen compounds (so-called drines), cadmium, asbestos, and hexachlorcyclohexan.[27] Only the two proposals regarding mercury[28] and that regarding cadmium[29] were adopted. Proposals were not submitted for heptachlor, chlordane, and arsenic because these substances are little used or dispersed in the Community,[30] a factor that may make it possible to considerably diminish the number of substances requiring priority action by the Community.

The second reason for difficulty in implementing the directive is that its deadlines (Art. 12) are largely unrealistic. The directive sets a non-binding deadline of twenty-seven months for submission of proposals for effluent standards for all list I substances. The Council is to vote on these proposals within an additional nine months. These deadlines have already been exceeded by more than two years, and the Commission has by no means made proposals for all list I substances. For this reason a recent Council resolution calls for intensified exchange of information among member states and urges them to take preliminary national measures for the control of list I substances.[31]

[26] *See* Council Resolution of 7 Feb. 1983 on the control of water pollution by dangerous substances, OJ No. C 46, 17 Feb. 1983, p. 17; Commission Communication on dangerous substances of 22 June 1982, OJ No. C 176, 14 July 1982, p. 3.

[27] Drines: OJ No. C 146, 12 June 1979, p. 5; mercury: OJ No. C 169, 6 July 1979, p. 2 and OJ No. C 20, 25 Jan. 1983, p. 5; asbestos: OJ No. C 78, 28 March 1980, p. 10; cadmium: OJ No. C 118, 21 May 1981, p. 3, as amended OJ No. C 16, 20 Jan. 1983, p. 8; HCH: OJ No. C 215, 11 Aug. 1983, p. 3.

[28] Directive 82/176/EEC of 22 March 1982 on limit values and quality objectives for mercury discharges by the chloralkali electrolysis industry, OJ No. L 81, 27 March 1982, p. 29. The declarations concerning this directive are *reprinted in* 9 ENVT'L POL'Y & L. 102 (1982); Directive 84/156/EEC of 8 March 1984 on limit values and quality objectives for mercury discharges other than by the chloralkali industry, OJ No. L 74, 17 March 1984, p. 49.

[29] Directive 83/513/EEC of 26 Sept. 1983 on limit values and quality objectives for cadmium discharges, OJ No. L 291, 24 Oct. 1983, p. 1.

[30] BULL. EC 12-1981, at p. 40, point 2.1.80; BULL. EC 6-1983, at p. 61, point 2.1.114; *see also* KUPFER, *Einflüsse der EG auf die deutsche Umweltpolitik*, IWL-FORUM 1981-II, 57, 73-74 (Institut für gewerbliche Wasserwirtschaft und Luftreinhaltung, Köln 1981).

[31] Council Resolution of 7 Feb. 1983, *supra* note 26.

Thirdly, from the proposals made to date, it is clear that the strategy of alternative harmonization has not resolved the conflict between the United Kingdom and the other member states on water pollution control strategy. This conflict continues to affect the bargaining on proposals mainly because the economic impacts of implementation measures under the two approaches are not easily comparable, and each side suspects the other of taking unfair advantage for its industry.[32]

There are two principal controversies. The first is whether all new facilities must employ state-of-the-art control techniques when a member state chooses to use water quality standards instead of effluent standards. The United Kingdom says no. During discussions on the mercury directive, the United Kingdom for the first time conceded that in principle all new sources must use the most recent control technology. However, an express declaration of the Council makes it clear that this concession is not to be considered as precedent. Second, there are fundamental differences of opinion between the United Kingdom and the other member states on the extent to which the quality standards provided for in the framework directive should be differentiated according to use of the waters. The treatment of transboundary pollution has also at times become controversial.

As for list II substances, only some member states have sent the Commission their improvement programs. The Commission, therefore, has as yet not been able to coordinate implementation of the directive.[33]

c. *Pollution of the Rhine*

With respect to the Rhine, the aquatic environment directive is supplemented by the Convention of 1976 on protection of the Rhine against chemical pollution[34] to which the Community, four member states, and Switzerland are parties. The Convention follows more or less the same system as the aquatic environment directive. The task of determining effluent standards for list I substances, which parallels and in practice follows progress under the aquatic environment directive,[35] has likewise proven to be very difficult.

[32] *See* von Moltke & Haigh, *EC - Major Issues for 1981*, 7 Envt'l Pol'y & L. 23, 27-28 (1981); Progress Report 1980, *supra* note 5, at 5.

[33] *See* Progress Report 1980, *supra* note 5, Annex I at 3; Action Programme of the European Communities, *supra* note 4, at 9.

[34] Of 3 Dec. 1976, 16 ILM 242 (1977). The convention was concluded in the framework of the Berne convention of 1963 for the protection of the Rhine, which was amended by a Supplementary Agreement to allow the Community to become a member (Council Decision 77/586/EEC of 25 July 1977, OJ No. L 240, 19 Sept. 1977, p. 35). *Cf.* Lammers, *New International Legal Developments concerning the Pollution of the Rhine*, 27 Neth. Int'l L. Rev. 171, 182 *et seq.* (1980); Scheuer, *Les travaux de la Commission de la C.E.E. concernant la pollution transfrontière du Rhin*, 1981 Revue Juridique de l'Environnement 314.

[35] *See* Krisor, *supra* note 25. However, there will be a regulation concerning chromium, a subject for which regulation is not yet envisaged within the EC.

The Convention of 1976 for protection of the Rhine against chloride pollution[36] had adopted a different strategy. It directly limited the chloride concentration of discharges from the state owned Alsatian alkali producers and created a fund financed by the other signatory states to underwrite 70% of the costs of the storage of chloride by France. The French government's refusal to submit this convention to parliament for ratification (justified by expectations that parliament would not ratify it) was no doubt a severe setback for Community environmental policy. New negotiations between the riverain states were accordingly necessary. In these negotiations three alternatives were discussed: discharge of chloride wastes into the North Sea through a pipeline, underground storage, and supply through a pipeline to soda factories in Lorraine.[37] After lengthy negotiations an agreement was reached in 1981. France is to reduce its chloride discharges by 20 kg/second. Seventy percent of this amount will be stored underground; the remainder will be used to produce salt. France committed itself to final ratification of the convention in 1983,[38] and has in fact recently ratified the convention.

d. Sector Specific Measures

Sector specific measures supplement directives of general application. Up to now the Community has focused on discharges from the pulp and paper industry and the titanium dioxide industry (discussed below under "Marine Pollution").

The Commission proposal of 1975 on water pollution from wood pulp mills[39] proposes to establish a system of effluent standards varying according to the manufacturing process employed. These standards were considered technically feasible, economically realistic, and an important first step in protection of the environment. Because the proposed effluent standards would have far-reaching economic consequences, the proposal provides that the assimilative capacity of the receiving waters as well as existing water uses and local social and economic conditions may be taken into account in implementing the standards. Competent authorities would accordingly be allowed to establish implementation programs, if necessary on a case by case basis, which would permit some departure from the effluent standards. Moreover, temporary exceptions were provided for discharges into tidal waters.

[36] Of 3 Dec. 1976, 16 ILM 265 (1977); *see* LAMMERS, *supra* note 34, at 172 *et seq.*; SCHEUER, *supra* note 34. JESSURUN D'OLIVEIRA, *Das Rheinchloridabkommen und die EWG*, 29 RECHT DER INTERNATIONALEN WIRTSCHAFT 322 (1982) considers the subsidization concept employed by the convention as in violation of Articles 92-94 of the EEC Treaty.

[37] BULL. EC 1-1981, at p. 21, point 2.1.29.

[38] BULL. EC 6-1981, at p. 39, point 2.1.78; *id.* 11-1981, at p. 35, point 2.1.72.

[39] Commission proposal of 20 Jan. 1975 for a directive on the reduction of water pollution caused by wood pulp mills in the Member States, OJ No. C 99, 2 May 1975, p. 2. *See* AMADUCCI, *Fresh and Sea Waters in the EEC: Common Solutions?*, 1975 DIRITTO COMUNITARIO E DEGLI SCAMBI INTERNAZIONALI 513, 523-524; S. JOHNSON, *supra* note 1, at 26 *et seq.*

The Council has not been able to reach an agreement on the Commission proposal, largely because of the far-reaching economic consequences adoption of the Commission proposal would have. The ten year adjustment period provided by the proposal for existing sources and the Commission's opinion that member states should subsidize adjustment by the industry have not been sufficient to overcome the concerns of the affected industry. Moreover, although the majority of the member states supported uniform effluent standards on the ground that they would most effectively eliminate water pollution while avoiding distortions of competition, the United Kingdom adamantly opposed them because it wanted to afford its industry the use of the absorptive capacity of the sea.[40] A compromise analogous to that found within the framework of the aquatic environment directive is not in sight.

The proposal is an example of the sectoral harmonization of national programs for list II substances anticipated by Art. 7 of the framework surface water pollution directive. The Council's inability to reach an agreement on this proposal casts serious doubt on the fate of list II substances regulation as a whole. Moreover, it is clear that the sectoral approach to water pollution control proclaimed in the environmental programs has failed to gain sufficient political support. Consequently, the Commission has decided not to press this approach.[41]

e. Detergents

The directive of 1973 on detergents,[42] the forerunner of more comprehensive Community activity in surface water pollution control, is designed to reduce water pollution by detergents. The legislative technique used by the directive is the setting of a product standard. The directive prohibits the marketing and use of detergents in which the average level of biodegradability of the surfactants is below 90%. A special directive[43] gives member states the choice of three methods to test for anionic substances. It allows relatively large tolerances for testing biodegradability of these substances so that the required minimum biodegradability in fact is 80% rather than 90%. Recently, a new directive has been adopted specifying methods for testing the biodegradability of non-ionic surfactants,[44] which have gained great importance as detergents.

[40] *See* VYGEN, *EG-Gewässerschutz - Erfolgreicher als erwartet*, 1978 UMWELT 426, at 429 (Verein deutscher Ingenieure, Düsseldorf 1978).

[41] *See* Progress Report 1980, *supra* note 5, Annex I, at 5; *cf.* Action Programme of the European Communities, *supra* note 4, at 9.

[42] Directive 73/404/EEC of 22 Nov. 1973 on the approximation of the laws of the Member States relating to detergents, OJ No. L 347, 17 Dec. 1973, p. 51.

[43] Directive 73/405/EEC of 22 Nov. 1973 on the approximation of the laws of the Member States relating to methods of testing the biodegradability of anionic surfactants, OJ No. L 347, 17 Dec. 1973, p. 53, as amended by Directive 82/243/EEC of 31 March 1982, OJ No. L 109, 22 April 1982, p. 18.

[44] Directive 82/242/EEC of 31 March 1982 on the approximation of the laws of the Member States relating to methods of testing the biodegradability of non-ionic surfactants and amending Directive 73/404/ EEC, OJ No. L 109, 22 April 1982, p. 1.

2. Marine Pollution

The Community approach to marine pollution has generally been to participate in international activities rather than to adopt specific Community measures.[45] The Community has encouraged member states to adhere to international conventions and sought to coordinate their negotiation and ratification activities. These attempts have often been unsuccessful. The most recent example is the UN Law of the Sea Convention which has been signed by only some of the member states. More recently, the Community has adhered, or proposed to adhere, to such conventions in its own right. Action oriented programs and directives calling for particular measures regarding marine pollution are relatively rare.[46] The reason for the modest Community role lies in the desire of member states to retain their powers in the field of foreign relations, especially in areas such as the protection of wildlife and natural resources where full internal legislative competence on the part of the Community has never been recognized. Even the adhesion of the Community along with that of member states to international conventions is opposed by some member states because they fear that this may amount to recognition of Community competences.

a. Dumping

Several member states are parties to the London Convention of 1972 on the dumping of wastes at sea.[47] This convention anticipates that the contracting parties will enter into regional agreements for prevention of pollution by dumping. Examples of the regional approach are the Oslo Agreement of 1972 which covers dumping in the North Sea,[48] the Helsinki Convention of 1974 on the protection of the Baltic Sea[49] to which some member states are parties, and the Barcelona Convention of 1976 for the prevention of pollution of the

[45] For a survey of Community policy in this area *see* CREMONA, *The Role of the EEC in the Control of Oil Pollution*, 17 COMMON MKT. L. REV. 171, 175 *et seq.* (1980); GÜNDLING, *Rechtsprobleme der Abfallbeseitigung auf See*, 4 NATUR UND RECHT 41 (1982); Fotheringham & Birnie, *supra* note 24; S. JOHNSON, *supra* note 1, at 40 *et seq.*; RAT VON SACHVERSTÄNDIGEN FÜR UMWELTFRAGEN, UMWELTPROBLEME DER NORDSEE, at No. 1110 *et seq.* (Kohlhammer, Stuttgart 1980); Koopmann, *Die internationalen Maßnahmen zur Reinhaltung des Meeres*, in DIE WIRTSCHAFTLICHE NUTZUNG DER NORDSEE UND DIE EUROPÄISCHE GEMEINSCHAFT 71 *et seq.* (H. R. Krämer ed., Nomos Verlag, Baden-Baden 1979); EUROPEAN ENVIRONMENTAL BUREAU, THE CONTROL OF THE DISPOSAL OF WASTES AT SEA 21 *et seq.* (Brussels 1981).

[46] *See* European Parliament Resolution of 16 Feb. 1978, OJ No. C 63, 13 March 1978, p. 28; *id.* of 16 Jan. 1981, OJ No. C 28, 9 Feb. 1981, p. 52.

[47] Convention of 13 Nov. 1972 on the Dumping of Wastes at Sea, 11 ILM 1291 (1972).

[48] Convention of 15 Feb. 1972 for the Prevention of Marine Pollution by Dumping from Ships and Aircraft, 11 ILM 262 (1972).

[49] Convention of 22 March 1974 on the Protection of the Marine Environment of the Baltic Sea Area, 13 ILM 546 (1974).

Mediterranean[50] to which three member states and the Community itself are parties. These conventions essentially follow the regulatory strategy of the aquatic environment directive in that they establish two or more lists of substances with control priorities varying as a function of their hazardousness. However, these lists are not fully coordinated.

In 1976 the Commission proposed a directive on waste dumping at sea[51] to supplement the existing regional conventions on ocean dumping. The proposal closely follows the regulatory concept of the Barcelona and London Conventions. The directive provides for three lists: dumping of some substances is prohibited altogether; other substances may only be dumped with a special permit; and the remaining substances may be dumped with a general permit. The role of the Commission is to coordinate information and review implementation of the directive. The proposal has not been adopted because the member states believe that existing conventions are sufficient.[52]

Finally, the titanium dioxide directive of 1978[53] is primarily designed to combat marine pollution from ocean dumping and discharge into the sea by pipeline. It is an expression of the sector oriented approach to water pollution control. It establishes a special, comprehensive system for the disposal (discharge, dumping, storage, tipping and injection) of waste from the titanium dioxide industry.

There are no common emission standards for new sources, but these sources are subject to the requirement of a prior authorization, which must be preceded by detailed environmental impact assessment. Authorization may only be granted when the applicant agrees to use commercially available materials, procedures, and techniques that are least harmful to the environment. The directive also provides that disposal must be accompanied by monitoring. A further directive[54] specifies procedures for surveys and monitoring. The member states must take further action when it is found that disposal of the titanium dioxide waste has adverse effects on the environment.

In the case of existing sources, member states are required to establish improvement programs setting general and intermediate targets for pollution reduction to be achieved by 1987 and describing the measures to be applied to

[50] Convention of 16 Feb. 1976 for the Protection of the Mediterranean Sea against Pollution, 15 ILM 285 (1976); First Protocol, 15 ILM 300 (1976); Second Protocol, 15 ILM 306 (1976); Third Protocol, 19 ILM 863 (1980); Fourth Protocol, BULL. EC 2-1982, at p. 28, point 2.1.44. For the adhesion of the Community, *see* OJ No. L 240, 19 Sept. 1977, p. 1; OJ No. L 162, 19 June 1981, p. 1; OJ No. L 67, 12 March 1983, p. 1; OJ No. L 68, 10 March 1983, p. 3.

[51] Proposal of 12 Jan. 1976, OJ No. C 40, 20 Feb. 1976, p. 3.

[52] *See* CREMONA, *supra* note 45, at 186.

[53] Directive 78/176/EEC of 20 Feb. 1978 on waste from the titanium dioxide industry, OJ No. L 54, 25 Feb. 1978, p. 19, as amended by Directive 83/29/EEC of 24 Jan. 1983, OJ No. L 32, 3 Feb. 1983, p. 28. *See also* S. JOHNSON, *supra* note 1, at 29 *et seq.*

[54] Directive 82/883/EEC of 3 Dec. 1982 on procedures for the surveillance and monitoring of the environments affected by waste from the titanium dioxide industry, OJ No. L 378, 31 Dec. 1982, p. 1.

each polluter. Exemptions of particular facilities from the improvement program require the Commission's agreement. These improvement programs will be harmonized by a further directive.[54a] However, the Council could not agree on a Commission proposal which provided for the eventual complete elimination of discharges by the titanium dioxide industry.[55] The United Kingdom as usual favored environmental quality standards over emission standards. West Germany opposed the Commission proposal because German producers create up to seven tons of waste per ton of end product since they use a poor quality Norwegian ore. Most other member countries are able to use richer ores which can be converted into the end product by a procedure producing less waste. On the other hand, West Germany believed that the German method of titanium dioxide waste disposal, namely dumping from ships into the ocean, is less harmful than the methods of other member states which discharge the wastes from pipelines in estuaries. Among the other member states, France and Italy favored the Commission proposal because both already had or were planning to introduce strict controls on the discharge of titanium dioxide wastes into the Mediterranean. They considered the directive necessary to reduce the competitive disadvantages faced by their own industries.

b. Operational Discharges

Community activity in the area of operational discharges at sea is mainly limited to coordinating member states' activities in the context of the London Convention of 1954 for the prevention of pollution of the sea by oil, as revised in 1962, 1969, 1971 and 1979 (OILPOL);[56] the follow up Convention of 1973 for the prevention of pollution from ships (MARPOL); and the Protocol of 1978 concerning chemicals,[57] which, in spite of a Community recommendation, has not been ratified by any member state[58] and is not yet in force. The Community also attempts to coordinate the member states' activities within the agencies implementing these conventions, such as the International Maritime Organization (IMO). Finally, the 1978 action program on the control and reduction of hydrocarbons discharged at sea[59] provides for additional measures to control operational discharges.

[54a] A proposal for a directive concerning the means of this harmonization was submitted to the Council on 18 Apr. 1983. *See* OJ No. C 138, 25 May 1983, p. 5.

[55] *See* Commission, State of the Environment: Second Report (Brussels 1979), at 48 *et seq.*; S. Johnson, *supra* note 1, at 31; Rat von Sachverständigen für Umweltfragen, *supra* note 22, at No. 1688-1689.

[56] 327 U.N.T.S. 3; 600 U.N.T.S. 332; 2 International Environmental Law: Multilateral Agreements 969: 77/1 (Erich Schmidt Verlag, Berlin, Looseleaf edition 1974); *id.* at 971: 77/1, 78/1. *See also* M. M'Gonigle & M. Zacher, Pollution, Politics and International Law: Tankers at Sea (University of California Press, Berkeley, Los Angeles, London 1979).

[57] 2 Nov. 1973, 12 ILM 1319 (1973); Protocol of 17 Feb. 1978, 17 ILM 546 (1978).

[58] *See* International Environmental Law, *supra* note 56, at 973: 84/1.

[59] Council Resolution of 26 June 1978, OJ No. C 162, 8 July 1978, p. 1.

c. *Marine Pollution from Land Based Sources*

The Community and all member states are parties to the Paris Convention of 1974 for the prevention of marine pollution from land based sources.[60] The Commission participates in working parties (PARCOM) established under this convention. The convention is to be implemented in the framework of the aquatic environment directive. It follows a similar regulatory system and faces similar implementation difficulties.[61] The Helsinki Convention for the protection of the Baltic Sea[62] and the Barcelona Convention for the Protection of the Mediterranean[63] also cover ocean pollution from land based sources.

d. *Accidental Pollution*

The action program of 1978 on the control and reduction of hydrocarbons discharged at sea[64] envisages a variety of measures intended to coordinate action by member states before or after oil accidents. Pursuant to this program two directives concerning the pilotage of vessels in the North Sea and the English Channel[65] have been issued. These directives establish minimum safety requirements for domestic and certain foreign tankers entering or leaving Community ports. They attempt to impose international standards for shipping safety and prevention of oil pollution.

The Commission has proposed a directive to require member states to impose international standards for shipping safety and pollution prevention on ships using Community ports.[66] The proposal would oblige member state governments to inspect ships and to immobilize substandard vessels. Another proposal calls for national contingency plans for combatting oil pollution caused by accidents.[67] The Community has also recently established a Com-

[60] Convention of 4 June 1974, 13 ILM 352 (1974), in force since 1978. For the adhesion of the Community, *see* Council Decision of 3 March 1975, OJ No. L 194, 25 July 1975, p. 5.

[61] *See* Rat von Sachverständigen für Umweltfragen, *supra* note 45, at No. 1114-1115.

[62] *Supra* note 49.

[63] *Supra* note 50.

[64] Council Resolution of 26 June 1978, OJ No. C 162, 8 July 1978, p. 1; *see also* Commission Decision 80/686/EEC of 25 June 1980, OJ No. L 188, 22 July 1980, p. 11, setting up an advisory committee on the control and reduction of pollution caused by hydrocarbons at sea.

[65] Directive 79/115/EEC of 21 Dec. 1978, OJ No. L 33, 8 Feb. 1979, p. 32; Directive 79/116/EEC of 21 Dec. 1978, OJ No. L 33, 8 Feb. 1979, p. 33, as amended by Directive 79/1034/EEC of 6 Dec. 1979, OJ No. L 315, 11 Dec. 1979, p. 16.

[66] Proposal for a directive concerning the enforcement, in respect of [*sic*] shipping using Community ports, of international standards for shipping safety and pollution prevention of 2 July 1980, OJ No. C 192, 30 July 1980, p. 8. *See* European Parliament Resolution of 16 Jan. 1981, OJ No. C 28, 9 Feb. 1981, p. 52 (criticizing the lack of such regulation).

[67] Proposal of 29 Sept. 1983 for a directive concerning the drawing up of contingency plans to combat accidental oil spills at sea, OJ No. C 273, 12 Oct. 1983, p. 3.

munity information system on hydrocarbon pollution of the sea.[68] Its purpose is to exchange technical information available from member states and the Community for combatting oil pollution. For example, it will establish a register of equipment and personnel available to combat oil pollution in all member states, thus enabling any member state to use the equipment of a neighboring member state in an emergency. Finally, the Commission has tried with limited success to induce member states to ratify various conventions for the promotion of safety at sea.

Most Community action in this area is based on the premise that the actions of the member states are sufficient and that supplementary Community measures, such as a Community monitoring system, are unnecessary. The European Parliament has criticized this position,[69] and the Commission itself would like the Community to take a greater role in controlling oil pollution, e. g. by establishing a Community coast guard service. Implementation of such ideas, however, is unlikely because member states insist on retaining their sovereignty, and the third environmental program does not mention them.[70]

C. Air Pollution

Community law on air pollution[71] presently covers only five problem areas: some automotive emissions, SO_2, NO_x and particulates emissions from stationary sources, and lead pollution from all sources. The extent and implementation of Community law in this field is far behind the targets of the first two environmental programs. Apart from the notorious personnel problems of the Commission, the explanation may be lack of sufficient scientific and technical information and the difficulty in reconciling economic, employment, and energy policy considerations.

1. Automotive Emissions

a. Motor Vehicles

The directive of 1970 on air pollution by motor vehicles, as amended,[72] is one of the many directives issued within the framework of the type-approval

[68] Decision of 3 Dec. 1981, OJ No. L 335, 10 Dec. 1981, p. 52. The European Parliament also called upon the Commission to initiate negotiations with non-member states to ensure their participation and to integrate the offshore industry into the information system. *See* Resolution of 16 Jan. 1981, OJ No. C 28, 9 Feb. 1981, p. 55.

[69] *See* Resolutions, *supra* note 46.

[70] *Supra* note 4.

[71] For a survey of (pre-1978) Community policy in this field *see* BRUSASCO-MACKENZIE & KISS, *supra* note 1, at 317. For Community policy on SO_2 *see* G. WETSTONE & A. ROSENCRANZ, ACID RAIN IN EUROPE AND NORTH AMERICA 149 *et seq.* (Environmental Law Institute, Washington 1983).

[72] Directive 70/220/EEC of 20 March 1970 on the approximation of the laws of the Member States relating to measures to be taken against air pollution by gases from positive-ignition engines of motor vehicles, JO No. L 76, 6 April 1970, p. 1 ([1970]

procedure for motor vehicles established by Directive 70/156/EEC.[73] Under this procedure, member states are obliged to grant, upon application, an EEC type-approval for a particular motor vehicle model if the requirements of the various special directives involving about seventy vehicle specifications are fulfilled. Until the few remaining unissued directives come into force, a national type-approval concerning specifications already established is granted. The approval is confirmed by a so-called EEC certificate recognized in all member states. Within the framework of this procedure, Directive 70/220/EEC sets emission standards for carbon monoxide, hydrocarbons, and nitrogen oxides and specifies testing methods.

Harmonization of emission standards is based on the cooperation of all major producer and consumer countries within the United Nations' Economic Commission for Europe (ECE).[74] It is composed of the West and East European member states of the United Nations, Switzerland, the United States and Canada; Japan participates in the harmonization work in a consultative capacity. The EEC member countries send the same experts to the technical committees of the EEC and the ECE, and they try to present a common view within the ECE. The emission standards agreed upon within the ECE are normally incorporated into Community directives, although the time limits for compliance are determined independently.

Initially, Community harmonization of automotive emission standards was designed to eliminate technical barriers to trade.[75] It sought to preserve the EEC type-approval system for gasoline cars, which was threatened by German and French initiatives to impose stricter emission controls within their respective jurisdictions. After adoption of the first Community environmental program, the first substantive amendment of the directive shifted the emphasis of Community policy to protection against atmospheric pollution.[76] Limitations on nitrogen oxides were instituted, and the existing permissible emission levels

OJ (special English ed.) at 171), as amended by Directive 74/290/EEC of 28 May 1974, OJ No. L 159, 15 June 1974, p. 61, Directive 77/102/EEC of 30 Nov. 1976, OJ No. L 32, 3 Feb. 1977, p. 32, Directive 78/665/EEC of 14 July 1978, OJ No. L 223, 14 Aug. 1978, p. 48, and Directive 83/351/EEC of 16 June 1983, OJ No. L 197, 20 July 1983, p. 1. *See* S. JOHNSON, *supra* note 1, at 69 *et seq.*, 74; RAT VON SACHVERSTÄNDIGEN FÜR UMWELTFRAGEN, *supra* note 22, at No. 1674 *et seq. See also* authors cited *infra* note 73.

[73] Directive 70/156/EEC of 6 Feb. 1970, JO No. L 42, 23 Feb. 1970, p. 1 ([1970] OJ (special English ed.) at 96), as amended. *See* Henssler, *Einige Aspekte des Abbaus technischer Handelshemmnisse im Verkehr*, in UMWELTSCHUTZ UND INTERNATIONALE WIRTSCHAFT 173 *et seq.* (V. Götz, D. Rauschning & G. Zieger eds., Carl Heymanns Verlag, Köln 1975); W. SCHMEDER, DIE RECHTSANGLEICHUNG ALS INTEGRATIONSINSTRUMENT IN DER EUROPÄISCHEN GEMEINSCHAFT 98 *et seq.* (Carl Heymanns Verlag, Köln 1978).

[74] *See* W. SCHMEDER, *supra* note 73, at 104-105.

[75] The motor vehicles emission directive was adopted in implementation of the General Programme of 28 May 1969 for the elimination of technical obstacles to trade, JO No. C 76, 17 June 1969, p. 1. *See also* P. J. SLOT, TECHNICAL AND ADMINISTRATIVE OBSTACLES TO TRADE IN THE EEC 101 *et seq.* (Sijthoff, Leyden 1975).

[76] *See* Henssler, *supra* note 73, at 177, 180-181.

of carbon monoxide and hydrocarbons were gradually lowered. The search for progressive solutions rather than the least common denominator now guides harmonization in this area.[77]

A member state that seeks more stringent controls may, however, be forced to sacrifice its objectives for the sake of maintaining uniformity throughout the Community. This is the problem with which West Germany is confronted. Under the German environmental program of 1971, the federal government envisaged reducing automotive emissions by 1989 to 10% of 1969 values. This mandate has recently gained new momentum because it appears that nitrogen oxides, a major component of vehicular emissions, contribute greatly to the widespread forest damage that has occurred in the last several years. West Germany is not the only European country seeking such drastic reductions. Switzerland recently ordered a drastic reduction, to take effect between 1982 and 1986, of the permissible emission levels for carbon monoxide, hydrocarbons, and nitrogen oxides. As compared with existing levels this reduction will ultimately amount to 75% for carbon monoxides, to 76.5% for hydrocarbons, and to between 76% and 58% for nitrogen oxides. The 1986 Swiss standards go beyond the ECE values (series 04) and correspond roughly to the US and Japanese standards and the German targets.

In June 1981, the West German government formally requested the Commission to make proposals for reduction of the existing standards. However, France, Italy, and initially the United Kingdom with their distressed car manufacturing industries were opposed to further — or at least speedy — reductions. They argued that the health and environmental necessity and the economic and energy impacts of these measures were not yet sufficiently clarified. From the German point of view the economic and technological difficulties are manageable. There are already technologies on the market whose utilization would enable European car manufacturers to comply with the new requirements, at least when lead-free gasoline is made widely available. Likewise, the energy policy objections to stricter standards are not well founded since the new generation of low emission motors are more efficient and consume less energy. Due to revision of its policy on lead emissions, the United Kingdom has abandoned its initial opposition. It is now committed to a policy of lead-free gasoline and favors far-reaching measures for the control of automobile emissions. However, France and Italy persist in opposing more stringent emission standards. The only agreement that could be reached was on compliance with the ECE series 04 standards beginning in 1986.[78] Recently, the Commission has proposed that the US standards should be achieved in three steps between 1989 and 1993, and that each member state be allowed to impose these standards on its industry beginning in 1986.[78a] West Germany considers this delay to be unwarranted and a possible source of wrong technical solutions and avoidable costs in the automobile industry. Together with

[77] *Id.* at 177.

[78] Directive 83/351/EEC, *supra* note 72.

[78a] Proposal of 12 June 1984, DOC COM (84) 226 final/22; OJ No. C 178, 6 July 1984, p. 9.

the controversy on lead-free gasoline (to be discussed below), the matter of automobiles emission controls is likely to generate further political conflict within the Community.

The original economic motivation for harmonization of automotive emission controls is still perceptible in the Community's focus on type-approval of new cars. The Community has not adopted requirements, demanded by the European Parliament,[79] for the maintenance of cars.

Under the motor vehicle air pollution directive,[80] an EEC type-approval and an EEC certificate, as well as a national type-approval, may not be refused when the requirements of the directive are met. As of 1 October 1979, compliance with emission standards is a prerequisite for granting the certificate. Cars that have an EEC type-approval or an EEC certificate may not be refused registration or prohibited from use within the Community (a principle already established by the framework directive 70/156/EEC). As of 1 October 1980, member states may also refuse national type-approval or prohibit use when a car does not comply with Community standards. The directive implements a form of optional harmonization by setting maximum requirements and leaving member states the power to allow operation of vehicles on their territory that do not meet the EEC emission standards.[81] However, it should be noted that the practical importance of this "maximum harmonization" strategy is attenuated by the fact that, due to the export orientation of the European car industry, an EEC certificate would normally be sought.[82] De facto, there is a system of total harmonization with respect to environmental requirements.

Similar rules apply to emissions from diesel automobiles. The directive of 1972 on emissions from diesel vehicles[83] and the directive of 1977 on emissions from diesel tractors[84] both provide for emission standards limiting particulate

[79] *See* European Parliament, Written Question No. 1447/80 by Mr. Linkohr and Mrs. Weber, OJ No. C 49, 9 March 1981, p. 23. *See also* Progress Report 1980, *supra* note 5, Annex I, at 11.

[80] *Supra* note 72.

[81] *See* Report of Transport Committee, EP Doc. 243/69, which proposed a new Art. 3a. The only exception to the principle of optional harmonization in this area is the requirement under Directive 77/143/EEC of 29 Dec. 1976 on the approximation of the laws of the Member States relating to roadworthiness tests for motor vehicles and their trailers, OJ No. L 47, 18 Feb. 1977, p. 47, that all buses, trucks, and trailers must undergo regular technical inspections covering exhaust emissions and noise. This directive, based on Art. 75 of the EEC Treaty, is clearly motivated by the desire to prevent distortions of competition in the transport business.

[82] *See* Henssler, *supra* note 73, at 174-5; W. SCHMEDER, *supra* note 73, at 91-2; Commission DOC COM (83) 633 final pp. 22-3.

[83] Directive 72/306/EEC of 2 Aug. 1972 on the approximation of the laws of the Member States relating to measures to be taken against the emission of pollutants from diesel engines for use in vehicles, JO No. L 190, 20 Aug. 1972, p. 1 ([1972] OJ (special English ed.) at 889).

[84] Directive 77/537/EEC of 28 June 1977 on the approximation of the laws of the Member States relating to the measures to be taken against the emission of pollutants

emissions from diesel engines. An extension of these directives to nitrogen oxides and hydrocarbons is envisaged, but as yet the Commission has not made any proposals.

b. Lead Emissions from Motor Vehicles

Quite a different strategy has been employed to deal with lead emissions from motor vehicle exhausts. The directive of 1978 on the lead content of petrol[85] limits inputs through product standards rather than regulating outputs directly through an emission standard. Since January 1981 the maximum permitted lead compound content of gasoline marketed in the Community is 0.4 g/l. Moreover, member states are obliged to ensure that the reduction of lead content does not cause a significant increase in other pollutants. The directive adopts a "straddle" strategy of harmonization which establishes both maximum and minimum permitted levels of control and leaves member states free to select a level of control within the range thus established. This strategy is very unusual for product related requirements and puts the very objectives of harmonization in question. A member state may require that the maximum lead content be less than 0.4 g/l, but it may not establish limits lower than 0.15 g/l. This is a compromise necessitated because West Germany had introduced a standard of 0.15 g/l as early as 1976 and was not prepared to consent to any deterioration. The other member states, most of which had national lead standards above 0.4 g/l, were unwilling to impose on their refining industry the heavy economic burden that West Germany had absorbed years before. (However, it must be noted that the United Kingdom will lower the lead content of gasoline to 0.15 g/l as of 1984.) As part of the compromise, Ireland was granted a five year exemption to permit marketing of gasoline that does not exceed its current level of 0.64 g/l. The exemption may be prolonged by the Council, acting by a qualified majority on a Commission proposal.

The compromise has a long history.[86] West Germany proposed national legislation in 1970 to reduce the lead content of gasoline to 0.4 g/l as of January 1972 and to 0.15 g/l as of January 1976. In response, the Commission, relying on the information/standstill agreement concluded within the framework of the 1969 program for the elimination of technical obstacles to trade, objected to the proposed legislation as erecting new barriers to trade and requested the federal government to defer its measure until Community harmonization was achieved. West Germany responded that its legislation was not covered by the standstill/notification agreement because under Art. 36 of the EEC Treaty, protection of health has priority over prevention of distortion of

from diesel engines for use in wheeled agricultural or forestry tractors, OJ No. L 220, 29 Aug. 1977, p. 38.

[85] Directive 78/611/EEC of 29 June 1978 on the approximation of the laws of the Member States concerning the lead content of petrol, OJ No. L 197, 22 July 1978, p. 19. *See also* S. JOHNSON, *supra* note 1, at 66-67.

[86] *See* H. BUNGARTEN, *supra* note 1, at 188 *et seq.*; RAT VON SACHVERSTÄNDIGEN FÜR UMWELTFRAGEN, *supra* note 22, at No. 1672/1673.

competition. Despite protests from the other member states and the Commission, the law was put into effect in January 1972. In 1974, the Commission submitted to the Council a draft directive for the reduction of the lead content of petrol.[87] It proposed to extend to 1976 the deadline for attaining the standard of 0.4 g/l. A standard of 0.15 g/l was proposed for 1978. The Commission proposal was rejected both by West Germany and the other member states. Adoption of a directive was possible only by introducing a double standard to enable West Germany to retain its stricter law.

The lead directive is the product of a political controversy between West Germany, on one side, and the Commission and the other member states, on the other, over the proper balance between economic interests and protection of human health. It demonstrates that Community environmental policy via harmonization is stalemated when member states' environmental policies are too far apart. Minimum harmonization may be an answer to this structural problem. However, in the case of product related requirements, minimum harmonization does not remove the technical obstacles to trade erected by different national requirements and therefore fails to fulfill the purpose of harmonization in the Common Market.

In the summer of 1983, the Netherlands, the United Kingdom and West Germany, supported also by Denmark, proposed that the Directive be amended so as to allow a member state to introduce lead-free gasoline. The United Kingdom wants lead-free gasoline for health reasons, and West Germany needs it as a prerequisite for stiffening the NO_x standards for car emissions. The proposal has met with stiff opposition from France and Italy, and the only agreement that could be reached as yet is a general commitment of all member states to lower the lead content of gasoline and a request to the Commission to study the problem and make mutually acceptable proposals. A recent Commission proposal[87a] empowers the member states to introduce lead-free gasoline in 1986 and requires them to do so beginning in 1989. However, pressures stemming from the problems of forest damage in West Germany are now such that West Germany thinks that an earlier mandatory introduction of lead-free gasoline in all member states is the only acceptable solution. This position is shared by Denmark and the Netherlands but it has not been possible to overcome the opposition of other member states. At the Council meeting of 28 June 1984, agreement could only be reached on the basis of the Commission proposal.

2. General Measures to Control Lead Pollution

The Community has not limited its lead control measures to reducing the lead content of gasoline. The directive of 1977 on biological screening of the pop-

[87] Proposal of 7 Dec. 1973 for a Directive concerning the approximation of the laws of the Member States relating to the composition of petrol, OJ No. C 8, 31 Jan. 1974, p. 28.

[87a] Proposals of 12 June 1984, DOC COM (84) 226 final/2, OJ No. C 178, 6 July 1984, p. 5; and of 5 Oct. 1984, DOC COM (84) 532 final.

ulation for lead[88] obliges member states to screen the general public for exposure to lead. It obliges member states to trace exposure sources when reference levels of lead concentrations in blood are exceeded. Remedial measures are completely at the member state's discretion. A more ambitious Commission proposal to set maximum blood concentration levels for the general public has not been accepted by the Council.

A proposal for a directive setting ambient air quality standards for lead[89] was made in 1975. West Germany originally supported this initiative because it believed that ambient air quality standards for lead could be attained only if the lead content of gasoline were reduced to the level mandated by German law. After the compromise allowing West Germany to maintain its gasoline lead content standard of 0.15 g/l, West Germany lost interest in the directive. However, the United Kingdom, which was reconsidering its lead pollution control policies, voiced its support for the Commission proposal. The directive was thus adopted in 1982.[90]

3. Sulfur Dioxide, Nitrogen Oxide and Particulates from Stationary Sources

In the case of air pollutants from stationary sources, the Community has so far focused on SO_2 and particulate matter pollution and recently extended its regulation to NO_x.

a. Sulfur Content of Fuels

With respect to SO_2, the strategy first applied was to regulate inputs by limiting the sulfur content of fuels. Sulfur emissions from domestic heating and small commercial installations fueled mainly with gas oil (light heating and diesel oil) was the first problem that the Community addressed. The gas oil directive of 1975[91] was adopted in response to West German and Dutch measures progressively reducing the sulfur content of gas oil. The directive provides for reduction by steps in 1976 and 1981 of the sulfur content of gas oil. It employs a regional strategy by distinguishing two grades of gas oil, namely type A and type B. The low sulfur content type A oil (ultimately 0.3%) may be used anywhere. Type B, with a higher sulfur content (ultimately 0.5%), may only be used in clean air areas and in heavily polluted areas where gas oil accounts for an insignificant portion of emissions.[92]

[88] Directive 77/312/EEC of 29 March 1977 on biological screening of the population for lead, OJ No. L 105, 28 April 1977, p. 10.

[89] Proposal of 24 April 1975 for a directive on air quality standards for lead, OJ No. C 151, 7 July 1975, p. 29.

[90] Directive 82/884/EEC of 3 Dec. 1982 concerning a limit value for lead concentration in the air, OJ No. L 378, 31 Dec. 1982, p. 15.

[91] Directive 75/716/EEC of 24 Nov. 1975 on the approximation of the laws of the Member States relating to the sulphur content of certain liquid fuels, OJ No. L 307, 25 Nov. 1975, p. 22. *See also* S. Johnson, *supra* note 1, at 58 *et seq.*

[92] However, there is a distinction between "ordinary" uses of gas oil and special uses, i. e. use in power plants, by ships, and by motor vehicles traveling from one zone to

The member states are to determine the zones where type B gas oil is permitted. To permit the Commission to verify the effectiveness of the Directive, member states are obliged to inform it of the criteria used to establish the zones. Some member states, such as West Germany, have required the use of type A (low sulfur) gas oil throughout the country.[93]

In 1975 the Commission also issued a proposal to reduce SO_2 emissions from large stationary sources using heavy fuel oil.[94] The basic strategy of the proposal was to limit the sulfur content of fuel oil. The various member states have employed or envisaged a large variety of strategies to deal with such emissions, such as specifying the type of fuel oil to be used in certain areas or installations, generally limiting the sulfur content of fuels, and limiting emissions at the source. The proposal provides for creation of zones of special protection in which only low sulfur fuel oil (2%) could be used. It also sets requirements for installations located outside these zones which contribute significantly to the ground level concentration of pollutants within the zones. The Commission recognized, however, that mandatory desulfurization of fuels might not always be the most economic solution. It therefore exempts installations which disperse SO_2 emissions by high stacks or that limit them by such techniques as gas desulfurization, fluidized bed combustion, and fuel gasification. The member states have not yet been able to agree on the Commission proposal. This is due to the divergence among member states' policies as well as the economic and energy implications of the proposal.

b. The SO_2 Limit Values Directive

The Community has recently adopted another strategy for controlling SO_2 pollution, namely air quality standards. The directive of 1980 on limit values for sulfur dioxide and suspended particulates[95] is, along with the vehicle emission directives, the most important Community regulation on air pollution. The directive, to some extent modeled on the Dutch system of air pollution control, establishes Community-wide mandatory ambient air quality standards and stricter non-binding guide values for SO_2 and suspended particulates. The mandatory air quality standards are to protect human health, and the guide values are intended as long-term precautions for health and the environment as well as points of reference for establishment of zones of special protection. The directive also specifies the associated measurement methods. There are three types of zones in which air quality standards for sulfur dioxide

the other or crossing a border between a non-member state and a member state. These special uses are uniformly subject to the less strict of the two input standards.

[93] *See* P. KNOEPFEL & H. WEIDNER, HANDBUCH DER SO_2-LUFTREINHALTEPOLITIK, vol. 2, at 45, 192, 313, 379, 467, 515, 592, 682 (Erich Schmidt Verlag, Berlin 1980).

[94] Proposal of 30 Dec. 1975 for a Directive on the use of fuel oils with the aim of decreasing sulphurous emissions, OJ No. C 54, 8 March 1976, p. 79. *See also* S. JOHNSON, *supra* note 1, at 60 *et seq.*

[95] Directive 80/779/EEC of 15 July 1980 on air quality limit values and guide values for sulphur dioxide and suspended particulates, OJ No. L 229, 30 Aug. 1980, p. 30.

and particulates may differ from the general standards: (1) nonattainment zones; (2) development zones; and (3) special protection zones. The concept of zones was not contained in the original Commission proposal.[96] The member states are obliged to take all appropriate measures to ensure that the mandatory standards are archieved by April 1983. In areas where the mandatory standards are likely to be exceeded (nonattainment zones), member states are obliged to progressively improve air quality on the basis of an improvement plan which is to describe in detail the implementation measures to be undertaken. The implementation plan is to provide for attainment of the mandatory standards as soon as possible, and by April 1993 at the latest.

Although the period for compliance is quite long, it is not very probable that the mandatory standards will be attained in all areas because of difficulties in monitoring air quality, devising appropriate implementation plans, translating the implementation plans into individual requirements, and enforcing these requirements. Although the member states may be justified in not relying on input standards for fuels because their possibly disproportionate cost offsets their ease of implementation, it is remarkable that the directive does not provide for emission standards, a strategy common to all member states. An explanation may be that the member states consider Community ambient air quality standards as a supplementary means of air pollution control for heavily polluted areas where generally applicable emission standards would not by themselves maintain appropriate air quality, as well as for special protection zones where particularly high air quality is desired.

The guide values are reference points for establishment of special protection and development zones. In zones where a member state considers it necessary to limit a foreseeable increase in pollution due to urban or industrial development (development zones), it may fix values lower than the limit values of the directive. In zones for which a member state desires special environmental protection (special protection zones), it may set values lower than the guide values of the directive. Determination of the two kinds of zones is fully within the discretion of member states since the directive contains no clear criteria for their establishment. However, the directive does oblige member states to inform the Commission of the values, deadlines, and time tables established for these zones and of any measures taken for attainment of the air quality objectives set for these zones. Moreover, member states are obliged to inform the Commission about violations of the limit values, the concentrations recorded, the reasons for nonattainment, the measures taken to meet the standards, and, at the request of the Commission, the concentrations in development and special protection zones.

Besides being a point of reference for establishment of quality standards in development and special protection zones, the guide values are also designed to serve as a general guideline for the member states' air pollution control pol-

[96] Proposal for a directive concerning health protection standards for sulphur dioxide and suspended particulate matter in urban atmospheres of 25 Feb. 1976, OJ No. C 63, 19 March 1976, p. 5.

icy. The member states are required to endeavor to move towards the guide values wherever existing concentrations exceed them.

In addition, the directive generally prohibits "significant" deterioration of air quality in areas where air pollution is low in relation to the mandatory standards. The Commission's proposal had contained an unconditional prohibition on deterioration of air quality like that contained in other recent environmental directives. The meaning of this modification and the interpretation to be given to environmental directives that prohibit deterioration but do not contain the qualifiying term "significant" are both unclear. Further, the relationship between the apparently mandatory prohibition of significant deterioration of air quality and the optional designation of special protection zones is also unclear.

The directive for control of SO_2 and particulates had been discussed for almost four years within the Council. One of the most controversial points of discussion was the choice of measurement method. Since West Germany insisted on retaining its own measurement method, which it considered environmentally superior to the measurement methods favored by the other member states, total harmonization of measurement methods was not possible. Therefore the directive allows member states to use either the measurement methods and corresponding standards set forth in the directive or the German measurement methods and associated standards contained in annex IV to the Directive.[97] Member states which decide to use the West German method (probably West Germany and Italy) must make parallel measurements under both methods to verify the correspondence of the measurement methods and standards. The monitoring results are to be reported to the Commission, which in turn is to report to the Council and make proposals concerning retention or abolition of the dual system of standards and associated measurement methods. Although it is generally thought that the German measurement method is more exact, the associated German ambient quality standards for particulates and SO_2 do not contain a separate winter standard. Since the winter standard of the directive is relatively strict (median limit value: 180 $\mu g/m^3$, guide value: 130 $\mu g/m^3$), it may be that the German standard is in this respect less stringent.

It is also worth noting that the SO_2 directive addresses itself to transboundary pollution. Member states are required to consult with the neighboring state or states before establishing development or special protection zones in border regions. Consultations are also required when the mandatory standards of the directive or the standards fixed by a member state for a border zone might be exceeded due to pollution which may have originated in the neighboring state. In addition to consultations, the member states have committed themselves to endeavor, in accordance with Directive 80/779/EEC, to

[97] The member states are also free to use, for the purpose of applying the standards established by the directive, other measurement methods provided they demonstrate to the Commission that the results correlate sufficiently well with those obtained using the Community reference method.

limit and as far as possible gradually reduce and prevent transboundary air pollution by sulfur dioxide and suspended particulates.[98] Finally the Community and the member states are parties to the 1979 ECE Convention on Long Range Transport of Air Pollutants.[99] This convention obliges the parties to endeavor gradually to reduce air pollution, especially by using the best available and economically feasible control technology, and to consult about transboundary air pollution originating in one contracting state and affecting another.

c. The NO_2 Limit Values Proposal

The approach used in the SO_2 directive was extended by a Commission proposal[99a] submitted in 1983 to introduce limit values and guidelines for NO_2 concentrations in the Community and to require the member states to determine air quality improvement plans in heavily polluted areas to meet these standards.

4. New Orientations in Community Air Pollution Control

As already mentioned, West Germany has in recent years suffered extensive damage to its large forests from air pollutants such as sulfur dioxide, nitrogen oxides, and ozone. As permitted by existing directives, West Germany has stiffened its own pollution control program by imposing new regulations on major fuel burning installations, especially power plants and industrial boilers. However, since half of West Germany's air pollution is imported, West Germany favors additional Community measures to control air pollution. It has proposed, as a first step, a new framework directive obliging member states to limit emissions of major industrial installations according to the state of the art; however, member states would have the power to define this term themselves, and harmonization of emission limitations reflecting the state of the art would be postponed for the future. Existing sources had to be gradually adjusted to the new source requirements. The Commission has recently made a proposal following the German suggestions.[100] It was anticipated that the United Kingdom, France, and Belgium, which have little forest damage because they have prevailing west winds and different soil structures, would not easily agree to any such proposal. However, agreement was reached easily,[100a] proba-

[98] Council Resolution of 15 July 1980, OJ No. C 222, 30 Aug. 1980, p. 1.

[99] INTERNATIONAL ENVIRONMENTAL LAW, *supra* note 56, at 979: 84/1. *See* ROSENCRANZ, *The ECE Convention of 1979 on Long-Range Transboundary Air Pollution*, 4 ZEITSCHRIFT FÜR UMWELTPOLITIK 511 (1981); KISS, *La convention sur la pollution transfrontière à longue distance*, 1981 REVUE JURIDIQUE DE L'ENVIRONNEMENT 30. The Council by its decision 81/462/EEC of 11 June 1981, OJ No. L 171, 27 June 1981, p. 11, adhered to the convention, which has recently gone into force.

[99a] Proposal of 19 Sept. 1983 for a directive on air quality limit values and guide values for nitrogen dioxide, OJ No. C 258, 27 Sept. 1983, p. 3

[100] OJ No. C 139, 27 May 1983, p. 5.

[100a] The proposal was adopted in the Council meeting of 1 March 1984: Directive 84/360/EEC of 28 June 1984 on the combating of air pollution from industrial plants, OJ No. L 188, 16 July 1984, p. 20.

bly because the obligations imposed by the directive are rather vague. Early in 1984, the Commission made a proposal for a directive on major combustion plants[100b] that provides emission standards for new sources and requires the member states to reduce total emissions from existing sources by a considerable percentage. It remains to be seen whether this proposal will be adopted as easily as the framework directive. In any case, the problem of forest damage has compelled the Community to step up regulatory efforts in an area that had not been considered a priority in the environmental program.

D. Noise

1. Traffic Noise

Community activity concerning noise pollution is primarily limited to traffic noise.[101] Its primary focus is harmonization of product standards rather than establishment of ambient noise levels. No proposals have as yet been submitted to implement the mandate of the environmental program to establish guidelines for determining noise quality objectives.

a. Motor Vehicles

The most important legislative text, the directive of 1970 on motor vehicle noise as amended,[102] closely resembles the motor vehicle emission directives. This is because both are implementing directives under the framework directive 70/156/EEC on EEC type-approval for motor vehicles.[103] As in the case of the emission directives, emphasis has shifted from elimination of technical barriers to trade towards protection of the general public.

The directive now establishes noise level standards, measurement methods, and specification standards for the exhaust systems of highway vehicles. The original directive was limited to specification standards for exhaust systems. Performance requirements were added in 1973. Pursuant to suggestions by France and the United Kingdom,[104] the noise levels and measurement methods have gradually been tightened in accordance with technical progress in motor

[100b] Proposal of 19 Dec. 1983 for a directive for the limitation of emissions from major combustion plants into the air, OJ No. C 49, 21 Feb. 1984, p. 1.

[101] *See* S. Johnson, *supra* note 1, at 100 *et seq.*; Bentil, *Environmental Improvement through Noise Control in the European Community*, 1978 Journal of Planning and Environmental Law 16.

[102] Directive 70/157/EEC of 6 Feb. 1970 on the approximation of the laws of the Member States relating to the permissible sound level and the exhaust system of motor vehicles, JO No. L 42, 23 Feb. 1970, p. 16 ([1970] OJ (special English ed.) at 111), as amended by Directive 73/350/EEC of 7 Nov. 1973, OJ No. L 321, 22 Nov. 1973, p. 33; Directive 77/212/EEC of 8 March 1977, OJ No. L 66, 12 March 1977, p. 33; and Directive 81/334/EEC of 13 April 1981, OJ No. L 131, 18 May 1981, p. 6.

[103] *Supra* note 73.

[104] Henssler, *supra* note 73, at 179; S. Johnson, *supra* note 1, at 100.

vehicle construction. However, the requirements are still relatively liberal. The directive contains deadlines for industry adjustment. Following a German initiative that called for further tightening of the standards by 1985, the Commission has recently made a proposal that would reduce the noise levels for cars and trucks by three decibels on the average; this proposal has been opposed by the Council.[105]

The EEC type-approval, EEC certificate, and national type-approval must be granted for vehicle models that comply with the directive's requirements. Harmonization, however, is optional. The directive empowers, but does not oblige, member states to refuse national type-approval or to prohibit initial entry into service, starting April 1980, to cars not meeting the noise level limits and, starting October 1982, to cars not meeting the exhaust specifications of the directive. Thus, member states may set more lenient requirements for their territory, but their manufacturers must seek an EEC certificate or a national type-approval of the importing state in order to export.

A similar system of noise control applies to agricultural tractors and motor cycles.[106]

b. Aircraft and Trains

The Community has also been active in regulating aircraft noise. The aircraft noise directive of 1979,[107] based on Art. 84(2) rather than Art. 100 of the EEC Treaty, adopts the system and standards established by annex 16 to the Convention on International Civil Aviation, adopted by the International Civil Aviation Organization (ICAO) Council on 3 April 1974 and operative from 27 February 1975. The directive establishes an EEC noise limitation certificate, a document by which the member state registering the aircraft certifies that it complies with the directive. This certificate must be recognized by all other member states. The directive also applies to civil aircraft of non-member countries landing or taking off in a member state. Finally, it applies to certain aircraft not covered by annex 16 to the Convention. These aircraft must meet re-

[105] Directive 84/372/EEC of 3 July 1984, OJ No. L 196, 26 July 1984, p. 47, and Directive 84/424/EEC of 3 Sept. 1984, OJ No. L 238, 6 Sept. 1984, p. 31.

[106] Directive 74/151/EEC of 4 March 1974 on the approximation of the laws of the Member States relating to certain parts and characteristics of wheeled agricultural or forestry tractors, OJ No. L 84, 28 March 1974, p. 25; Directive 78/1015/EEC of 23 Nov. 1978 on the approximation of the laws of the Member States on the permissible sound level and exhaust system of motorcycles, OJ No. L 349, 13 Dec. 1978, p. 21. Another directive dealing with motor vehicle noise, namely Directive 77/311/ EEC of 29 March 1977 on the approximation of the laws of the Member States relating to the driver-perceived noise level of wheeled agricultural or forestry tractors, OJ No. L 105, 28 April 1977, p. 1, is exclusively designed to protect occupational health.

[107] Directive 80/51/EEC of 20 Dec. 1979 on the limitation of noise emissions from subsonic aircraft, OJ No. L 18, 24 Jan. 1980, p. 26. The directive was initiated by West Germany. *See* Close, *Art. 84 EEC: The Development of Transport Policy in the Sea and Air Sectors*, 5 European L. Rev. 188, 198 (1980).

quirements similar to those established by the Convention.[108] There is a Commission proposal to limit helicopter noise according to ICAO rules.[109] Finally, a proposal seeks to limit noise originating from new trains.[109a]

2. Other Areas of Noise Control

Another subject of Community activity is construction and equipment noise.[110] A 1979 directive[111] attempts to harmonize measurement methods for noise emissions of construction machinery and equipment. In addition to this general directive, the Commission has submitted a series of specific proposals relating to certain types of machinery, such as pneumatic jackhammers, electric generators, current generators for welding, power cranes, compressors, and lawnmowers.[112] These proposals create emission standards and a type-approval procedure for the various kinds of machinery. Like the traffic noise directives, they follow the principle of optional harmonization, allowing member states to permit the operation of machinery in their territory that does not comply with Community emission standards. However, the Commission proposal on earth-moving machines[113] follows the principle of total harmonization. The same is true of the recent Commission proposal on household appliances[114] which obliges all manufacturers to test the noise level of their products and provide the buyer with adequate information.

Some of the proposals have been pending in the Council for quite some time. The major reason for delay seems to be that the preference of the majority of member states for total harmonization is not shared by the remaining member states. A secondary reason is that some member states believe uniform noise requirements may open the Community market to third countries without the necessary counter-concessions.[115]

108 The Commission proposal of 28 Sept. 1981, OJ No. C 276, 28 Oct. 1981, p. 5, provides for adjustment of the Directive to amendments of the ICAO rules.

109 Proposal of 13 Oct. 1981 for a directive on the limitation of noise emissions from helicopters, OJ No. C 275, 27 Oct. 1981, p. 2.

109a Proposal of 29 Sept. 1983 for a directive on the approximation of the laws of the member states relating to noise emissions of trains, OJ No. C 354, 29 Dec. 1983, p. 4.

110 For a survey of Community policy in this field *see* S. JOHNSON, *supra* note 1, at 103-104.

111 Directive 79/113/EEC of 19 Dec. 1979 on the approximation of the laws of the Member States relating to the determination of the noise emission of construction plant and equipment, OJ No. L 33, 8 Feb. 1979, p. 15, as amended by Directive 81/1051/EEC of 7 Dec. 1981, OJ No. L 376, 30 Dec. 1981, p. 49.

112 OJ No. C 82, 14 April 1975, p. 112; OJ No. C 54, 8 March 1976, p. 75; *id.* p. 71; *id.* p. 63; OJ No. C 94, 19 April 1978, p. 2; OJ No. C 86, 2 April 1979, p. 9.

113 Proposal of 28 Nov. 1980, OJ No. C 356, 3 Dec. 1980, p. 3, amended on 9 Oct. 1981, OJ No. C 302, 29 Nov. 1981, p. 7.

114 Proposal of 12 Jan. 1982, OJ No. C 181, 19 July 1982, p. 1, amended on 23 Nov. 1983, OJ No. C 334, 10 Dec. 1983, p. 15.

115 *See* Progress Report 1980, *supra* note 5, Annex I, at 14.

E. Waste Disposal

Regulation of waste disposal[116] is a Community activity in which the preventive approach plays a prominent role not only in policy announcements, such as the environmental programs, but also in Community legislation itself. Prevention of waste generation and recycling of waste are important goals of Community activity. The establishment of a Waste Management Committee in 1976 was designed to provide the Commission with the scientific expertise and information on national experience necessary to develop new proposals. However, lack of staff and money has greatly impeded the process of implementation by the Commission.[117]

Waste disposal and recovery are covered by a framework directive which establishes general principles of waste disposal, by a more specific directive on disposal of toxic and dangerous wastes, and by several specific directives applicable to particular types of hazardous wastes.

1. General Regulation of Waste Disposal

Under the waste directive of 1975[118] the fundamental obligation of member states is to ensure that waste is disposed of without injury to health and the environment. To meet this obligation, member states must formulate waste disposal plans; establish permitting systems for waste disposal, treatment or storage installations; and prevent the uncontrolled disposal of wastes. They must submit a situation report to the Commission every three years. The directive endorses the polluter-pays principle as the guiding principle for cost allocation. Finally, the directive contains a general member state obligation to encourage the prevention of waste generation and re-use of waste.

2. Special Regulation of Particular Wastes

The directive of 1978 on toxic and dangerous waste[119] applies to wastes containing substances considered to be extremely dangerous and therefore to require priority consideration. Examples of substances to which the directive applies are heavy metals, pesticides, organic halogen compounds, and asbestos. The directive gives member states some discretion in applying the directive because it covers only wastes which contain the listed substances in such quantities as to constitute a risk to health or the environment.[120] The directive

[116] *See* J. P. Hannequart, La Politique de Gestion des Déchets 76 *et seq.* (Erich Schmidt Verlag, Berlin 1983); Offermann-Clas, *supra* note 9, at 1128 *et seq.* For a survey of Community policy on waste *see also* Brusasco-Mackenzie & Kiss, *supra* note 1, at 316-317; S. Johnson, *supra* note 1, at 77 *et seq.*

[117] Progress Report 1980, *supra* note 5, Annex I, at 42.

[118] Directive 75/442/EEC of 15 July 1975 on waste, OJ No. L 194, 25 July 1975, p. 39.

[119] Directive 78/319/EEC of 20 March 1978 on toxic and dangerous waste, OJ No. L 84, 31 March 1978, p. 43.

[120] This qualification was not contained in Art. 1(b) of the Commission proposal of 28 July 1976, OJ No. C 194, 19 Aug. 1976, p. 2.

repeats and details the general principles of the framework directive, particularly those regarding disposal of toxic and dangerous waste, application of the polluter-pays principle, formulation of waste disposal plans, reporting obligations, and the principles concerning prevention of waste generation and re-use of waste.

Although the Commission was at one time considering a proposal on disposal of toxic and dangerous wastes,[121] there are currently no Community rules for such disposal. Instead, the directive sets up a mechanism of joint Community and member state coordination of the waste disposal plans established by member states. It establishes a uniform system of permitting for installations that store, treat and/or dispose of toxic and dangerous waste and obliges the holders of such wastes to use the facilities of authorized enterprises. The directive provides for extensive monitoring and supervision of installations, establishments, and enterprises which produce, hold or dispose of toxic and dangerous wastes. It creates rights of inspection and obligations to keep records regarding disposal and carriage of such wastes.

An earlier directive on the disposal of PCBs[122] repeats the general principles of the framework directive, but places particular emphasis on the recovery of PCB waste and requires that member states make compulsory the disposal of PCB waste contained in equipment. This directive is atypical of Community environmental policy in that no specific provision existed regulating PCBs in the member states prior to its adoption.

The titanium dioxide directive has already been discussed in connection with marine pollution.

There also is a special regime for waste oils. The waste oil directive[123] of 1976 sets out guiding principles for disposal of used oil which are similar to those of the framework directive on waste, but gives more emphasis to recycling through regeneration or combustion for generation of energy. The directive follows existing legislation in West Germany and similar legislative proposals in France and the Netherlands. An important question not settled by the directive is whether waste oil should be re-used by refining or by burning. Burning causes concern due to release into the atmosphere of the large quantities of heavy metals and other hazardous substances contained in waste oil. The probable solution is not to emphasize regeneration, but rather to require pretreatment of waste oils before burning.

The directive requires member states to prohibit discharge of used oil into water, prevent soil pollution caused by the deposit or discharge of used oil, and control air pollution from waste oil processing. In order to attain these basic objectives, they must if necessary establish a system of waste oil collection and

[121] Progress Report 1980, *supra* note 5, Annex I, at 43.

[122] Directive 76/403/EEC of 6 April 1976 on the disposal of polychlorinated biphenyls and polychlorinated terphenyls, OJ No. L 108, 26 April 1976, p. 41. *See also* S. JOHNSON, *supra* note 1, at 81.

[123] Directive 75/439/EEC of 16 June 1975 on the disposal of waste oils, OJ No. L 194, 25 July 1975, p. 23. *See also* Progress Report 1980, *supra* note 5, Annex I, at 43.

disposal by special enterprises. Strict record keeping, reporting and inspection requirements must be imposed on enterprises producing, collecting and/or disposing of waste oil in large quantities. Finally, the directive allows member states to subsidize collection and/or disposal enterprises and to levy waste oil charges. The subsidy may be financed, in accordance with the polluter-pays principle, by a charge imposed on waste oil or on products eventually transformed into waste oil.

Problems with international transport and disposal of dangerous wastes in the Community caused the Commission to submit a proposal in early 1983 for the surveillance and control of such international transactions.[124] The proposal covers toxic and dangerous wastes, PCBs, and waste oil. It provides for reporting all transfrontier transport of such wastes to the countries of origin, destination, and transit; requires carriers to take out insurance; and imposes packaging and labeling obligations. Some member states, such as West Germany and Denmark, would prefer a permit requirement and, in spite of the trade implications, want to retain the power to set stricter national regulations (e. g. prescribe that dangerous wastes must in principle be disposed of in the state of origin).[124a] The agreement reached at the Council meeting of 28 June 1984 arguably allows the introduction of a permit requirement that also covers their exportation, but hazardous wastes transported for re-use or recycling are partly excluded.

Finally, a recent Commission proposal[125] provides that sewage may be used for agricultural purposes only if specified concentration levels of heavy metals are not exceeded.

3. Prevention of Waste

The recent legislative activities of the Community show a stronger emphasis on prevention of waste.

In late 1981 the Council endorsed a modest recommendation to the member states on the recovery and re-use of waste paper and cardboard.[126] It encourages the member states to define and implement policies to promote the use of recycled paper and cardboard, especially by public authorities. It does not con-

[124] Proposal for a directive on the surveillance and control of transfrontier disposal of dangerous waste in the Community, OJ No. C 53, 25 Feb. 1983, p. 3, as amended OJ No. C 186, 12 July 1983, p. 3.

[124a] It is not clear whether the decision of the European Court of Justice, case 172/82, Syndicat national des fabricants raffineurs d'huile de graissage v. Groupement d'intérêt économique "Inter-Huiles," [1983] ECR 555, has disposed of the applicability of Articles 30 and 36 to hazardous waste because that decision concerned waste oil which is a commercial product.

[125] Proposal of 13 Sept. 1982 for a directive on the use of sewage sludge in agriculture, OJ No. C 264, 8 Oct. 1982, p. 3, as amended OJ No. C 154, 14 June 1984, p. 6.

[126] Recommendation 81/972/EEC of 3 Dec. 1981 concerning the re-use of waste paper and the use of recycled paper, OJ No. L 355, 10 Dec. 1981, p. 56.

tain a quantitative target for the use of recycled paper and cardboard such as the 60% target proposed by the European Parliament.[127]

The most prominent example of the preventive approach is the Commission proposal for a directive on beverage containers.[128] The proposal, which is the ninth version of an original draft, would require member states to take appropriate measures to save energy and raw materials in beverage packaging. The member states are obliged to fix annual target values by weight and volume for the reduction of wastes from beverage packages. They are also obliged to fix annual targets for re-use and recycling. Furthermore, they are obliged to promote utilization of returnable containers, the recycling of packaging materials, and technological innovation (reduction of weight). They are also to improve consumer awareness of the utilization and disposal of packages. They are obliged to gradually introduce common standards for such packages in order to facilitate re-use by persons other than the original distributor. As of 1984, they must prohibit the use of beverage packages that can not be re-used or recycled.

The Commission proposal, which would implement the member states' obligation under the framework directive to encourage the prevention and re-use of waste, contains elements of the waste control programs of West Germany, France, and Denmark.[129] However, there are differences of emphasis and approach in the various national programs. Moreover, this directive has met with stiff opposition from the powerful European packaging industry, especially since there is still much controversy about the comparative environmental costs and benefits of one-way and returnable packages. As long as Community policy for waste control pursued the traditional objective of regulating pollution it could count on widespread consensus. The more it ventures into waste prevention, the more it will encounter difficulties stemming from the fact that implementation of preventive strategies often requires administrative reorganization and large appropriations, threatens vested economic interests, and must cope with unresolved scientific issues. These considerations are aggravated by the complexity of the Community policy process and the need to coordinate diverse interests at several levels of decisionmaking.[130] Probably the Council will adopt the proposal only in the form of a recommendation.

[127] Resolution of 16 Jan. 1981, No. C 28, 9 Feb. 1981, p. 66.

[128] Proposal of 23 April 1981 for a directive on containers of liquids for human consumption, OJ No. C 204, 13 Aug. 1981, p. 6.

[129] For Denmark *see* C. H. JENSEN, THE LAW AND PRACTICE RELATING TO POLLUTION CONTROL IN DENMARK 143-144, 151-152 (Graham & Trotman, London, 2d ed. 1982).

[130] *See also* Progress Report 1980, *supra* note 5, Annex I, at 40 *et seq.*

F. Hazardous Substances

Regulation of hazardous substances[131] became a Community concern relatively early because of the trade implications of non-uniform national requirements. Although protection of health was nominally a goal of harmonization, the early Community law was basically limited to disclosure. It required disclosure in a standardized form of information, based on existing scientific knowledge, about the health risks of a particular substance. It did not attempt to develop additional health and safety data. It is only recently that testing requirements for new substances were introduced, thereby improving the basis for public information. There are few examples of substantive regulation of hazardous substances by prohibitions and restrictions on production, marketing, and use. Community procedure is characterized by a selective, *ad hoc* approach whereby only very hazardous substances and, more recently, major chemical accidents are subject to harmonized substantive regulation. One factor contributing to this lack of comprehensive approach is the need to take priority action on harmonization of substances covered by proposed national regulations communicated to the Commission under the information/standstill agreement.

1. Classification, Packaging, and Labeling of Chemicals

a. The Framework Directive of 1967 on Dangerous Substances

The basic legislative text regulating chemicals is the original directive of 1967 on dangerous substances.[132] It is a framework directive providing for a uniform system of listing, classification, packaging, and labeling of hazardous substances. The directive contained a lengthy annex in which all existing substances marketed in Europe and considered hazardous were listed and classified into eight risk categories. The fourth amendment listed 123 further substances, changed the labeling required of substances previously listed, and provided a special procedure for adjusting the list to the development of scientific knowl-

[131] For a survey of Community policy in this field *see* S. JOHNSON, *supra* note 1, at 90 *et seq.*; R. BRICKMANN, S. JASANOFF & T. ILGEN, CHEMICAL REGULATION AND CANCER: A CROSS-NATIONAL STUDY OF POLICY AND POLITICS 320 *et seq.* (Cornell U. Press, Ithaca 1982); FARQUHAR, *The Politics of the European Community Towards the Environment - The Dangerous Substances Directive,* 1983 JOURNAL OF PLANNING AND ENVIRONMENTAL LAW 145.

[132] Directive 67/548/EEC of 27 June 1967 on the approximation of laws, regulations and administrative provisions relating to the classification, packaging and labelling of dangerous substances, JO No. 196, 16 Aug. 1967, p. 1 ([1967] OJ (special English ed.) at 234), as amended by Directive 73/146/EEC of 21 May 1973, OJ No. L 167, 25 June 1973, p. 1, Directive 75/409/EEC of 24 June 1975, OJ No. L 183, 14 July 1975, p. 22, Directive 79/831/EEC of 18 Sept. 1979, OJ No. L 259, 15 Oct. 1979, p. 10 and Directive 83/467/EEC of 29 July 1983, OJ No. L 257, 16 Sept. 1983, p. 1. Some other amendments only postponed the deadlines for member states' adjustment to the directive or changed annex I, the list of classified substances. One later amendment adjusted the directive to Greece's accession to the Community.

edge. The fifth amendment altered the provisions on packaging and labeling and empowered member states to take preliminary measures to protect human health. The seventh amendment listed fifty new substances in the annex.

b. Special Directives

The classification, packaging, and labeling strategy of the 1967 directive was followed in the 1973 directive on solvents[133] and the 1977 directive on paints,[134] although the preambles to these directives place more emphasis on protection of health. There is also the directive of 1978 on classification, packaging, and labeling of pesticides.[135] The directive covers all kinds of pesticides, including herbicides, wood preservatives, and rodenticides. Its purpose is principally to protect human health and only indirectly the environment. Although it is a special directive under the 1967 directive on dangerous substances and basically follows the listing and classification system established by the framework directive, its risk classification is limited to two categories, namely "poisonous" and "harmful to health." It also obliges producers to perform simple tests to determine the toxicity of a pesticide unless its toxicity can be derived from the toxicity of its components. Since the list of existing pesticides could not be compiled by January 1981, the effective date of the directive had to be indefinitely postponed.

2. Pre-Market Control of Chemicals

The sixth amendment to the directive of 1967, directive 79/831/EEC,[136] completely restructured the original directive. The legislative model was French legislation for registration and pre-market testing of chemicals, which was postponed in view of the envisaged harmonization. While retaining the system of Community classification and uniform packaging and labeling require-

[133] Directive 73/173/EEC of 4 June 1973 on the approximation of Member States' laws, regulations and administrative provisions relating to the classification, packaging and labelling of dangerous preparations (solvents), OJ No. L 189, 11 July 1973, p. 7, as amended by Directive 76/907/EEC of 14 July 1976, OJ No. L 360, 30 Dec. 1976, p. 1, Directive 80/781/EEC of 22 July 1980, OJ No. L 229, 30 Aug. 1980, p. 57, and Directive 82/473/EEC of 10 June 1982, OJ No. L 213, 21 July 1982, p. 17.

[134] Directive 77/728/EEC of 7 Nov. 1977 on the approximation of the laws, regulations and administrative provisions of the Member States relating to the classification, packaging and labelling of paints, varnishes, printing inks, adhesives and similar products, OJ No. L 303, 28 Nov. 1977, p. 23, as amended by Commission Directive 81/916/EEC of 5 Oct. 1981, OJ No. L 342, 28 Nov. 1981, p. 7 and Directive 83/265/EEC of 16 May 1983, OJ No. L 147, 6 June 1983, p. 11.

[135] Directive 78/631/EEC of 26 June 1978 on the approximation of the laws of the Member States relating to the classification, packaging and labelling of dangerous preparations (pesticides), OJ No. L 206, 29 July 1978, p. 13, as amended by Directive 81/187/EEC of 26 March 1981, OJ No. L 88, 2 April 1981, p. 29.

[136] *Supra* note 132. For the history of the sixth amendment *see* 1978/79 JAHRESBERICHT DES VERBANDES DER CHEMISCHEN INDUSTRIE 50-51 (Köln 1979); *id.* 1979/80, at 53 (Köln 1980).

ments, the directive emphasizes development of health and safety data by establishing uniform registration and testing requirements for new chemical substances. The directive further departs from the 1967 directive because its stated purpose is to protect the natural environment as well as human health; the classification of risk categories has been correspondingly enlarged. In this respect, it reflects a preventive approach to environmental policy.

Under the directive, any producer or importer of more than one ton of a new substance must register the substance with the competent national authority forty-five days before placing it on the market. This registration must be recognized by all other member states. This is the first instance of recognition of foreign decisions as a harmonization technique in Community environmental law. Fear of lax regulation by other member states' authorities was dispelled by harmonization of testing methods and the establishment of a system of information exchange among member states and the Commission.

The producer must supply the national authority with specified test data designed to allow assessment of the health and environmental hazards presented by the substance. The directive provides for a three tier system of tests, consisting of a base set and two further steps triggered by reaching certain threshold production volumes as well as by the results of previous tests and other available health and safety data. The tiered system of testing was not contained in the original Commission proposal,[137] but was instead introduced by West Germany which for economic reasons originally opposed the proposal altogether and then tried to water it down. The Germans remained uncompromising on the economic question during Council discussions starting in 1977, and under the German presidency in 1978 the tiered system was endorsed by all member states as a compromise between what was considered necessary from a health and environmental point of view and what was acceptable in light of the administrative and economic costs involved in an ambitious testing scheme. In all other respects, the Netherlands appears to have exercised the strongest influence on the final form of the directive.

The directive's registration and testing requirements do not apply to existing chemicals, which are those marketed in the Community before the effective date of the directive and contained in an inventory the Commission is to compile. These substances are subject only to classification, labeling, and packaging provisions. This situation raises the controversial question, which the directive does not address, of whether member states can individually impose registration and testing requirements on existing chemicals.

The directive is basically limited to registration, testing, packaging, and disclosure. Apart from requiring the forty-five day waiting period between registration and marketing, the directive does not provide Community authorities with power to prohibit or limit the production, marketing, and use of chemicals. The waiting period certainly does not amount to a disguised Community approval procedure for new chemicals. It is a compromise between the Commission proposal, which provided for a thirty day waiting peri-

[137] Proposal of 21 Sept. 1976, OJ No. C 260, 5 Nov. 1976, p. 4.

od, and the Netherlands' which preferred adherence to the American system of registration of new chemicals that would include the power to prohibit or limit production or use of chemicals deemed to be unduly dangerous. The directive also fails to refer to the 1976 PCB directive (discussed in the heading immediately following) which provides for substantive regulation of several chemicals. Despite these evident limitations, it is sometimes asserted that the directive preempts all regulation of chemicals. However, it seems that the member states have retained the power to prohibit, or at least restrict, production, marketing, and use of registered new or existing chemicals provided the problem to be addressed does not have its source in classification, packaging, and labeling but rather in the hazards presented by the chemical.

The sixth amendment has given the Commission a major and novel administrative task. The Commission is to establish the inventory of existing substances and define methods of determining the properties of substances. Moreover, within the Community system of exchange of national registrations and accompanying test data, the Commission will have to act as a moderator and conciliator when conflicting national claims as to secrecy of data threaten the information flow. It remains to be seen whether the Commission can appropriately discharge these responsibilities without clashing with member state bureaucracies and neglecting its other obligations in this area.[138] Compilation of the inventory of existing substances is progressing well. More than 34 000 existing substances have already been listed and another 50 000 substances notified by the member states. The final inventory will probably be published in 1985.[139]

A 1976 Commission proposal for introduction of an optional Community approval procedure for pesticides[140] has not yet been endorsed by the Council. The proposal was very controversial. The Commission has since changed its position and now favors a system whereby pesticides approved by any member state are automatically admitted throughout the Community unless the Community Permanent Committee on Pesticides decides by a majority against admission. The proposal to allow decision by a majority, rather than requiring unanimity, is opposed by West Germany, France, and Italy. In contrast, the Netherlands and Denmark demand decision by majority at the Community level and harmonization of the substantive requirements for approval of pesticides.

3. Restrictions on Marketing and Use

The major legislative text providing for substantive Community regulation of chemicals is the PCB directive of 1976.[141] It restricts the marketing and indus-

[138] *See also* Progress Report 1980, *supra* note 5, Annex I, at 18.

[139] *See* OJ No. C 79, 31 March 1982, vol. II; *cf.* BULL. EC 10-82, at p. 30, point 2.1.57.

[140] Proposal of 4 Aug. 1976, OJ No. C 212, 9 Sept. 1976, p. 3. *See also* S. JOHNSON, *supra* note 1, at 94 *et seq.*; Progress Report 1980, *supra* note 5, Annex I, at 23.

[141] Directive 76/769/EEC of 27 July 1976 on the approximation of the laws, regulations and administrative provisions of the Member States relating to restrictions on the

trial use of certain substances considered to be extremely hazardous, namely PCBs, PCT, their products, and vinylchloride. The directive was originally intended to serve as a kind of "umbrella" for general Community regulation of the production, marketing, and use of chemical substances. But the version adopted by the Council does not reflect this objective. Extensions of the directive to other chemicals must be authorized by the normal Community procedure for adoption of a new directive.

Between 1976 and 1983 the directive was amended several times,[142] and further amendments have been proposed by the Commission.[143] For example, the use of certain polychlorinated terphenyls (TRIS) in the treatment of textiles and as a component of certain household goods was prohibited; the marketing and use of asbestos was restricted (subject to temporary and permanent exceptions). The proposals would restrict the marketing of certain PCT products after 1985, and would prohibit the use of benzene in toys.[144]

Regulation of hazardous substances under the 1976 directive has been supplemented by a 1979 directive on agricultural pesticides containing specified active ingredients.[145] The directive is designed to protect health and the environment from the adverse effects of certain very hazardous substances used in pesticides, such as mercury and organo-chlorine compounds. It bans use of some substances as ingredients in agricultural pesticides, restricts other substances to particular uses, and provides timetables for phasing out use of some of them.

In addition to harmonization by way of regulatory directives, Community environmental policy has also sought to encourage stronger national measures. For example, the Council resolution of 1978 on fluorocarbons[146] called upon member states to encourage manufacturers and users of certain fluorocarbons to eliminate their discharge and prevent increase in production capacity. Based on a Commission communication reporting an overall decrease of 22% in certain regulated uses of fluorocarbons (accompanied, however, by an increase in unregulated uses such as foam plastics, refrigeration, and air

marketing and use of certain dangerous substances and preparations, OJ No. L 262, 27 Sept. 1976, p. 201.

142 *See especially* Directive 79/663/EEC of 24 July 1979, OJ No. L 197, 3 Aug. 1979, p. 37; Directive 83/264/EEC of 16 May 1983, OJ No. L 147, 6 June 1983, p. 9; Directive 83/478/EEC of 19 Sept. 1983, OJ No. L 263, 24 Sept. 1983, p. 33.

143 Proposal of 23 Jan. 1980, OJ No. C 31, 5 Feb. 1980, p. 9; proposal of 14 Oct. 1980, OJ No. C 285, 4 Nov. 1980, p. 2.

144 *See also* Economic and Social Committee, Resolution of 10-11 Dec. 1980, OJ No. C 353, 31 Dec. 1980, p. 31 (criticizing the limitation of the restriction on benzene to toys).

145 Directive 79/117/EEC of 21 Dec. 1978 prohibiting the placing on the market and use of plant protection products containing certain active substances, OJ No. L 33, 8 Feb. 1979, p. 36.

146 Council Resolution of 30 May 1978 on fluorocarbons in the environment, OJ No. C 133, 7 June 1978, p. 1.

conditioning), the Council decided in March 1980[147] to require member states to reduce, by the end of 1981, the use of fluorocarbons in aerosol cans to 70% of the 1976 levels. West Germany, Denmark, and the Netherlands reserved the right to mandate larger reductions. Fluorocarbon use in aerosols has now decreased by 34%.[148] A June 1982 Council decision[149] freezes the production capacity for fluorocarbons for use in aerosol cans and calls upon the Commission to make new proposals by mid 1983. However, nor further action was deemed necessary.

4. Prevention of Chemical Accidents

Prevention of accidents from the operation of plants producing or handling hazardous substances and from large facilities storing such substances is the purpose of the 1981 directive for the prevention of major accidents.[150] The directive requires industrial enterprises using a poisonous, inflammable or explosive substance within the meaning of the 1967 directive on dangerous substances to evaluate the risk of accident and to take adequate measures to prevent or minimize such risk. A more detailed risk analysis, stricter safety requirements and reporting obligations are provided for enterprises using ultrahazardous substances.

With respect to these latter enterprises, the directive also has provisions regarding safety equipment, emergency plans, public information, and cooperation with competent authorities. The competent authorities are to review the risk analysis and, if necessary, carry out their own evaluation and require appropriate corrective measures. The directive is primarily concerned with new installations but its provisions will eventually extend to existing plants as well.

The directive was very controversial.[151] West Germany tried to modify the Commission proposal along the lines of the proposed German regulation for the prevention of major accidents (now in force). In particular, it voiced reservations as to the broad scope of the proposed directive. The issues were whether the directive should be confined to chemical accidents or also extend to accidents caused by the explosion of boilers containing substances under pressure and whether it should be confined to a limited list of ultrahazardous substances used in specific quantities. The ultimate directive reached a compromise by adopting a two-tier system of regulation that confines the more stringent safety obligations to enterprises using specified ultrahazardous substances in certain quantities.

[147] Council Decision 80/372/EEC of 26 March 1980 concerning chlorofluorocarbons in the environment, OJ No. L 90, 3 April 1980, p. 45.

[148] 90 UMWELT, MITTEILUNGEN DES BUNDESMINISTERS DES INNEREN 37 (5 Aug. 1982).

[149] Council Decision 82/795/EEC of 15 Nov. 1982 on the consolidation of precautionary measures concerning chlorofluorocarbons in the environment, OJ No. L 329, 25 Nov. 1982, p. 29.

[150] Directive 82/501/EEC of 24 June 1982 on the major accident hazards of certain industrial activities, OJ No. L 230, 5 Aug. 1982, p. 1, corrigendum OJ No. L 289, 13 Oct. 1982, p. 35.

[151] For the history of the directive *see* VON MOLTKE & HAIGH, *supra* note 32, at 24.

The directive's provision for consultation relating to installations that are liable to have transboundary effects in case of a major accident was another major source of dispute.[152] This provision was added to the original proposal upon request of the European Parliament.[153] France opposed a Community consultation procedure as a limitation of its sovereignty, fearing prejudicial impact on its plans to locate nuclear power plants in border areas. As a compromise solution, it was proposed to adopt the provisions concerning transboundary consultation as a mere resolution. However, Belgium blocked this compromise because it believed that the proposal did not adequately protect its interest in its ongoing conflict with France over France's installation of a nuclear power plant just across the border. The final agreement, achieved because France ultimately did not want to block a compromise supported by the Commission and all other member states, provides for "bilateral" consultations. Where a polluting installation has transboundary impacts, bilateral consultations are to be held between the states concerned on the basis of the information to be supplied to neighbors and workers pursuant to Articles 5 and 8(2) of the directive.

G. Radioactivity

The Euratom Treaty entrusts the Community with the tasks of promoting the peaceful use of nuclear energy, preventing the misuse of nuclear materials, and creating a common market for substances and equipment used in the nuclear industry. However, it contains little authority for Community institutions to legislate for the protection of health and the environment against the risks presented by the peaceful use of nuclear energy. Consequently, the legislative activities of the Community in this area have remained narrow. Various attempts by the Commission to expand them have met with stiff opposition from some member states such as France, which consider nuclear energy policy a matter of high politics not amenable to harmonization.

1. Health Standards

The traditional area of Community involvement is the establishment of health standards expressly mandated by Articles 2(b), 30 and 37 of the Euratom Treaty. Superseding an earlier 1959 directive, a 1976 directive[154] establishes a

[152] Von Moltke & Haigh, *supra* note 32, at 25.

[153] European Parliament Resolution of 19 June 1980, OJ No. C 175, 14 July 1980, p. 49; EP Doc. 1-220/80, 16 June 1980.

[154] Directive 76/579/Euratom of 1 June 1976 laying down the revised basic safety standards for the health protection of the general public and the workers against the dangers of ionizing radiation, OJ No. L 187, 12 July 1976, p. 1, as amended by Directive 79/343/Euratom of 27 March 1979,OJ No. L 83, 3 April 1979, p. 18, and Directive 80/836/Euratom of 15 July 1980, OJ No. L 246, 17 Sept. 1980, p. 1. The original directive is Directive (Euratom) of 2 Feb. 1959 laying down the basic stan-

comprehensive system of basic health standards by setting maximum permissible doses of radiation for various categories of workers and the general public. It also requires monitoring of exposure levels and medical surveillance of exposed workers and the general public. Member states may set stricter standards.[155] It requires prior authorization for most uses of radioactive substances in consumer goods. The production, processing, storage, transport, and disposal of radioactive substances must also receive prior authorization whenever necessary in light of possible dangers. Compliance with these obligations is to some extent supervised by the Commission under the consultation procedure of Art. 37 of the Euratom Treaty, which provides that any plan for the discharge of radioactive substances which may affect other member states must be submitted to the Commission.[156] The Commission, after consultation with an expert group, may comment on it. Article 38 of the Euratom Treaty permits the Commission to issue directives for enforcing the basic health standards and, in case of non-compliance, to institute infringement proceedings before the European Court of Justice.

2. Nuclear Safety

Until 1975, the Community was not involved in the safety aspects of the design and location of nuclear power stations, aside from the consultation procedure under Article 37 of the Euratom Treaty. However, the Council Resolution of 22 July 1975[157] proclaimed the Community's intention progressively to harmonize safety requirements for nuclear power stations. While the intent is both to promote trade and protect health and safety, the resolution specifies that the present level of nuclear safety must not be relaxed. Pursuant to this resolution, the Commission in 1976 proposed a regulation concerning establishment of a Community consultation procedure for power plants in border areas.[158] In response to criticism by member states as well as the European Par-

dards for the protection of the health of workers and the general public against the dangers arising from ionising radiations, 1959 JO, 20 Feb. 1959, p. 221 ([1959-62] OJ (special English ed.) at 7). *See* Recht & Erikat, *La révision des normes de base Euratom*, in NUCLEAR INTER JURA '75, at 215 *et seq.* (Association internationale de droit nucléaire, Bougival 1976).

155 Bischof, *Internationale Rechtsgrundlagen des Entstehens der Strahlenschutzverordnung*, in VIERTES DEUTSCHES ATOMRECHTS-SYMPOSIUM 1975, at 39, 56-57 (Institut für Völkerrecht der Universität Göttingen und Bundesministerium des Inneren ed., Carl Heymanns Verlag, Köln 1976); H. P. IPSEN, EUROPÄISCHES GEMEINSCHAFTSRECHT 458-459 (Mohr Siebeck, Tübingen 1972).

156 *See* Recommendation of 16 Nov. 1960, 1960 JO, 21 Dec. 1960, p. 1893. For a recent proposal for amendment *see* BULL. EC 2-82, at p. 37, point 2.1.105.

157 Council Resolution of 22 July 1975 on the technological problems of nuclear safety, OJ No. C 185, 14 Aug. 1975, p. 1.

158 Proposal of 13 Dec. 1976 for a Regulation concerning the introduction of a Community consultation procedure in respect of [*sic*] power stations likely to affect the territory of another Member State, OJ No. C 31, 8 Feb. 1977, p. 3. *See also* EP Doc. 506/76, 11 Jan. 1977.

liament,[159] the Commission modified its proposal in 1979.[160] In its present form, the proposal provides for a Community consultation procedure prior to establishment and expansion of power plants. Existing regulations[161] already require member states to inform the Commission of investment projects in this area. The Commission in turn routinely informs the other member states. The innovation of the amended proposal is that either on its own initiative or on that of a member state, the Commission will consult experts and, on the basis of the expert opinion, render an opinion to the member states concerned.

This proposal is limited to consultation procedures. It does not develop common criteria for the location of power plants within the Community. The development of a common policy concerning the location of power plants has been demanded by the European Parliament.[162]

The proposal has not yet been adopted by the Council. This reflects the opposition of France, which fears that the mandatory consultation procedure and common criteria for the siting of power plants would endanger its independent nuclear energy policy and the competitive advantages to its industry from the cheap electricity which that policy is designed to provide. France has proposed an amendment providing for bilateral cooperation of the member states concerned. This proposal is opposed by the European Parliament. It is still uncertain whether the proposal of the Commission will be adopted.[163]

3. Nuclear Waste

The consultation procedure under Art. 37 of the Euratom Treaty provides one basis for Community action on nuclear waste. The first Community program specifically aimed at the nuclear waste problem was adopted by the Council in 1975.[164] It merely defines the relevant problems and calls for additional research efforts. In 1980 the Council adopted a comprehensive Community plan of action for radioactive wastes.[165] Based on the long standing Community activity in research and development concerning radioactive wastes, the resolution provides for measures aimed at creating a Community

[159] Council Resolution of 20 Nov. 1978, OJ No. C 286, 30 Nov. 1978, p. 1; European Parliament Resolution of 7 July 1977, OJ No. C 183, 1 Aug. 1977, p. 56. *See also* the Resolution of 13 Jan. 1976, OJ No. C 28, 9 Feb. 1976, p. 12.

[160] Amended proposal of 17 May 1979, OJ No. C 149, 15 June 1979, p. 2.

[161] Regulation 1056/72/EEC of 18 May 1972, JO No. L 120, 25 May 1972, p. 7 ([1972] OJ (special English ed.) at 466), as amended by Regulation 1215/76/EEC of 4 May 1976, OJ No. L 140, 28 May 1976, p. 1.

[162] Resolution of 20 Nov. 1980, OJ No. C 327, 15 Dec. 1980, p. 34. *See also* resolutions cited *supra* note 159.

[163] *See* Written question 1217/80 by Mrs. Lizin, OJ No. C 352, 31 Dec. 1980, p. 9.

[164] Council Decision 75/406/Euratom of 26 May 1975 adopting a programme on the management and storage of radioactive waste, OJ No. L 178, 9 July 1975, p. 28. *See* J. P. HANNEQUART, LES COMMUNAUTÉS EUROPÉENNES ET LE PROBLÈME DES DÉCHETS RADIOACTIFS (SERES, Louvain-la-Neuve 1979).

[165] Council Resolution of 18 Feb. 1980 on a Community plan of action in the field of radioactive wastes, OJ No. C 51, 29 Feb. 1980, p. 1.

network of sites for storing radioactive wastes and gradually harmonizing waste management practices, quality standards for treated wastes, and waste disposal conditions. Other resolutions relate to the problems of reprocessing and fast breeder reactors.[166] None of these programs impose binding obligations on the member states. They merely call for new studies and analyses.[167] The only proposal for a directive, the Commission proposal of 1976 on dumping of waste at sea,[168] which includes radioactive waste, has not yet been adopted by the Council.

4. Further Activities

After the Three Mile Island accident near Harrisburg, Pennsylvania, the Community increased its efforts in the area of nuclear energy and established a working group to consider the following questions:
- safety standards, criteria, practices, and regulations of member states,
- the procedures for a Community information system concerning accidents and incidents at nuclear power plants,
- the present application of the health and safety provisions of the Euratom Treaty, particularly with regard to waste, and
- the siting of nuclear power plants.[169]

This working group submitted its report and recommendations in 1980. The Commission has acted on the report by laying down safety principles for future harmonization and by setting up a framework for future Community action.[170]

H. Agriculture, Forestry, Land Use Planning, Protection of Flora and Fauna

Apart from pesticide regulation, Community environmental activities in this field fall within the framework of the common agricultural and regional policies and focus on financial aids to agriculture, e. g. for farmers in mountain

[166] Council Resolution of 18 Feb. 1980 on the reprocessing of irradiated nuclear fuels, OJ No. C 51, 29 Feb. 1980, p. 4. *See also* Commission Recommendation 82/74/Euratom of 3 Feb. 1982 on the storage and reprocessing of irradiated nuclear fuels, OJ No. L 37, 10 Feb. 1982, p. 36; Council Resolution of 18 Feb. 1980 on fast breeder reactors, OJ No. C 51, 29 Feb. 1980, p. 5.

[167] *See* the criticism of the European Parliament, Resolution of 17 March 1978, OJ No. C 85, 10 April 1978, p. 46.

[168] Proposal of 12 Jan. 1976 for a Council Directive concerning the dumping of wastes at sea, OJ No. C 40, 20 Feb. 1976, p. 3. *See* EUROPEAN ENVIRONMENTAL BUREAU, *supra* note 45, at 22 *et seq.*

[169] Commission Decision 79/520/Euratom of 16 May 1979, OJ No. L 141, 9 June 1979, p. 26; Commission Decision 79/828/Euratom of 2 Oct. 1979, OJ No. L 251, 5 Oct. 1979, p. 26.

[170] *See* BULL. EC 9–1981, at p. 39, point 2.1.128; *id.* 2-1982, at. p. 37, point 2.1.104; *id.* 7/8-1982, at p. 52, point 2.1.176.

areas and reforestation in certain Mediterranean zones, and on management of fisheries. Because these financial aids were judged insufficient to protect and enhance the natural environment, the Commission has proposed a Council resolution for the implementation of the directive on farming in mountain and less favored areas that contains a clause designed to ensure that proposed action is environmentally acceptable.[171] Moreover, the Commission has proposed a Council resolution calling for a forestry policy compatible with the social functions of the forest.[172] Both proposals have not been adopted. As for the protection of fisheries, conflicting national interests have until recently impeded implementation of a common policy in this area.[173] Community activities in the field of land use planning are for the present limited to research, information exchange, and similiar non-regulatory activities.

There are some legislative texts concerning protection of wild fauna. Migratory birds are protected under the 1979 directive on the conservation of wild birds.[174] This directive restricts the number of species that can be hunted or commercially traded, regulates hunting methods, and contains general rules for habitat conservation. It is assertedly based on Art. 235 of the EEC Treaty, but its legal authority is somewhat doubtful because of the tenuous linkage between protection of birds and the functioning of the Common Market.[175]

The Commission has tried to overcome doubts as to the legislative competence of the Community in this area by basing proposals on Art. 43 of the EEC Treaty and on regulations made under the common agriculture policy. However, the member states have, as a matter of principle, rejected this procedure. It was followed in only one case, namely the recent regulation on importation of whale products.[176] The regulation bans the import of whale products after a two year transition period. Since substitutes for whale products already exist, the Council believes this period is sufficient for industry adjustment.[177] On the other hand the Council has continued to use Art. 235 of the EEC Treaty to conclude international conventions for the protection of flora and fauna and

[171] *See* Progress Report 1980, *supra* note 5, Annex I, at 24.

[172] *See* OJ No. C 301, 15 Dec. 1978, p. 8; *see also* BULL. EC 1979, Supplement 3-79, at 35.

[173] *See* new Regulation 170/83/EEC of 25 Jan. 1983 establishing a Community system for the conservation and management of fisheries resources, OJ No. L 24, 27 Jan. 1983, p. 1, and the implementing Regulation 171/83/EEC of 25 Jan. 1983, OJ No. L 24, 27 Jan. 1983, p. 14.

[174] Directive 79/409/EEC of 2 April 1979 on the conservation of wild birds, OJ No. L 103, 25 April 1979, p. 1.

[175] This doubt is admitted by the Commission. *See* Progress Report 1980, *supra* note 5, Annex I, at 36, 37. *See also* the discussion *supra* at pp. 26–28. Moreover, those member states in which bird hunting is widely practiced, such as Italy and Belgium, have not yet taken steps to implement the directive.

[176] Regulation 348/81/EEC of 20 Jan. 1981 on common rules for imports of whale or other cetacean products, OJ No. L 39, 12 Feb. 1981, p. 1. To implement this regulation the Commission promulgated Regulation 3786/81/EEC of 22 Dec. 1981, OJ No. L 377, 31 Dec. 1981, p. 42.

[177] *See* Written question 1640/79 by Mr. Coppietas, OJ No. C 137, 9 June 1980, p. 31.

to implement them domestically. The Community and most member states are parties to the Bonn Convention on the Conservation of Migratory Species of Wild Animals.[178] Likewise, the Community and all member states are parties to the Washington Convention on the International Trade in Endangered Species of Wild Fauna and Flora.[179] In June 1982, the Council adopted a regulation on its implementation.[180] The regulation attempts to ensure that the free movement of goods within the Community is not disturbed by the application of the Convention and to harmonize national measures so that no distortions of competition arise. The Community and all member states are also parties to the Berne Convention of the Council of Europe on the Conservation of European Wildlife and Natural Habitats.[181]

Finally, in 1982 the Commission proposed a ban on the import of baby seal furs. This proposal aroused much interest in the member states and at the same time stiff opposition from some governments. Since public opinion demanded speedy action, the Council first developed an interim solution. In January 1983 it passed a resolution empowering member states to take preliminary national measures to restrict import of baby seal furs into their territory. In its meeting of 28 March 1983 it then issued a directive – instead of a regulation as proposed by the Commission — that provides for a two year prohibition on importation of baby seal furs into the Community starting 1 October 1983.[182] Meanwhile, the Commission was to negotiate with the states concerned in the hope of finding a solution that would render the directive superfluous. (These negotiations have been unsuccessful.) The choice of a directive rather than a regulation was based on the Council's view that Community competence rests not on Art. 43 of the EEC Treaty dealing with the common agriculture and fishery policies, but rather on Art. 235 of the EEC Treaty. The Council believes that, under Art. 235, regulations may be made only under exceptional circumstances.

Community policy in the field of protection of wild flora and fauna is not easy to assess. There are certainly jurisdictional problems. Moreover, the measures so far instituted are insufficient to prevent extinction of several species. The Commission has announced that it will make greater efforts in the future to preserve the habitats of these species. This runs counter to the position of the majority of member states that protection of nature should in principle remain within their exclusive jurisdiction.

[178] 19 ILM 15 (1980); OJ No. L 210, 19 July 1982, p. 10.

[179] INTERNATIONAL ENVIRONMENTAL LAW, *supra* note 56, at 973: 18/1; OJ No. C 243, 22 Sept. 1980, p. 16.

[180] Regulation 3626/82/EEC of 3 Dec. 1982, OJ No. L 384, 31 Dec. 1982, p. 1, as amended by Regulations (EEC) 3645/83 of 28 Nov. 1983 and 3646/83 of 12 Dec. 1983, OJ No. L 367, 28 Dec. 1983, pp. 1 & 2.

[181] INTERNATIONAL ENVIRONMENTAL LAW, *supra* note 55, at 979: 70/1; OJ No. L 38, 10 Feb. 1982, p. 1.

[182] Directive 129/83/EEC of 28 March 1983, OJ No. L 91, 9 April 1983, p. 30. *See also* BULL. EC 2-83, at p. 29, point 2.1.76. For the previous Resolution *see* OJ No. C 14, 18 Jan. 1983, p. 1.

I. Environmental Impact Assessment

As provided by both environmental programs, the Commission has submitted to the Council a proposal to introduce environmental impact assessment. The proposal ultimately transmitted to the Council is the result of about twenty consecutive drafts[183] and differs substantially from the preliminary drafts. It is much less detailed and does not attempt to resolve many of the procedural issues initially covered by the drafts. The major difference is that the notion of an impact statement contained in a single document patterned on the US model has been replaced by a more flexible procedure designed to ensure consideration of environmental effects both by the sponsor of a project and the competent national authority.

The proposal obliges sponsors of public and private projects liable to have major impacts on the environment and subject under national law to the requirement of a planning permission or similar governmental authorization, or, in the case of a public project, an equivalent decision by the competent national authority, to perform an environmental impact assessment before the planning permission can be granted. Annexes to the directive list those projects which are always subject to the requirement of a full environmental impact assessment and those for which the assessment procedure is simplified. Projects normally requiring only the simplified procedure may be subjected to a full assessment if their potential environmental effects so require.

The environmental impact assessment would extend to all environmental effects of the project, including effects on water, air, soil, climate, flora, fauna, their interrelationships, and effects on the built up environment including cultural heritage and landscape. The effects on these resources are assessed with a view to protecting and enhancing human health and living conditions and to conserving the productive capacity of resources on a sustained yield basis. Article 6 of the proposal prescribes the essential elements of the environmental impact statement which the sponsor of the project is to submit to the competent national authority along with an application for a planning permission.

[183] Proposal of 16 June 1980 for a Council directive concerning the assessment of environmental effects of certain public and private projects, OJ No. C 169, 9 July 1980, p. 14, amended on 1 April 1982, OJ No. C 110, 1 May 1982, p. 5. *See* LEE & WOOD, *Environmental Impact Assessment in the EEC*, 1 ENVT'L IMPACT ASSESSMENT REV. 287 (1980); KENNEDY, *The Directive on Environmental Impact Assessment*, 8 ENVT'L POL'Y & L. 84 (1982); VON MOLTKE & HAIGH, *EC – Major Issues for 1981*, 7 ENVT'L POL'Y & L. 23 (1981); WANDESFORDE-SMITH, *Environmental Impact Assessment in the European Community*, 2 ZEITSCHRIFT FÜR UMWELTPOLITIK 35 (1979); G. ZELLENTIN, *Sozialökonomische Bedingungen einer "harmonischen Entwicklung des Wirtschaftslebens" (Artikel 2, EWGV) in der Europäischen Gemeinschaft*, 5 ZEITSCHRIFT FÜR UMWELTPOLITIK 1, 13 *et seq.* (1982); GRECO, *Procedimento e partecipazione amministrativa nella gestione dell'ambiente: dal modello USA al progetto della CEE*, 1980 RIVISTA TRIMESTRIALE DI SCIENZA AMMINISTRATIVA 1; O'RIORDAN, *Beware Binding Commitments: The British Approach to EIA*, 2 ENVT'L IMPACT ASSESSMENT REV. 89 (1981); HAIGH, *The EEC Directive on Environmental Assessment of Development Projects*, 1983 JOURNAL OF PLANNING AND ENVIRONMENTAL LAW 585.

The competent authority has the power to request the sponsor to supplement its assessment; it may also assist in supplementing the assessment. Interested authorities must be consulted. The application and environmental impact statement together with any supplementary information given by the sponsor must be published, and the public concerned by the project must be consulted. The forms of notice and public participation are within the discretion of the competent authority (Articles 7 and 8). The competent authority is obliged to consider the environmental impact statement as well as comments by interested agencies and the general public. As part of its consideration of the application for planning permission it must assess the impacts of the project on the environment (Art. 10). The final decision on the project and its justification must be published.

The European Parliament commented critically on the proposal and advanced it with various proposals for amendments. Discussions in a working group established by the Committee of Permanent Representatives as well as in the Environmental Council showed that there were many reservations about the proposal. In view of this criticism, the Commission amended its draft by adopting several of the Parliament's proposals.[184] These amendments clarify the contents of the impact assessment and the requirement of consideration of alternatives, provide for greater participation by interested private associations, and provide for consultation and participation in the case of transboundary pollution beyond the model of the major accidents directive. The proposal also aroused much public interest within some member states.[185] It was one of the rare occasions where political bargaining over a proposal was not limited to discussions behind the closed doors of the Committee of Permanent Representatives and the Council and formal opinions by institutions such as the European Parliament and the Economic and Social Committee. National parliaments, environmental organizations, and the mass media exercised a relatively high degree of pressure on national governments to adopt a directive which preserved much of the impetus of the original proposal. The major points of controversy were the relative responsibilities of the project's sponsor and the competent authority, transboundary pollution, public participation, whether assessment is mandatory or discretionary, and especially the scope of the assessment.

Extensive involvement of the authorities in performing the impact assessment may amount to an indirect subsidy, which would be inconsistent with the polluter-pays principle. It is anticipated that the problem will be treated in a declaration that public assistance may not be so substantial that it amounts to a subsidy. The question of transboundary pollution is part of an ongoing controversy within the Community between France on one side and the other member states and the Commission on the other.[186] However, this controversy

[184] Resolution of 18 Feb. 1981, OJ No. C 66, 15 March 1981, p. 76; EP Doc. 1-569/81.

[185] *See* KENNEDY, *supra* note 183, at 88 *et seq.* for further references.

[186] The European Parliament had strongly demanded action concerning transboundary pollution. *See* Resolution of 18 Feb. 1981 and the Report of the Environmental Com-

seems largely settled by the compromise formula of "bilateral" consultations agreed upon under the major accidents directive. The more radical Commission proposal to require participation of foreign neighbors was rejected by the Council.

Perhaps the most weighty reservations stemmed from the fact that the directive would cover an area where much procedural legislation already exists and that several member states would be compelled to substantially modify traditional administrative procedures.[187] France and the Netherlands, which had or were about to introduce specific legislation in this area, favored the proposal in principle. However, France opposed the inclusion of nuclear power plants, and the Netherlands wanted the procedure extended to programs and plans as well as specific projects.[188] Denmark wanted an exception for decisions on projects taken by Parliament. Although the Commission proposal was greatly influenced by British experts who based their suggestions on the English system of planning permission,[189] and although it would seem that the English system of planning permission for private projects and of decisionmaking on public projects is essentially compatible with the Commission proposal, the British government and the House of Commons opposed mandatory impact assessment because they believed that it would unduly protract government decisions.[190]

West Germany favored less stringent assessment and public information requirements. It feared that its codified, complex planning system, often extending over various levels of government and involving various levels of decisions, would be threatened.[191] In particular, West Germany was anxious to retain procedures such as the permit procedure under the Federal Emission Control Act. Under this procedure the competent authority is required only to ensure that the applicant complies with the applicable zoning ordinance and the ambient air quality and emission standards administratively established under the Act. It was anticipated that the Community environmental impact assessment procedure would compel West Germany to completely modify its system of authorization under this Act because all environmental impacts would have to be considered. It has been doubted in West Germany that the present state of environmental science allows such comprehensive assessment. Even if such an assessment is feasible, it was thought that although environmental impact assessment was a suitable procedural device for improving the rationality of official decisions with large margins of discretion, it was not appropriate

mittee, *supra* note 184. The revised Commission draft (new Art. 8, II) now provides for consultation and participation in cases of projects having transboundary impact. *See also* KENNEDY, *supra* note 183, at 87-88.

[187] *See* VON MOLTKE & HAIGH, *supra* note 183, at 25.

[188] *See also* KENNEDY, *supra* note 183, at 85.

[189] *See* LEE & WOOD, *The Assessment of Environmental Impacts in Project Appraisal in the European Community*, 16 J. OF COMMON MKT. STUD. 189 (1978).

[190] *See* VON MOLTKE & HAIGH, *supra* note 183, at 25; O'RIORDAN, *supra* note 183, at 96; KENNEDY, *supra* note 183, at 88 *et seq.* (for further references).

[191] *See* KENNEDY, *supra* note 183, at 91.

where the law itself, by mandating the establishment of standards, has already made an assessment of the environmental impacts of a particular project.[192]

West Germany would maintain that the West German Emission Control Act, together with national procedures for scrutinizing environmental effects not covered by the Act, accomplish in several steps what a single environmental impact assessment seeks to accomplish in one. Article 2 of the amended Commission proposal[193] may allow this multiple approach for dealing with environmental effects by basing assessment requirements on the decisions of the competent "agency or agencies." This reference might be interpreted to allow a specific environmental aspect of a project, such as air pollution, to be handled through a permit procedure like that of West Germany. Apparently, all member states agree that the existing structure of national law and procedures must be preserved and that therefore much flexibility is needed.

In evaluating the various criticisms of the Commission proposal, it should be noted that the scope and contents of the proposed environmental impact assessment requirement is rather modest. Only projects, not plans and programs, are subject to the impact assessment requirement. Furthermore, by listing in an annex the categories of major projects subject to full impact assessment and of minor projects to be assessed in a simplified procedure, the proposal takes into account considerations of practicality and legal certainty, although somewhat neglecting environmental impacts stemming from location, size, and other individual characteristics of a project.[194] The provisions for public participation are formulated so vaguely that member states have a wide margin of discretion in incorporating them into existing administrative procedures. Almost any provisions for public participation — from last minute notification to a full-fledged hearing, from standing limited to neighboring property owners to standing for the general public — seem compatible with the proposal.[195]

On the other hand, it is remarkable that apparently no member state has objected to the appropriateness of procedural harmonization in areas where they apply nonharmonized national environmental law rather than Community law. The premise of the Commission proposal that providing a broadly comparable procedure for environmental assessment of major projects will help eliminate distortions of competition is highly arguable as long as the competent national agency has full substantive discretion. The objections of the Ger-

[192] *See* Bundesrat, Resolution of 30 Jan. 1981, Bundesrats-Drucksache 413/80 (Beschluß), translated in: 7 ENVT'L POL'Y & L. 85 (1981). The Bundestag Committee on the Interior and the House are generally more in favor of the Commission proposal. *See* Innenausschuß, Umweltverträglichkeitsprüfung, Bundestag-Drucksache 9/166 (June 1981). Bundestag, Resolution of 25 Nov. 1983, Bundestag-Drucksache 10/38 (Nov. 1983). *See also* KENNEDY, *supra* note 183, at 90-91; MALANCZUK, *EC - Developments*, 7 ENVT'L POL'Y & L. 85 (1981); VON MOLTKE & HAIGH, *supra* note 183, at 26.

[193] *See supra* note 183.

[194] *See* KENNEDY, *supra* note 183, at 87.

[195] KENNEDY, *supra* note 183, at 88; G. ZELLENTIN, *supra* note 183, at 19 *et seq.*

man Bundesrat, which were not, however, shared by the Bundestag,[196] focussed on this problem. Member state governments appreciate that it is difficult in principle to justify the proposal as a measure to eliminate distortions of competition. Accordingly, the Council, in contrast to the Commission and the European Parliament,[197] will base the new directive exclusively on Art. 235 of the EEC Treaty rather than on Art. 100. However, as a policy matter all member states in principle consider harmonization of national procedures for environmental impact assessment, even without concomitant substantive law harmonization, a useful application of the principle of prevention.

The debate on environmental impact assessment indicates the high complexity of Community environmental policymaking, which often involves a large measure of political bargaining. Many rounds of negotiation in the Environmental Council were necessary to produce final agreement on the major controversial issues. A new draft submitted by the Commission in the spring of 1984[198] embodies all the changes the original proposal has undergone during the negotiations. The only question that is as yet unresolved is the Danish reservation on project decisions taken by Parliament. The new draft provides that the impact assessment is mandatory only for a few projects, whereas in the majority of cases the member states would have flexibility; it dispenses the member states from mandatory consideration of alternatives; it allows the assessment to be carried out in the framework of existing procedures; and it diminishes the extent of prescribed participation. All this has the result that the procedure will have lost many of its teeth. In any case it is clear that the environmental impact assessment procedure will not be the beginning of a new kind of Community-wide participatory public decisionmaking for conflicts between development and local environmental and preservation interests,[199] but only a modest development of existing administrative procedures in the member states.

[196] *Supra* note 192.

[197] Report of the Legal Committee, EP Doc. 1-569/81/rev., at No. 33-34. *Accord*, MALANCZUK, *supra* note 192, at 85.

[198] Not officially published.

[199] *See* G. ZELLENTIN, *supra* note 183, at 19 *et seq.*

V. Overview of US Substantive Environmental Law

A. Introduction: The Federal Legislative Process

For nearly four decades following the New Deal, "reform" legislation establishing new regulatory or social welfare programs resulted primarily from executive branch initiatives. The White House and the interested executive departments and agencies would draft, advocate, and generate political support for such legislation. Environmental, health, and safety legislation since 1968 has not generally followed this pattern. Statutory initiatives – most notably those in the areas of pollution and toxic substances control – have largely resulted from the initiatives of key congressional leaders, committees and staff, advocacy by environmental groups, and media publicity. This change of pattern reflects the conjunction of Democratic Congresses and Republican presidencies during much of the period; the sensitivity of the White House to the performance of the economy and the economic burdens attributed to environmental measures; the development of politics dominated by special issues and ideologies; and decline in the ability of political parties, Congress, and the administration to form a consensus on priorities and strategies. The statutes which emerge from this process are not coordinated with one another and embody quite different and often inconsistent principles and strategies.

The air and water pollution control statutes represent the most extensive and fully developed federal environmental legislation. Air and water pollution were the first environmental problems to generate widespread public concern. Federal legislation in these fields, which dates back to the 1950s, moved steadily in the direction of centralization during the 1960s and early 1970s. Air pollution is a highly visible problem, particularly in scenic urban areas such as Los Angeles. The Public Health Service invested considerable resources during the 1960s in research identifying the health hazards associated with air pollution. Water pollution is a special concern of recreation and fishing interests, but also attracted widespread attention from the general public. Particularly in the case of municipal waste treatment systems, construction interests have been an important political force supporting federal requirements and subsidies. Industries and unions located in the industrialized central and northeastern parts of the United States have supported uniform federal air and water pollution controls in order to reduce the competitive advantage that less developed regions with abundant air and water resources might otherwise enjoy. Federal efforts in pollution control originally focussed on pollutants, such as particulates, sulfur oxides, and organic wastes, that are emitted in large quantities.

During the 1970s, attention turned to hazardous chemicals and wastes, reinforced by widespread public concern with cancer and dramatic instances of improper hazardous waste dumping. It may be sheer happenstance that ugly incidents involving serious health injury from toxic chemicals, similar to those occurring in the 1960s in Japan, did not occur earlier in the United States and focus the first wave of federal legislation on toxic chemical and waste problems.

Public concern about the hazards of nuclear energy, including nuclear waste disposal, has steadily increased since the mid 1960s, but the powerful constituencies supporting nuclear power have blocked significant congressional response to these concerns. Opponents of nuclear power have exploited the federal licensing process to delay construction of new nuclear plants, and have secured state and logical legislation limiting nuclear power and waste disposal.[1]

Concern about conservation of natural resources and preservation of federal lands from environmentally destructive development has also increased since 1965. This concern was a major factor in the 1969 enactment of the National Environmental Policy Act, requiring preparation of environmental impact assessments for federal actions. But appart from wilderness legislation (including the Alaska Lands Bill), stripmine regulation, and the Endangered Species Act, this concern has generally not been translated into significant statutory restrictions on the discretion of federal resource managers in balancing economic and environmental goals.

In recent years, enthusiasm for environmental causes has been tempered by concern about availability of domestic energy resources and poor performance of the economy. But environmental advocates have retained a powerful position within the decentralized committee structure of Congress, and the political importance of environmental concerns has remained high; as a result, no major reversals in federal environmental legislation have occured. Basic changes have, however, been initiated at the executive level. While every president since Nixon has resisted Congressional enthusiasm for broad environmental measures because of concern over their economic implications, President Reagan has gone far to reverse the historic trend in favor of more stringent environmental measures. He appointed several administrators who are markedly less sympathetic to environmental goals than their predecessors,[2]

[1] *E. g.*, California's Warren-Alquist Act puts a moratorium on further construction of nuclear power plants until a federally approved method of nuclear waste disposal is established. The Act was recently upheld by the Supreme Court against the contention that it is preempted by the Atomic Energy Act. Pacific Gas & Electric Co. v. State Energy Resources Conservation & Development Commission, 103 S.Ct. 1713 (1983).

[2] *E. g.*, former Secretary of the Interior James Watt and Environmental Protection Agency Administrator Anne Gorsuch.

cut the budget for environmental protection programs,[3] sought to delegate further implementation and enforcement responsibilities to the states, and imposed an extensive system of economic impact assessment and review to control environmental regulatory proposals.[4] The administration has, however, been largely unsuccessful in its efforts to persuade Congress to weaken the basic provisions of the environmental statutes themselves.

B. Air Pollution Control Regulation

1. Background

During the 1950s and early 1960s, the federal government undertook research concerning the health effects of air pollution and provided administrative grants to states that adopted air pollution control measures. Congressional legislation in 1965 and 1967 established federal controls on new automobile emissions and a far reaching program for state adoption and enforcement of air quality standards based on federal research and planning. But leading members of Congress, such as Senator Muskie, and environmentalists viewed the implementation of these measures by the administration and the states as tardy and lax. The 1970 Clean Air Act amendments imposed a far more centralized system of regulatory controls. Refinements and modifications were made by substantial amendments in 1977 as well as by a number of more specialized measures adopted at various points throughout the 1970s. The Act is currently the subject of extensive consideration in Congress, but no major changes seem likely to emerge in the near future.

2. Control of Air Pollution from Industrial Sources

The basic strategy of the Clean Air Act is for the federal government to adopt uniform environmental quality standards for widespread pollutants, and for the states to adopt and carry out, under federal supervision, implementation measures to achieve and maintain those standards. EPA is directed to adopt geographically uniform primary air quality standards designed "to protect the public health" with an "adequate margin of safety," and secondary standards to protect against welfare effects (statutorily defined to include economic, aesthetic, and ecological harms).[5] The statute does not provide for consideration of economic costs or implementation burdens in the adoption of standards. EPA has adopted standards for SO_2, NO_2, CO, ozone, hydrocarbons, lead, and particulate matter.[6]

Following adoption of standards by EPA, states must adopt state implementation plans (SIPs) imposing controls on sources that will reduce emissions suf-

[3] PETERSON, *Laissez-Faire Landscape*, N.Y. Times, Oct. 31, 1982, § 6 (Magazine), 26, 36.
[4] *See infra* Ch. VII, text accompanying note 14.
[5] 42 U.S.C. § 7409(a).
[6] 40 C.F.R. Part 50.

ficiently to achieve compliance with the federal standards.[7] SIPs are subject to approval by EPA; if a SIP is inadequate, EPA may require the state to adopt an adequate SIP or may promulgate its own SIP for the state. SIPs are to be implemented through permits or other methods of control on individual sources. SIP requirements are enforceable as federal law by federal administrative authorities or citizen suits in federal court.[8] Subject to certain exceptions in the case of new automobiles, fuel additives, and aircraft, states may adopt and enforce more stringent standards and requirements than those mandated by federal law.[9]

The 1970 Amendments to the Clean Air Act originally provided that the primary ambient standards must be achieved by 1975, with limited provisions for extension of this deadline to 1977. Secondary standards were to be achieved within a "reasonable time." Difficulties in achieving the standards in polluted areas led Congress in 1977 to push the primary standard deadline back to 1983, with extensions to 1988 in the case of automotive pollutants. Although substantial progress in achieving compliance has been made, the burdens of meeting the standards in heavily polluted areas such as Los Angeles make further deadline postponements inevitable. The 1983 deadlines have already passed, but Congress has as yet been unable to agree on amendments to deal with the problem of continuing non-compliance.

The 1970 Amendments also required EPA to adopt uniform, technology-based emission controls for major new industrial sources of widespread pollutants.[10] The rationale for these new source performance standards (NSPS) — to be established on an industry by industry basis — was to ensure adoption by new sources of state-of-the-art technology as a hedge against the continuing increases in total emissions that would occur with continuing economic development. In addition, industry and labor in the midwest and northeast supported the measure in order to reduce the incentive of industry to locate in areas of the south and west with air quality better than that required by the federal ambient standards. Without NSPS, these areas could allow new sources to be constructed with little or no air pollution control.

Implementation of the 1970 Amendments soon presented the question whether states with air cleaner than that required by the federal ambient standards were free to pollute their air up to the level of the standards. As a result of litigation initiated by an environmental group, the courts held that the Act precludes "significant deterioration" of air quality in clean air areas, without defining precisely what "significant deterioration" means.[11] EPA then adopted regulations limiting the increments of pollution concentrations per-

[7] 42 U.S.C. § 7410.

[8] *Id.* §§ 7413(a)(1) (federal enforcement); 7604(f)(3) (citizen suits).

[9] *Id.* § 7416.

[10] Current version codified at 42 U.S.C. § 7411.

[11] Sierra Club v. Ruckelshaus, 344 F. Supp. 253 (D.D.C.), *aff'd per curiam* 4 Env't Rep. Cas. (BNA) 1815 (D.C. Cir. 1972), *aff'd by an equally divided court sub nom.* Fri v. Sierra Club, 412 U.S. 541 (1973).

mitted in clean air areas. EPA's approach was codified by Congress in the 1977 Amendments, which established three classes of clean air regions and specified graduated amounts of permitted increments in the different classes.[12] An elaborate review system for new sources in clean air areas — now termed prevention of significant deterioration or PSD areas — was established to assure that the increment requirements were not violated, and stringent controls on new sources (in some cases more stringent than NSPS) were imposed.

In addition to extending the deadline for attaining the ambient standards in dirty air areas, the 1977 Amendments adopted special measures to deal with such "nonattainment" regions.[13] In theory, SIPs were supposed to mandate achievement of the ambient standards by 1977. But in practice state and federal administrators and courts were unwilling to shut down plants that failed to meet stringent control deadlines, so long as they were making reasonable progress in installing available control technology. The 1977 Amendments sanctioned the continued use of "delayed compliance orders" in these circumstances. The 1977 Amendments also require that new sources in nonattainment regions obtain more than compensating reductions in emissions from existing sources, and that such new sources employ especially stringent pollution controls.

Although the 1970 Amendments had provided for uniform air quality standards everywhere in the nation, the 1977 Amendments thus established a zoned system of clean and dirty air areas. This zoning system — together with associated new source review provisions — would appear to have significant but as yet unquantified effects on the incentives to invest in new plants and on locational decisions.

The tradeoff system for allowing new sources to be built in nonattainment areas, and the previously described "bubble" policy, which encourages a more cost-effective allocation of abatement burdens, represent limited efforts to introduce incentives for more cost-effective approaches to abatement and to take the first steps towards creation of a market in pollution rights. But the basic thrust of the Clean Air Act has been to impose command and control regulation on private conduct. Congressional interest in use of economic incentives has been extremely limited, and the bubble and tradeoff initiatives originated in EPA have had scant endorsement from Congress.

3. Motor Vehicle Pollution Control

A federal program for regulation of motor vehicle emissions was initiated in 1965. Dissatisfaction with the pace of administrative implementation became acute. The 1970 Amendments mandated a 90% reduction of existing emission levels of nitrogen oxides, hydrocarbons, and carbon monoxide by 1975-1976, with provision for a single one year administrative extension by EPA. The mandated reductions were supposedly necessary to guarantee

[12] 42 U.S.C. §§ 7470-7491 (Supp. II 1978). *See generally* TERZIEV, *PSD: New Regulations and Old Problems*, 5 HARV. ENVT'L L. REV. 130 (1981).

[13] 42 U.S.C. §§ 7501-7508.

achievement of projected federal ambient standards in heavily polluted areas such as Los Angeles. They were to be enforced through a program of EPA testing and certifications of new model prototypes. The required reductions were supposed to be achieved throughout the life of the automobile, statutorily defined as 50 000 miles. Firms which manufactured uncertified models were subject to fines of $10 000 per car.[14]

While the 1970 Amendments have resulted in substantial reductions of emissions from new automobiles, the US automobile industry has still not met the 90% reductions originally targeted for 1975-1976. Repeated amendments to the Act have extended the deadline. Critics of the automobile industry attribute this failure to lack of innovative capability in the industry and its refusal to give full support to environmental values. The industry asserts that the 90% reduction requirements are excessively stringent and unrealistic. The draconian nature of the sanction for violation and the political impossibility of shutting down the domestic automobile industry have also been important factors in the failure to meet the "technology forcing" goals originally set in 1970.

In 1967, Congress, responding to auto industry fears of multiple and inconsistent state regulations, preempted state controls on automobile emissions that were more stringent than federal controls. The 1970 Amendments authorized EPA to exempt California from preemption, in recognition of the acute automobile pollution problems in California and the political power of the California delegation in the House of Representatives. EPA has authorized California to adopt different and in most respects more stringent standards. The 1977 Amendments allow states with areas that have not achieved compliance with federal standards for automotive pollutants to adopt standards identical to California's.[15] The result is a two tier system of controls on new automobile emissions.

Although the federal automotive emission control provisions in the Clean Air Act apply only to new motor vehicles, states are subject to the overriding SIP requirement of achieving the federal ambient standards. Emissions from automobiles already in use are an important source of pollution. The delays in imposing emission reductions from stationary sources, the postponements of the federal timetable for 90% reduction of emissions from new vehicles, and the fact that emission control equipment in new vehicles is subject to deterioration or dismantlement, all generated political and legal pressure for states to impose controls on automobiles in use. Litigation by environmental groups and administrative steps by EPA required states to implement transportation control plans (TCPs).[16] TCPs included such measures as retrofitting older

[14] Current version at 42 U.S.C. §§ 7521-7551. In addition, EPA is to establish emission limitations for aircraft pollution in conjunction with the Secretary of Transportation. 42 U.S.C. §§ 7571-7574.

[15] 42 U.S.C. § 7543.

[16] *See generally* R. Stewart & J. Krier, Environmental Law & Policy 441-445 (Bobbs-Merrill, Indianapolis, Indiana, 2d ed. 1978).

cars with control devices, inspection and maintenance of vehicles' pollution control equipment to ensure its proper functioning, restrictions on express highway access for cars with only one or two riders, physical restrictions on access and parking by private automobiles in center city areas, increased tolls and parking surcharges, gasoline rationing, and promotion of mass transit. These measures, which by their very nature could only be adequately implemented and enforced by state and local authorities, were bitterly resisted by those authorities. Congress amended the Act to strip EPA of its power to require certain TCP controls, such as parking surcharges, and litigation resulted in decisions which severely limited EPA's authority to impose coercive sanctions on states or state officials that failed to implement such controls.

In the 1977 Amendments, Congress gave EPA the authority to cut off highway construction funds and other related federal grants and to prohibit construction of new stationary sources releasing automotive-type pollutants in states that had failed to achieve federal ambient standards for such pollutants and has also failed to adopt inspection and maintenance plans to regulate emissions from existing automobiles.[17] EPA has invoked or threatened to invoke this authority with considerable success. Most nonattainment states have adopted or are in the process of adopting emissions monitoring and maintenance programs for cars in use, although their implementation has barely begun and their contribution to pollution control is still problematic.[18]

The 1970 Amendments authorized EPA to regulate the content of lead and other additives in automotive fuels for two purposes: to prevent the fouling of pollution control devices (such as exhaust system catalysts) and to protect public health against air pollution resulting from the combustion of fuels with additives.[19] Contrary state measures are preempted.[20] EPA originally exercised this authority to require refiners and distributors to manufacture and sell essentially lead-free gasoline for new cars with catalytic control devices. More recently, EPA adopted regulations requiring that the lead content of all automotive fuels be gradually decreased in order to prevent health risks associated with elevated lead levels in children's blood.[21]

C. Water Pollution Control

1. Background

Prior to 1956, the federal water pollution control effort was limited to research and the dissemination of information. In that year, Congress authorized a conference procedure, convened at federal initiative in the case of interstate

[17] 42 U.S.C. § 7506.
[18] *See generally* R. Stewart & J. Krier, Environmental Law & Policy 80-82 (Supp. 1982) (Bobbs-Merrill, Indianapolis).
[19] Current version at 42 U.S.C. § 7545(c)(1).
[20] *Id.* at § 7545(c)(4).
[21] 47 Fed. Reg. 38,078 (1982).

waters or at the request of a state governor in the case of intrastate waters. The conference procedure was cumbersome and federal enforcement responsibility limited. In 1965, Congress enacted a program of state-adopted water quality standards and implementation procedures. States were called upon to "zone" the use of various waters within the state (e. g., for swimming, fishing or "industrial use"), adopt ambient water quality standards appropriate to those uses, and enforce limitations on effluent discharges from sources in order to assure that standards were achieved. State standards and plans were subject to federal approval, but the extent of federal authority to take action unilaterally in the face of inadequate state measures was unclear. Moreover, water quality standards were applicable only to interstate waters, a category representing less than one sixth of all navigable water bodies. Progress in implementing the system was slow.

During the late 1960s, the Supreme Court interpreted the Refuse Act of 1899,[22] prohibiting the discharge or deposit of "refuse matter of any kind" into the navigable waters of the United States without a permit from the Army Corps of Engineers, as prohibiting pollution without a permit.[23] This ruling gave the federal government a powerful weapon to deal with water pollution. An administrative licensing program was instituted to require sources to adopt technology-based limitations on effluents.

2. Control of Discharges from Industrial Sources

The current federal water pollution control program was established by the 1972 Amendments to the Federal Water Pollution Control Act (now known as the Clean Water Act).[24] While the earlier system of state water quality standards was maintained, the Act proclaimed broad goals of "fishable and swimmable" water everywhere in the nation by 1983 and "zero discharge" of pollutants into waters by 1985. The operative focus of the Act, however, was a system of geographically uniform technology-based effluent standards, established by EPA, for major pollution sources. All "point sources" of pollution discharges into any waters were required to obtain a permit from the federal government incorporating these standards.[25] The EPA could delegate licensing authority to qualifying state agencies.[26]

The 1972 Amendments required industrial sources to achieve "best practical technology" limitations (BPT) (representing the better practice of pollution control within an industry) by 1977 and "best available technology" limitations (BAT) (representing the state of the technological art) by 1983.[27] The Act has been judicially interpreted to require that such effluent limitations be geo-

[22] The Refuse Act is codified as § 13 of the Rivers and Harbors Act, 33 U.S.C. §§ 401-418.

[23] *See* United States v. Standard Oil Co., 384 U.S. 224 (1966).

[24] 33 U.S.C. §§ 1251-1375.

[25] 33 U.S.C. § 1342.

[26] *Id.*

[27] *Id.* § 1311.

graphically uniform for each industry category, with only limited exceptions to accommodate variations in production processes or feasible control technologies.[28] A waiver or exemption from the uniform standards generally can not be obtained simply on the grounds that compliance is too costly for a given source or that a lesser degree of control would achieve adequate water quality because of the nature of the particular source's receiving water body and the absence of other dischargers.

Congress's reliance on technology-based effluent limitations reflected a number of considerations. It believed that the prior system of water quality standards was too cumbersome and difficult to implement because of the large number of water pollutants and the difficulty of translating ambient water quality standards into enforceable controls on the often numerous sources discharging into the same water body. Initial experience under the 1970 Clean Air Act Amendments seemed to confirm the problems of complexity and delay in a regulatory program based on environmental quality standards. It was thought that a system of technology-based standards would be easier to institute and implement. It was also believed that a system of uniform technology-based controls was more "equitable" because it would impose the same controls on all plants in an industry, eliminating the "competitive distortions" and relocation incentives in favor of regions with relatively clean water generated by a system based on water quality standards. Members of Congress and labor unions feared movement of industry from the northeast and midwest to the south if such an approach were adopted.

In any event, EPA ended up adopting over 500 separate effluent limitations for different categories and subcategories of industries. The proliferation of industry subcategories was aimed in part at accommodating differences in control costs among plants in a given industry. The process was time consuming and controversial, and a large percentage of the limitations eventually adopted were overturned in court.[29]

Moreover, the extent of uniformity actually achieved within an industrial category or subcategory under this system is problematic. Considerable discretion is involved in translating effluent limitation regulations into enforceable controls on particular plants. Particularly where this function has been delegated to a state agency, the goal of uniformity may be compromised.

The BPT and BAT limitations are aimed at widespread conditions of pollution: biochemical oxygen demand, total suspended solids, pH and fecal coliform. A separate system of effluent limitations for toxic substances such as heavy metals or organic chemicals that pose serious health and ecological risks even in small quantities was also authorized by the 1972 Amendments. The expectation was that the effluent limitations would be established on a pol-

[28] EPA v. National Crushed Stone Association, 449 U.S. 64 (1980) (no variance from uniform standards for plants claiming economic infeasibility); Appalachian Power Co. v. Train, 430 F. 2d 1040 (4th Cir. 1980) (no variance from uniform standards because local environmental benefits from compliance low).

[29] *E. g.*, Appalachian Power Co. v. Train, 545 F.2d 1351 (4th Cir. 1976).

lutant by pollutant basis and that controls (including, if necessary, a total prohibition on discharges) would be established to prevent adverse effects without regard to economic costs or even, perhaps, technological feasibility. Burdensome procedural requirements for the adoption of standards were imposed, and only a handful of toxic limitations were adopted. Environmental groups brought litigation which resulted in an EPA settlement agreement to use a system of technology-based controls to control discharges of a wide range of toxic substances from various types of industrial sources.[30]

Several modifications in the structure and timing of industrial source controls were achieved by the 1977 Amendments to the Act. The BPT deadline was pushed back from 1977 to 1983, provided plants are making "good faith" efforts to comply. For a new category of "conventional" pollutants (BOD, suspended solids, pH, fecal coliform) the BAT requirement was eliminated, and a new control objective of best conventional technology (intermediate between BPT and BAT) was to be met by 1984. The Act adopted a system of technology-based source controls for various industrial categories to deal with toxic pollutants. BAT standards for toxic pollutants were to be met by 1984. The Act also created a new category of "non-conventional" pollutants, the chief example being oil and grease. For this category, BAT standards must be met by 1987. Many sources will not meet these revised deadlines, and proposals for further deadline extensions are pending in Congress.

3. Municipal Waste Treatment

The 1972 Amendments instituted an ambitious program for treatment of municipal sewage, funded primarily by federal grants.[31] Municipal treatment systems were to achieve "secondary treatment" (sludge removal plus mechanical aeration or its equivalent) by 1977 and "best practical waste treatment" technology by 1983. The latter would be defined in relation to the ambitious ambient water quality goal of fishable and swimmable water everywhere by 1983, and could require greater control in some areas than others. The federal government undertook to finance up to 90% of the capital costs of municipal waste treatment projects meeting federal requirements. Waste treatment facilities that could handle industrial as well as municipal wastes were encouraged, but industrial sources discharging into a municipal plant were required to bear an appropriate part of its capital and operating costs, and were also required to pretreat industrial wastes to make them compatible with municipal waste treatment technology. A "section 208" state and local process of planning to coordinate water supply, storm and sanitary sewage facilities, municipal waste treatment, and industrial, commercial and residential development was also funded by the federal government.[32]

[30] Natural Resources Defense Council, Inc. v. Train, 8 Env't Rep. Cas. (BNA) 2120 (D.D.C. 1976) (approving consent decree).

[31] Current version at 33 U.S.C. §§ 1281-1293.

[32] 33 U.S.C. § 1288.

The 1972 Amendments authorized $18 billion for funding construction of municipal treatment plants. This amount proved inadequate, and there were administrative delays in implementing the grant program. By 1977 only one third of 12 500 US municipalities had met the secondary treatment requirement. In 1977 Congress extended the secondary treatment deadline to 1983, authorized an additional $25 billion in federal grants for construction of waste treatment facilities, required states and EPA to establish a firmer set of priorities among municipal projects, and attempted to promote innovative alternatives (such as recycling or spray disposal) to conventional sewer treatment systems. The program had led to overbuilding by municipalities of capital intensive sewage treatment facilities that were sometimes inappropriate and often poorly maintained (the federal government provides no operating subsidies). The future of the program is jeopardized by the Reagan administration's determination to reduce the federal budget. Deadline postponement and budget reauthorization proposals are pending in Congress.

4. Ambient Standards and Nondegradation

The technology-based effluent limitations established by the Act have at best a loose relation to the vague and unrealistic water quality goals proclaimed by the federal statute. But the system of state water quality standards carried over from the pre-1972 law still has, in theory, legally controlling significance.[33] If the system of technology-based federal effluent limitations does not control discharges into a given water body sufficiently to achieve applicable state water quality standards, more rigorous controls are supposed to be enforced through the federal permit process. It is estimated that more than 25% of all sources would have to adopt more stringent controls in order to meet state water quality standards. In response to this prospect, some states are attempting to relax existing water quality standards. Environmentalists, on the other hand, assert that such standards are often inadequate, and that EPA has responsibility and authority under the Act to review and correct deficiencies in state water quality standards. Environmentalists also contend that the Water Act contains a principle of nondegradation of clean waters similar to that recognized in the Clean Air Act. On the other hand, the Reagan administration has proposed to cut back on municipal waste treatment grants in areas where further controls are not needed to meet state water quality standards.

5. Non-Point Sources and Groundwater

The system of permits and controls established under the Water Act applies only to "point sources" of pollution, and does not reach runoff from agriculture and forestry operations, or other dispersed sources of pollution.[34] The sec-

[33] *Id.* §§ 1312-13.

[34] "Point source" is defined in the Act as: "any discernible, confined and discrete conveyance, including but not limited to any pipe, ditch, channel, tunnel, conduit, well, discrete fissure, container, rolling stock, concentrated animal feeding operation, or

tion 208 planning process is supposed to deal with non-point pollution sources and groundwater problems, but progress in many states has been slow.[35] The Safe Drinking Water Act of 1974[36] requires EPA to establish primary and secondary standards and treatment technologies for public drinking water supplies. Subtitle C of the Act is designed to prevent contamination of groundwater from underground injection wells. A state having standards at least as strict as the federal standards may take over authority to enforce the statute.[37]

6. Dredge and Fill Operations in Navigable Waters

Section 404 of the Clean Water Act requires that persons engaging in dredge and fill operations in navigable waters obtain a permit from the Army Corps of Engineers.[38] In most instances, such permits must be consistent with concurrent EPA regulations. Enforcement and implementation authority may be delegated to state agencies. One state supreme court has held that state regulation of dredge and fill activities is not preempted where federal navigability is not affected.[39]

These provisions have been used to control development of commercial and residential facilities in the coastal zone and along "navigable" waterways. Although courts and administrators have construed the term "navigable" very liberally, the Reagan administration has recently attempted to limit the Section's reach. The Act has been applied to regulate the conversion of swamp land to agricultural purposes by draining and clearance, and has also been directed at obstructions or diversions of streams. Some of these more far reaching regulatory applications have resulted from litigation by environmental groups.

7. Marine Pollution

The US legal system for regulation of pollution of the marine environment is a complex statutory maze. Only the most important elements will be summarized here.

Section 311 of the Clean Water Act prohibits the discharge from vessels or other facilities of oil or hazardous substances into or upon the navigable waters of the United States or the waters of the contiguous zone (twelve miles

vessel or other floating craft, from which pollutants are or may be discharged. This term does not include return flows from irrigated agriculture." 33 U.S.C. § 1362(14).

[35] *See generally* Tripp & Jaffe, *Preventing Groundwater Pollution: Towards a Coordinated Strategy to Protect Critical Recharge Zones*, 3 Harv. Envt'l L. Rev. 1 (1979).

[36] 42 U.S.C. §§ 300f-300j-9.

[37] *Id.* § 300g-2.

[38] 33 U.S.C. § 1344. *See generally* Blumm, *The Clean Water Act's Section 404 Permit Program Enters its Adolescence: An Institutional and Programmatic Perspective*, 8 Ecology L. Q. 409 (1980).

[39] Bartell and Barko Hydraulics, Inc. v. Minnesota, 284 N.W.2d 834, 14 Env't Rep. Cas. (BNA) 1263 (Minn. 1979).

from shore).[40] The United States is authorized to assess civil penalties for violations. In addition, Section 312 of the Act authorizes the United States to recover cleanup costs and the costs of "repair or restitution" of natural resources attributable to oil spills within twelve miles of shore or resulting from outer continental shelf activities or in connection with damage to fishery resources within 200 miles of the coast.[41] Certain limitations on liability are provided. State compensation funds are not preempted, and the federal limitations on liability have been held not to apply to such funds.[42]

Section 312 of the Clean Water Act provides for federal technology-based standards for marine sanitation devices to prevent the discharge of untreated or inadequately treated sewage. States concluding that federal controls are inadequate may adopt a total ban on all sewage discharges, provided that the EPA determines that adequate facilities for safe and sanitary removal and treatment of sewage are available. The EPA itself may also, upon finding of need for more stringent controls, ban all discharges in specified waters.

The Ports and Waterway Safety Act deals with the problem of safety and vessel-source pollution attributable to ballasting, washing, collisions, groundings, and accidents through an extensive system of regulation of port traffic and through mandatory design and construction standards for new vessels.[43] These measures are administered by the Coast Guard in the Department of Transportation. There has been some effort to coordinate these regulatory controls with international conventions. *Ray v. Atlantic Richfield Company*[44] held that the federal system of regulation preempted more stringent state vessel design requirements, and also preempted a ban by the State of Washington on tankers in excess of 125 000 tons in Puget Sound, although certain state pilotage requirements were upheld.

The Marine Protection, Research and Sanctuaries Act requires a permit for all dumping within twelve nautical miles of the United States and all transportation for ocean dumping through that zone.[45] Administration of the permit authority is divided between the Army Corps of Engineers and EPA.

Offshore extraction of oil is regulated under the Outer Continental Shelf Lands Act.[46] The Interior Department must take environmental considerations into account in determining which areas may be leased for exploration and development. The Act calls for adoption of regulatory standards to prevent pollution from drilling, storage, and transportation operations. These requirements are enforced by the Coast Guard, although routine discharges of oil and disposal of drilling muds are subject to regulation by EPA. The Act imposes liability for cleanup costs and damages, and establishes a fund, financed

[40] 33 U.S.C. § 1321.
[41] *Id.* § 1322.
[42] Askew v. American Waterways Operators, Inc., 411 U.S. 325 (1973).
[43] 33 U.S.C. §§ 1221-1232.
[44] 435 U.S. 151 (1978).
[45] 16 U.S.C. §§ 1431-1434 & 33 U.S.C. §§ 1401-1444.
[46] 43 U.S.C. §§ 1331-1343.

by a fee on offshore production, for losses not otherwise compensated. Supplementary state funds have been held not to be preempted,[47] although state efforts to impose more stringent regulatory controls on federally leased and licensed offshore facilities would almost certainly be held to be preempted.

D. Noise Pollution

Under the Noise Control Act of 1972,[48] EPA has adopted technology-based standards to control noise from construction, transportation, and electrical equipment and engines. EPA may also require notices or labels on consumer products to disclose the level of noise emitted by the product. The Act preempts state regulation of sources subject to federal standards. Noise standards for aircraft are established by the Federal Aviation Administration after consultation with EPA.

E. Waste Disposal

1. Resource Conservation and Recovery Act (RCRA)

a. Hazardous Wastes

RCRA, enacted in 1976, provides a comprehensive regulatory program to ensure proper treatment and disposal of hazardous wastes, but its implementation is still in a beginning stage.[49] The Act reflects public concern with the hazards of toxic chemicals disposal and a history of inadequate or nonexistent state and local regulation. EPA is required to develop criteria for identifying and listing hazardous wastes, taking into account their toxicity, persistence, degradability, flammability, and corrosiveness. Listing triggers a series of regulatory controls on the generation, transportation, and disposal of listed wastes. EPA must adopt regulations requiring generators to keep records on hazardous wastes generated, to store and label them properly in containers, and to report each offsite shipment of waste in accordance with a manifest system. Transporters of hazardous waste from generators are also subject to regulatory controls and must participate in the manifest system by documenting their acquisition of waste from generators and their disposition of waste to treatment, storage, and disposal facilities. These facilities are in turn subject to the manifest system and to regulatory controls designed to ensure environmen-

[47] Askew v. American Waterways Operators, Inc., 411 U.S. 325 (1973).

[48] 42 U.S.C. §§ 4901-4918.

[49] 42 U.S.C. §§ 6901-6987. *See generally* Worobeck, *An Analysis of the Resource Conservation and Recovery Act*, 11 [Curr. Dev.] Env't Rep. (BNA) 633 (1980). The hazardous waste regulatory provisions are found in subtitle C, §§ 6921-6934. The regulations implementing those provisions appear at 40 C.F.R. §§ 260-267. *See generally* Friedland, *The New Hazardous Waste Management System: Regulation of Waste or Wasted Regulation?*, 5 Harv. Envt'l L. Rev. 89 (1981).

tally acceptable treatment, storage, and disposal. The manifest system is supposed to generate a "cradle to grave" paper trail to ensure that hazardous wastes find their way to proper treatment and disposal facilities. The regulatory standards to be adopted by EPA must be "such standards . . . as may be necessary as to protect human health and the environment."

Treatment, storage, and disposal facilities must obtain a permit from EPA which incorporates regulatory requirements, including assurances of long term financial responsibility to meet future cleanup or damage costs. EPA may delegate implementation and enforcement of the regulatory scheme to states with programs that meet federal standards.[50]

RCRA also grants EPA the authority to seek federal court injunctions to prevent handling, storage, treatment, transportation or disposal of any waste which "may present an imminent and substantial endangerment to health or the environment."[51]

Although RCRA mandated that EPA promulgate a complete set of hazardous waste regulations by May 1978, the major portion of the regulations were not issued until May 1980.[52] Standards for what is arguably the most important element of the RCRA program — governing design and operation of hazardous waste landfills — were not promulgated until July 1982.[53] Many of these standards are subject to pending court challenges. The delays in adopting these various regulations reflected EPA's limited resources, the sheer magnitude of the regulatory problem (it is estimated that the US generates as much as 150 000 000 metric tons of hazardous waste per year and that there are some 760 000 generators of hazardous waste),[54] and technical and political controversy over the details of implementation.[55] Among the controversial issues have been the procedures and criteria for determining which wastes to list as hazardous; the cut-off point for exempting small generators from certain regulatory requirements; and the respective roles of technology-based

[50] 42 U.S.C. §§ 6926.

[51] 42 U.S.C. § 7003. The government has filed a number of "imminent hazard" suits under this provision, and has succeeded in many cases in imposing strict liability on generators of wastes to finance cleanup of sites where their wastes were dumped. *See generally* MOTT, *Liability for Cleanup of Inactive Hazardous Waste Disposal Sites*, 14 NAT. RESOURCES LAW. 379 (1982).

[52] 45 Fed. Reg. 33,066 (1980). The delay prompted a lawsuit by several environmental groups and the state of Illinois in an attempt to hasten promulgation. Illinois v. Costle, 12 Env't Rep. Cas. (BNA) 1597 (D.D.C. 1979).

[53] 47 Fed. Reg. 32,274. The regulations were promulgated in "interim final" form, meaning that EPA would accept public comment on the regulations, but that, absent amendment, the regulations automatically took effect six months later, on January 26, 1983.

[54] 14 [CURR. DEV.] ENV'T REP. (BNA) 715 (1983); U.S. General Accounting Office, Hazardous Waste Facilities with Interim Status May Be Endangering Public Health and the Environment (1981) (Doc. No. CED-81-158).

[55] The 1980 hazardous waste regulations were challenged in over forty lawsuits, which were consolidated in Shell Oil v. Costle, No. 80-1532 (D.C. Cir.).

standards and environmental quality-based standards in regulation of treatment and disposal. At one extreme, for example, EPA could require a uniform set of containment controls for landfills, regardless of soil type or the presence of groundwater resources in the area. At the other extreme, it could adopt environmental quality standards limiting the nature and extent of groundwater pollution from disposal sites. The precise type of controls selected will have important implications for the location of waste disposal facilities and the cost and reliability of disposal. There is also controversy over the extent to which the regulations should encourage alternatives to land disposal, such as incineration.

The Act presents some difficult issues of preemption that have not yet been resolved.[56] In order to qualify for delegated implementation and enforcement responsibility and federal financial assistance, a state program must be "equivalent to" and "consistent with" the federal program.[57] In another provision, the Act provides that nothing in it shall be construed "to prohibit any State ... from imposing any requirements, including those for site selection, which are more stringent than those imposed" by EPA.[58] The latter provision is seemingly an express disclaimer of any federal preemption, and would allow states to ban or tightly restrict waste disposal. But EPA has interpreted the "consistency" requirement to limit states from unduly restricting waste disposal within their borders.[59]

EPA's concern is grounded in public fear of the hazards of toxic waste disposal and consequent efforts by states to prohibit or restrict disposal within their borders of wastes originating from other states, or to ban new waste disposal sites entirely. Such bans could preclude use of the most suitable disposal sites and encourage unauthorized dumping. In *Philadelphia v. New Jersey*[60] the Supreme Court invalidated as unconstitutional a New Jersey ban on out of state waste on the ground that it was discriminatory and therefore violated negative commerce clause principles. RCRA had not yet been enacted when the controversy between Philadelphia and New Jersey arose. EPA is now concerned that states will invoke RCRA to legalize unduly restrictive measures contained in state programs to implement that Act. Accordingly, under EPA regulations a state program will not be authorized as "consistent with" the federal program if any aspect of a state program "unreasonably restricts" the free movement into the state of hazardous wastes from other states or "has no basis in human health or environmental protection" and acts as a prohibition on the treatment, storage, and disposal of hazardous wastes within the state.[61] The legal validity of these provisions is an open question.

[56] *See generally* FLORINI, *Issues of Federalism in Hazardous Waste Control: Cooperation or Confusion?*, 5 HARV. ENVT'L L. REV. 307, 310-18 (1982).

[57] 42 U.S.C. § 6926.

[58] *Id.* § 6929.

[59] 40 C.F.R. § 123.32(a).

[60] 437 U.S. 617 (1978).

[61] 40 C.F.R. § 123.32(a),(b).

b. Solid Wastes

Solid wastes that are not classified by EPA as hazardous are subject to other RCRA provisions designed to encourage state and regional planning and implementation of good waste management practices.[62] EPA is to issue guidelines and information identifying appropriate methods for dealing with solid wastes through recycling, resource recovery, and landfill disposal. States are encouraged to promote regional planning programs to accomplish these goals. Qualifying state programs are entitled to receive federal financial assistance. EPA, as required by RCRA, has established criteria for identifying those solid waste disposal sites that are environmentally unacceptable "open dumps."[63] In order to receive federal financial aid, states must have a program to upgrade such disposal facilities in accordance with a specific timetable.

2. Comprehensive Environmental Response, Compensation and Liability Act

The 1980 Comprehensive Environmental Response, Compensation, and Liability Act (CERCLA) (commonly referred to as "Superfund") addresses the problems created by hazardous waste spills and waste dumps.[64] EPA has estimated that one to two thousand of the thirty to fifty thousand existing waste disposal sites pose potential threats to public health or the environment, and that the estimated costs of needed cleanup range from 26 to 40 billion dollars. In addition, an unknown quantity of hazardous wastes has simply been dumped by roadsides, parks, forests, and streams. The Act establishes a $1.6 billion hazardous substances response trust fund, 87.5% of which is financed by taxes on petroleum products and petrochemical feedstocks, with the balance supplied by the federal treasury.[65]

The fund is to be used to underwrite the cost of cleanup and to provide compensation for damage to governmentally owned natural resources. Federal cleanup responses must be consistent with a national contingency plan to be designed after consultation with the states.[66] The federal response actions are limited in time and amount unless a state in which the site is located agrees to a variety of conditions, including payment of 10% of present and future remedial and maintenance costs, assumption of responsibility for overseeing future maintenance of the site, and assurance of a satisfactory waste disposal facility to receive cleaned up wastes. In lieu of federal action, the President may allow qualifying states to take remedial action and receive federal reimbursement for costs less 10%. The Act creates a federal cause of action against persons re-

[62] The solid waste management provisions of RCRA are in subtitle D, 42 U.S.C. §§ 6941-6950. EPA's guidelines for state solid waste management plans appear at 40 C.F.R. § 256.

[63] 40 C.F.R. § 257.

[64] 42 U.S.C. §§ 9601-9657.

[65] *See supra* Ch. III, at note 43.

[66] 42 U.S.C. § 9605. EPA promulgated the National Contingency Plan on July 16, 1982, 47 Fed. Reg. 31, 180 (to be codified at 40 C.F.R. § 300).

sponsible for wastes or waste facilities for cleanup costs and damages caused to governmentally owned natural resources.[67]

The Act is a compromise measure falling far short of what environmental advocates and the Senate had sought. The Senate version provided for a $4.1 billion fund and provided for compensation and damage liability for personal injuries and private property damage. Another major compromise secured by industry interests was the inclusion of several preemptive provisions. The Act does not prevent states from imposing additional liability or regulatory controls with respect to the release of hazardous substances within the state. But any person receiving compensation under the federal act "shall be precluded from recovering compensation for the same removal costs or damages or *claims* pursuant to any other law, and vice versa" (emphasis added).[68] Although the federal fund is not available for compensating personal injuries or private property damage, a broad construction of "claims" might forbid a person who had received compensation from the fund from pursuing such compensation through state remedies. In addition, the Act provides that "no person may be required to contribute to any fund, the purpose of which is to pay compensation for claims for any costs of response or damages or claims which may be compensated" under the federal act, subject to limited exceptions. The phrase "may be compensated" has critical significance in light of the fact that the level of funding for the federal fund is far too low to cover all estimated response and natural resource damage costs. On a broad interpretation of this phrase, a person receiving partial compensation under the federal fund would be precluded from receiving any additional compensation from state funds for the same injury or industry would be exempted from contributing to the state fund.

The legal issues are important because a number of states have instituted their own funds to supplement or go beyond the coverage provided under the federal act. The reach of the preemptive provisions is currently the subject of litigation.[69]

F. Production and Sale of Hazardous Chemicals

1. Pesticides

The federal pesticide statutes date back to 1947. The current version, known as the Federal Insecticide, Fungicide, and Rodenticide Act,[70] requires EPA registration (licensing) of all pesticides.[71] In order to be registered, EPA must

[67] 42 U.S.C. § 9607(a).

[68] *Id.* § 9614(c).

[69] Exxon v. Hunt, 4 N.J. Tax 294 (1982), 12 Envt'l L. Rep. (ELI) 20,734 (1982). The court rejected plaintiff's claim that the New Jersey Spill Compensation and Control Act was preempted by CERCLA. *Cf.* Exxon v. Hunt, 683 F.2d 69 (3d Cir. 1982), *cert. denied,* 103 S. Ct. 727 (1983).

[70] 7 U.S.C. § 136-136y (Supp. IV 1980).

[71] *Id.* § 136a.

determine that the pesticide is effective for its intended use and that its labeling (including indicated uses and directions for application) is accurate. In addition, EPA must determine that it will not cause "unreasonable adverse effects on the environment," defined as "any unreasonable risk to man or the environment, taking into account the economic, social and environmental costs and benefits of the use of any pesticides."[72] Nearly 30 000 pesticides are currently registered by EPA. Registrations may be cancelled by EPA upon a determination that the conditions for registration are no longer satisfied, and manufacture and use of the pesticide may be suspended immediately, pending completion of cancellation proceedings, if EPA finds "imminent hazard" in continued use.[73] Time-consuming and burdensome procedural requirements are imposed on EPA in cancellation proceedings. As a result of 1972 Amendments, registrations must be reviewed by EPA every five years.[74]

EPA may limit the uses for which the pesticide is licensed.[75] If it determines that a pesticide is highly toxic to man or the environment, it must be classified for restricted use, and applied only under the direct supervision of a certified applicator or under other special restrictions. EPA is granted authority to certify applicators, but this responsibility may be and often is delegated to the states.[76]

States, subject to EPA approval, may register pesticides for intrastate distribution and use to meet "special local needs."[77] Environmentalists have attacked this provision as a loophole in the system of federal control. Conversely, states may prohibit pesticides certified by EPA or impose more stringent restrictions on their use. Environmentalists have been critical of the failure of the federal government to develop non-chemical methods of dealing with pests, including use of changed farming practices. Several states are attempting to encourage such alternatives. The pesticide industry recently won administration backing for legislation to preempt certain aspects of state pesticide regulation, including testing and disclosure of data on adverse effects, but Congress has thus far refused to adopt the necessary legislation.

2. Toxic Substances Control Act

The Toxic Substances Control Act (TSCA) was enacted in 1976 as a comprehensive program of federal regulatory control of manufacture and use of toxic chemicals.[78] Certain toxic chemicals and their residues are subject to federal regulation under the pesticide statutes, the air and water pollution control laws, RCRA, and CERCLA. TSCA was designed as a comprehensive regulato-

[72] 7 U.S.C. § 136a(c)(5), as defined at § 136(bb).
[73] *Id.* § 136d.
[74] *Id.* § 136d(a).
[75] *Id.* § 136a(d).
[76] *Id.* § 136b.
[77] *Id.* § 136v.
[78] 15 U.S.C. §§ 2601-2629. *See generally* 1A F. Grad, Treatise on Environmental Law § 4A.02. (Matthew Bender & Co., New York 1981).

ry program to deal with the tens of thousands of chemicals already in commercial use and the thousand or more commercially significant new chemicals that appear each year, many of which would not be subject to control under the various statutes noted above.

TSCA requires manufacturers of new chemicals (or of existing chemicals destined for a "significant new use") to notify EPA before commencing manufacture.[79] The notice must include considerable information, including all known data on health and environmental effects. The EPA may limit or delay manufacture or use of a chemical on a finding that data are "insufficient to permit a reasoned evaluation of the health and environmental effects" of the chemical or because anticipated uses "may present an unreasonable risk of injury to health or environment." This power enables EPA to demand additional information and testing concerning the effects of a chemical. EPA must take action within ninety days of receipt of notice, but the ninety day period can be renewed for "good cause."

Chemical substances already on the market are subject to EPA "testing orders," adopted by regulation, under which manufacturers may be required to test their chemicals for health and environmental effects.[80] Tests are supposed to generate information to enable EPA to determine whether continued manufacture and use of a chemical should be permitted. If EPA determines that there is a "reasonable basis" for concluding that manufacture, use, or disposal of a chemical "presents or will present an unreasonable risk of injury to health or to the environment" it may restrict uses of the chemical or ban it entirely.[81]

In making determinations about unreasonableness of risk with respect to both new and existing chemicals, EPA must balance health and environmental considerations with the benefits of a chemical and the economic consequences of restricting or prohibiting its use. EPA is also authorized to seek judicial relief against manufacture or use of "imminently hazardous" chemicals.[82] There is also a special provision requiring EPA to regulate and restrict use of polychlorinated biphenyls (PCBs).[83]

To date, EPA has made only limited use of its powers under TSCA. For example, the agency has not issued any final rules requiring testing of chemicals already in use.[84] Instead, the agency has attempted to arrange "voluntary" testing agreements. Environmentalists criticize these voluntary agreements on the ground that EPA does not have adequate control over testing protocols and

[79] 15 U.S.C. § 2604. For a comparison of this provision to analogous statutes in Europe, *see* Note, *Control of Toxic Substances: the Attempt to Harmonize the Notification Requirements of the U.S. Toxic Substances Control Act and the European Community Sixth Amendment*, 20 VIR. J. INT. L. 417 (1980).

[80] 15 U.S.C. § 2603.

[81] *Id.* § 2605.

[82] *Id.* § 2606.

[83] *Id.* § 2605(e).

[84] EPA's failure to use its testing authority prompted the Natural Resources Defense Council to sue. NRDC v. Costle, 10 ENVT'L L. REP. (ELI) 20,274 (S.D.N.Y. 1980).

procedures. Environmentalists also criticized, and successfully litigated, EPA's initial PCB regulations, which would have exempted 99.3% of the PCBs then in use.[85]

Implementation of TSCA has been hampered by limited EPA resources, debates over appropriate testing policies, limited testing personnel and laboratories, and the huge number of chemicals subject to regulation. EPA has attempted to develop generic approaches to testing that would require a set battery of tests for different types of chemicals depending on their structure, expected use and volume. Industry has claimed that this approach is technically flawed, overinclusive, and too expensive, and that a case by case determination of the adequacy of testing data should be made. Implementation has also been slowed by legal controversies among industry, environmental groups, and EPA concerning the confidentiality of testing and other data submitted by manufacturers to EPA.[86]

TSCA contains several provisions involving preemption of state law. If EPA promulgates a rule for testing a chemical, no state may establish a testing requirement for similar purposes.[87] Also, if EPA restricts use of a chemical in order to protect against an unreasonable risk, no state may regulate the substance to protect against the same risk unless the state regulation is identical to that of EPA; or is adopted under authority of another federal law, such as the Clean Air Act; or prohibits completely the use of the chemical.[88] States may apply to EPA for an exemption from these preemption provisions, which EPA may grant if the exemption would not lead to a violation of TSCA and provides a significantly higher degree of protection from the risk than the federal regulation without unduly burdening interstate commerce.[89] EPA had argued to Congress against inclusion of the exemption provision, contending that it was better equipped to assess risks than state authorities, and that the hazards posed by a chemical were unlikely to vary geographically.

G. Radioactivity

The Atomic Energy Act gives the Nuclear Regulatory Commission (formerly the Atomic Energy Commission) broad regulatory and licensing authority over the use of nuclear materials (uranium, thorium, plutonium, enriched uranium, their by-products, and materials that have been made radioactive by exposure to them).[90] The most significant responsibility of the Nuclear Regulato-

[85] Environmental Defense Fund, Inc. v. EPA, 636 F.2d 1267 (D.C. Cir. 1980).

[86] For discussion of the trade secrets issue, *see* Latovick, *Protection for Trade Secrets under the Toxic Substances Control Act of 1976*, 13 J. L. Reform 329 (1980); McGarity & Shapiro, *The Trade Secret Status of Health and Safety Testing Information: Reforming Agency Disclosure Policies*, 93 Harv. L. Rev. 837 (1980).

[87] 15 U.S.C. § 2617(a).

[88] *Id.*

[89] *Id.* § 2617(b).

[90] 42 U.S.C. §§ 2011-2296.

ry Commission (NRC) has been to regulate nuclear reactors for electricity generation, although it also regulates the use of radioactive materials for medical, industrial, commercial, and research uses. The NRC also has jurisdiction, some of it shared with other federal agencies, over the mining, transportation, and disposal of nuclear materials.

Facilities, including nuclear power plants, which use nuclear materials must receive a permit from the NRC. The NRC has adopted environmental quality standards and guidelines limiting the permitted exposures to radioactivity of workers within a facility, and of the general public at the border of the facility's property line during normal operation.[91] The guidelines and standards also include technology-based requirements obliging facilities to reduce radioactivity releases to a level "as low as is practicably achievable" taking into account the availability and costs of control technology and the benefits from the use of nuclear materials. Nuclear power plants are subject to special regulations designed to minimize the danger of an accident generating massive releases of material.

Nuclear generating plants are subject to a two step licensing process.[92] They must receive one license at commencement of construction and another at commencement of operation. Because of the volatile state of nuclear generating control technology and fierce opposition from environmental and other groups to nuclear power, the licensing process has been extremely protracted.

The Act was amended in 1959 to authorize the NRC to delegate to qualifying states regulatory and licensing authority over radioisotopes and other less hazardous materials. But the NRC retains sole responsibility for regulating certain more hazardous activities, including the construction and operation of any nuclear generating facility. However, the same provision which retains such authority for the NRC also provides that it should not be "construed to affect the authority of any State or local agency to regulate activities for purposes other than protection against radiation hazards."[93] There is also a provision stating that nothing in the Act "shall be construed to affect the authority or regulations of any Federal, State or local agency with respect to the generation, sale or . . . transmission of electric power produced through the use of nuclear facilities."[94]

The effect of these provisions on state efforts to curb use of nuclear power has been hotly disputed. A state clearly may not impose controls limiting emissions from nuclear plants or regulate their design or operation. On the other hand, a state can probably impose regulations on the siting of nuclear power plants so long as the provisions are applied to nuclear and non-nuclear plants in a non-discriminatory fashion. A much more difficult case was presented in *Pacific Gas & Electric Co. v. State Energy Resource Conservation &*

[91] 10 C.F.R. § 20.
[92] *Id.* § 50.
[93] 42 U.S.C. § 2021(c),(k).
[94] *Id.* § 2018.

Develop. Comm'n.,[95] in which the Supreme Court upheld a California statute precluding construction of new nuclear plants until the state Energy Commission had determined that a federally approved method of disposing of nuclear wastes exists. The Court found that the primary aim of the statute was economic, being designed to protect ratepayers against the future financial exposure associated with unresolved nuclear waste disposal problems rather than to regulate radioactive hazards associated with nuclear wastes themselves. The Court's decision is likely to encourage a variety of ingenious state and local measures to restrict or ban nuclear facilities.[96]

The problem of preemption is complicated by amendments to the Clean Air Act and the Clean Water Act that make it clear that EPA and states may adopt ambient air or water quality radioactivity standards.[97] EPA or state ambient environmental quality standards for radioactivity would provide a basis for regulatory controls that could restrict or block the development of nuclear power. However, the standards would have to be applied to all sources of radioactivity.

There is also a question whether the Atomic Energy Act might preempt state measures to ban or restrict the disposal of nuclear generating wastes within their borders. Many states and localities have enacted such measures, and states containing existing disposal sites for low level radioactive wastes are phasing down their operation. The federal government has thus far been unsuccessful in demonstrating an acceptable technology for permanent disposal of high level wastes. Given the failure to deal explicitly with nuclear wastes in the Act, and the traditional primacy of the states in matters of land use control, it seems most unlikely that a court would construe the Atomic Energy Act to preempt restrictive state measures, particularly in light of the Supreme Court's decision in *Pacific Gas & Electric*. Advocates of nuclear power favor an express preemption by Congress, but political support for such a measure is lacking.[98] The federal government has explored a variety of compromise measures to enlist consultation and concurrence with the states in the solution of this problem. For example, in 1980 Congress enacted the Low-Level Radioactive Waste Policy Act.[99] It declares that "each state is responsible for providing for the availability of capacity either within or outside the state for providing for the disposal of low-level radioactive waste generated within its borders," and authorizes states to enter into interstate compacts governing the establishment and operation of disposal facilities.[100] Radioactive tailings from uranium

[95] 103 S.Ct. 1713 (1983).

[96] *See generally* MEEKS, *Nuclear Power and State Radiation Protection Measures: The Impotence of Preemption*, 10 ENVT'L L. 1 (1979); TRIBE, *California Declines the Nuclear Gamble: Is Such a State Choice Preempted?*, 7 ECOLOGY L. Q. 679 (1979).

[97] Clean Air Act, 42 U.S.C. § 7422(a); Clean Water Act, §§ 1311(f), 1319.

[98] *See generally* HART & GLASER, *A Failure to Enact: A Review of Radioactive Waste Issues and Legislation Considered by the Ninety-Sixth Congress*, 32 S.C.L. REV. 639 (1981).

[99] 42 U.S.C. § 2021b-d (Supp. IV 1980).

[100] *Id.* § 2021d(a)(1)(A). Such compacts, however, do not take effect until individually ratified by Congress.

mining operations are subject to federal regulation by EPA under the Uranium Mill Tailings Radiation Control Act of 1978.[101]

Another set of federalism issues in the nuclear power context is presented by the Price-Anderson Act, which limits the total liability of nuclear power plants, contractors, and suppliers to $560 million, and provides a system of industry-wide reinsurance to reduce the exposure of any single utility still further.[102] Environmental plaintiffs challenged the constitutionality of the Act on the ground that it violated due process and equal protection by abolishing their state law right to unlimited compensation for injuries attributable to nuclear power plant accidents. The Supreme Court sustained the constitutionality of the Act in *Duke Power Company v. Carolina Environmental Study Group.*[103]

H. Land Use Planning, Protection of Nature, Landscape, Flora and Fauna

Although there is extensive federal legislation in the US concerning land use planning and environmental conservation, the relative dearth of such law in the EC make its appropriate to summarize the US law very briefly.[104]

Approximately one third of US land and a higher percentage of its valuable mineral resources are owned by the federal government. The Forest Service in the Agriculture Department manages the national forests, comprising about one fourth of all federally owned land.[105] Most of the remaining federal lands, including lands valuable for grazing and rich in minerals, are managed by the Bureau of Land Management (BLM) in the Interior Department.[106] The Fish and Wildlife Service[107] and the National Park Service[108] in the Interior Department manage smaller amounts of public lands which are, however, of great environmental significance. The Forest Service and the BLM enjoy wide statutory discretion in the management of lands within their jurisdiction. The

[101] 92 Stat. 3021 (codified in various sections of 42 U.S.C.).

[102] 42 U.S.C. § 2210 (1976). *See generally* GREEN, *Nuclear Power: Risk, Liability, and Indemnity*, 71 MICH. L. REV. 479 (1973).

[103] 438 U.S. 59 (1978).

[104] For a more detailed explanation of relevant US statutes, *see* CULHANE & FRIESEMA, *Land Use Planning for the Public Lands*, 19 NAT. RESOURCES J. 43 (1979).

[105] The organic act authorizing the Forest Service is codified at 16 U.S.C. §§ 471-542 (1974 & West. Supp. 1981). The National Forest Service is responsible for administering over 150 forests and other areas. *See* 36 C.F.R. § 200.1(c)(2) (listing components of the forest system).

[106] The organic act for the Bureau of Land Management is the Federal Land Policy and Management Act, 43 U.S.C. §§ 1731-1748 (1976).

[107] The Fish and Wildlife Service operates primarily under the authority of the Fish and Wildlife Coordination Act, 16 U.S.C. §§ 661-668, and the National Wildlife Refuge System Act, 16 U.S.C. §§ 668dd-668ee.

[108] The National Park Service was established by Act of Congress in 1916, current version at 16 U.S.C. §§ 1-460.

Fish and Wildlife Service and the National Park Service operate under statutes which give paramount weight to conservation and environmental values.

The discretion of the Forest Service and the BLM (and of all other federal land and resource managers) is, however, limited by generic statutes aimed at securing specific conservation and environmental values. The Wilderness Act of 1964 forbids any significant development of certain public lands designated by Congress.[109] The Act also provides an administrative system for studying and recommending designation of additional wilderness areas by the Agriculture and Interior Departments. Development within wilderness areas is severely restricted. The Wild and Scenic Rivers Act imposes similar restrictions on development of river systems designated by Congress.[110]

Federal land and resource management decisions, as well as federally funded and licensed projects, are subject to the National Environmental Policy Act (NEPA) (considered below), and the Endangered Species Act,[111] which prohibits actions which would jeopardize "critical habitats" of species listed by Interior as endangered; a limited exemption process is provided.[112] The Surface Mining Control and Reclamation Act limits and regulates stripmining activities on federal as well as private lands.[113]

The Outer Continental Shelf Lands Act governs the BLM's leasing and regulation of oil and gas development activities on the outer continental shelf.[114] BLM must balance energy and environmental concerns and impose controls designed to minimize harm to the environment. Development of minerals on public land is governed by the Mineral Leasing Act,[115] which gives BLM considerable discretion, and by the 1872 Mining law,[116] which grants discoverers of valuable minerals on public lands property rights in their discovery.[117]

A wide variety of federal agencies have statutory authority and funding to undertake water resource and navigation projects. These agencies include the Army Corps of Engineers, the Federal Water and Power Service in the Interior Department, the Soil Conservation Service in the Agriculture Department, the Tennessee Valley Authority, and others. A variety of statutes, including NEPA, have attempted to inject consideration of environmental impacts and economic efficiency into the planning and execution of such projects, but with only moderate success. The Federal Energy Regulatory Commission in the Energy Department is responsible for licensing hydroelectric projects under the Federal Power Act, which requires it to consider conservation and recrea-

[109] 16 U.S.C. §§ 1131-1136.

[110] *Id.* §§ 1271-1287.

[111] *Id.* §§ 1531-1543.

[112] *Id.* § 1536(g). The Act also makes it unlawful for private persons to take, possess, sell, transport, import or export any species listed as endangered. *Id.* § 1538 (a).

[113] 30 U.S.C. §§ 1201-1328.

[114] 43 U.S.C. §§ 1331-1356.

[115] 30 U.S.C. §§ 181-287, 351-359.

[116] *Id.* §§ 22-54.

[117] For an overview of these and related statutes, *see* 3 F. Grad, *supra* note 78, at § 12.03 [2].

tional values.[118] Section 404 of the Clean Water Act requires that persons undertaking dredge and fill activities in navigable waters obtain a permit from the Army Corps of Engineers, with the EPA playing a role in the development of guidelines governing the permit process.[119] The permit process is used to control development in coastal areas and those bordering rivers and lakes. The Coastal Zone Management Act provides federal financial and planning assistance to encourage states to engage in land use and development planning for the coastal zone, and allows states with federally approved plans to exercise regulatory authority over federally controlled developments on the outer continental shelf adjacent to the state.[120]

I. Environmental Assessment

The National Environmental Policy Act of 1969 (NEPA)[121] has two basic objectives. One is to provide each federal agency with legal authority to protect and further environmental values unless squarely inconsistent with the mission defined by its organic statute. The second is to establish a set of guidelines and procedures under which federal agencies are required to generate information on the environmental effects of their activities; identify and develop information on alternatives that might be less environmentally damaging; and use environmental analysis to promote environmental considerations in their decisionmaking. The provisions of the Act are quite general. It was a broad-brush congressional response to rising concern with environmental values and the perception that many federal agencies whose primary mission was not environmental protection would neglect environmental considerations in their policies and decisions.

NEPA established a Council on Environmental Quality (CEQ) to oversee implementation of the Act by executive agencies,[122] but the primary responsibility for enforcement of the Act has been assumed by federal courts.[123] Although there is no provision in the Act for judicial review, courts quickly asserted the power to require agency compliance with NEPA's Environmental Impact Statement (EIS) provision.[124] The Act requires responsible federal agencies to "include in every recommendation or report on proposals for legislation and other major Federal actions significantly affecting the quality of the human environment," a "detailed statement" on "the environmental impact

[118] 16 U.S.C. §§ 791a-828c.

[119] 33 U.S.C. § 1344.

[120] 16 U.S.C. §§ 1451-1464.

[121] 42 U.S.C. §§ 4321-4347.

[122] *Id.* § 4342. The council consists of three members, appointed by the President.

[123] *See generally* F. Anderson, NEPA in the Courts: A Legal Analysis of the National Environmental Policy Act (Johns Hopkins Press, Baltimore, Maryland 1973); R. Liroff, A National Policy for the Environment: NEPA and its Aftermath (Indiana University Press, Bloomington, Indiana 1976).

[124] 42 U.S.C. § 4332(2)(c).

of the proposed action," alternatives to the proposed action, the relation between short term uses of the environment and the maintenance and enhancement of its long term productivity, and other irreversible and irretrievable commitments of resources involved in the proposed action.

The courts interpreted these provisions to require the preparation of a draft EIS in the case of any federal action involving potentially significant environmental effects; circulation of the draft to interested state and federal agencies and the general public; receipt of comments; and preparation of a final EIS incorporating or responding to criticisms of the draft statement. These requirements were incorporated in the NEPA regulations issued by the CEQ in 1978.[125] The courts have interpreted the threshold of "major" federal actions "significantly affecting" the human environment in a fashion that required preparation of Impact Statements on hundreds of projects annually. Federal "actions" have been interpreted to include not only actions and projects directly undertaken by the federal government, but also federally funded projects undertaken by state or local authorities and private projects licensed by the federal government. There is, however, continuing litigation over the precise extent of federal financial or regulatory involvement in state or local projects necessary to trigger the federal EIS requirement. Other issues of controversy include the scope of an EIS and the extent to which agencies must prepare a "comprehensive" or "programmatic" EIS dealing with the cumulative interrelated effects of numerous individual projects or decisions.[126]

Courts have engaged in rather searching review of the adequacy of impact statements, often setting aside statements for failure to deal adequately with environmental issues raised by opponents of the particular project.[127] While enforcing a good deal of procedural rigor in the impact statement process, the federal courts have refused to turn NEPA into a vehicle for judicial creation of a federal common law of the environment that would empower federal courts to set aside the balance struck by agencies between environmental and other values.[128] The Supreme Court has reiterated on several occasions that the thrust of the Act is "essentially procedural" and does not empower federal courts to set aside agency decisions which prefer development over environmental values so long as the impact statement accompanying the decision is reasonably complete and accurate.[129]

Some environmentalists and students of the EIS process contend that it has had little effect on agency decisions, and has merely served to generate elaborate studies that have little operational significance.[130] Other observers believe

[125] 40 C.F.R. §§ 1500-1508.

[126] *See generally* BARNEY, *The Programmatic Environmental Impact Statement and the National Environmental Policy Act Regulations*, 16 LAND & WATER L. REV. 1 (1981).

[127] *E. g.*, Chelsea Neighborhood Associations v. US Postal Service, 516 F.2d 378 (2d Cir. 1975).

[128] *See* Note, *The Last Adverse Alternative Approach to Substantive Review Under NEPA*, 88 HARV. L. REV. 735, 743, 746 (1975).

[129] *E. g.*, Strycker's Bay Neighborhood Council, Inc. v. Karlen, 444 U.S. 223 (1980).

[130] *E. g.*, SAX, *The (Unhappy) Truth About NEPA*, 26 OK. L. REV. 239 (1973).

that the process has had significant effects despite the refusal of the federal courts to find judicially enforceable "substantive" commands in NEPA.[131] They argue that NEPA has led agencies to give greater weight to environmental values by forcing them to generate information on environmental effects and hire environmental analysts to prepare studies, and by obliging them to acknowledge the relevance and legitimacy of environmental interests and to engage in dialogue with environmentally minded federal and state agencies and private groups on the environmental merits of proposed actions.

NEPA does not preempt any state measures, and many states have adopted similar environmental impact assessment requirements for projects undertaken, funded, or licensed by state authorities.[132]

[131] *E.g.*, Comment, *The National Environmental Policy Act: How It Is Working, How It Should Work*, 4 Envt'l L. Rep. (ELI) 10,003 (citing CEQ report noting that Army Corps of Engineers had cancelled 24 projects and modified 197 others because of NEPA).

[132] *See generally* Pearlman, *State Environmental Policy Acts: Local Decisionmaking and Land Use Planning*, 43 J. Am. Inst. Planners 42 (1977).

VI. Implementation and Enforcement in the Community

A. Role of Legislative and Administrative Institutions of the Community and Member States

Implementation and enforcement of environmental directives are in principle the sole responsibility of member states. The Commission has no power to act as an executive agency. It can not give directions to national authorities, and it has no powers to designate the competent national authorities. Under Art. 5 of the EEC Treaty or under special provisions of environmental directives, member states are to organize appropriate authorities to implement Community policy and to provide the necessary staff, equipment, and funding.[1] It is their task to issue the appropriate substantive and procedural provisions for implementation of a particular directive, to translate the directive (as incorporated into national law) into requirements for individual polluters, to monitor the activities of polluters, and to take enforcement action in case of noncompliance.

1. Implementation and Integration Mechanisms

However, this description of the roles of the Commission and member states in the implementation and enforcement process conveys only a rough picture. The actual balance of powers between the Community and member states and the latitude of member states in implementing and enforcing directives depends on the integration mechanisms used and the depth of harmonization required by a particular directive.

In Community environmental policy, there are three types of integration mechanisms, each of which give the Community and member states different roles in implementation and enforcement. There are regulation-type-directives, directives setting quality objectives, and directives establishing environmental protection principles or coordinating member state policies.

In many areas of environmental policy, the Community has not followed the mandate of Art. 189(3) of the EEC Treaty to fix only the results to be achieved and to leave member states the choice of form and methods. Instead,

[1] European Court of Justice, case 71/76, Thieffrey v. Conseil de l'ordre des avocats à la cour de Paris, [1977] ECR 765, 777; BLECKMANN, *Die Rechtsprechung des Europäischen Gerichtshofs zur Gemeinschaftstreue*, 27 RECHT DER INTERNATIONALEN WIRTSCHAFT 653, 654 (1981).

it has issued directives which comprehensively regulate the environmental area concerned, thus leaving member states no discretion. Such directives are therefore hardly distinguishable from regulations. These directives do not merely harmonize a particular area of environmental law. They effectuate a full unification of substantive law. In many other areas of environmental policy, the relevant directives do follow the mandate of Art. 189(3).[2] Although sometimes the Community goals established by these directives are fairly specific, e. g. attainment of ambient quality standards, they are also sometimes rather vague, e. g. an obligation to give priority to re–use of wastes or to prevent injury to the environment from waste disposal. In either case the directives normally establish principles for implementation of these goals, such as an obligation to control polluting activities through permit requirements, implementation plans, or recordkeeping and monitoring.

a. Regulation–Type Directives

Detailed regulation of a particular field of environmental protection is sometimes accomplished by a single regulation–type directive covering that field. In other instances, a two–tier process is used. First, a framework directive is adopted that sets policy goals, principles, and strategies applicable to a broad field of environmental protection. Second, the framework is filled out by later implementing special regulation–type directives covering all or part of the field. Under this two–tier system of harmonization, general agreement on policy goals, principles, and strategies is followed by agreement on specific instruments for addressing a particular environmental problem. Examples are the mercury and cadmium directives and other Commission proposals for implementing directives under the aquatic environment framework directive. The directive and proposals are based not only on Articles 100 and 235 of the EEC Treaty, but also on the framework directive.[3]

Regulation–type directives may take different forms. For example, directives may set forth: prohibitions on polluting activities; emission, specification, and input standards or similar product related requirements; testing obligations for manufacturers; and packaging and labeling obligations. They may also specify associated testing or measurement methods. Member states do not have much latitude in implementing such directives. They have only to incorporate them into national law. Their role in implementing the directives is essentially confined to applying them to particular cases and enforcing them.

[2] The contrary view of WEINSTOCK, *Nur eine Umwelt? Europäische Umweltpolitik zwischen ökologischer Vielfalt und ökonomischer Einheit,* 6 ZEITSCHRIFT FÜR UMWELTPOLITIK 1, 4, 20, 21 (1983) (that regulation–type directives are the rule in the Community) is based on a rather selective assessment of Community environmental policy.

[3] For a discussion of this approach *see* Salzwedel, *Auswirkungen der EG–Richtlinien mit wasserrechtlichem Bezug auf den Vollzug des deutschen Wasserrechts,* in GESELLSCHAFT FÜR UMWELTRECHT, DOKUMENTATION DER FACHTAGUNG 1979, at 139, 146–147 (Erich Schmidt Verlag, Berlin 1980).

This technique of comprehensive, substantive Community legislation is used for two reasons.[4]

The first relates to elimination of obstacles to free trade and of distortions of competition within the Community. Setting only broad policy goals and leaving member states the choice of how to implement them would probably result in divergent requirements that would hamper the free flow of goods or affect the competitive position of firms within the Common Market. Virtually all product related directives (toxic substances, solvents, paints, pesticides, vehicles, tractors, motorcycles, aircraft, construction machinery, fuels, detergents) follow the technique of detailed and comprehensive substantive Community regulation.

However, this trade rationale does not necessarily require environmental uniformity. There are legislative techniques to reconcile the goal of equal access to national markets with the interest of member states in environmental diversity. The concept of partial harmonization, whereby the Community sets uniform requirements for products that cross national borders and leaves member states free to legislate for domestic products, has in principle been rejected in Community practice. Another legislative technique, widely used in Community environmental law, is that of optional harmonization. Under this concept, harmonization covers both interstate and domestic transactions. However, member states may retain their domestic regulation, and producers have the choice of complying with either the harmonized or domestic requirements. If a producer decides to comply with the harmonized requirements, it must be allowed access to the markets of all member states.

Comprehensiveness in process regulation can similarly be explained by the Community's desire to avoid distortion to competition by divergent national implementation. Such considerations have, for example, been paramount in the case of the aquatic environment directive. The same is true of the titanium dioxide directive. However, not all directives can be explained in this way, and indeed many process related directives employ integration mechanisms other than comprehensive and detailed regulation. Since the economic impacts of regulation in these areas may be less significant than in product regulation, and particularly since access of foreign firms to domestic markets is not at stake, there is more latitude for environmental diversity. Hence, most directives in this area set only minimum standards; the member states may retain or introduce stricter standards.

The second rationale for comprehensive, substantive regulation of a particular environmental problem seems to be the perceived seriousness of the environmental problem itself. This rationale may afford an additional explanation for some of the product and process related directives, especially the uniform manufacturer testing requirements and the emission standards and prohibitions in toxic substances regulation. At any rate, it explains the comprehensive and detailed regulation of PCB use and disposal and of radioactivity.

[4] *See* F. Behrens, Rechtsgrundlagen der Umweltpolitik der Europäischen Gemeinschaften 252 (Erich Schmidt Verlag, Berlin 1976).

Finally, there are also more palpable explanations for comprehensive regulation arising from the policy process. Community environmental policy is bureaucratic policy. The perfectionist attitudes of those in the Commission's environmental service undoubtedly play a role. Also, a member state may prefer detailed regulation. For example, Italy regularly favors detailed provisions because it can then simply incorporate the directive into national law without undergoing the lengthy and, under the Italian political system, risky process of enacting implementing provisions.

b. Directives Setting Environmental Quality Standards

Several kinds of air and water pollution problems have been dealt with by Community quality standards. Normally, the relevant directives not only set ambient quality standards, but also require establishment of implementation plans and/or monitoring systems. They usually leave member states a wide margin of discretion in applying the standards to individual polluters.

Generally speaking, this approach is chosen where the regulation has no direct trade impacts and the environmental problem is either well suited to ambient standards or is somewhat less serious so that some variation among member states can be accepted. This approach is designed to accord member states more flexibility. However, there is a recent trend in Community legislation to limit this flexibility by establishing some Community or joint Community/member state mechanism of supervising and sometimes even coordinating implementation of the directive. Thus, under the directives setting quality standards for drinking water, sources of drinking water, bathing water, and shellfish water and the SO_2 limit values directive, the Commission has the right to oversee the improvement plans each member state is to establish. Some of these directives provide that, in cases where such plans are considered inadequate, the Commission may make proposals for further harmonization.

The reasons why some directives give the Community a greater role in implementation and why different methods of supervising member state implementation have been chosen are unclear. Often, the greater Community role in implementation appears to be a means of compensating for the Council's failure to agree on substantive policies, such as deadlines for improvements, emission standards, etc. Accordingly, it would not be correct to interpret the increasing Community role in implementation as a deepening of political integration in environmental protection. However, the greater Community involvement in implementation may establish a precedent for future evolution of the Community role in environmental protection.

c. Directives Establishing Environmental Protection Principles or Coordinating Member State Policies

Often the Community confines itself to setting broad environmental policy goals and encouraging implementation of these goals through coordination of member state policies. One example is the regulation of less dangerous substances under the aquatic environment directive. The directive establishes the goal of considerably reducing pollution from such substances within ten years. For that purpose, it requires member states to establish implementation programs for the reduction of water pollution. These plans must contain water quality standards, whose determination is fully within the responsibility of individual member states. There is, however, provision for joint Community/member state coordination of the national implementation plans.

A similar procedure is established for existing sources by the titanium dioxide directive. The national improvement plans required under the directive must set pollution reduction targets to be achieved by 1987. They must be submitted to the Commission, which is to submit proposals for harmonization of these programs. Other examples are presented by the major directives on waste (waste, toxic and hazardous waste, used oil) which fix only broad principles for the control mechanisms to be implemented by member states. Although the framework directive on waste and the waste oil directive do not give the Community any role in their implementation, the toxic wastes directive makes the task of supervising and coordinating member state waste disposal plans a joint Community/member state responsibility.

The ground water directive requires a member state to notify the Commission when it grants a regulatory exception allowing a discharge liable to cause ground water pollution. A similar requirement exists under the mercury directive. The SO_2 limit values, gas oil, and some water quality directives establish geographically differentiated standards but leave the zoning of areas to member states. They also establish extensive reporting requirements concerning the criteria applied in zoning. It is assumed that these reporting requirements will prevent member states from frustrating the objective of the directive by excessive creation of high pollution zones or insufficient creation of protected areas. Finally, the proposed regulation on the location of power plants in border areas does not set forth substantive criteria for the siting of nuclear and conventional power plants; rather, it attempts to coordinate member state policies by establishing a Community consultation procedure.

Here again, the greater Community role in implementation is motivated by the desire to offset the lack of agreement on detailed substantive standards for the relevant environmental sector. This approach uses the policy formulating activities of the member states as a basis for development of harmonized policies at the Community level. It may be a response to political disagreement as well as simply to the complexity of the relevant problem. For example, in the area of toxic wastes and ground water, it might have been difficult or premature to develop detailed Community standards in the absence of more exact knowledge about the problem in each member state.

The strategy of Community coordination of policies developed by member states may be illusory because without firm Community guidance the national measures may in fact be too different to allow real coordination. For example, national programs for list II substances under the aquatic environment directive give priority to so many different substances and control measures that the Commission is for practical purposes confined to collecting data from member states. However, the experience with some of the directives providing for area classification shows that reporting requirements may indeed have a coordinating effect.

2. Substantive Standards of Implementation

Apart from the cases just analyzed in which an environmental directive establishes criteria for its implementation, member states are in principle free to follow their political priorities and established administrative practices in implementing a directive. This division of labor between the Community and member states is articulated in Art. 189(3) of the EEC Treaty which accords member states a substantial degree of discretion in implementing a directive. Only in exceptional cases do Community rules limiting this discretion come into play.

One case is failure to implement a directive. Although it might be maintained that an isolated nonapplication or misapplication of an environmental directive (as incorporated into national law) by national authorities does not constitute an infringement of Art. 5 of the EEC Treaty,[5] it is clear that a member state is in violation of the Treaty when it does not take appropriate steps to ensure application of the directive, as for example, when it promulgates administrative guidelines or establishes an administrative practice inconsistent with the directive. A permanent failure to apply or enforce the directive clearly constitutes an infringement of the Treaty.

Furthermore, Articles 30 and 36 of the EEC Treaty may restrict member states' implementation of a product-related directive through measures such as national testing requirements, border inspections, and approval schemes that have the same effect as quantitative restrictions on trade. Here, the public policy (reasonableness) test developed by the European Court of Justice beginning with its decision in *Cassis de Dijon*[6] is applicable. It generally allows national regulation of products insofar as it is not a disguised restriction of trade but instead designed to protect health or the environment. Under this test the regulating state has a certain degree of discretion[7] in evaluating the risks of the product and determining the safety or quality objectives to be pursued

[5] Regarding misapplication of Art. 177 of the EEC Treaty by national courts *see* MERTENS DE WILMARS & VEROUGHSTRAETE, *Proceedings Against Member States for Failure to Fulfill Their Obligations?*, 7 COMMON MKT. L. REV. 385, 390 (1970); EVANS, *The Enforcement Procedure of Article 169 EEC: Commission Discretion*, 4 EUROPEAN L. REV. 442, 452–453 (1979) (stating that the Commission normally does not challenge isolated administrative decisions because they do not threaten the unity of the common market); *contra*, H.A.H. AUDRETSCH, SUPERVISION IN COMMUNITY LAW 64–65 (North Holland Publishing Co., Amsterdam 1978).

[6] Case 120/78, Rewe-Zentrale-AG v. Bundesmonopolverwaltung für Branntwein (*Cassis de Dijon*), [1979] ECR 649.

[7] As for the applicability of the *Cassis de Dijon* doctrine to the problem of the discretion left to member states in the implementation of a directive, *see* European Court of Justice, case 53/80, Officier van Justitie v. Koninklijke Kaasfabriek Eyssen BV (Nisin), [1981] ECR 409.

and the regulatory instruments to be used.[8] Consequently, national measures for implementing a product related directive are within the discretion of member states provided they are reasonable in light of the regulatory problem addressed by the directive. For example, some divergence in national requirements for testing the biodegradability of detergents not yet covered by a measurement directive or for testing toxic substances under the tiered procedure of directive 79/831/EEC does not violate the Treaty. Overall, the impact of Articles 30 and 36 of the EEC Treaty on implementation of environmental directives appears to be small.

3. The Commission as an Executive Authority

In rare cases, the Commission functions as an executive authority per se. Thus, under the titanium dioxide directive, the Commission's agreement must be sought when a member state desires not to include a particular existing source in the improvement program because the state considers the measures already implemented by the polluter to be sufficient. The sixth amendment to the 1967 hazardous substances directive entrusts the Commission with the major administrative tasks of compiling the inventory of existing substances and organizing the Community system of information exchange, although for the latter task controversies among member states as to the adequacy of data generated by the producer and reported to another member state will ultimately be decided by a management committee in an abbreviated procedure. The Commission role under the titanium dioxide directive may be explained as an extension of the "offset" approach – compensating for lack of substantive standards – described above. The Commission's administrative task under the sixth amendment is a novel one; it is a consequence of the common screening procedure for new chemicals established by the directive and the concomitant need for central administrative activities.

4. Supervision

Apart from these exceptional responsibilities for implementation and enforcement, the Commission is limited to its role as guardian of the Treaty (Art. 155 EEC Treaty). It is the member states which are primarily responsible for the incorporation, implementation, and enforcement of directives. Aside from some treaty provisions conferring general supervisory powers not normally relevant in the present context (except for Art. 93 of the EEC Treaty with respect to subsidies granted for investments to protect the environment), Art. 169 of the EEC Treaty is the fundamental provision granting the Community powers to supervise national incorporation, implementation, and enforcement activities. Oversight under this provision is political in that the Commission has some flexibility in interpreting the allegedly violated rules and deciding when

[8] *See* the *Nisin* case, *supra* note 7, and text *supra* at pp. 29–31.

to initiate administrative proceedings.[9] It also has some discretion in instituting judicial proceedings before the European Court of Justice when its own reasoned opinion finding a violation has not been complied with.[10] Although the method for ensuring observance of directives is flexible, it is legal in the formal sense that the European Court of Justice may ultimately pass on infringements. The emphasis of Commission enforcement activities regarding environmental protection is clearly on incorporation of directives into national law. While the Commission has instituted numerous infringement proceedings against member states for lack of appropriate legislative incorporation of environmental directives, there is not a single proceeding concerning administrative implementation and enforcement.[11] The infringement procedure is not well suited for this latter kind of problem: The existence of several layers of decisionmaking between the Commission and the ultimate actors, the lack of direct information concerning these actors, and the discretion of member states in implementing and enforcing environmental directives render the infringement procedure rather inefficient. In short, there is an undeniable discrepancy, inherent in the Community's constitutional structure, between adoption of harmonized legislation and implementation of such legislation.[12] The power of Community institutions effectively reaches as far as the incorporation of environmental directives into national law, which is in fact nothing other than the second part of the two tier Community lawmaking process. Except perhaps for the compliance with formal member state obligations, it does not reach the implementation and enforcement process. In parallel to the constitutional order of West Germany, the Community is indeed a supranational institution in the field of legislation, but only a "weak confederation" in the field of implementation and enforcement.

B. Role of Litigation

This section treats the role of litigation and of "subjective rights" in ensuring the effective implementation of harmonized environmental policies and laws.[13]

[9] European Court of Justice, case 9/75, Meyer-Burckhardt v. Commission, [1975] ECR 1171, 1187 (Opinion of Warner, Advocate-General); EVANS, *supra* note 5, at 445; SCHERMERS, *The Law as It Stands Against Treaty Violation by States*, 1 LEGAL ISSUES OF EUROPEAN INTEGRATION 111, 125 (1974); *contra*, H. SMIT & P. HERZOG, THE LAW OF THE EUROPEAN COMMUNITY, vol. 5, 321 (Matthew Bender, Albany 1976); H. A. H. AUDRETSCH, *supra* note 5, at 20, 179–180.

[10] European Court of Justice, case 7/71, Commission v. France, [1971] ECR 1003; EVERLING, *Die Mitgliedstaaten der Europäischen Gemeinschaft vor ihrem Gerichtshof*, 18 EUROPARECHT 101, 106 (1983); H. A. H. AUDRETSCH, *supra* note 5, at 36.

[11] *See* WEINSTOCK, *supra* note 2, at 22–23; EVANS, *supra* note 5, at 452–453.

[12] *See generally* Krislov, Ehlermann & Weiler, *Political Organs and the Decision-Making Process in the U.S. and the European Communities*, at §§ VI & VII.D.2, in INTEGRATION THROUGH LAW, Vol. 1, Book 2.

[13] For a survey of the available remedies *see* Jacobs & Karst, *The "Federal" Legal Order: The U.S.A. and Europe Compared – A Juridical Perspective*, at §§ III.A.1.b & III.A.2.b,

1. Litigation Initiated by Community Authorities

a. Litigation Against Member States

The infringement action under Art. 169 of the EEC Treaty is the Commission's judicial remedy against a member state for failure to incorporate, implement, or enforce environmental directives. It can also be used to review member state regulatory measures which violate Articles 30 and 36 of the EEC Treaty. The Art. 169 action may be instituted when a member state does not comply with the reasoned opinion issued by the Commission pursuant to Art. 169 finding a violation of that member state's obligations under the Treaty. These obligations of course include the duty to incorporate, implement, or enforce an environmental directive. Similar rules exist under Articles 38(3) and 143 of the Euratom Treaty.

Several legal limitations restrict the efficacy and availability of the infringement action.[14] Under Art. 169 of the EEC Treaty and the corresponding provisions of the Euratom Treaty, the European Court of Justice has no enforcement jurisdiction. It can only render a declaratory judgment or, in case of urgency, a declaratory interim injunction. Because of this restriction the member states are the ultimate guardians of the Treaty. Moreover, it is generally assumed that the Commission has discretion on whether to institute Court proceedings and that this decision is not reviewable at the request of an affected private party.[15] This discretion and restriction of standing constitute a central weakness of the infringement action and make it more a political than a legal device for securing compliance with the Treaty.

b. Litigation Against Regulated Firms

The Community can not directly enforce environmental directives against regulated firms. The enforcement of directives incorporated into national law is part of member states' obligation to enforce directives and is therefore their exclusive responsibility.

2. Privately Initiated Judicial Review of Community Implementation

Community institutions, apart from implementing a framework directive by issuing specific directives, play a rather limited role in implementation and enforcement of environmental directives. In some instances, the Commission has a coordinating function and may, if it finds member state implementation unsatisfactory, propose additional legislation to the Council. However, the Commission normally does not have executive powers. The titanium dioxide

in INTEGRATION THROUGH LAW, Vol. 1, Book 1; J. Weiler, Supranationalism Revisited – Retrospective and Prospective, EUI Working Paper No. 2, at 53 *et seq.;* H. G. SCHERMERS, JUDICIAL PROTECTION IN THE EUROPEAN COMMUNITIES (Kluwer, Deventer 1979).

[14] *See* MERTENS DE WILMARS & VEROUGHSTRAETE, *supra* note 5, at 385 *et seq.*

[15] European Court of Justice, cases 6 and 11/69, Commission v. French Republic, [1969] ECR 523, 542.

directive provides the only exception. Under this directive, the exclusion of an existing source from a member state improvement program requires the Commission's agreement, which is granted or refused by a decision addressed, pursuant to Art. 189(4) of the EEC Treaty, to the relevant member state. Finally, the Commission has the task of monitoring member state compliance with the obligations imposed by environmental directives, particularly the obligation to incorporate directives into national law. Because of the limited Community role in implementing harmonized environmental policies and the primary reliance on coordination and legislation where Community institutions do have a role, the potential scope for judicial review of Community action is also very limited.

a. Review by the European Court of Justice

Under Art. 173(1) of the EEC Treaty member states may challenge the legality, i. e. conformity with the Treaty, of implementing directives and Commission decisions. However, implementing directives are not directly subject to judicial review instituted by a private party. This is so even when the directive has direct legal effect and therefore resembles a regulation. Article 173(2) of the EEC Treaty allows review of a regulation at the request of private parties only where it is de facto an individual decision. The reviewability of directives can not extend further.[16] However, to the extent that Community measures can be reviewed by state courts, indirect review by the European Court of Justice under the preliminary ruling procedure (Art. 177 EEC Treaty) may be available. The restrictions on direct review expressed by the Treaty and reinforced by the Court make this type of joint state and Community court review of primary importance.[17]

The situation is only slightly different in the rare case of a Commission decision. Under Art. 173(2) decisions are generally reviewable on grounds of incompetence, infringement of an essential procedural requirement, infringement of the Treaty or any rule relating to its application, or misuse of powers. Article 175 of the Treaty extends this remedy to failure to make a decision. The action is also available for private parties affected by a Commission decision. However, the narrow standing criteria developed by the European Court of Justice have the effect of making judicial review of Commission decisions exceptional.[18]

[16] *See* European Court of Justice, cases 16 and 17/62, Fruit and vegetable cases, [1962] ECR 471; case 100/74, Société C.A.M. SA v. Commission, [1975] ECR 1393, 1403.

[17] J. Weiler, *supra* note 13, at 55.

[18] *See* STEIN & VINING, *Citizen Access to Judicial Review of Administrative Action in a Transnational and Federal Contex*, 70 AM. J. of INT'L L. 219 (1976); U. KOCH, DIE KLAGEBEFUGNIS DRITTER GEGENÜBER EUROPÄISCHEN ENTSCHEIDUNGEN GEMÄSS ART. 173 ABS. 2 EWG-VERTRAG (Peter Lang, Frankfurt, Bern 1978); A. W. GREEN, POLITICAL INTEGRATION BY JURISPRUDENCE – THE WORK OF THE COURT OF JUSTICE of the EUROPEAN COMMUNITIES IN EUROPEAN POLITICAL INTEGRATION 107 *et seq.* (Sijthoff, Leyden 1969).

Under Art. 173(2), a third party is accorded standing only where the relevant decision is of "direct and individual concern" to that party. It is true that violation of a legally protected interest is not necessary for standing to be granted. A plaintiff may assert violation of a legal rule designed solely to protect public interests. The plaintiff need not even assert interests arguably within the zone of interests protected by the particular directive.[19] The prerequisite of "direct" concern is also liberally interpreted. In particular, a decision may be addressed to a state, but nevertheless directly concern a private party.[20]

However, the European Court of Justice has interpreted the prerequisite of "individual" concern very narrowly.[21] It is necessary that the plaintiff (and at most a small number of other persons) be affected in a specific way that distinguishes the plaintiff from other persons affected by the decision. Thus, an importer affected by abolition of a customs tariff or by a price-fixing decision was held not to be individually concerned because all other importers were also affected by the decision.[22] In contrast, a decision affecting only importers who had already concluded contracts was held to be of individual concern.[23] Under these criteria, it is probable that the plaintiffs in the two pending, but presently dormant, titanium dioxide cases would have been granted standing.[24] In these cases the plaintiffs challenged the legality of a Commission decision addressed to a member state in which the Commission refused to agree to the exclusion of the plaintiffs from the member state improvement program. That the decision was addressed to a member state does not necessarily rule out a conclusion that it directly concerns the enterprises whose inclusion in the improvement plan is at issue.[25] They are individually concerned because the decision affects only the two individual enterprises rather than a larger group. However, it should be emphasized that this is an exceptional case that does not invalidate the general proposition that access of individuals to the Eu-

[19] European Court of Justice, cases 83 and 94/76, 4, 15 and 40/77, Skimmed milk powder, [1978] ECR 1209; cases 116 and 124/77, Isoglucose, [1979] ECR 3497; case 238/78, Ireks-Arkady GmbH v. Council and Commission, [1979] ECR 2955.

[20] European Court of Justice, cases 106 and 107/63, Toepfer v. Commission, [1965] ECR 405; case 62/70, Bock, [1971] ECR 897, at 907; cases 41–44/70, NV International Fruit Co. v. Commission, [1971] ECR 411; case 26/76, Metro v. Commission, [1977] ECR 1875; case 100/74, C.A.M. SA v. Commission, [1975] ECR 1393.

[21] European Court of Justice, case 25/62, Plaumann v. Commission, [1963] ECR 95; case 38/64, Getreide-Import v. Commission, [1965] ECR 203; case 113/77, NTN Toyo Bearing Co. Ltd. v. Council, [1979] ECR 1185, at 1205; case 139/79, Isoglucose, [1980] ECR 3393.

[22] Plaumann, *supra* note 21.

[23] Toepfer, *supra* note 20.

[24] Pending case 78/79, BTP Tioxide Ltd. v. Commission, pending case 79/79, Laporte Industries Ltd. v. Commission, OJ No. C 153, 20 June 1979, p.5.

[25] *Cf.* European Court of Justice, case 730/79, Philip Morris Holland BV, [1980] ECR 2671 (recipient of national subsidy which the Commission had refused to authorize under Art. 93 of the EEC Treaty was granted standing).

ropean Court of Justice is extremely restricted.[26] For example, it is highly improbable that a manufacturer would be granted standing to challenge a Commission decision not to include a chemical in the inventory of existing chemicals compiled under the sixth amendment to the 1967 hazardous substances directive. The consequence of such exclusion is that registration as a new substance would be required. Standing would be denied because the decision concerns a whole group of producers.

Also, the European Court of Justice does not grant associations standing. There are some older cases decided under the European Coal and Steel Community Treaty that accorded standing to associations representing members which, when suing as individuals, would have standing. More recent cases have taken the contrary position, reasoning that associations by their nature can not be individually affected by decisions concerning their members and that aggregating the interests of the members is not acceptable.[27]

The distinction drawn by the European Court of Justice between individual and group concerns as well as the rejection of association suits has been sharply criticized.[28] A speculative explanation is that the Court, by limiting direct access of plaintiffs, is pursuing a deliberate policy of becoming the appellate court for the Community and leaving national courts the role of first reviewing national measures implementing the Community measure to be potentially challenged.

With respect to the Commission's supervision of member state implementation of directives, it is established law that the Commission has discretion whether to institute court infringement proceedings under Art. 169 and that this decision is not reviewable at the request of an affected private party.[29] However, it is another question whether the Commission can be compelled by a private party to institute the Art. 169 administrative infringement proceedings preceding court action. The wording of Art. 169(1) of the EEC Treaty seems to support the view that the Commission is under a legal duty to institute administrative proceedings for infringement of the Treaty and that only the institution of court proceedings, as one means of remedying an infringement, is at its discretion. If so, refusal to institute administrative proceedings would be appealable by an individual affected by the infringement, provided

[26] *See* J. Seybold, Das Individuum vor dem Gerichtshof der Europäischen Gemeinschaften 132 (Unpublished Thesis, Würzburg 1971).

[27] Case 8/55, Fédération Charbonnière de Belgique v. High Authority of the ECSC (Fédéchar), [1954–56] ECR 245; cases 16 and 17/62, Fruit and vegetable cases, [1962] ECR 471; case 175/73, Union syndicale v. Council, [1974] ECR 917, at 925; case 72/74, Union syndicale v. Council, [1975] ECR 401, at 409–410.

[28] Especially by Stein & Vining, *supra* note 18; A. W. Green, *supra* note 18; Rasmussen, *Why is Article 173 Interpreted Against Private Plaintiffs?*, 5 European L. Rev. 112 *et seq.* (1980].

[29] European Court of Justice, case 30/59, Limburg v. High Authority of the ECSC, [1961] ECR 1; case 48/65, Lütticke GmbH v. Commission, [1966] ECR 19, 40.

that the individual meets the narrow standing criteria established by the European Court of Justice.[30]

b. Review by State Courts

Member state courts can indirectly review action taken by Community institutions for implementation and enforcement of environmental directives. Special directives or decisions can not be voided by a member state court because they are issued by authorities over which the European Court of Justice has exclusive jurisdiction (Art. 183 EEC Treaty). However, where a special directive or decision requires further implementation by member states, the implementing measures may be challenged before state courts. This gives state courts, pursuant to Art. 177 of the EEC Treaty, the opportunity of indirectly reviewing the validity of the directive or decision.[31] The state court can find that the relevant Community directive or decision is inconsistent with a framework directive or the Treaty. For example, a special directive for the implementation of a framework directive may become subject to indirect member state court review, irrespective of whether the member state has incorporated the directive, when a state agency has based a decision on the directive and the addressee of the decision challenges the conformity of the special directive and the national decision with the framework directive or the Treaty. In this situation the state court may indirectly review the directive's validity or may – or perhaps even must – refer the matter to the European Court of Justice for a preliminary ruling pursuant to Art. 177 of the EEC Treaty. On the whole, however, member state court review of Community environmental law has little practical importance.

3. Privately Initiated Administrative and Judicial Review of State Implementation[32]

a. State Law

Review under state law of administrative implementation and enforcement has the objective of ensuring that environmental directives as incorporated

[30] The decision of the European Court of Justice, cases 6 and 11/69, Commission v. French Republic, [1969] ECR 523, 542 (denying the appealability of a reasoned opinion at the request of the affected state), is not in point because here the Court argued that the reasoned opinion was an integral part of the infringement proceeding and that the affected state could have the Court scrutinize its consistency with the Treaty in the court proceedings following the state's failure to comply with the reasoned opinion; *cf.* H. A. H. Audretsch, *supra* note 5, at 25. *But see* European Court of Justice, case 246/81, William, Lord Bethel v. Commission, [1982] ECR 2277 (no standing for an individual to require the Commission to institute proceedings against a third party for violation of EC antitrust law).

[31] *See, e. g.*, European Court of Justice, case 106/77, Amministrazione delle Finanze dello Stato v. Simmenthal S.p.A., [1978] ECR 629.

[32] The following analysis is primarily based on E. Rehbinder, Right of Associations and other Legal and Natural Persons to Sue in Cases concerned with the Protection of

into national law are appropriately applied. Such review may take place by public participation in administrative proceedings and later in the implementation process by administrative and judicial review of official action. Although primarily designed to safeguard individual rights against the state and to control the proper functioning of the national administration, review under state law indirectly contributes to enforcement of directives. Given the prominent role of member states in implementing and enforcing environmental directives, it may even be the most important device for enforcing environmental directives. However, a major complication is the great diversity in member state legal systems.

i. Public Participation in Administrative Proceedings

To begin to understand the law applying to participation in administrative proceedings, the types of administrative decisions must be distinguished. Generally speaking, public participation in Europe focuses on individual decisions rather than on administrative rulemaking. Many member states have established advisory councils which are to be consulted on proposed administrative action and in which environmental interests often have some representation. Along with informal participation of selected interest groups, these advisory councils are extensively used in administrative rulemaking. These represent weak forms of participation, however, because the administration retains wide discretion.

With respect to individual decisions, some states, especially Italy (except for the province of Bolzano), do not provide for substantial citizen participation in environmental decisionmaking. Others limit citizen participation to the

the Environment under the Law of the Member States of the European Economic Community, Report submitted to the Commission of the European Communities, ENV. 738/77 (1977 – not published). *See also* J. M. AUBY & M. FROMONT, LES RECOURS CONTRE LES ACTES ADMINISTRATIFS DANS LES PAYS DE LA COMMUNAUTÉ EUROPÉENNE (Dalloz, Paris 1971); Despax, *Défense collective de l'environnement et recevabilité des actions en matière de pollution transfrontalière,* in ENVIRONMENTAL PROTECTION IN FRONTIER REGIONS 199, 208 *et seq.* (OECD, Paris 1979); DUE PROCESS IN THE ADMINISTRATIVE PROCEDURE, vol. 3 (Fédération Internationale pour le Droit Européen, Copenhagen 1978); OECD Secretariat, *Equal Right of Access in Matters of Transboundary Pollution,* in LEGAL ASPECTS OF TRANSFRONTIER POLLUTION 54 (OECD, Paris 1977); R. LUMMERT & V. THIEM, RECHTE DES BÜRGERS ZUR VERHÜTUNG UND ZUM ERSATZ VON UMWELTSCHÄDEN 43 *et seq.* (Berichte 3/80 des Umweltbundesamtes, Erich Schmidt Verlag, Berlin 1980); R. MACRORY & M. LAFONTAINE, PUBLIC INQUIRY AND ENQUÊTE PUBLIQUE, FORMS OF PUBLIC PARTICIPATION IN ENGLAND AND FRANCE (Environmental Data Services Ltd., London 1982); LEGAL PROTECTION AGAINST THE EXECUTIVE, vols. 1–3 (H. Mosler ed., Max–Planck–Institut für ausländisches öffentliches und Völkerrecht, Heidelberg 1969–71); ENVIRONMENTAL POLLUTION AND INDIVIDUAL RIGHTS (S. McCaffrey & R. Lutz eds., Kluwer, Deventer 1978); T. OPPERMANN & M. KILIAN, GLEICHSTELLUNG AUSLÄNDISCHER GRENZNACHBARN IN DEUTSCHEN UMWELTVERFAHREN? 52 *et seq.* (Berichte 8/81 des Umweltbundesamtes, Erich Schmidt Verlag, Berlin 1981); THE PROTECTION OF THE INDIVIDUAL IN RELATION TO ACTS OF ADMINISTRATIVE AUTHORITIES (Council of Europe, Strasbourg 1975).

making of written or oral objections (the "public inquiry" procedure as used particularly in France and Belgium), sometimes accompanied by a discretionary "public meeting" (as in France for major projects, especially those subject to environmental impact assessment). Finally, there are states such as the United Kingdom, West Germany, and the Netherlands whose law or administrative practice provide, at least for major projects, an opportunity to make objections and participate in a subsequent public hearing. Even here there are significant differences. For example, in West Germany the hearing is normally on the objections only whereas in the United Kingdom its scope may be broader. The extent of advance notice of proposed administrative action normally depends on the kind of participation allowed and the nature of standing requirements, but some states have information statutes providing access to public files independent of particular proceedings.[33]

These general procedural systems are subject to many exceptions and variations. In each member state there are environmental decisions not subject to any participation or subject to a form of participation other than that usually provided. Participation requirements generally vary according to substantive environmental law. For example, participation in formulation of development plans is quite extensive; the laws regulating air and noise pollution and nuclear installations permit less broad participation; and participation under water law and frequently under waste disposal law is rather restricted. These differences may be justified by the varying impact of the different decisions, i. e. effects on the general population, on neighbors, or only on specific water users, but they are hardly reconcilable with the modern conception of environmental law as a means for protecting and enhancing the environment in the long term interest of all people.

Standing to participate in environmental proceedings is generally broad. However, there are considerable differences among member states and even within a particular state depending upon the type of environmental statute involved. Property owners and occupiers, neighbors, municipal residents, and even the general public may be entitled to participate in the proceeding. Standing does not necessarily correspond to the kind and extent of participation granted by a particular statute. For example, it does not necessarily follow that standing is granted more generously whenever the procedures provided are more informal or restricted in scope. The Netherlands, United Kingdom and recently also France offer the broadest access to environmental proceedings.[34]

[33] *Denmark*: Act on Access of the Public to Documents in Administrative Files, Act No. 280 of 10 June 1970, 1980 Official Journal at 708; *see also* Holm, *Danish Report*, in Due Process, *supra* note 32, at 3.4 *et seq.*; *France*: Law No. 78–753, 1978 J. O. 2851 (18 July 1978); *Netherlands*: Act of 1978 on Public Access to the Administration, 1978 Staatsblad No. 571 (in force since 1 May 1980).

[34] In the Netherlands, Articles 20–22, 28, and 38 of the Environmental Protection Act of 1979 (Wet allgemene bepalingen milieuhygiene) (1979 Staatsblad No. 442), now in principle grant everybody standing to participate in administrative proceedings. This statute replaces standing provisions in special statutes that had partially limited standing to interested parties. *See* K. von Moltke & N. Visser, Die Rolle der Um-

Almost all states accord anyone standing to participate in preparation of development plans. Many grant equally broad standing, although sometimes on a discretionary basis, for proceedings relating to major polluting installations (except for water pollution proceedings) and public facilities. Others limit standing in such proceedings to neighbors.

Added complexity is presented by the rules governing the standing of organizations to participate. When the relevant statute grants standing to anyone, associations may avail themselves of the rights of the individual. In all other cases standing of associations is usually narrower than that of individuals, although neighbors' associations are usually entitled to participate or are at least allowed on a discretionary basis.

There are great differences among member states in the treatment of associations specifically created to promote environmental goals. In West Germany public interest organizations are normally allowed to participate in proceedings concerning the preparation of development plans, the siting of major polluting installations, and the siting of public facilities. Certain associations have statutory standing with respect to major projects generally affecting nature and landscape or specific nature reserves and national parks.[35] In the United Kingdom, apart from proceedings open to anyone (development plans, decisions on waste disposal sites and, in the future, water permits), associations may be and in practice often are admitted as third parties to public hearings at the discretion of the hearing examiner.[36] The Netherlands grants standing to anyone and hence to any public interest organization to participate in administrative proceedings concerning the environment.[37] Belgium, France, and Italy,

WELTSCHUTZVERBÄNDE IM POLITISCHEN ENTSCHEIDUNGSPROZESS DER NIEDERLANDE 82 *et seq.* (E. Schmidt Verlag, Berlin 1982); Kok, *Netherlands Report*, in DUE PROCESS, *supra* note 32, at 9.8–9. Furthermore, Art. 23 of the Town and Country Planning Act of 1962 accords anyone standing in planning procedures.

In the United Kingdom, the Town and Country Planning Act 1971, especially §§ 9(3), 12–14 on structure and local plans, § 29(2) on "bad-neighbourhood" development, and Administrative Guidelines on development conflicting with an existing plan allow for broad citizen participation (*see* Hamilton, *Recourse for Environmental Harm – England*, in ENVIRONMENTAL POLLUTION AND INDIVIDUAL RIGHTS, *supra* note 32, at 30 *et seq.*; R. MACRORY & M. LAFONTAINE, *supra* note 32, at 28 *et seq.*, 34 *et seq.*, 43 *et seq.*).

In France, the recent Law No. 83–630 of 12 July 1983 concerning the democratization of public inquiries and the protection of the environment, 1983 J. O. p. 2156 (13 July 1983), Art. 4, accords anyone access to procedures or projects subject to a public inquiry, which includes all projects likely to have an adverse impact on the environment.

[35] § 29 Protection of Nature Act of 20 Dec. 1976, 1976 BGBl I at 3574.

[36] Hamilton, *supra* note 34, at 31; D. A. BIGHAM, THE LAW AND ADMINISTRATION RELATING TO PROTECTION OF THE ENVIRONMENT 15 (Oyez Publications, London 1973).

[37] Articles 20–22, 28, and 38, Environmental Protection Act of 1979, *supra* note 34, which consolidates previous administrative practice and special legislation. *See also* authors cited *supra* note 34.

which do not have a strong tradition of participation, at first glance seem much less liberal. However, in Belgium any association may make objections in proceedings subject to the requirement of a public inquiry since they are open to everybody. Such proceedings include those involving major polluting installations and development plans.[38] In France, any association may participate in the permit proceedings concerning classified installations and in proceedings concerning projects subject to environmental impact assessment; a recent law seems to grant associations access to all proceedings on projects subject to a public inquiry, a category which includes projects likely to have an adverse impact on the environment.[39] Under the Building Code, recognized associations have standing in proceedings concerning local zoning, although not in those concerning regional zoning.[40] The Protection of Nature Act provides that such associations may be allowed to participate in proceedings at the discretion of the deciding authority.[41] Except for land use plans, Denmark used to confine participation to local associations, but a recent amendment to its Environmental Protection Act accords four national associations standing in a number of particular substantive areas.[42] Italy in principle denies standing to associations.[43]

ii. Judicial and Administrative Review

There are substantial differences among member states in the extent to which they rely upon administrative versus judicial review of administrative action. Judicial review of administrative action relating to the environment is unimportant or even unavailable in the United Kingdom, Denmark, and the Netherlands. In these countries administrative review is in practice the decisive method for controlling the legality of environmental decisionmaking. In West Germany, France, Belgium, and Italy the situation is more or less the reverse, although all these states also provide for administrative review. Despite the differences between the two control devices, especially those regarding the status of the persons deciding the appeal and the scope of review, they are to a large extent functionally equivalent, especially where (as in the Netherlands and

[38] *See* Conseil d'État, 13 Oct. 1959, Hollaert, 1959 Recueil des décisions du Conseil d'État No. 7.282; E. Rehbinder, *supra* note 32, at 340 *et seq.*

[39] *See supra*, note 34; previously standing existed at least to the same extent as for judicial review; *see* E. Rehbinder, *supra* note 32, at 116–117, and *infra* note 56.

[40] Art. L. 121–8 Code de l'urbanisme, introduced by Art. 8, Act. No. 76–1285 of 31 Dec. 1976 portant réforme de l'urbanisme, 1977 J. O. p. 4 (1 Jan. 1977).

[41] Art. 40 II Law No. 76–629 of 10 July 1976 concerning the Protection of Nature, 1976 J. O. p. 4203 (13 July 1976).

[42] Art. 74 II–V, 80 of the Environmental Protection Act as amended by the Law No. 204 of 18 May 1982, 1982 Official Journal p. 471. For the previous law *see* C. H. Jensen, Law and Practice Relating to Pollution Control in Denmark 24 *et seq.* (Graham & Trotman, London, 2d ed. 1982). Art. 24 II, 58 Protection of Nature Act of 1972 had recognized association standing in the field of protection of nature.

[43] *See* E. Rehbinder, *supra* note 32, at 427, 432–433, 437–438.

Denmark) administrative review may be considered quasi-judicial. In general, the available remedies in all member states are more or less sufficient to ensure ex post facto review of individual decisions. However, in many member states administrative rules and programs are subject to review only in the context of challenges to an individual decision based on such rule or program.[44]

Problems arise when an appellant or plaintiff wishes to stay execution of the challenged decision pending review. With the exception of West Germany, the Netherlands, and to some extent Denmark, the member states do not automatically suspend a decision while an appeal or suit is pending. Most states, however, permit some preliminary injunctive relief to be granted. The criteria for granting such relief vary, particularly with respect to the relevance of the merits of the case.

iii. Standing to Secure Review

The principles governing access to higher authorities, tribunals, or courts to secure administrative or judicial review vary widely. With respect to administrative review, the procedural law or specific environmental statutes of many states (France, Belgium, and the Netherlands) allow anyone or, somewhat more narrowly, any objector, i. e. any person who made objections in the preceding administrative proceedings, to appeal the resulting decision.[45] If, as is often the case, the group of persons having standing to participate in administrative proceedings is large, this approach, as a practical matter, permits general citizen suits. The Netherlands now openly recognizes citizen actions. But such liberal standing principles have little significance in states, such as France, where administrative review is little used. Other states (West Germany, Denmark, and Italy) normally limit administrative (as well as judicial) standing to neighbors.[46] The United Kingdom is extremely restrictive. Third parties may not appeal a decision granting an application; however, the applicant can appeal a negative decision, and then there is broad participation of third parties.[47]

Standing to secure judicial review is generally accorded to neighbors whose property, health, or immediate living environment is affected by the challenged administrative decision. The general interest of an individual in environmental

[44] A notable exception is France; *see* Conseil d'État, 26 June 1959, Syndicat Général des Ingénieurs–Conseils, 1959 DALLOZ JURISPRUDENCE 541.

[45] *France:* Conseil d'État, 23 Nov. 1962, Association des anciens élèves de l'Institut commercial de Nancy, 1962 Recueil des décisions du Conseil d'État 625; *Belgium:* Conseil d'État, 20 Jan. 1980, Bond Beter Leefmilieu–Interenvironnement, 1980 Recueil des décisions du Conseil d'État No. 20.021; *Netherlands:* Art. 44, 49 Environmental Protection (General Rules) Act; *see* K. VON MOLTKE & N. VISSER, *supra* note 34, at 84. *See also* Kok, *supra* note 34, at 9.9.

[46] *West Germany:* F. KOPP, VERWALTUNGSGERICHTSORDNUNG § 69 note 6 (C. H. Beck, München, 5th ed. 1981); *Denmark:* C. H. JENSEN, *supra* note 42, at 28 *et seq.*; *Italy:* A. SANDULLI, MANUALE DI DIRITTO AMMINISTRATIVO 661 *et seq.* (E. Jovene, Naples, 10th ed. 1969).

[47] D. A. BIGHAM, *supra* note 36, at 14–15; Hamilton, *supra* note 34, at 32.

protection does not normally confer standing, nor does European law grant standing based on mere "injury in fact."

In France and, to some extent Italy, neighbors to a polluting installation or public facility can also assert, as an encroachment upon their living environment, violation of a statute exclusively designed to protect the public interest (such as a statue for the protection of nature or landscape). France also grants standing to persons who are affected by environmental harm in a more diffuse way, e. g. as inhabitants of a residential neighborhood.[48] However, persons who merely visit a place for recreation and other transients do not generally have standing to challenge the legality of an administrative decision affecting the environment.

In other states the standing criteria for judicial review are much narrower. This is especially true of the United Kingdom and West Germany. In the United Kingdom it is still doubtful whether a neighbor to a source of pollution would always have standing, although recent cases evidence a trend towards liberalization of the traditionally narrow standing criteria.[49] West Germany normally limits standing to persons who assert infringement of environmental statutes designed to protect individual interests, thereby limiting relief in planning law and almost completely excluding private suits in areas like protection of nature, landscape, water resources, and recreation.[50] Moreover, under some West German environmental laws a plaintiff who has not participated in the preceding administrative proceedings will be denied standing to seek judicial review. In Italy, persons who are not neighbors are generally denied standing on the ground that they are affected only in a diffuse manner, as a member of a larger group.

[48] *See* PRIEUR, *Le recours devant les juridictions administratives en matière d'installations classées pour la protection de l'environnement*, 1978 REVUE JURIDIQUE DE L'ENVIRONNEMENT 121, 123 *et seq.;* E. Rehbinder, *supra* note 32, at 136 *et seq.;* M. DESPAX, LE DROIT DE L'ENVIRONNEMENT 42 *et seq.*, 814 *et seq.* (Librairies techniques, Paris 1980); R. LUMMERT & V. THIEM, *supra* note 32, at 71–72.

[49] This seems to depend on the remedy (in spite of the attempt of Order 53 of the Rules of the Supreme Court to establish the requirement of "sufficient interest" as the unique standing criterion at least for common law remedies). *Cf.* HARLOW, *Note,* 1978 PUBLIC LAW 1. *See* R. v. Henderson R. D. C. *ex parte* Chorley, (1933) 2 K. B. 696 (certiorari); Gregory v. Camden L. B. C., (1966) 1 W. L. R. 899 (declaration); Turner v. Sec. of State of Environment, (1973) 228 ESTATE GAZETTE 355 (planning appeal); R. v. Hammersmith & Fulham B. C. *ex parte* People Before Profit Ltd., (1982) 80 LOCAL GOVERNMENT REPORTS 322, a planning appeal case, now has considerably liberalized the standing criteria by requiring, to qualify as a "person aggrieved," only a "legitimate bona fide reason," which might include people who visited the place for holiday and even "ideological" objectors. *See* R. MACRORY & M. LAFONTAINE, *supra* note 32, at 58.

[50] Bundesverwaltungsgericht, 16 July 1980, 1981 NEUE JURISTISCHE WOCHENSCHRIFT 362. *See* Rehbinder, *German Report,* in ENVIRONMENTAL POLLUTION AND INDIVIDUAL RIGHTS, *supra* note 32, at 41–42, 45 *et seq.;* R. LUMMERT & V. THIEM, *supra* note 32, at 69–70.

The European law of standing for associations is varied, but the dominant tendency, particularly in West Germany, Italy, and the United Kingdom, is individual oriented.

In West Germany, associations can only assert their own "personal" interests; any other claims are strictly disallowed.[51] Various proposals have been made in West Germany to statutorily create standing at the federal level for public interest associations in politically sensitive areas such as nuclear energy and nature protection law. These proposals have so far been unsuccessful. However, some of the German states (Länder) have introduced an association suit in the field of protection of nature and landscape. In Italy a decision rendered by a chamber of the supreme administrative court,[52] which had held that a national public interest organization (Italia Nostra) had standing to secure judicial review of administrative decisions regarding protection of nature, has been reversed by the united chambers of the Court of Cassation.[53] The United Kingdom, however, shows at least some tendency toward recognition of the association suit[54] and freely allows association appeals in administrative review proceedings.

Belgium allows appeals and suits by associations representing individuals who independently have standing.[55] France, the Netherlands, and recently also Denmark go beyond that. In France, representation of individuals who would have standing is not necessary; it suffices that the association represents, by virtue of its charter, interests which are encompassed by the statute allegedly violated.[56] The Netherlands now generally accords environmental associations standing.[57] Denmark used to limit standing to groups representing individuals who would have standing as individuals but, as already mentioned, recently

[51] Bundesverwaltungsgericht, *supra* note 50. *See* E. Rehbinder, *supra* note 32, at 43–44, 51; R. LUMMERT & V. THIEM, *supra* note 32, at 87–88.

[52] Consiglio di Stato, Sezione V, 9 March 1973, No. 253, Associazione "Italia Nostra," 1974 FORO ITALIANO III, 33.

[53] Corte di Cassazione, Sezioni unite civili, Provincia autonoma di Trento c. Associazione "Italia Nostra," 8 May 1978, No. 2207, 1978 FORO ITALIANO I, 1090 (with annotation by C. M. Barone).

[54] Turner v. Sec. of State of the Environment, *supra* note 49.

[55] Conseil d'État, 25 Nov. 1969, 1969 Recueil des décisions du Conseil d'État No. 13802; 11 Feb. 1977, 1977 Recueil des décisions du Conseil d'État No. 18101.

[56] The previous practice of the French Conseil d'État has been codified in Art. 40 III, Protection of Nature Act, *supra* note 41. With respect to polluting installations where the standing criteria used to be narrower (Conseil d'État, 3 November 1972, consorts Reulos, 1972 Droit administratif 380), standing has also been broadened by Art. 14, Act No. 76–663 of 19 July 1976 sur les installations classées pour la protection de l'environnement, 1976 J. O. p. 4320 (20 July 1976). *See* Conseil d'État, 26 July 1978, Ministre de la Qualité de Vie c. Sieur Tissandier, 1978 DROIT ADMINISTRATIF 320; E. Rehbinder, *supra* note 32, at 139 *et seq.*

[57] This follows from the concept of the Environmental Protection (General Rules) Act, *supra* notes 34 and 45, which accords anybody standing in administrative proceedings and any objector in review proceedings.

accorded four major national organizations standing in a number of specific areas.[58]

iv. Scope of Review

The differences in the scope of review in member states appear, at least at first glance, even more fundamental than those already discussed.[59] Here the distinction between administrative and judicial review becomes relevant. Administrative review is generally full review of the merits. Where, however, administrative review is quasi-judicial as in the Netherlands and to some extent Denmark, the scope of review is very similar to that of judicial review. With respect to judicial review, West Germany and Belgium accord broad review powers to the courts, while the United Kingdom and to a lesser degree France are reluctant to allow review of the merits. However, a broad scope of judicial review exists in France with respect to major polluting installations.

v. Conclusions

The conclusions to be drawn about the controls exercised under state law by state agencies and courts over implementation of Community environmental directives are far from encouraging from the viewpoint of harmonization. It is true that there is a common core of basic controls in all member states. Moreover, the net functional differences among member states are narrower than the formal ones. For example, states that grant their courts broad review powers are not identical with those having liberal standing requirements, and vice versa. Indeed, although this is an overstatement, it may be concluded that narrow review powers and narrow standing criteria are two functionally equivalent mechanisms for limiting the number of environmental decisions subject to effective review and that member states use either one or the other mechanism. Nevertheless, the variations among the legal systems of member states remain considerable. It would be an oversimplification to explain these variations by the classic distinction of common and civil law systems.[60] Far more important than this distinction are the differences in development of the relevant political societies, in the relationship between citizen and administration, the power of the executive branch, and the relationship between public and private interest.[61] The consequence of these various differences is that the uniform application of directives, one of the central predicates of the Com-

[58] Articles 74 II–V, 80 II Environmental Protection Act as amended, *supra* note 42; Articles 24 II, 58 Protection of Nature Act, *supra* note 42.

[59] *See* J. M. Auby & M. Fromont, *supra* note 32, at 88 *et seq.*, 167 *et seq.*, 239 *et seq.*, 316 *et seq.*, 402 *et seq.*; H. W. Rengeling, Rechtsgrundsätze beim Verwaltungsvollzug des Europäischen Gemeinschaftsrechts 252 *et seq.* (Carl Heymanns Verlag, Köln 1977).

[60] *See* Rivero, *Vers un Droit Commun Européen: Nouvelles Perspectives en Droit Administratif*, in New Perspectives for a Common Law of Europe 389 *et seq.* (M. Cappelletti ed., Sijthof, Leyden, London, Boston 1978).

[61] J. Weiler, *supra* note 13, at 75.

munity, can not be ensured by review exercised under state law. Uniform or at least roughly equivalent control over the implementation and enforcement of environmental directives would require, at a minimum, comparable remedies, standing criteria, and court powers in all member states. These requirements are far from being fulfilled in the Community.

European Community law does not offer principles which, in the interest of uniform application of directives, could be used to correct these variations among the administrative procedure laws of member states. The European Court of Justice has repeatedly held that in the present state of development of Community law, and especially in view of member states' responsibility to implement Community law, member states are in principle free to apply their domestic administrative procedure law, provided it does not discriminate against foreigners, is not unreasonable, and does not entirely preclude judicial review.[62] In particular, the Court has not recognized any affirmative obligation to provide effective judicial review. This jurisprudence can be explained by the great diversity of national rules, the consequent lack of common principles, and the Court's preference for harmonization via Articles 100 and 235 of the EEC Treaty rather than harmonization by the Court at the lowest common denominator.[63]

[62] European Court of Justice, case 33/76, Rewe v. Landwirtschaftskammer, [1976] ECR 1989; case 45/76, Comet v. Produktschap voor Siergewassen, [1976] ECR 2043; case 13/68, SpA Salgoil v. Italian Ministry for Foreign Trade, [1968] ECR 453; case 811/79, Amministrazione delle finanze dello stato v. Arieta SpA, [1980] ECR 2545; case 93/71, Leonesio v. Italian Ministry for Agriculture and Forestry, [1972] ECR 287; case 61/79, Amministrazione delle finanze dello stato v. Denkavit Italiana S.r.l., [1980] ECR 1205; case 68/79, Just v. Danish Ministry for Fiscal Affairs, [1980] ECR 501; case 265/78, Ferwerda BV, [1980] ECR 617; cases 66, 127 and 128/79, Salumi, [1980] ECR 1237; case 130/79, Express Dairy Foods Ltd. v. Intervention Board for Agricultural Produce, [1980] ECR 1887; case 158/80, Rewe v. Hauptzollamt Kiel (Butterfahrten), [1981] ECR 1805. In the case of subsidies, state law may entirely deny a remedy to an unsuccessful applicant. *See* case 152/79, Kevin Lee v. Minister for Agriculture, [1980] ECR 1495. For decisions in the same line of cases concerning prescription of claims for restitution of subsidies unlawfully received, *see id.;* cases 119 and 126/79, Lippische Hauptgenossenschaft e. G. v. Bundesanstalt (Denaturierungsprämien), [1980] ECR 1863. *See* Bebr, *Community Report*, in REMEDIES FOR BREACH OF COMMUNITY LAW 10.5–6 (Fédération Internationale pour le Droit Européen, London 1980); Rengeling, *Europäisches Gemeinschaftsrecht und nationaler Rechtsschutz – unter besonderer Berücksichtigung der Rechtsprechung des Europäischen Gerichtshofs und der deutschen Gerichte*, in DAS EUROPA DER ZWEITEN GENERATION, GEDÄCHTNISSCHRIFT FÜR C. SASSE, vol. 1, 197, 201 *et seq.* (R. Bieber, A. Bleckmann & F. Capotorti eds., Nomos Verlag, Baden–Baden 1981) (in favor of broader limits on national procedure law); J. Weiler, *supra* note 13, at 73–74 (ditto); Hilf, *Möglichkeiten und Grenzen des Rückgriffs auf nationale verwaltungsrechtliche Regeln bei der Durchführung des Gemeinschaftsrechts*, in EUROPÄISCHES VERWALTUNGSRECHT IM WERDEN 67, 76 *et seq.* (J. Schwarze ed., Nomos Verlag, Baden–Baden, 1982) (more cautious).

[63] *See* Hilf, *supra* note 62, at 89 *et seq.*

However, in evaluating the differences between legal systems, it must be remembered that there are many other informal means of influencing administrative environmental decisions besides exercise of legal rights. The political culture of a country has perhaps a much greater impact on environmental protection than statutes and court cases. Therefore, an exclusively juridical evaluation is perhaps insufficient.

b. Community Law

i. The Direct Effect and Standard of Review Doctrines

There is no Community court system comparable to that existing in developed federal states.[64] The European Court of Justice does not have competence to decide at the request of a member state citizen whether state incorporation, implementation, and enforcement of environmental directives are legal and particularly whether they conform with the relevant directive. Nor is the Court a sort of Community court of appeal which can decide on appeals against member state court decisions on these questions. Rather, the primary responsibility for reviewing state incorporation, implementation, and enforcement of environmental directives is vested in member state courts.

Jurisdiction of the member state courts can be invoked only under the same conditions (e. g., type of action subject to challenge, standing, scope of review) as applicable to governmental action based on nonharmonized national law. Normally, state courts exercise their review powers by applying domestic law. However, where the question is raised of whether a particular national statute, regulation, or binding administrative provision incorporating or implementing a Community environmental directive conforms with the directive or of whether a particular interpretation or application of that statute, regulation, or provision is mandated by, or consistent with, the directive, the private party may invoke the directive, and the national courts must directly apply it. There are four situations to be distinguished: (1) the member state has not incorporated the relevant environmental directive; (2) the national provision does not conform with the directive; (3) in implementing or enforcing the directive, the member state has exceeded its allowable discretion; (4) the national law is unclear, with only some of its possible interpretations consistent with the directive.

Which course the national court is to take under Community law largely depends on the specificity of the environmental directive in question.[65] Where the relevant Community provision does not leave the national authorities discretion for implementing it, but simply mandates its incorporation into national law, the provision normally has direct effect. Direct effect of a directive

[64] For this section *see generally* REMEDIES FOR BREACH OF COMMUNITY LAW (Fédération Internationale pour le Droit Européen, London 1980).

[65] Moreover, as a preliminary question there may be review of the validity of Community law, including its conformity with general principles of law and fundamental rights, and the interpretation of Community law.

means the citizen has an individual right against the state (arguably not against another individual) which can be enforced in member state courts. Where the directive leaves the national authority a choice between various solutions, the directive serves as a standard for judicial review of the conformity of national law or administrative practice with the directive. Thus, individuals may invoke provisions of a directive before a national court for a ruling whether the competent national authorities, in exercising their discretion as to the form and methods for implementing the directive, have kept within the limits of the directive.[66] The directive has a negative function: It is limited to invalidating national law that exceeds the limits of the directive. It is up to the national legislature or courts to develop new rules conforming to the directive.

The question of whether a provision contained in a directive is sufficiently clear to have direct effect or is only a standard for review of national law (because it leaves the member states a margin of discretion) is not always easy to decide. In environmental law this question, for example, arises with respect to provisions, contained in many recent directives, prohibiting (significant) deterioration of existing ambient environmental quality.

In the *VNO* case[67] the Court concluded that the notion of "capital good," contained in a directive for the harmonization of value added taxes, referred to the law of the member states for the definition of such qualities of a capital good as durability, value, and methods of depreciation. The member states were therefore held to have a margin of discretion, limited by the requirement that the essential difference between capital goods and other goods be taken into account. On the other hand, in the *Grunert* case[68] the Court held differently. At issue was a provision in a directive for the harmonization of food preservative law that required member states to select preservatives to be allowed as food additives from a list of generally approved preservatives. The directive's statement that a member state may not "totally exclude the use of a substance" on the list was held to be sufficiently clear to have direct effect in the legal order of member states. It would not have been altogether surprising if the Court had decided the other way around.

As the case law of the European Court of Justice now stands, it is therefore unpredictable what meaning would be given to a provision mandating no (significant) deterioration. Judging from the US experience with a similar prohibition under its Clean Air Act, it would seem absolutely necessary to grant member states some discretion in implementing such prohibitions. If this is correct, then such prohibitions would merely serve as a standard for review of national law.

[66] European Court of Justice, case 51/76, Verbond van Nederlandse Ondernemingen v. Inspecteur der Invoerrechten en Accijnzen (VNO), [1977] ECR 113, 127; case 21/78, Delkvist v. Anklagemyndigheden, [1978] ECR 2327, 2336. *See supra* p. 39, at notes 88–89.

[67] *Supra* note 66, at 124–125.

[68] European Court of Justice, case 88/79, Ministère Public v. Grunert, [1980] ECR 1827. *See also* case 108/80, Ministère Public v. Kugelmann, [1981] ECR 433.

The impact of the direct effect and standard of review doctrines as means for controlling national incorporation of Community law is limited by the fact that a directive can be invoked by a private party only to secure a decision which is advantageous to it and does not create obligations enforceable against other private parties. Where a member state has not yet formally incorporated an environmental directive into its legislation, its authorities are required to apply directive provisions which are more stringent than national law or administrative practice only if national law grants them discretion to do so. Otherwise, the directive is not applicable regarding an individual, and incorporation must be awaited. On the other hand, as demonstrated by the *Ratti* case,[69] a polluter can rely on a directive to challenge a national decision on the ground that the directive is less stringent than national law.

However, there are a host of unresolved legal issues regarding efforts by third parties, such as neighbors or environmental associations, to invoke a directive to challenge the legality of an authorization granted to a polluter on the ground that the authorization is based on national law not in conformity with a directive or does not sufficiently respect a directive. Whether such an action can be sustained at all would seem to depend on the national rules relating to standing to sue. Assuming that such parties have standing, it could be argued that recognition of direct effect or standard of review doctrines in favor of third parties would amount to imposing obligations on the polluter and is therefore impermissible. On the other hand, the legal proceeding in question formally concerns only the relationship between the third party and the relevant member state authority. It could therefore be argued that the holdings of the European Court of Justice on the direct effect of directives and on invocation of directives as a standard of review are applicable.

In West Germany the prevailing view is that water quality and emission standards established under the water pollution directives do not require member states to grant legal protection to third parties. In contrast, a Dutch court has held that the Community basic safety standards for the protection from radiation could be invoked by third parties.[70] Although the German position at first view seems to be a mere corollary of Germany's legal tradition of using the protective law theory as a standard for granting standing and delimiting the scope of judicial review, it has more general importance because it

[69] European Court of Justice, case 148/78, Pubblico Ministero v. Ratti, [1979] ECR 1629.

[70] Dahme, *Auswirkungen der EG-Richtlinien mit wasserrechtlichem Bezug auf den Vollzug des deutschen Wasserrechts*, in Gesellschaft für Umweltrecht, Dokumentation zur Wissenschaftlichen Fachtagung 1979, at 158 (Erich Schmidt Verlag, Berlin 1980); Zuleeg, *EG-Richtlinien auf dem Gebiete des Wasserrechts und ihre nationalen Auswirkungen*, 14 Zeitschrift für Wasserrecht 133, 143–144 (1975) (the relevant directives do not protect individuals; grant of standing would amount to recognizing direct obligations of private parties); *contra* Rest, *Pollution du Rhin*, 12 Envt'l Pol. & L. 37, 40 (1984); Rechtsbank s'Gravenhage, 23 Oct. 1974, 1975 Nederlandse Jurisprudentie No. 115 (direct applicability of EC nuclear health standards).

claims the right to make the determination under national law as to whether, as a matter of substantive law, a directive provides third party protection. If accepted by all member states, this position would make the direct effect and standard of review doctrines much less effective as instruments for controlling the incorporation, implementation, and enforcement of environmental directives with a view to ensuring better protection of the environment.[71] Thus, it would reinforce the traditional bias of European judicial review in favor of economic interests and against environmental interests.

ii. The European Court of Justice

The European Court of Justice has no powers to directly review the conformity with Community law of state incorporation, implementation, and enforcement of environmental directives. However, the Court is vested with indirect review powers which to a certain extent remedy this inherent structural deficiency. In litigation instituted by a private party (a regulated firm, or a third party or environmental organization having standing under state law) before a state court for review of an administrative decision or possibly in an administrative or criminal proceeding instituted against a regulated firm before a state court, the decision as to whether the official action violates a directive may depend on interpretation of the Treaty or the validity or interpretation of a directive. These questions may be, and, where a member state court or administrative tribunal of last instance is involved, must be referred to the European Court of Justice for a preliminary ruling (Art. 177 EEC Treaty).

The preliminary ruling procedure is an important device for ensuring the supremacy of European law and, although not relevant here, for controlling Community institutions. The European Court of Justice has expressly recognized that referral of questions from private suits before national courts through the Article 177 procedure is an important contribution to the enforcement of the Treaty; consequently, it has held that a pending infringement proceeding under Article 169 or 170 of the EEC Treaty does not exclude the Article 177 procedure.[72] The great majority of cases (with the exception of competition cases and labor disputes between the Community and its staff) decided by the European Court of Justice are preliminary rulings.

In environmental law, however, infringement proceedings instituted by the Commission have so far been far more important than preliminary rulings. There are to date only three environmental decisions rendered under the preliminary ruling procedure, namely the *Ratti* case[73] which concerned the direct applicability of the 1973 directive on solvents and the *Biological Products*

[71] European Court of Justice, case 158/80, Rewe v. Hauptzollamt Kiel, [1981] ECR 1805, 1838, held only that third parties have standing to sue public authorities to oblige them to enforce directives to the extent that such remedies exist under national law.

[72] European Court of Justice, case 26/62, Van Gend, [1963] ECR 1; case 31/69, Export rebates case, [1970] ECR 25, 33–34.

[73] *Supra* note 69.

case[74] and the *Waste Oil* case[75] which were rendered under Articles 30, 34 and 36 of the Treaty. In *Ratti* the conformity of an Italian law establishing stricter labeling requirements than the directive for solvents was at issue. In the *Biological Products* case the question was whether tests made under the pesticide law of the state of origin must be recognized by the importing state. In the *Waste Oil* case, the Court had to decide on the conformity of the French restrictions on the exportation of waste oil with the waste oil directive and with Articles 34 and 36 of the Treaty. It can be anticipated that the preliminary ruling procedure will in the future gain greater importance in environmental matters.

The preliminary ruling procedure has some important shortcomings. First, access to the procedure is conditional on access to state courts; it is therefore not uniform in all member states. Second, the powers of the European Court of Justice are limited.

In the preliminary ruling procedure the Court has jurisdiction to decide on the interpretation of the Treaty and the validity and interpretation of directives. This includes the issues of whether a directive is directly applicable or of what kind of incorporation or implementation action it requires a member state to take. The Court does not have powers to apply Community law to the facts of a particular case. In particular, it can not determine whether a particular action of incorporation, implementation, or enforcement (or non–action) violates a directive. It remains the member state courts' responsibility to draw the necessary conclusions from the holding of the European Court of Justice.[76] But it is clear that in practice the Court has often crossed the border between stating Community law and applying it to the individual case.[77] In any event, member state courts will in general defer to the supremacy of Community law as stated by the European Court and abstain from applying or interpreting a national law contrary to the spirit of the opinion of the European Court of Justice. This loyal behavior is especially to be expected of lower courts that have voluntarily referred the matter to the European Court of Justice and thereby become "partners" in a venture of cooperative judicial decisionmaking. There may be exceptions in those presumably rare cases where an unwilling high court has referred the matter or where an environmental conflict is or has become politicized.

Although the jurisdiction of the European Court of Justice adequately reaches the incorporation problem, it does not effectively reach administrative implementation and enforcement. The typical case where indirect review un-

[74] European Court of Justice, case 272/80, Biologische Producten (Pesticides), [1981] ECR 3277.

[75] European Court of Justice, case 172/82, Syndicat national des fabricants d'huile de graissage v. Groupement d'intérêt économique "Inter-Huiles," [1983] ECR 555.

[76] European Court of Justice, case 6/64, Costa v. ENEL, [1964] ECR 585; case 30/70, Otto Scheer v. Einfuhr- und Vorratsstelle für Getreide und Futtermittel, [1970] ECR 1197; cases 314, 315, 316/81 and 83/82, Waterkeyn, [1982] ECR 4337.

[77] Rasmussen, *supra* note 28, at 115.

der Art. 177 occurs is when the conformity with an environmental directive of the national agency's interpretation of a statute or regulation is challenged directly, or, more frequently, challenged in a criminal proceeding, a permit proceeding, or a proceeding for failure to take enforcement action. The application of harmonized environmental law to the facts of such particular cases is normally beyond the reach of Community jurisdiction. This limitation of the review powers of the European Court of Justice goes beyond those typical for courts of last instance and is a structural deficiency of the Community legal system. Specifically, there is no Community appellate court empowered to review state court decisions as to their conformity with Community law.

4. Enforcement Actions

Citizen enforcement actions against polluting sources are not possible under either Community or member state law. However, the normal private law remedies, especially tort and nuisance actions, may have the function of indirectly enforcing harmonized environmental requirements against polluters. Under tort law, the infringement of an environmental statute often constitutes a tort or establishes a presumption of illegality and/or negligence. In a nuisance action, environmental standards may be taken as guidelines as to whether an emission is substantial and not customary in the vicinity of a polluting installation. If so, it may be enjoined, or compensation may be required for harm resulting from its continuing operation. As yet, there is no practical experience with this kind of indirect enforcement of Community environmental law.

5. The Role of Litigation in Special Cases

a. Transboundary Pollution

i. Public Involvement

There are no common law actions available to member states to seek redress from another member state for transboundary pollution. An increasing number of directives provide for mandatory consultation or collaboration among member states where issues of transboundary pollution impede achieving the directives' goals of attaining quality standards or regulating particular polluting activities.[78] Furthermore, there are consultation or conflict resolu-

[78] Art. 4, Directive 80/778/EEC of 15 July 1980, OJ No. L 229, 30 Aug. 1980, p. 11 (drinking water directive); Art. 10, Directive 79/923/EEC of 30 Oct. 1979, OJ No. L 281, 10 Nov. 1979, p. 47 (shellfish water directive); Art. 10, Directive 78/659/EEC of 18 July 1978, OJ No. L 222, 14 Aug. 1978, p. 1 (fish waters directive); Art. 4(2), Directive 75/440/EEC of 16 June 1975, OJ No. L 194, 25 July 1975, p. 26 (bathing water directive); Art. 17, Directive 80/68/EEC of 17 Dec. 1979, OJ No. L 20, 26 Jan. 1980, p. 43 (ground water directive); Art. 11, Directive 80/779/EEC of 15 July 1980, OJ No. L 229, 30 Aug. 1980, p. 30 (sulfur dioxide limit values directive); Art. 8(2), Directive 82/501/EEC of 24 June 1982, OJ No. L 230, 5 Aug. 1982, p. 1 (major acci-

tion procedures provided under conventions on pollution of the Rhine and marine pollution. There are also bilateral and trilateral conventions covering certain kinds of transboundary pollution.[79] In recent years, a considerable degree of regional consultation and cooperation for prevention of pollution and for land use planning in border areas of member states has developed.[80] Where these coordination mechanisms fail, a member state may institute infringement proceedings under Art. 170 of the EEC Treaty against a neighboring state to redress violations of treaty obligations. This procedure is available where the transboundary pollution allegedly violates the Treaty obligations of another member state, including obligations arising under an environmental directive. Where these conditions are not fulfilled, a member state attacking transboundary pollution has recourse only to the dispute settlement mechanisms recognized under general public international law.

The efficacy of the remedies described is somewhat doubtful. It is not known whether the consultation procedures provided under some directives have yet been used. The infringement procedure under Art. 170 of the EEC Treaty is legally broad but in fact is rarely used. The action is a "public" action. The complaining state need not have a particular interest in the matter; it may act solely in the interest of the Community and for the defense of Community law. The action is subject to exhaustion of "administrative" remedies, i. e. the complaining state must first submit the matter to the Commission. But it may file the infringement suit with the European Court of Justice three months after the submission of the matter to the Commission if the Commission has failed to deliver a reasoned opinion to deal with the complaint.[81] Finally, the

dents directive); with respect to monitoring: Art. 7(2), Directive 78/176/EEC of 20 Feb. 1978, OJ No. L 54, 25 Feb. 1978, p. 19 (titanium dioxide directive); Art. 4, Directive 82/176/EEC of 22 March 1982, OJ No. L 81, 27 March 1982, p. 29 (first mercury directive).

[79] *See* RAT VON SACHVERSTÄNDIGEN FÜR UMWELTFRAGEN, UMWELTPROBLEME DES RHEINS, at No. 430 *et seq.* (Kohlhammer, Stuttgart 1976).

[80] *See* OECD, Recommendation for Strengthening International Cooperation on Environmental Protection in Frontier Regions, OECD Doc. C(78)77; EUROPEAN FRAMEWORK CONVENTION ON TRANSBOUNDARY COOPERATION BETWEEN MUNICIPALITIES (Council of Europe, Strasbourg 1980); ENVIRONMENTAL PROTECTION IN FRONTIER REGIONS (OECD, Paris 1979); TRANSFRONTIER POLLUTION AND THE ROLE OF STATES (OECD, Paris 1981); Bothe, *Transfrontier Environmental Management*, in TRENDS IN ENVIRONMENTAL LAW 391 *et seq.* (M. Bothe ed., International Union for the Conservation of Nature and Natural Resources, Gland 1980); ERCMAN & STORSBERG, *Auswertung der Erfahrungen mit den Methoden der grenzüberschreitenden Zusammenarbeit auf nationaler, regionaler und örtlicher Ebene: Alternativvorschläge*, 3 ZEITSCHRIFT FÜR UMWELTPOLITIK 553 (1980); B. SCHLÖGEL, GRENZÜBERSCHREITENDE INTERKOMMUNALE ZUSAMMENARBEIT (Erich Schmidt Verlag, Berlin 1982).

[81] The role of the Commission in Art. 170 proceedings is not that of a mediator, but rather of an arbitrator between the states concerned. *See* H. A. H. AUDRETSCH, *supra* note 5, at 115; MERTENS DE WILMARS & VEROUGHSTRAETE, *supra* note 5, at 393.

action may even be instituted in parallel to a proceeding brought by the Commission under Art. 169 of the EEC Treaty.[82]

In practice, however, state infringement actions have only a supplementary function. Because of the political implications of a direct infringement action instituted under Art. 170, member states normally prefer to bring a complaint to the Commission and have the Commission institute an infringement proceeding under Art. 169. There is as yet only one Court decision rendered under Art. 170.[83] This case concerns the controversy between France and the United Kingdom on fishing rights in the English economic zone subject to Treaty rules. There are several recent cases in which member states have threatened to institute proceedings in fishery or trade matters, but then acquiesced in a negotiated settlement. It remains to be seen whether this reflects a new trend in member state behavior with regard to infringements by other member states. All of these controversies have dealt with very sensitive political issues.

ii. Private Involvement

Private involvement in control of transboundary pollution can take two forms: first, administrative interventions and suits by individuals against a foreign state, especially for review of administrative action having transboundary effects, and second, suits among individuals based on private law. In both cases, private activity may have the function of ensuring the effective implementation and enforcement of harmonized environmental policy decisions or of stimulating new central initiatives. On the other hand, it appears highly unlikely that private initiatives alone could bring about direct harmonization of environmental law and policies of member states since the competent national courts, in the absence of Community environmental directives, will invariably apply a national law selected in application of (administrative or private) domestic conflict of law rules.

There is as yet little Community activity to promote private participation in administrative proceedings and review of state administrative action having transboundary effects on individuals in another member state. The amended Commission proposal for environmental impact assessment for the first time calls for full fledged rights of participation for affected foreign neighbors.[84] However, this proposal has not been accepted by the Council. Therefore, the development of appropriate rules at present remains essentially the responsibility of member states. A developed case law does not yet exist. Two major and a series of minor problems arise.

[82] H. A. H. AUDRETSCH, *supra* note 5, at 117; Wohlfahrt, in DIE EUROPÄISCHE WIRTSCHAFTGEMEINSCHAFT, KOMMENTAR ZUM VERTRAG 484 (E. Wohlfahrt, U. Everling, H. Glaesner & R. Sprung, Vahlen, Frankfurt, Berlin 1960).

[83] European Court of Justice, case 141/78, France v. United Kingdom, [1979] ECR 2923.

[84] Art. 8(2), Commission proposal of 1 April 1982 to amend the proposal for a Council Directive concerning the assessment of the environmental effects of certain public and private projects, OJ No. C 110, 1 May 1982, p. 5.

One major problem is the standing of foreigners to participate in administrative proceedings and secure judicial review by national courts. An Austrian decision concerning the permit proceedings for the border airport of Salzburg[85] denied standing to Bavarian neighbors on the ground that the principle of territoriality prevented Austrian authorities from considering foreign impacts of their decision and that therefore violation of a protected interest of foreign neighbors was inconceivable. The political rationale underlying the decision is the view that transboundary pollution conflicts should be a matter for the states concerned, i. e. for consultation and negotiation between them, rather than a matter for legal action by individuals. However, its value as a precedent is weakened by the fact that since then Austria has amended its domestic law so as to protect foreign neighbors, provided there is reciprocity.[86]

In any case, the narrow view would probably not be followed by the courts of Common Market countries since member states are bound by the prohibition against discrimination on the basis of nationality under Art. 7 of the EEC Treaty. This interpretation is supported by various OECD recommendations that rely on the principle of nondiscrimination to establish the proposition that in case of transboundary pollution, foreigners should have access to administrative and civil court proceedings to the same extent as nationals.[87] Although Community practice clearly emphasizes consultation and negotiation between the states, regions, and municipalities concerned,[88] either within or without Community institutions, it would seem that nationals of another member state must be granted standing to the same extent as nationals before national administrative agencies and courts in order to challenge the legality of administrative action having transboundary environmental impact.[89] Of

[85] Österreichischer Verwaltungsgerichtshof, 30 May 1969, 1969 Entscheidungen des Verwaltungsgerichtshofs No. 7582(A) 264, 99 JOURNAL DU DROIT INTERNATIONAL 647 (1972).

[86] Amendment of the Gewerbeordnung of 13 June 1973, § 75 III, 1974 Official Journal, vol. 3, No. 50.

[87] Recommendation on Principles Concerning Transfrontier Pollution, OECD Doc. C(74)224; Recommendation on Equal Right of Access in Relation to Transfrontier Pollution, OECD Doc. C(76)55(Final); Recommendation for the Implementation of Equal Right of Access and Nondiscrimination in Relation to Transfrontier Pollution, OECD Doc. C(77)28 (Final); OECD Recommendation C(78)77, *supra* note 80. The first three recommendations are *reprinted in* LEGAL ASPECTS OF TRANSFRONTIER POLLUTION 11 *et seq.*, 19 *et seq.*, 29 *et seq.* (OECD, Paris 1977). The latter is *reprinted in* 4 ENVT'L POL'Y & L. 195 (1978). *See* LANG, *Cinq Ans d'Activité du Groupe de L'OCDE sur la Pollution Transfrontière,* 7 ENVT'L POL'Y & L. 161 (1981). *See also* International Law Association, *Rules of International Law Applicable to Transfrontier Pollution, Report of the Committee on Legal Aspects of the Conservation of the Environment* (Montreal Conference 1982); *Resolution of the Montreal Conference,* 10 ENVT'L POL'Y & L. 27 (1983).

[88] *See supra* note 78.

[89] *E. g.*, in French practice, *see* Conseil d'État, 4 May 1979, Départment de la Savoie et autres (Creys–Malville nuclear power plant), 1979 Recueil des décisions du Conseil d'État 185, 1979 REVUE JURIDIQUE DE L'ENVIRONNEMENT 188; 23 Dec. 1981, Commune

course, it is doubtful whether a merely "passive" grant of formal access to foreigners really amounts to equal treatment of foreigners and nationals. The problem of unequal access to information can only be overcome if a state, when significant transboundary effects are anticipated, actively seeks to inform and consult with the public in the neighboring state. This may imply modification of the normal procedures applicable in purely national cases, (e. g. organization of foreign participants, language, etc.). Moreover, normal procedural barriers such as time limits, laches, and legal costs may impose excessive burdens on foreigners.

The second major problem is to what extent an administrative agency, when making a decision that potentially affects individuals in a neighboring state, must take transboundary effects into consideration. Conceptually, the application of national law implementing Community directives should be distinguished from the application of nonharmonized law.

Community directives, even if not containing specific provisions on transboundary pollution, ought to be interpreted to require consideration of transboundary effects. This interpretation is suggested by Art. 5 of the EEC Treaty

de Thionville (Cattenom nuclear power plant), 1981 Recueil 484 (parts of decision containing lists of plaintiffs not published); Tribunal administratif Strasbourg, 27 July 1983, 1983 REVUE JURIDIQUE DE L'ENVIRONNEMENT 343 (Rhinewater case); Pacteau, *The Principle of Equal Right of Access of Foreigners in Cases of Transfrontier Pollution and Prospects of Its Incorporation into French Law,* in LEGAL ASPECTS OF TRANSFRONTIER POLLUTION 203, at 211–212 (OECD, Paris 1977). For the Netherlands *see* T. OPPERMANN & M. KILIAN, *supra* note 32, at 65–66. In West Germany, the prevailing opinion in legal literature favors granting standing to foreigners in administrative proceedings. *See* Bothe, *Der Rechtsschutz ausländischer Nachbarn gegen umweltbelastende Anlagen im Grenzbereich,* in FESTSCHRIFT ZUR 150-JAHR-FEIER DES RECHTSANWALTSVEREINS HANNOVER 42, 50 *et seq.* (Hannover 1982); KÜPPERS, *Die Stellung ausländischer Nachbarn bei Genehmigung gefährlicher Anlagen im Inland,* 93 DEUTSCHES VERWALTUNGSBLATT 686, 689 (1978); WEBER, *Beteiligung und Rechtsschutz ausländischer Nachbarn im atomrechtlichen Genehmigungsverfahren,* 95 DEUTSCHES VERWALTUNGSBLATT 330 *et seq.* (1980); SIEHR, *Grenzüberschreitender Umweltschutz,* 45 RABELS ZEITSCHRIFT FÜR AUSLÄNDISCHES UND INTERNATIONALES PRIVATRECHT 377, 394 (1981); L. FRÖHLER & F. ZEHETNER, RECHTSSCHUTZPROBLEME BEI GRENZÜBERSCHREITENDEN UMWELTBEEINTRÄCHTIGUNGEN, vol. 2, at 92 (Institut für Raumordnung und Umweltgestaltung, Linz 1979–1980). For an opinion favoring only "voluntary" participation *see* T. OPPERMANN & M. KILIAN, *supra* note 32, at 96 *et seq.* For the practice of German authorities in cases of transfrontier pollution *see id.* at 84.

Due to the limitations of the German "protective law theory," it is more difficult to grant standing to foreigners in court proceedings; however, in two decisions concerning nuclear power plants, German administrative courts denied foreign plaintiffs standing solely on the ground of excessive distance. *See* Oberverwaltungsgericht Lüneburg, 21 May 1980 (7 OVGA 32/78, unpublished); Verwaltungsgericht Schleswig, 14 Dec. 1979, 1980 ENERGIEWIRTSCHAFTLICHE TAGESFRAGEN 363. For arguments in favor of granting standing, *see* BOTHE, *Grenzüberschreitender Verwaltungsrechtsschutz gegen umweltbelastende Anlagen,* 1983 UMWELT- UND PLANUNGSRECHT 1 *et seq.;* KÜPPERS, *supra,* at 689; WEBER, *supra,* at 334; L. FRÖHLER & F. ZEHETNER, *supra,* at 90 *et seq.* *Contra* T. OPPERMANN & M. KILIAN, *supra,* at 135–136.

which requires member states to facilitate the achievement of Community tasks and to abstain from any measure which could jeopardize attainment of the Treaty's objectives. This provision obliges member states to implement Community environmental directives in good faith. The principal purpose of Community environmental legislation is to establish a centralized system of environmental protection subject to harmonized requirements. This system would be threatened if member states could, in making decisions on the application of Community environmental law that have significant transboundary effects, simply ignore these effects. However, given the dearth of case law in this area, this interpretation is not yet established law. As a minimum requirement, the rules applicable to nonharmonized national environmental law must be observed.

It remains the primary responsibility of member states to determine the scope of application of nonharmonized national environmental law. The OECD[90] relies on the principle of nondiscrimination to support its proposition that extraterritorial effects of environmental decisions should be considered by national authorities to the same extent as domestic ones, thereby creating "soft" international law that may influence the future practice of member states. It is, however, doubtful whether Art. 7 of the EEC Treaty in fact requires member states to actively protect the environment of a neighboring member state by applying the same quality standards as are applicable to domestic effects. It can not be assumed that the traditional limitation of administrative law to defense of territorial interests has been entirely eroded by Art. 7.[91]

French jurisprudence has for quite some time taken the view that a domestic administrative decision must consider transfrontier environmental effects; in a recent judgment, the Administrative Court of Strasbourg has voided the permit granted the operators of the Alsatian alkali mines to discharge chloride into the Rhine on the grounds that the ensuing deterioration in the quality of Rhine water in the Netherlands was not considered in granting the permit.[92] Among West German legal writers the opinion prevails that in view of the national constitution's emphasis on international cooperation (Art. 24, 25), transboundary effects should be considered insofar as the relevant statute

[90] *Supra* note 87.

[91] The European Court of Justice has several times held that application of the principle of territoriality does not violate the Treaty. *See* case 31/78, Bussone v. Italian Ministry for Agriculture and Forestry (Labeling of eggs), [1978] ECR 2429, 2445; cases 3, 4 and 6/76, Kramer (Biological resources of the sea), [1976] ECR 1279, 1313; case 155/80, Oebel (Prohibition on baking bread at night), [1982] ECR 1993.

[92] Tribunal administratif Strasbourg, *supra* note 89. *See also* Conseil d'État, *supra* note 89; Pacteau, *supra* note 89; Despax, *supra* note 32, at 738–739; Bischoff, *The Territorial Limits of Public Law and Their Implications in Regard to the Principles of Non-Discrimination and Equal Right of Access as Recognised in Connection with Transfrontier Pollution*, in LEGAL ASPECTS OF TRANSFRONTIER POLLUTION 128, 143–144 (OECD, Paris 1977).

does not contain a territorial limitation.[93] The same view now seems to be gaining ground in the Netherlands.[94] However, application of this principle, already advocated by Karl Neumeyer, the founder of German administrative conflict of law, and Walter Jellinek,[95] poses several unresolved problems.

An extreme consequence of the principle of "nondiscrimination" would be that a polluting facility located, e. g., in West Germany must be refused authorization where the German ambient quality standards are exceeded not in West Germany but, rather, in a neighboring member state, even if the neighboring state has less stringent ambient quality standards or follows a system of emission standards and therefore would not refuse an application for the installation on its own territory. As an alternative, compliance with the standards applicable in the receiving state could be required. This is a possible solution where the receiving state has lower standards; however, it can not be reversed in order to protect a receiving state having higher standards. Another possibility is for the emitting state to formulate some ad hoc standard intermediate between its own standard and that of the neighboring state (as this is done under German law in the case of conflicts between different use related noise standards).

These issues show that the problem is far from solution, and this makes the conservative counter–position of ignoring extraterritorial effects quite attractive. The member states have expressed their willingness to consider adverse environmental effects outside their territory arising from a domestic activity by agreeing on several directives providing for consultation between governments. Apart from the environmental impact assessment proposal, there is no indication that the member states desire to facilitate participation or consideration of foreign effects in administrative proceedings concerning transboundary pollution. From the perspective of the governments concerned, consultations have the advantage of permitting the executive to retain control over the extent of accommodation of foreign interests. Therefore, it may be presumed that future development will focus on political management of transboundary pollution conflicts rather than legal mechanisms of conflict resolution, even in cases where harmonized requirements already exist. The far–reaching right of participation in case of potential transboundary pollution under the Commission proposal for environmental impact assessment, which arguably includes an implied right for affected foreigners to require consideration of out of state

[93] BOTHE, 1983 UMWELT- UND PLANUNGSRECHT, *supra* note 89, at 4 *et seq.;* L. FRÖHLER & F. ZEHETNER, *supra* note 89, at 75 *et seq.;* KÜPPERS, *supra* note 89, at 688–689; K. VOGEL, DER RÄUMLICHE ANWENDUNGSBEREICH DER VERWALTUNGSRECHTSNORM 408, 419 *et seq.* (Metzner Berlin, Frankfurt 1965); WEBER, *supra* note 89, at 331–332. *Contra,* T. OPPERMANN & M. KILIAN, *supra* note 32, at 111 *et seq.* (prerogative of the executive).

[94] *See* T. OPPERMANN & M. KILIAN, *supra* note 32, at 65–66.

[95] K. NEUMEYER, INTERNATIONALES VERWALTUNGSRECHT, vol. 2, at 26 *et seq.* (J. Schweitzer Verlag, München, Berlin 1922); W. JELLINEK, VERWALTUNGSRECHT 148–149 (Springer, Berlin, 3d ed. 1931).

impacts by the originating state authorities, has not been agreed to by the Council.

iii. Private Litigation

Litigation over transboundary pollution between private parties is facilitated by the Convention of 1968 on jurisdiction and the enforcement of civil and commercial judgments in conjunction with the Protocol of 1971 concerning its interpretation[96] by the Court of Justice. The new member states have acceded to this convention, and it will soon be in force in them. The Convention establishes uniform criteria for personal jurisdiction. Most important with respect to transboundary pollution is its Article 5(3). This provision vests personal jurisdiction over a tort in the state where the tort was committed. In the leading *Rhinewater (Alsatian alkali)* case,[97] Dutch farmers instituted a suit in the Netherlands against the French alkali works in Alsace, the main source of chloride pollution of the Rhine, for crop damage suffered when using water polluted by leaking Rhine water for irrigation. The European Court of Justice held in a preliminary ruling that the place of the wrong within the meaning of the convention was not only the place where the constituent acts of the tort were performed, but also the place where the injury was suffered. Hence, the Dutch courts did have personal jurisdiction over the matter, and a lower Dutch court[98] has since held the French defendant liable for a certain share of the damages (under Dutch law, where several sources of pollution have contributed to a single injury, each contributor is liable only pro rata).

Recognition by the European Court of Justice of long-arm jurisdiction over torts clears the way for victims of transboundary pollution to bring tort actions in their domestic courts, which are probably more favorable to the victim's action than the national courts of the tortfeasor. Long-arm jurisdiction probably also applies to injunctive relief.[99] The potential of the *Rhinewater* holding

[96] Convention on Jurisdiction and Enforcement of Judgments in Civil and Commercial Matters of 27 Sept. 1968, 8 ILM 229 (1969), OJ No. L 299, 31 Dec. 1972, p. 32; Protocol (75/464/EEC) of 3 June 1971, OJ No. L. 204, 2 Aug. 1975, p. 28. For the accession of Denmark, Ireland, and the United Kingdom, *see* Agreement of 9 Oct. 1978, OJ No. L 304, 30 Oct. 1978, p. 1 (not yet in force).

[97] Case 21/76, Handelskwekerij G. J. Bier B. V. v. Mines de Potasse d'Alsace S. A., [1976] ECR 1735. *See* the favorable annotation by Rest, *Wahl des zuständigen Gerichts bei Distanzdelikten nach dem EG-Zuständigkeits- und Vollstreckungsübereinkommen*, 23 Recht der internationalen Wirtschaft 669 (1977). *See also* Jessurun d'Oliveira, *La pollution du Rhin et le droit international privé*, in Rhine Pollution/La Pollution du Rhin 81, 104 *et seq.* (Tjeenk Willink, Zwolle 1978). *But see* Droz, *annotation*, 1977 Dalloz-Sirey 615.

[98] Rechtsbank Rotterdam, 8 Jan. 1979, 1979 Nederlandse Jurisprudentie No. 113, 1979 European Community Cases 206; 16 Dec. 1983, 33 Ars Aequi 133 (1984). The court did not only apply Dutch municipal law but also based its judgment on public international law. *See* Lammers, *New International Legal Developments Concerning the Pollution of the Rhine*, 27 Neth. Int'l L. J. 171, 186 *et seq.* (1980).

[99] *See* Jessurun d'Oliveira, *supra* note 97, at 114 *et seq.*

is demonstrated by two later cases. French courts held an Italian manufacturer liable for losses to French fishermen caused by the dumping of titanium dioxide wastes in the Tyrrhenian Sea beyond Italian territorial waters.[100] A German court granted compensation to German farmers for cattle and crop damage originating from a French pesticide factory.[101]

It should be noted, however, that the *Rhinewater* holding is limited to torts. In some European countries, such as West Germany and Italy, the primary basis for maintaining a damage suit for transboundary pollution would not be tort but rather nuisance, which is considered part of the law of property (neighborhood relations). Article 16(1) of the Convention vests exclusive personal jurisdiction for matters involving rights in real property in the courts where the property is situated. It remains to be seen whether this provision will be interpreted as encompassing neighborhood relations or whether they will be considered quasi-tort relations. In the former case it would be unclear whether the location of the emitting or receiving property controls.[102]

The nonharmonized conflicts rules of the forum state govern the choice of substantive law.[103] The national conflicts rules of the member states concerning tort actions are more or less parallel to the jurisdictional rules of the Convention, although the laws of some member states are not well settled. There is a trend towards relying on the law of the place where the injury occurs rather than on that of the place where the tortious act was committed. Some states combine both criteria and then apply the law more favorable to the plaintiff or chosen by the plaintiff.[104] With respect to legal rules regulating the behavior of

[100] Tribunal grande instance Bastia, 6 Dec. 1976, 1977 DALLOZ–SIREY JURISPRUDENCE 427; *aff'd*, Cour d'Appel Bastia, 28 Feb. 1977, 1980 FORO ITALIANO IV 406, at 408; *aff'd*, Cour de Cassation Civile, 3 April 1978, 1978 DALLOZ–SIREY JURISPRUDENCE I 367.

[101] Oberlandesgericht Karlsruhe, 4 Aug. 1977, 23 RECHT DER INTERNATIONALEN WIRTSCHAFT 718 (1977), DIE DEUTSCHE RECHTSPRECHUNG AUF DEM GEBIET DES INTERNATIONALEN PRIVATRECHTS IM JAHRE 1977, at No. 27 (Mohr Siebeck, Tübingen 1979).

[102] The German courts apply the lex rei sitae. *See* Landgericht Waldshut–Tiengen, 11 Feb. 1982, 1983 UMWELT- UND PLANUNGSRECHT 14 (Zurich–Kloten airport); Landgericht Traunstein, 16 April 1975, DIE DEUTSCHE RECHTSPRECHUNG AUF DEM GEBIET DES INTERNATIONALEN PRIVATRECHTS IM JAHRE 1976, at No. 29a (Mohr Siebeck, Tübingen 1978); *aff'd*, Oberlandesgericht München, 29 Jan. 1976, *id.* No. 29b.

[103] A Commission proposal for a convention on harmonized conflict of law rules for tort law (Text: 38 RABELS ZEITSCHRIFT FÜR AUSLÄNDISCHES UND INTERNATIONALES PRIVATRECHT 211 (1974)) will not be pursued further.

[104] West Germany applies the law more favorable to the plaintiff. *See* Reichsgericht, 30 March 1903, 54 REICHSGERICHT IN ZIVILSACHEN 198 (1903); G. KEGEL, INTERNATIONALES PRIVATRECHT 301 (C. H. Beck, München, 4th ed. 1977); LUMMERT, *Zur Frage des anwendbaren Rechts bei zivilrechtlichen Schadenersatz – und Unterlassungsklagen wegen grenzüberschreitender Umweltbeeinträchtigungen*, 1982 NATUR UND RECHT 241 *et seq.;* SIEHR, *supra* note 89, at 379 note 4, all with further references. *See also* A. REST, THE MORE FAVORABLE LAW PRINCIPLE IN TRANSFRONTIER ENVIRONMENTAL LAW 59 *et seq.*, 69 *et seq.* (Erich Schmidt Verlag, Berlin 1980). With respect to neighbor relations the lex rei sitae (of the affected land) is applied. *See* Bundesgerichtshof, 10

a person – in contrast to the rules concerning relief – the law of the place where the act was committed is often applied and thus the lawfulness of the act determined by reference to that law.

A major problem is the question whether an authorization lawfully granted under the law of the place where the source is located to the operator of a source of pollution would be relevant in a suit instituted by a domestic victim of transboundary pollution. This is not an issue in states which apply the law of the place where the act was performed or at least as a preliminary matter apply that rule to determine the effect of a foreign permit. In jurisdictions in which the law of the place of injury governs, the majority opinion is to deny any relevance to a foreign permit because its effects are strictly territorial.[105] Others acknowledge that foreign permits may be recognized if three conditions are satisfied: residents of the receptor state were able to participate in the administrative proceedings granting the permit; the granting authority considered the receptor state's interests (but query: to what extent?); and a domestic permit would bar or limit a claim for damages.[106] This theory is the conflict of law expression of the ever increasing interrelationship of private and administrative law in the field of pollution control. The Dutch court in the *Rhinewater* case[107] was able to disregard this issue because the substantive law of both the Netherlands and France grants the victim compensation for pollution damage irrespective of whether the operator has a permit. Under the sub-

March 1978, 94 DEUTSCHES VERWALTUNGSBLATT 226 (1979); Landgericht Waldshut-Tiengen, *supra* note 102. In France, the legal literature and the lower courts favor the place of injury. *See* H. BATIFFOL & P. LAGARDE, DROIT INTERNATIONAL PRIVÉ, vol. 2, at 220–221 (Lib. générale de droit et de jurisprudence, Paris, 6th ed. 1976); BOUREL, *Droit international, Responsabilité civile,* RÉPERTOIRE DALLOZ, No. 45 *et seq.;* A. REST, *supra,* at 58–59. In the Netherlands the law is not well settled: *see* Jessurun d'Oliveira, *supra* note 97, at 94 *et seq.;* A. REST, *supra,* at 58. For a comparative analysis, *see* P. MCNAMARA, THE AVAILABILITY OF CIVIL REMEDIES TO PROTECT PERSONS AND PROPERTY FROM TRANSFRONTIER POLLUTION INJURY (Metzner Verlag, Frankfurt 1981).

105 As for West Germany *see* Bundesgerichtshof, *supra* note 104, at 227; Landgericht Waldshut-Tiengen, *supra* note 102; KÜPPERS, *supra* note 89, at 263–264; ROSSBACH, *Der Einfluß der im Ausland erteilten Bewilligung zur Gewässernutzung auf Schadensersatzansprüche wegen grenzüberschreitender Gewässerverunreinigungen,* 18 ZEITSCHRIFT FÜR WASSERRECHT 16, 19 *et seq.* (1979) (but based on the premise that transboundary participation is not possible); REST, *Berücksichtigung grenzüberschreitender Umweltaspekte im Recht der Bundesrepublik Deutschland?,* 32 ÖSTERREICHISCHE ZEITSCHRIFT FÜR ÖFFENTLICHES RECHT UND VÖLKERRECHT 59, 79–80 (1981) (same argument); STOLL, *Der Schutz der Sachenrechte nach internationalem Privatrecht,* 37 RABELS ZEITSCHRIFT FÜR AUSLÄNDISCHES UND INTERNATIONALES PRIVATRECHT 357, 375 (1973).

106 M. KLOEPFER & C. KOHLER, KERNKRAFTWERKE UND STAATSGRENZE 167 *et seq.* (Duncker & Humblot, Berlin 1981); SIEHR, *supra* note 89, at 387; LUMMERT, *supra* note 104, at 243 *et seq.;* also in principle ROSSBACH, *supra* note 105; Rechtsbank Rotterdam, *supra* note 98.

107 *Supra* note 98.

stantive law of other member states a permit would bar a private damage remedy if the source has complied with permit conditions. Such compliance would bar private injunctive relief in all member states.

Even if the domestic victim of transboundary pollution obtains a judgment for compensation or injunctive relief, the execution of that judgment in the foreign state may cause difficulties. Under Article 27 of the Convention a member state may refuse recognition and execution of a foreign judgment only where it violates its public policy. There are no precedents. However, it is safe to assume that no state will give its consent to execution of a foreign judgment that would directly or indirectly interfere with its administrative control and management of pollution and natural resources and that the European Court of Justice would support this view.[108] Therefore, injunctions and damages awarded by a receptor state court in cases where the polluting facility has a permit which under the law of the originating state bars damages or other relief, might be unenforceable in the originating state.

b. Environmental Impact Assessment

Since the Commission proposal for Community environmental impact assessment has not yet been adopted, litigation to force compliance with impact assessment procedures is not yet a real issue.

The litigation aspects of the Community environmental impact assessment procedure have been grossly neglected in the ongoing discussion. In particular, national differences in compliance due to differences in access to the courts, court powers, and the scope of judicial review have not been discussed.[109] France introduced environmental impact assessment in 1976.[110] There already is some experience with judicial reaction to the procedure which, although primarily relevant in the context of the French legal system, allows some comparative conclusions.[111]

Four remarks are apposite at this point. First, there is no chance that national standing requirements will be affected by the directive. Second, whether inadequacy of an environmental impact assessment will necessarily lead to annulment of the relevant administrative decision depends on national administrative procedure law. In France, the doctrine of *"vice de forme"* normally leads to annulment of the relevant decision. In West Germany, one would have to ask whether the environmental impact assessment procedure is de-

[108] *See* Siehr, *supra* note 89, at 381; Jessurun d'Oliveira, *supra* note 97, at 117 *et seq. See also* Rest, *Transfrontier Environmental Damages: Judicial Competences and Forum Delicti Commissi*, 1 Envt'l Pol'y & L. 127, 130 (1975).

[109] *But see* E. Rehbinder, *supra* note 32, at 523 *et seq.*

[110] Art. 2, *supra* note 41.

[111] *See* Conseil d'État, 27 Feb. 1981, Commune de Lias, No. 5865 (unpublished); Hebrard, *Les études d'impact sur l'environnement devant le juge administratif*, 1981 Revue juridique de l'environnement 129, 135 *et seq.* (with further references). *See also* Prieur, *Le respect de l'environnement et les études d'impact*, 1981 Revue juridique de l'environnement 103, 124 *et seq.*

signed to protect individual interests. Third, since almost all member states allow review of procedural errors only as part of review of a final administrative decision, it is highly improbable that the relevant authority or the project's sponsor can be directly compelled by interim injunctions to conduct an adequate impact assessment. The best that could be hoped for is that all member state courts and tribunals, including those in states not recognizing automatic suspensory effect of administrative suits, would grant interim injunctions against the immediate execution of a final decision violating the impact assessment requirement. Fourth, it is uncertain whether the obligation to consider the results of the impact assessment, as proposed under Article 10 of the draft directive, will broaden and harmonize the very unequal scope of review of administrative decisions in the various member states.

c. State Measures Prohibited by Articles 30, 34 and 36 of the EEC Treaty

The Commission or a member state may challenge before the European Court of Justice the conformity with Articles 30, 34 and 36 of the EEC Treaty of another state's regulatory measures for the protection of the environment. Likewise, a private party can challenge state action as in violation of Articles 30 and 36 before a national court, and the national court may or must refer the case to the European Court of Justice for a preliminary ruling under Art. 177 of the EEC Treaty. The recent *Biological Products* case[112] and *Waste Oil* case[113] are examples of the preliminary ruling procedure in an environmental context.

[112] *Supra* note 74.
[113] *Supra* note 75.

VII. Implementation and Enforcement in the US

A. Federal Mechanisms of Integration and Implementation

1. Regulatory Programs

As already noted,[1] federal environmental regulatory initiatives cover three basic categories of activity:

- Nationally marketed products (autos, airplanes, noise-generating equipment, pesticides, and chemicals)
- Industrial processes (air and water pollution; radiation; toxic waste facilities; stripmining)
- Private, state and local land and natural resource use and infrastructure investment (coastal zone management; water resource planning; water supply and sewage facilities; solid waste management)

Programs in the first category generally involve direct federal regulation. Those in the second category generally rely on state implementation and enforcement of federal standards. The third category of programs relies upon federal guidance and financial incentives for states and localities to engage in planning and regulation. These differences in the nature and extent of the federal role do not directly reflect the perceived seriousness of the environmental problems involved; rather, they arise more from the relative advantages and disadvantages of centralized standard setting, implementation, and enforcement in relation to the problems involved and the existing allocation of related governmental functions.

Nationally marketed products present an obvious case for direct federal regulation because of the scale efficiencies in uniform, centralized regulation and the potential inconsistencies and cumulative burdens threatened by multiple, decentralized state regulation. Manufacturers are often large national concerns, and the implementation and enforcement task is within federal capabilities. Programs of direct federal regulation not infrequently preempt inconsistent state measures. In most cases, however, no substantial state regulation existed before the adoption of federal programs. This pattern reflects the circumstance that the product markets in question were already nationally integrated and subject to other forms of federal regulation; when environmental problems became a matter of concern, additional federal regulation was the natural response.

The primary reasons for federal regulation of major industrial processes include fear that industry will induce states to adopt lax standards by threaten-

[1] *See supra* pp. 46–50.

ing to relocate or make new plant investment elsewhere and by exercising other forms of political power; economies of scale in dealing with scientific and technological issues; interstate pollution spillovers; and the need to preserve pristine environments in scenic areas of national significance. The number of regulated facilities, however, is typically large (100 000 to 200 000 in the case of air and water pollution controls), and the nature and impact of appropriate control measures often varies depending on local conditions.

While direct federal implementation and enforcement would not be infeasible if adequate administrative resources were provided, several factors call for a substantial state role in implementation and enforcement. These include the need to avoid duplication of pre-existing state programs; the comparative advantages of state and local authorities in monitoring and collecting other relevant information; and the need for a measure of flexibility in adjusting controls to varied local circumstances. Accordingly, implementation and enforcement is either delegated to states in the first instance, subject to federal takeover in the event of inadequacy, or federal agencies are authorized to delegate implementation and enforcement to the states, provided that the states comply with federal directives and are subject to federal supervision. Because national product markets are not threatened, and because the dangers of excessive state regulatory stringency are damped by capital and labor mobility, federal law generally leaves states free to impose more stringent controls than federal law itself requires.

Programs involving state implementation and enforcement of federal standards involve a series of steps not dissimilar to those involved in EC environmental directives. After the federal authority has adopted standards and regulations governing their implementation, states undertaking implementation and enforcement must first demonstrate that they have legal authority, as a matter of state law, to do so. In order to show such authority, states may have to enact statutes explicitly granting state agencies the necessary competence, although recently EPA, anxious to delegate regulatory responsibilities to the states, has accepted certifications by state Attorney Generals that state authorities already have such competence.[2] The state's administrative authorities must then undertake actual implementation and enforcement. Inadequate efforts or outright resistance by states that place a low value on environmental goals can lead to a severe "implementation gap" and substantial variations in actual enforcement levels among states. Industry compliance with state requirements is often limited because state judges are reluctant to impose sanctions on first offenders or require payment to the state of fines that could otherwise be invested by firms in pollution controls.[3] Federal agency resource lim-

[2] For example, EPA accepts certifications by state Attorney Generals in assessing whether a state is qualifed under RCRA. 40 C. F. R. § 123.5. This certificate would not, of course, preclude a regulated firm from judicially challenging the state's legal authority as a matter of state law.

[3] *See* Roberts & Farrell, *The Political Economy of Implementation: the Clean Air Act and Stationary Sources,* in APPROACHES TO CONTROLLING AIR POLLUTION (A. Friedlander ed., M. I. T. Press, Cambridge, Ma. 1978).

itations, political constraints, and the substantive and procedural complexities involved make federal takeover of implementation and enforcement a rather weak threat. Federal administrators generally have considerable statutory discretion whether to take over implementation and enforcement. Federal court litigation by environmental groups against reluctant federal officials is unlikely to be a very effective corrective. The largely successful efforts of the state of Ohio to sabotage implementation of Clean Air Act controls within the state are a particulary notorious example of the implementation gap problem.

Federal encouragement of state measures is a strategy that has been followed in areas such as land use, sewage treatment and water supply planning, solid waste disposal, automobile use, non–point water pollution, and other forms of activity that involve many individual actors and have traditionally been the responsibility of the states. Problems are too varied, the interrelations with local functions are too intimate, and federal resources are too limited to permit direct federal regulation. Because such regulations would involve centralized direction of the day to day activities of millions of individuals, it would also be highly unpopular politically. Most forms of direct federal regulation are in fact aimed at large industrial firms. For all of these various reasons, federal programs in this category consist largely of efforts to encourage stronger state and local measures through conditional grants, provision of information and so on.

The second and third categories of federal regulatory programs aim for a precarious balance between ensuring adequate implementation and enforcement on the one hand, and acknowledging the political and functional advantages of decentralized flexibility on the other. The federal government lacks, and politically could not obtain, the resources to undertake direct implementation and enforcement of all of these programs. It must therefore concentrate its limited resources on ensuring that central initiatives are adequately carried out by others. These central initiatives are frequently uniform measures that may be economically and environmentally inappropriate. Clean Water Act effluent limitations and Clean Air Act ambient standards are examples. In the implementation process, such uniformities must be modified by the need to accommodate economic and environmental realities, as the development of the PSD and nonattainment programs under the Clean Air Act illustrates. But these non–uniform measures greatly increase the burden on the federal government of ensuring adequate enforcement. Introduction of flexibility – such as adjusting Clean Water Act effluent limitations in accordance with local water quality conditions – involves either massive complexity in centrally directed programs, or an effective loss of central control.

As a rough generalization, one can say that existing programs give greatest responsibility to the federal government in those areas where the economic and environmental costs of centralized implementation and enforcement are least. The evolution of policy over time, however, moves dialectically, reacting to the relative advantages and disadvantages of centralized and decentralized implementation. After a period of centralization, the United States has recently been moving in the direction of decentralization. But it would be a mistake to conclude that this will involve a return to the weak state environmental programs of the 1960s. Institutional capability and political support for environmental programs are considerably stronger in most states today than fifteen years ago, in part because of federal programs designed to develop the state role in implementation and enforcement. However, the vigor of state environmental programs is threatened by the Reagan administration's steps to cut back federal grants earmarked for support of such programs.

2. Management of Public Resources

The promotion of environmental objectives in connection with the management of federal resources takes two basic forms: organic statutes defining the authority and responsibility of particular resource management agencies, and generic statutes that impose environmental obligations on all federal resource managers.

The organic statutes governing federal land and natural resource management typically grant administrative officials considerable discretion to balance economic and development goals against conservation and environmental protection goals. In most instances, conservation and environmental values were part of the agency's mission from the outset, although in some instances (for example, the Outer Continental Shelf Lands Act governing offshore oil development[4]) such values have been given greater and more explicit importance through recent statutory amendments. In a few instances, environmental and conservation advocates have succeeded in obtaining legislation that gives their interests dominant or overriding weight. Examples include the establishment of specialized agencies to manage designated public lands for restricted uses (National Park Service, Fish and Wildlife Service), or the adoption of legislation sharply limiting the discretion otherwise enjoyed by multiple use land managers (Wilderness Act, Surface Mining Control and Reclamation Act).[5]

The second form of federal legislation designed to promote environmental considerations in connection with federal resource management is represented by generic statutes, such as NEPA and the Endangered Species Act, that apply to all federal resource agencies.

The effort to ensure that federal resource managers give greater consideration to environmental values presents a dilemma. Given the wide variety of public lands and resources, attempts to contain resource manager discretion through specific, uniform substantive limitations are likely to be procrustean, as examples like the Endangered Species Act attest. Congress can to some extent avoid these difficulties by classifying specific lands for specific uses, but there are obvious limits to this technique. On the other hand, broad injunctions that managers must take environmental values into account will likely have little effect if the agency (such as the Tennessee Valley Authority or the

[4] *See* Outer Continental Shelf Lands Act Amendments of 1976, Pub. L. No. 95–372, 92 Stat. 629 (1978) amending 43 U. S. C. §§ 1331–1343.

[5] *See supra* pp. 132–134.

Army Corps of Engineers) conceives of its mission in terms of commercial development or massive project construction and enjoys strong political support from development interests. The problem of controlling managerial discretion is often exacerbated when, as is frequently the case, decisional authority is decentralized within the federal government to local and regional offices. For example, the decentralization of decisional authority over coal leasing during the late 1960s and early 1970s within the Interior Department resulted in a series of decisions granting large numbers of industry lease applications without coordinated consideration of whether the aggregate amount and pattern of leases was environmentally or economically appropriate.

The requirements of generic statutes like NEPA and the Endangered Species Act apply not only to management of federal lands and natural resources, and to projects built and owned by the federal government, but also to state, local, and private projects financed or licensed by the federal government. This indirect extension of federal environmental policies is politically more feasible than direct federal regulation.[6]

The interplay between the various federal resource management statutes and programs on the one hand, and state and local environmental and resource policies on the other, is a complex process not easily summarized. The process of interaction occurs in legislative, judicial, and administrative fora at the national, state, and local governmental levels. On the one hand, states (allied with development interests) often oppose federal policies that limit development of federal resources and consequently limit economic development in the states where those resources are located. This opposition may take the form of lobbying against congressional legislation giving paramount weight to preservation and conservation values, participating in administrative proceedings in order to persuade federal resource managers to adopt policies favoring development, and litigation against those managers when they fail to do so.

Alternatively, states may utilize the same fora to oppose or restrict development on federal lands which will cause environmental disruption within the state or deplete scarce resources. Examples include state opposition to continental shelf development off their shores and to oil shale development. States, unless specifically preempted by statute, may generally regulate pollution and resource use on federal lands, so long as they do so on a non-discriminatory basis.

Federal land and resource managers have in the past often been more sensitive to or effective in championing environmental and conservation values than many of their state counterparts. But the Reagan administration's strenuous effort to develop or dispose of federally owned resources may necessitate revision of this judgment. Today, the states may be a stronger force for conservation than the federal government.

[6] The Endangered Species Act, however, also prohibits private takings of endangered species. *See* 16 U.S.C. § 1538(a).

3. Transboundary Spillovers and Interstate Resource Conflicts

Despite the Clean Air Act, two major transboundary air pollution problems have emerged. One problem is transboundary drift of photochemical oxidants, particularly in the northeast United States.[7] It has been extraordinarily difficult to establish the precise amount of such drift or to adjust state by state control strategies to deal with it. Downwind states dispute the amount of drift and disclaim any legal responsibility for assuming some of the additional abatement burden which spillovers impose on downwind states. Moreover, an upwind state will claim that much of its oxidant problem is the responsibility of other states even further upwind.

The second problem is acid precipitation and sulfate and nitrate deposition caused by the atmospheric transport and transformation of sulfur and nitrogen emissions.[8] The problem is most serious in the northeast, but is becoming significant in the west as well. Existing air pollution control strategies do not deal with this problem because the standards are directed at ground level concentrations of NO_2 and SO_2 rather than the ultimate sulfate and nitrate products of emissions. Strategies, such as construction of tall stacks, to meet local SO_2 and NO_2 standards have exacerbated the acid precipitation and deposition problem. The precise quantitative and geographic relation between sulfur and nitrogen emissions and acid precipitation and deposition is hotly debated. There is support in Congress for adopting specific measures to deal with acid precipitation, but the administration has not yet made or supported any proposals for legislation.

A belated and inadequate effort to deal with transboundary problems was made in the 1977 Clean Air Act Amendments, which provide that one state's SIP shall not prevent "attainment and maintenance" of federal air quality standards in other states by reason of transboundary pollution.[9] In addition, there is a special procedure governing the construction of major new stationary air pollution sources that may cause pollution levels in neighboring states to exceed applicable federal standards.[10] But the substantive criteria for determining extent of abatement responsibility in the originating state are vague, and EPA has shown little taste for taking on controversial problems of interstate pollution control. The provisions are keyed to existing air quality standards, and thus do not deal with the acid precipitation and deposition problem. They also do not deal with pollution from motor vehicles, which is an important element in the oxidant problem.

Transboundary problems have not been as conspicuous in the water pollution area, although the reliance on uniform technology based controls in the federal program may not secure adequate cleanup in certain interstate waters. The continuing controversy between Illinois and the City of Milwaukee over

[7] *See generally* R. Stewart & J. Krier, Environmental Law and Policy 96–98 (Supp. 1982) (Bobbs-Merill, Indianapolis, Indiana).

[8] *Id.*

[9] 42 U. S. C. § 7410(a)(2)(e).

[10] *Id.* § 7426(a).

the adequacy of Milwaukee's treatment and control of sewage wastes dumped into Lake Michigan is an example.[11] The Clean Water Act provides that EPA is to take transboundary effects into consideration in issuing permits, but EPA has shown little willingness to take on transboundary controversies.

The legislative branch of the federal government is ill–suited to resolve directly transboundary spillover controversies and other interstate resource conflicts. The states enjoy powerful representation in Congress. They are distrustful of administrative discretion that might be exercised in a manner seriously adverse to their economic interests. Accordingly, Congress has generally been unwilling to give strong powers to federal administrators to resolve spillover or other interstate resource controversies. For similar reasons, it has been difficult to reach agreement in Congress on specific measures directed at interstate controversies. An effort is made to deal with such problems indirectly through uniform national measures, such as the national ambient air quality standards or nationally uniform effluent limitations, aimed at all sources of pollution. But these responses are often inadequate to resolve particularized interstate spillover problems. The limited power granted EPA under the Clean Air and Water Acts to deal with spillovers has not been vigorously exercised, in large part because of administrative reluctance to become involved in politically charged interstate disputes.

Congress has also failed to deal effectively with a variety of important interstate or inter–regional resource conflicts other than pollution spillovers. These include state bans on nuclear or toxic waste disposal, heavy taxes by energy producing states on energy development, and state restrictions on particular forms of energy development. An effective solution to many of these problems would involve total federal preemption or strict federal control of state land use regulation and state taxation. Strong interests in state autonomy, represented through the Congress, have blocked the necessary legislation, as illustrated by President Carter's failure to secure congressional adoption of an Energy Mobilization Board to impose restrictions on state regulation of major energy facilities.[12]

B. Cooperative Harmonization of Law Among States

The Constitution provides for congressional ratification of compacts negotiated among states; when ratified, the compacts have the force of federal law. Some compacts exist for the management of interstate rivers, including the Colorado and the Delaware. Their use has been limited by difficulties in

[11] *See infra* text accompanying notes 48–50.

[12] *See* Note, *The Energy Mobilization Board*, 8 Ecology L. Q. 727 (1980). For general discussion of interstate resource conflicts, *see* Stewart, *Interstate Resource Conflicts: The Role of the Federal Courts*, 6 Harv. Envt'l L. Rev. 241 (1982).

reaching agreement on terms, and enforcement problems presented by vague or ambiguous language in compacts.[13]

No substantial effort has been made to harmonize state environmental law through the Commission on Uniform State Law, the Restatements of Law, and so on. The federal courts have not, through the exercise of their diversity jurisdiction or otherwise, contributed appreciably to the harmonization of state environmental law.

C. Role of Litigation and Remedies

1. Introduction: Federal Administrative Procedures and the Judicial System

Federal agencies and courts have played a major role in the shaping and implementation of federal environmental policy, and must be considered in any assessment of the US experience. This subsection provides some basic background information.

a. Administrative Procedures

Federal environmental statutes delegate major responsibilities for implementation and enforcement to federal administrative authorities, the most important of which are the Environmental Protection Agency (air and water pollution, toxic chemicals and wastes, solid wastes, uranium tailings, noise); the Interior Department (management of public lands except national forests); the Forest Service in the Agriculture Department (national forests); the National Oceanic and Atmospheric Administration in the Commerce Department (fisheries and coastal zone management); and the Nuclear Regulatory Commission (nuclear radiation hazards). Other federal agencies whose actions have major environmental implications include the Energy Department, the Army Corps of Engineers, and the Transportation Department.

Many of the regulatory statutes adopted by Democratic Congresses between 1968 and 1976 reflect a sharp distrust of the incumbent Republican presidential

[13] *See generally,* Muys, *Allocation and Management of Interstate Water Resources: The Emergence of the Federal Interstate Compact,* 6 Denver J. Int. L. & Pol. 307 (1976).

Interstate compacts have also been used in the context of air pollution control. *See generally,* Hirsch & Abramovitz, *Clearing the Air: Some Legal Aspects of Interstate Air Pollution Problems,* 18 Duquesne L. Rev. 53 (1979); Weakly, *Interstate Compacts in the Law of Air and Water Pollution,* 3 Nat. Resources Law. 81 (1970). Several federal statutes encourage states to form interstate pollution control compacts. *E. g.,* RCRA, 42 U. S. C. § 6904(b); Clean Air Act, 42 U. S. C. § 7402(c). Such compacts, however, do not take effect until approved by Congress. Congress has refused to ratify any of the few compacts that have been proposed to date. *See* 1 F. Grad, Treatise on Environmental Law §§ 2.127–2.134 (Matthew Bender & Co., New York, NY 1973). As previously noted, the Low-Level Radioactive Waste Policy Act seeks to encourage interstate compacts to deal with disposal of such waste on a cooperative basis. *See supra* Ch. V notes 99–100 and accompanying text.

administration's commitment to environmental concerns. This distrust is often reflected in detailed statutory provisions designed to limit administrative discretion and force implementation of specific environmental measures. For example, the Clean Air Act and the Clean Water Act specify with great particularity the strategies to be used in implementing pollution controls and impose specific deadlines for the accomplishment of various steps in the implementation process. They provide for "citizen suits" against the Environmental Protection Agency for failure to adhere to these "action forcing" requirements.[14] The highly detailed character of these statutes has made it necessary to amend them frequently because deadlines have not been met or the policy specified by Congress has proved unworkable or unwise. Nevertheless, these statutes involve considerable administrative discretion in setting standards, establishing priorities, and devising strategies of implementation. At the other extreme are statutes, such as the so-called Bureau of Land Management Organic Act, that grant very broad discretion to federal administrators in the management of public resources.

In implementing environmental statutes, administrators rely heavily on regulations adopted through notice and comment rulemaking procedures.[15] This process is used to specify pollution standards and implementing measures and to establish procedures and criteria for public resource management decisions.

The notice and comment rulemaking procedures require the responsible federal agency to publish its proposed regulation in the Federal Register, and make publicly available information and analysis generated by the agency in connection with the proposal. The public is then given a minimum of sixty days to submit comments on the proposal. Industry groups, developers, environmental groups, and concerned state and local authorities all participate actively in important rulemaking procedures, submitting extensive comments that include their own data and analysis. In adopting a final regulation, the agency must accompany its decision with an elaborate opinion explaining the basis for its action and dealing with contrary data, analysis, and criticisms submitted by outside groups. The decision must be based on a documentary record consisting of the agency's studies and information and all submissions by outside parties.[16] Controversial regulations are frequently challenged in court. Major rulemaking proceedings, such as those involving the adoption of environmental quality standards or technology-based emission standards for industrial plants, often take several years.

[14] Clean Air Act, 42 U. S. C. § 7604; Clean Water Act, 33 U. S. C. § 1365. *See also* Noise Control Act, 42 U. S. C. § 4911; Safe Drinking Water Act, 42 U. S. C. § 300j–8; Marine Protection Research and Sanctuaries Act, 33 U. S. C. § 1416(g); Resource Conservation and Recovery Act, 42 U. S. C. § 6974.

[15] Administrative Procedure Act, 5 U. S. C. § 553.

[16] *See generally* Stewart, *The Development of Administrative and Quasi-Constitutional Law in Judicial Review of Environmental Decisionmaking: Lessons from the Clean Air Act*, 62 Iowa L. Rev. 713, 733–40 (1977).

The standards adopted in these regulations are implemented through decisions on individual plants and projects. In the context of pollution and toxic waste control, firms must generally obtain licenses or permits specifying their compliance with the standards established in the regulations. Regulation of pesticides, toxic chemicals, manufacture and sale of chemical products, and major facilities siting is generally accomplished through case by case screening of varying individual products or projects under general criteria. Firms or other interested parties (including environmental groups) contesting the agency's application of regulatory standards or criteria to particular facilities, projects, or products can generally obtain a trial-type administrative hearing if they can demonstrate the existence of material disputed facts.

Policies regarding public resources are developed and implemented through case by case decisions on particular investments of federal moneys in projects or particular decisions to develop public lands. These decisions generally are made through a relatively informal process involving federal officials, state officials who also have licensing or planning responsibility for the project, the responsible industry or project developer, and, less frequently, environmental groups. Preparation of an environmental impact statement is normally required. In addition, some form of hearing is generally provided in contested cases. Depending on the applicable statute, the "hearing" may be no more than the opportunity to submit written comments and perhaps oral argument, or may amount to a full-fledged trial with testimony by witnesses and cross-examination.[17] Most proceedings are relatively informal.

Relations between federal agencies whose prime mission is environmental protection and those whose mission is development frequently assume an adversary character. For example, EPA air pollution regulations have an important impact on the development of oil shale. The Department of Energy actively participates in EPA rulemaking proceedings, often voicing strong criticism of EPA proposals and submitting extensive data and analysis to justify less stringent controls. By the same token, EPA participates in Energy Department proceedings, arguing that regulations implementing programs to encourage conversion by utilities and industry from oil to coal should include stringent environmental controls. Even within a given Department, such as the Interior, sharp conflicts exist between development-minded bureaus such as the Bureau of Land Management, and conservationist bureaus such as the National Park Service.

If controversies between departments or agencies become acute, they may attract the attention of the Office of Management and Budget (OMB) and even the President, although such intervention is sporadic. In addition, every president since Nixon has sought to assert White House and OMB control over the costs imposed by environmental, health, and safety regulation. In its present version, this system of control (established by Executive Order 12,291)

[17] For general discussion of the procedures and administrative law principles governing federal environmental agency decisionmaking, *see* R. Stewart & J. Krier, Environmental Law & Policy Ch. 7 (Bobbs-Merrill Co., Charlottesville, Va. 1978).

requires that regulatory agencies prepare an economic analysis of "major" regulatory proposals likely to impose significant costs on the American economy.[18] These assessments must include determination of proposals' economic and social costs and benefits and a study of alternative measures that would produce greater net benefits or be more cost–effective. These procedures provide a mechanism whereby industry or others critical of environmental controls can attempt to moderate initiatives by regulatory agencies. Administrators are also required by the Executive Order to consider these assessments and adopt the alternative that is most cost–effective or yields greatest net benefits, to the extent that such consideration and action is not precluded by the relevant statute specifically governing the action in question. Draft and final assessments must be presented to the Office of Management and Budget prior to final action. The Office of Management and Budget and the staff of the Council of Economic Advisors include a substantial number of economists and other analysts who review these statements.

OMB also reviews proposed regulations that impose paperwork burdens under the Paperwork Reduction Act of 1980.[19] Unless OMB approves, no federal agency may issue or revise reporting, record keeping, or similar information collection requirements. Given the extensive data collection provisions in many federal environmental laws, this statute may significantly affect future regulatory policies.

OMB and, on a few occasions, White House staff have intervened to hold up regulations that they perceive as excessively costly. A few of these cases have involved the President.[20] In many instances, the regulatory agency (generally the Environmental Protection Agency or the Occupational Health and Safety Administration) has substantially prevailed. On the other hand, the economic impact assessment procedures, the provision for OMB review, and the possibility of White House intervention have undoubtedly had a restraining effect on the stringency of environmental regulations. The requirements of regulatory analysis and OMB review have undoubtedly been used by the administration as a political/bureaucratic weapon to moderate initiatives by regulation minded agencies which the White House views as extreme or unthinking. But from a longer term perspective, such measures could serve as a useful institutional innovation to coordinate and discipline a decentralized and often parochial regulatory system. Existing congressional and judicial controls over that system are fragmented, intermittent, and sometimes technically ill–informed.

[18] Exec. Order No. 12, 291, 46 Fed. Reg. 13, 193 (1981). Under the Order, "major" proposals include all those with estimated compliance costs over $100 million. Exec. Order No. 12, 291 § 1(b).

The order has generated considerable commentary and controversy, *e. g.*, Rosenberg, *Beyond the Limits of Executive Power: Presidential Control of Agency Rulemaking Under Executive Order 12, 291*, 80 Mich. L. Rev. 193 (1981).

[19] 44 U. S. C. §§ 3501–3520.

[20] *See, e. g.*, Sierra Club v. Costle, 657 F. 2d 298 (D. C. Cir. 1981).

The implementation of federal environmental and resource management programs entails considerable informal consulation and negotiation among federal administrative officials and their state and local counterparts. EPA has ten regional offices through which liaison with counterpart state agencies is maintained. In addition to regional offices, the Interior Department has officials located on federal lands and major federal project sites. As previously noted, the Reagan administration is shifting a great deal of implementation and enforcement responsibility for environmental regulatory statutes to the states. It has also promised states in which federal lands and projects are located considerable say in their management and development. Federal funding of state programs through conditional grants has been an important factor in state–federal relations in the past, but the amount of such funding has been reduced or limited by the Reagan administration.

Environmental advocates and federal officials often regard state environmental programs as inadequate either because of lack of political commitment to environmental measures or inadequate resources or both. State and local officials typically complain that federal supervision and review procedures are excessively time–consuming and cumbersome. They claim that the federal government takes too long to develop governing regulations, and that, once adopted, such regulations and associated policies are subject to frequent and confusing changes.

b. The Judicial System

Pursuant to Article III of the Constitution, federal district courts have "federal question" jurisdiction to entertain controversies arising under the "Constitution and laws" of the United States. Constitutional issues are rare in environmental controversies; the effort by environmentalists in the early 1970s to win federal court recognition of a constitutional right to the environment failed totally.[21] However, the federal courts have played a major role in overseeing administrative enforcement and implementation of environmental statutes and administrative management of public resources.

Administrative law, particularly in the environmental area, has been aggressively developed by federal judges over the past fifteen years in order to control administrative decisionmaking. Traditionally, only industries subject to regulatory controls or persons claiming private property interest in public resources could challenge federal administrative actions in court. But the courts have recently relaxed doctrines of standing and ripeness to allow environmental and conservation groups as well as interested state and local authorities to obtain review.

Under current law, a person seeking federal court review of federal agency action (or inaction) must generally show that it has or will cause him "injury in fact."[22] The Supreme Court has interpreted "injury in fact" quite liberally.

[21] *See* R. Stewart & J. Krier, *supra* note 17, at 300–312.

[22] Association of Data Processing Service Organizations v. Camp, 397 U. S. 150 (1970). The requirements of *Data Processing* and the APA apply when (as is usually the case)

Although a purely ideological interest in a problem is generally not sufficient to confer standing, "injury in fact" includes adverse aesthetic effects and health risks as well as economic injury. Moreover, a membership association can obtain standing if it has at least one member who suffers such injury. Finally, the fact that the injury is individually small and that many other individuals – even the entire population – also suffer the same injury is not a bar to standing.[23] Under this approach, for example, any resident of the northeastern US would have standing to seek review of EPA decisions allowing increased sulfur emission from midwest sources that contributed to acid deposition in the northeast. In addition to showing injury, a person must be "arguably within the zone of interests regulated or protected" by a statute and must show that a favorable judgment on the merits will prevent or redress the injury. These requirements, however, are generally not difficult to satisfy. Review can be sought immediately after regulations have been adopted or after a final decision has been made to commence a project. In addition, environmental groups generally may obtain review of agency failure to adopt regulations or to take enforcement action to implement environmental programs. In many federal environmental statutes, this right to obtain judicial review of agency failure to act or enforce is codified in "citizen suit" provisions.[24]

A high percentage of agency decisions are challenged in court by industry and environmental groups. Courts review agencies' compliance with applicable substantive statutes and regulations and also consider whether agency exercise of discretion is "arbitrary and capricious."[25] They also review the evidentiary foundation for agency factual determinations and enforce often demanding procedural requirements. On matters of discretion, courts will rarely overrule agency choices as impermissibly arbitrary, but will conduct a searching review of the administrative record and the agency's explanation for its decision in order to determine whether it has taken a "hard look" at all relevant data, analyses, and policy considerations, including those offered by outside parties.[26] Failure to satisfy this standard results in remand for further proceedings, a frequent occurrence. Both industry and environmental interests devote substantial resources to litigation, although industry outspends environmental groups by a large margin. Successful environmental group litigants sometimes

the statute providing for court jurisdiction or review fails to specify who may seek review. But sometimes particular environmental statutes deal explicitly with standing. The most notable are the "citizen suit" provisions providing that "any person" may seek review of an agency's failure to carry out statutory duties. See *supra* note 14.

[23] Sierra Club v. Morton, 405 U. S. 727 (1972); United States v. Students Challenging Regulatory Agency Procedures (SCRAP), 412 U. S. 669 (1973).

[24] *See supra* note 14. For general discussion of remedies for inadequate agency implementation and enforcement, *see* Stewart & Sunstein, *Public Programs and Private Rights,* 95 Harv. L. Rev. 1193 (1982).

[25] The "arbitrary and capricious" standard in the Administrative Procedure Act, 5 U. S. C. § 706(2)(A), governs federal judicial review of most federal agencies' decisions. *See* Citizens to Preserve Overton Park, Inc. v. Volpe, 401 U. S. 402 (1971).

[26] *See* Stewart, *supra* note 16, at 133–40.

obtain an award of attorney's fees from the government. Such awards are authorized by many federal environmental regulatory statutes.[27]

Suits under the National Environmental Policy Act challenging an agency's failure to prepare environmental impact stratements or challenging such statements as inadequate are also an important staple of federal environmental litigation.

Federal courts have substantial additional environmental business arising under federal statutes, including civil and criminal enforcement actions initiated by the government, citizen enforcement suits against industry and developers for violation of federal regulatory requirements (in most instances, such suits must be and often are explicitly authorized by statute), disputes with states and contractors in connection with federal grants, and miscellaneous other actions.

A potentially important category of federal jurisdiction is that involving disputes among states with respect to transboundary pollution spillovers or the use and apportionment of interstate waters. This topic is examined in greater detail below.

Under the negative commerce clause doctrine, federal courts review and invalidate state environmental measures that discriminate against or unduly burden interstate commerce. Under the Supremacy Clause in the Constitution, federal courts must also determine the ultimate allocation of authority between federal statutes and programs and state statutes and programs. These questions typically turn on the interpretation of often silent or ambiguous federal statutes in order to determine the extent of their preemptive effect.[28]

Most private litigation for damages is brought in state courts under state tort and property law. Under their diversity jurisdiction, however, federal courts hear controversies based on state law when the parties are citizens of different states. Federal statutes rarely authorize private damage actions and the Supreme Court has recently curtailed the tendency of lower federal courts to imply damage actions for violations of federal environmental statutes.[29] Most state courts have adopted some version of strict liability in connection with environmental or consumer–product harms, although proving injury and causa-

[27] *See, e. g.*, Clean Air Act § 307(f), 42 U. S. C. § 7607(f), and other statutes collected in Ruckleshaus v. Sierra Club, 103 S. Ct. 3274, 3275–6 n. 1 (1983). In that decision the Court took a highly restrictive interpretation of § 307(f), which authorizes court award of attorney's fees to a party whenever the court determines that such an award is "appropriate." Despite the fact that § 307(f) was deliberately intended to go beyond statutes authorizing such awards only to a "prevailing party," the Court held that § 307(f) authorizes awards only to parties who have prevailed in whole or in part, reversing a lower court decision awarding fees to an environmental group that had not prevailed but had raised important and weighty legal claims whose resolution, in the court's view, had helped clarify the applicable law.

[28] *See* Stewart, *supra* note 12.

[29] *E. g.*, Middlesex County Sewerage Authority v. National Sea Clammers Association, 453 U. S. 1 (1981).

tion is often a significant obstacle.[30] Issues of state statutory and administrative law are normally heard and decided in state courts, although on occasion a controversy may involve issues of both state and federal law, and the issues of federal law may support federal jurisdiction. In such cases, federal courts may decide the state issues under the principle of pendent jurisdiction.

Complicated problems of jurisdiction arise under federal environmental programs involving a substantial state implementation and enforcement role. Consider, for example, cases where implementation and enforcement has been delegated by a federal agency to a state agency; the state agency either takes or refuses to take certain action; and the responsible federal agency takes no steps to veto or modify the state agency's decision. The question arises whether the state agency's conduct or the federal agency's failure to act may be reviewed in federal court. The results are mixed, although the recent tendency has been to limit federal court jurisdiction.[31] The allocation of competence problem becomes even more complicated when administrative remedies must be exhausted prior to judicial action and both state and federal administrative agencies may provide (or must concur in) the relief sought.

2. Remedies Initiated by Federal Authorities

The remedies here discussed are limited to the three categories of federal regulatory programs: direct federal regulation, state implementation of federal standards, and federal encouragement of state regulation.

a. Against Private Persons

Federal programs of direct federal regulation of private persons provide for a wide variety of enforcement powers and sanctions. Administratively instituted sanctions include cease and desist orders, license revocation, and civil penalties. Their imposition is subject to judicial review, and coercive enforcement ordinarily requires some form of judicial order. Alternatively, agencies may request the Justice Department to seek judicially imposed sanctions, including injunctions, criminal penalties, or civil penalties.

In programs involving state implementation of federal standards, the federal government as a general matter either has the power to enforce implementing state measures directly against private violators, or the power to take over enforcement responsibility by revoking the delegation of such responsibility to the state.

Federal enforcement against private persons is generally not available under programs of federal encouragement of state regulation. Federal authorities may seek to induce state enforcement by withdrawing approval of state programs as not conforming to federal standards and threatening withdrawal of federal funds that support state programs.

[30] *See generally* Ginsberg & Weiss, *Common Law Liability for Toxic Torts: A Phantom Remedy*, 9 Hofstra L. Rev. 859 (1981).

[31] Shell Oil v. Train, 415 F. Supp. 70 (N. D. Cal. 1977), *aff'd*, 585 F. 2d 408 (9th Cir. 1978); District of Columbia v. Schramm, 631 F. 2d 854, 861 (D. C. Cir. 1980).

b. Against States

State–owned enterprises which generate pollution or cause other forms of environmental degradation are subject to federal enforcement in the same fashion as private persons. Otherwise the question of federal remedies against states arises only in the context of state implementation of federal standards or programs designed to encourage state regulation. We first discuss the remedies potentially available in the case of state implementation of federal standards.

Federal agencies generally lack authority to require states to undertake implementation and enforcement of federal regulatory programs against private actors, and federal courts have in several cases refused to grant injunctive or declaratory relief imposing such an obligation.[32] Despite the broad reach of Congress' commerce power, courts have been reluctant to find such authority in relevant statutes, and have suggested or held that coercive federal conscription of states in regulatory implementation would violate principles of state autonomy recognized by the federal structure of the US Constitution and the Tenth Amendment. These decisions are based on the Supreme Court's *National League of Cities* decision, which forbids federal impositions on states that violate their independence and capacity for self–determination.[33] However, courts have upheld EPA authority to require a state not to register or permit use of its highways by automobiles that do not meet federal air pollution requirements.[34]

When federal grants are provided to fund state implementation and enforcement, the responsible federal agency normally has administrative authority to terminate such funding on a determination that the state's program fails to meet federal requirements. This remedy is an unpalatable one from the viewpoint of federal administrators, because a cut–off of federal funds defeats the ultimate objectives of the federal program. Alternatively, the federal agency may obtain a declaratory judgment from a federal court that a state is obliged to adhere to federal standards so long as it continues to receive federal funds (adversely affected private citizens can also obtain such a judgment). Thus far, federal courts have refused to entertain or uphold claims that the use of conditional grants to induce states to carry out federal requirements violates the principles of federalism recognized in *National League of Cities* by empow-

[32] *E. g.*, Brown v. EPA, 566 F. 2d 665 (9th Cir. 1977). For discussion, see STEWART, *Pyramids of Sacrifice? Problems of Federalism in Mandating State Implementation of National Environmental Policy*, 86 YALE L. J. 1196 (1977).

[33] 426 U. S. 833 (1976) (invalidating application of federal minimum wage requirements to state employees). The precedental strength of *National League of Cities* was diminished by E. E. O. C. v. Wyoming, 103 S. Ct. 1054 (1983) (upholding application of federal age discrimination regulations to state employees).

[34] United States v. Ohio Department of Highway Safety, 635 F. 2d 1195 (6th Cir. 1980), *cert. denied*, 451 U. S. 949 (1981).

ering federal authorities to secure indirectly what they can not require directly.[35]

In order to induce states to adopt automobile emission control inspection and maintenance plans, the Clean Air Act authorizes EPA to cut off federal highway grants to states that fail to adopt and enforce such plans. It also authorizes EPA to ban construction in such states of new stationary sources emitting automotive-type pollutants.[36] These measures, which are apparently constitutional, have been successfully employed by EPA to induce most states that have not attained the federal ambient standards for automotive-type pollutants to adopt inspection and maintenance plans.

In the case of federal programs designed to encourage state regulation, the only statutory sanctions generally provided for state non-cooperation are termination of federal financial assistance or, alternatively, a declaratory judgment of state duty to comply with federal standards so long as the state continues to receive funds. The Coastal Zone Management Act provides the additional incentive of granting states with qualifying coastal zone management plans authority to regulate outer continental shelf developments otherwise within exclusive federal regulatory competence.

3. Private Remedies

a. Federal Agency Compliance with Federal Resource Management Laws

Development and environmental groups and concerned state and local authorities enjoy ready access to administrative proceedings and court review to challenge federal agency decisions with respect to management of federal resources. Most often suit is brought by plaintiffs challenging decisions in favor of development, but industrial firms and organizations favoring development have successfully challenged administrative decisions to withhold resources from development. With a few notable exceptions, such as the Endangered Species Act, relevant statutes generally grant administrators considerable discretion. Because organic statutes generally provide little in the way of formal procedures for administrative resource decisions, NEPA is the principal source of procedural requirements. Although NEPA does not explicitly provide for judicial review, courts have vigorously enforced the environmental impact statement requirement in NEPA while at the same time emphasizing that NEPA's requirements are "essentially procedural" and that substantive review must largely be based on other relevant statutes.

b. Federal Regulatory Agency Implementation and Enforcement

Those subject to regulation can secure judicial review of implementing regulations when issued; of permit decisions; and of enforcement actions. Environmental groups and others complaining of inadequate implementation and en-

[35] *See generally* Note, *Taking Federalism Seriously: Limiting State Acceptance of National Grants*, 90 YALE L. J. 1694 (1981).

[36] 42 U. S. C. § 7506.

forcement face a somewhat more difficult situation because of traditional doctrines barring judicial review of prosecutorial discretion. These doctrines have, however, been considerabley eroded. Environmental plaintiffs can ordinarily challenge implementing regulations as inadequate. They can also challenge a failure to issue implementing regulations or to take enforcement action if such initiatives are mandated by statute. Such "action forcing" mandates are common in many federal environmental statutes. The Clean Air Act and the Clean Water Act, for example, require EPA to issue implementing regulations by specified deadlines and provide that EPA "shall" institute enforcement proceedings against designated types of violation.[37] Many statutes contain "citizen suit" provisions empowering "any person" to seek judicial relief against EPA for failure to perform a non–discretionary duty.[38]

Moreover, courts have reviewed agencies' failure to take action even when the relevant statute grants them substantial discretion in implementation and enforcement.[39] As a generalization, if a plaintiff makes out a prima facie case that agency failure to undertake implementation and enforcement measures is contrary to statutory purposes or unreasonable, the court will grant review and require a reasoned justification by the agency for its conduct.

The greatest difficulty faced by environmental plaintiffs is obtaining effective judicial relief against agency failure to take implementation and enforcement action. Even where a statute mandates issuance of regulations by a deadline or compels agency enforcement action against violations, federal judges are reluctant to impose contempt sanctions on agencies or administrators who claim (often with considerable justification) that their resources are too limited to discharge all of the duties mandated by Congress in "action forcing" statutes, that action requires information and analyses that are not readily available, and that statutory deadlines are hopelessly unrealistic. The usual remedy is the negotiation, under judicial prodding, of a timetable for action, although such timetables are often subject to further postponements.[40] Where statutes grant administrators greater discretion, courts show correspondingly greater deference, and agencies may, by pointing to limited resources and a host of complex and burdensome responsibilities, rather easily persuade a court that their failure to take action in a particular instance was not unreasonable.[41] In some instances, the agency's discretion may be so extensive that courts will dismiss the case at the outset on the ground that the matter is committed to agency discretion by law and therefore unreviewable.

[37] For example, the Clean Air Act requires EPA to take action against major stationary sources that violate applicable standards. 42 U. S. C. § 7413.

[38] *See supra* note 14. These provisions also authorize courts to grant attorneys' fees to plaintiffs.

[39] *See, e. g.*, Environmental Defense Fund, Inc. v. Ruckleshaus, 439 F. 2d 584 (D. C. Cir. 1971). For discussion, *see* STEWART & SUNSTEIN, *supra* note 24, at 1267–1289.

[40] *See* Illinois v. Gorsuch, 530 F. Supp. 337 (D. D. C 1981), *aff'd* 684 F. 2d 1033 (D. C. Cir. 1982) (recounting "years of futility" experienced by court in attempt to force EPA to promulgate regulations concerning hazardous waste land disposal facilities).

[41] *See* STEWART & SUNSTEIN, *supra* note 24, at 1283–84.

c. State Implementation of Federal Standards and Programs

Mixed federal–state regulatory programs involve complex issues of federal and state remedial law.[42]

Standards or implementing regulations issued by a federal agency, as well as its failure to issue standards or regulations, are reviewable under the principles governing direct federal regulatory programs. Complexities arise when litigants challenge or seek relief from state agency decisions.

A person subject to regulation may challenge a state agency's requirements as contrary to federal law. Such challenges raise substantive and procedural problems. The substantive problem is that states are generally free to impose controls more rigorous than those required by federal law. Unless the plaintiff can establish some form of federal preemption, or perhaps that the state agency relied exclusively upon an erroneous interpretation of federal law, he will have no substantial federal claim, and must show that the state agency has exceeded its authority under state law. The procedural problems are several. One is the difficulty of obtaining federal court review of federal agency failure to correct the state agency's assertedly erroneous action. Unless the federal agency has specific authority to veto or override particular state agency decisions, such review will not be available. Even if the federal agency has such authority, failure to exercise it in particular cases may be held non–reviewable as committed to agency discretion. The state agency's action may be reviewable in federal court if the agency is regarded as "federal" because it is executing a federal program, but this will depend upon the details of the statutory program. If such review is not available, the litigant will have to seek state court review of the state agency's action and raise his federal claim in the state proceedings.

Alternatively, a regulated firm may seek discretionary relief from a state agency. Where federal agency concurrence is not required, the problems of judicial review are the same as those discussed in the previous paragraph. But where federal concurrence is required (as in the case of revision of a State Implementation Plan under the Clean Air Act), plaintiff may have to seek administrative relief from both state and federal agencies and, upon its denial, seek judicial review of the state agency's decision on state (and possibly federal) grounds in state court, and simultaneously seek review of the federal agency's decision in federal court.

Now take the case where an environmental or similar plaintiff complains of (a) a state agency's grant of regulatory permission or relief as contrary to federal law, or (b) state agency failure to take implementation and enforcement action.

Direct federal court review of the state agency's action (or inaction) would ordinarily not be available, although in cases of type (a) the state agency may,

[42] Many of the issues discussed in this section are examined in greater detail, with discussion of relevant decisions, in D. Currie, Air Pollution: Federal Law and Analysis §§ 9.02–9.06, 9.10–9.13, 9.22–9.23 (Callaghan & Co., Wilmette, Illinois) (1981 with 1983 cumulative Supp.)

depending on the statutory scheme, be regarded as a federal instrumentality. In most cases plaintiff must look to one or more of the following alternative remedies, none of which may be satisfactory: First, relief could be sought from the federal agency responsible for supervising state implementation and enforcement. The agency could be asked to veto state actions of type (a) if it has such authority. In cases of type (b), it could be asked to revoke a delegation and initiate direct federal enforcement, or cut off funds to the state agency. Judicial review of the federal agency's response would often (though not always) be available in the federal courts, but if so, the standard of review would be highly deferential. A second potential remedy would be judicial review in the state courts of the state agency's failure to conform with federal law. A third avenue of relief is a declaratory judgment action in federal court that a state agency receiving federal conditional grants is obliged to obey those conditions so long as it continues to receive federal funds. None of these remedies is likely to be very successful unless federal obligations are clearly defined and the responsible federal agency has a strong interest in seeing them honored.

There are instances where both federal and state agencies are simultaneously playing an active role in implementation and enforcement, thus creating quite difficult problems of the availability and timing of remedy in state and federal courts; these problems will not be elaborated here.

d. Private Enforcement Actions Against Regulated Enterprises

Citizen suit provisions in many federal environmental statutes, such as the Clean Air Act, authorize direct citizen enforcement of regulations and permit requirements through actions in federal district court against individuals and enterprises subject to regulation, although thirty days' notice must be given to the responsible state or federal enforcement agency. Permits issued by state agencies pursuant to programs providing for state implementation of federal standards are generally federally enforceable in the same fashion.[43] Statutes generally limit relief to injunctive remedies and do not authorize recovery of damages. Despite the fact that the citizen suit provisions provide for reimbursement of successful plaintiffs' litigation expenses, these provisions have not been widely used because of difficulties in establishing violations, which may involve complex monitoring and other technical issues, and the focus of national environmental advocacy groups on national issues rather than case by case enforcement.

Until recently, federal courts had frequently created private damage and injunctive remedies in favor of members of the class of persons intended to be protected by regulatory requirements, unless the relevant statute vested unusual discretion in the agency responsible for implementing it or there was some other special reason to conclude that private judicial remedies were inappropriate. But in several recent decisions, some involving environmental statutes, the Supreme Court has sharply restricted this practice and virtually eliminated

[43] *E. g.*, Clean Air Act, 42 U. S. C. § 7604(f); Clean Water Act, 33 U. S. C. § 1365(f)(6).

private enforcement actions unless specifically authorized by statute.[44] The Court has been concerned about the need for political responsibility for the implementation and enforcement process, the dangers that private enforcement might pose to coordinated and consistent regulatory policy, and the burdens such enforcement actions impose on the courts.

Nonetheless, given the prevalence of citizen suit provisions in federal environmental statutes, environmental plaintiffs can in most cases generally obtain prospective relief in federal court against clear regulatory violations either by requiring federal agencies to initiate enforcement measures or through direct private enforcement actions. Claims for damages, however, must ordinarily be based on state law.

State courts have increasingly embraced principles of strict liability in tort or nuisance suits arising from environmental and consumer–product injuries.[45] In addition, state courts have shown greater willingness to create private damage remedies for violation of state statutes and regulations including, presumably, those established under federal programs. In light of the Supreme Court's recent restriction of private remedies under federal statutes, one may expect increased litigation in state courts seeking damages for violation of federal (as well as state) statutes and regulations as negligence or nuisance *per se.*

The greatest obstacles to recovery in private actions for damages are the requirements that plaintiff prove the existence of some present compensable injury (as opposed to the risk of future injury attributable to current exposure), and also prove that defendant's activities caused the injury.[46] Substantial damage awards have, however, been recovered in cases of single–source exposure to toxic substances and residues.[47] The threat of strict liability in damages is one of great concern to firms, and undoubtedly has a substantial deterrent effect. The availability of damage compensation under state law is an important supplement to federal regulatory programs, which generally do not provide for victim compensation.

4. Special Situations

a. Transboundary Pollution - Public Plaintiffs

The Supreme Court has traditionally acted as a common law tribunal when exercising its original jurisdiction to resolve disputes between states over borders and the apportionment of interstate waters. In a 1972 decision involving a dispute between Illinois and the City of Milwaukee, Wisconsin, over the latter's pollution of Lake Michigan, the Supreme Court recognized a federal common law of interstate pollution to govern disputes between a plaintiff state,

[44] *E. g.*, Middlesex County Sewerage Authority v. National Sea Clammers Association, 453 U. S. 1 (1981). For discussion, *see* Stewart & Sunstein, *supra* note 24.

[45] *See* 1A F. Grad, Treatise on Environmental Law § 4A.05 (Matthew Bender & Co., New York, NY 1982).

[46] Ginsberg & Weiss, *supra* note 30.

[47] *E. g.*, Bichler v. Eli Lilly & Co., 79 A. D. 2d 317, 436 N. Y. S. 2d 625 (1981).

suing *parens patriae* on behalf of its citizens, and a defendant state or state or local authority.[48] Such suits may be brought under the original jurisdiction of the Supreme Court or the federal question jurisdiction of the federal district courts. Some lower federal courts have applied the federal common law of interstate pollution to state suits against private defendants in other states.[49]

The federal common law remedy for interstate spillovers was, however, sharply restricted by the Supreme Court's second decision in the *Illinois v. Milwaukee* controversy, holding that the Clean Water Act had preempted the federal common law of interstate pollution,[50] and that Illinois was accordingly obliged to seek an administrative remedy from the federal Environmental Protection Agency. In so ruling, the Court emphasized the limitations of courts in dealing with the scientific and technical issues presented by interstate pollution controversies, and the absence of standards for deciding such controversies. Given the breadth of most federal regulatory statutes and the willingness of the Supreme Court to find regulatory preemption, little federal common law seems likely to survive.

In most cases, therefore, states will have to seek relief against transboundary spillovers from federal regulatory authorities. However, the discretion enjoyed by such authorities and their reluctance, already noted, to take on politically sensitive and administratively cumbersome interstate controversies make this a weak remedy. Despairing of effective relief from EPA, states suffering from acid rain are contemplating litigation under the federal common law of interstate pollution, even though there is a substantial probability that the suit will be held preempted by the Clean Air Act.

Alternatively, states suffering from interstate spillovers may seek to use their own municipal law and courts to obtain relief against transboundary spillovers. Suits against other states would be barred by sovereign immunity, but a receiving state could constitutionally exercise "long arm" jurisdiction over private sources in other states causing damage within the receiving state. Damage judgments against the defendant would be enforceable in the state where the defendant resides under the full faith and credit clause of the Constitution. A state might conceivably obtain damages as *parens patriae* on behalf of its citizens, but these would ordinarily be quite difficult to prove. It may well be – although the issue has not been authoritatively resolved – that the full faith and credit clause does not oblige the originating state to enforce an injunction issued by a receiving state court against the polluting source.[51] Unless the defendant has operations or property within the receiving state, an effective

[48] Illinois v. City of Milwaukee, 406 U. S. 91 (1972).

[49] *E. g.*, State of Texas v. Pankey, 441 F. 2d 236 (10th Cir. 1971). *See generally* ELLICKSON, *Public Property Rights: A Government's Rights and Duties When Its Landowners Come Into Conflict with Outsiders*, 52 S. C. L. REV. 1627 (1979).

[50] City of Milwaukee v. Illinois, 451 U. S. 304 (1981).

[51] U. S. Const. art. IV, § 1. Traditionally, courts have refused to issue or enforce injunctive remedies pertaining to the ownership or disposition of land in another jurisdiction. *See* 11 C. WRIGHT & A. MILLER, FEDERAL PRACTICE & PROCEDURE: Civil § 2945 (1973 & Supp. 1981) (West Publishing, St. Paul, Minnesota).

remedy will be difficult to obtain. (Ironically, it was these deficiencies in the remedies otherwise available that led to creation of a federal common law of interstate disputes in the first *Illinois* v. *Milwaukee* decision.) Moreover, under the two successive *Illinois* v. *Milwaukee* decisions, it might be held first, that state law, as applied to interstate pollution controversies, had been, preempted by federal common law; and second, that federal common law had been preempted by federal regulatory statutes.[52]

b. Transboundary Pollution - Private Plaintiffs

Although lower federal courts have held that private plaintiffs may invoke the federal common law of interstate pollution to obtain redress against pollution of interstate waters,[53] this question is now largely moot in light of the Supreme Court's readiness to find preemption of federal common law by federal regulatory statutes.

Private plaintiffs can seek relief against interstate spillovers from federal regulatory authorities and can enforce federal orders or regulations against non-complying sources in other states through federal court "citizen suits." However, the typical problem is that existing federal statutes and regulations are not adequate to deal with interstate spillovers. Given the considerable discretion enjoyed by federal administrators and their reluctance to take on interstate controversies, judicial remedies are unlikely to be of great value.

Federal law guarantees access, on a nondiscriminatory basis, by citizens of one state to administrative and judicial tribunals in other states.[54] The obstacles to effective relief by pursuing remedies in the state where pollution originates are the general inadequacy of state laws in controlling discharges resulting in distant pollution and the parochial tendency of an originating state to ignore or discount out of state impacts.

There are also obstacles to effective private relief in the courts or agencies of the receiving state. Traditional administrative remedies generally do not apply to out of state sources. Court jurisdiction over out of state polluters could be obtained in most jurisdictions under "long arm" statutes, but damages are rarely obtainable because of difficulty in proving compensable injury and causation. Courts are reluctant to enter injunctive decrees that must be enforced against out of state activities, and, as already noted, it is doubtful whether the originating state would be obliged to give full faith and credit to such a decree.

[52] This logic is implicit in Middlesex County Sewage Authority v. Natural Sea Clammers Association, 453 U.S. 1 (1981), holding private damage actions for interstate and offshore water pollution preempted by the Clear Water Act, even though that Act fails to provide a damage remedy and expressly saves state law remedies.

[53] National Sea Clammers Association v. City of New York, 616 F. 2d. 1222 (3d Cir. 1980), *rev'd on other grounds sub nom.* Middlesex County Sewerage Authority v. National Sea Clammers Association, 453 U. S. 1 (1981).

[54] "Citizens of each state shall be entitled to all the Privileges and Immunities of Citizens in the General States," U. S. Const. art. IV, § 2, cl. 1. *See* L. Tribe, American Constitutional Law § 6–32 (Foundation Press, Minneola, NY 1978).

c. *Challenges to State Environmental and Resource Measures as an Unconstitutional Burden on Commerce*

A person subject to or injured by state regulation or taxation may challenge the measure as an unconstitutional burden on interstate commerce under the negative commerce clause doctrine.[55] The federal courts have construed the Constitution's grant of power to regulate commerce as a mandate for the federal courts, when Congress has not acted, to promote freedom of interstate commerce by striking down discriminatory or unduly burdensome state measures.[56] Because of federal statutes prohibiting initiation in federal district court of suits challenging state taxes and other limitations on federal district court jurisdiction, a private person challenging a state measure must often pursue his claim through the state courts and seek Supreme Court review of an adverse decision. The state courts are, however, required to apply federal law, and often invalidate state measures as an unconstitutional burden on commerce.[57] A state may also challenge another state's measure as an infringement of interstate commerce, invoking the original jurisdiction of the Supreme Court (such suits are rare).

Federal courts have invalidated state taxes on energy and national resource development that openly discriminate against out of state consumers, but have sustained nondiscriminatory taxes even though most of the resource is exported.[58] Discriminatory regulatory measures, such as a ban by New Jersey on disposal of out of state wastes within its borders, have likewise been invalidated.[59] Courts have generally sustained nondiscriminatory regulatory measures, including detergent bans, bans on nonreturnable containers, and bottle deposit legislation.[60] Unless a state statute by its terms discriminates against out of state producers or consumers or imposes an obviously disproportionate burden on them which otherwise lacks rational foundation, state regulation and taxation of environmental and natural resources will generally be sustained against commerce clause attack.[61]

[55] *See, e. g.*, Philadelphia v. New Jersey, 437 U. S. 617 (1978) (invalidating New Jersey ban on in–state disposal of waste generated out of state); Hughes v. Oklahoma, 441 U. S. 322 (1979) (invalidating Oklahoma statute that prohibited export of minnows).

[56] *See* Kommers & Waelbroeck, ***Legal Integration and the Free Movement of Goods: The American and European Experience,*** at § II, in INTEGRATION THROUGH LAW, Vol. 1, Book 3. *See also generally* T. DAINTITH & S. WILLIAMS, ENERGY POLICY (Vol. 5, INTEGRATION THROUGH LAW SERIES, forthcoming).

[57] *See, e. g.*, Robert Emmet & Son Oil & Supply Co. v. Sullivan, 259 A. 2d 636, 639 (1969) ("A state may not, through the guise of taxation or otherwise, prohibit or unduly impede the flow of products from other states.").

[58] *See* Commonwealth Edison Co. v. Montana, 453 U. S. 609 (1981).

[59] City of Philadelphia v. New Jersey, 437 U. S. 617 (1978).

[60] *E. g.*, Minnesota v. Clover Leaf Creamery Co., 449 U. S. 456 (1981) (ban on nonreturnable containers upheld).

[61] *See* T. DAINTITH & S. WILLIAMS, *supra* note 56; STEWART, *supra* note 12.

d. Challenges to State Measures as Preempted by Federal Statute

Those subject to state regulation may challenge state regulation or taxation in federal court on the ground that it is preempted by federal statutes or regulations.[62] These controversies present difficult cases for federal courts when, as is frequently the case, the relevant federal statute is silent on the question of preemption or contains a preemption provision that is ambiguous or incomplete. There is a general presumption against preemption but federal courts have, for example, invalidated state or local controls on airline flights, nuclear reactors, and oil tanker operations, and other activities thought to implicate important national interests even though the relevant federal statute did not expressly provide for such preemption.[63]

[62] *See generally* L. Tribe, *supra* note 53, at 376–90.
[63] *See* Stewart, *supra* note 12.

VIII. The Policy Process in the Community

A. Political Choices in Environmental Law

1. Environmental Problems Addressed and Solutions Chosen

a. Lack of Focus, Depth, and Comprehensiveness

Perhaps the most striking feature of Community environmental law is its lack of focus, depth, and comprehensiveness.[1] Critical problems covered by federal legislation in all developed federal systems are not addressed while less important problems are often minutely regulated. Water pollution and wastes have received relative priority while air and noise pollution have been neglected. No environmental sector is comprehensively regulated by the Community. Even waste disposal is no exception. Although it is covered by a framework directive, the framework is applied by only a few implementing directives for particular kinds of waste. Widely marketed products such as motor vehicles, detergents, and chemicals are rather comprehensively regulated. However, the emphasis is on regulating new products, while existing products are relatively ignored. As compared with the multitude of environmental problems arising in an industrial society and normally addressed by federal environmental law, Community environmental law is no more than a kind of regulatory patchwork covering at most a fifth of the relevant problem areas.

This is primarily due to the pragmatic, *ad hoc* approach taken by the Commission in identifying and developing subjects for harmonization. Community environmental policy does not function by identifying priority areas of environmental protection for Community harmonization and leaving less important areas to member state legislation. Instead, it identifies narrow, manageable problems of varying environmental importance. However, the recently adopted third environmental program represents some departure from this pattern.

[1] BOTHE, *The Trends in Both National and International Politics for Achieving a Uniformity of Standards in Pollution Matters*, 2 ZEITSCHRIFT FÜR UMWELTPOLITIK 293, 303 (1979). *Contra*, WEINSTOCK, *Nur eine europäische Umwelt? Europäische Umweltpolitik im Spannungsverhältnis zwischen ökologischer Vielfalt und ökonomischer Einheit*, 6 ZEITSCHRIFT FÜR UMWELTPOLITIK 1, 13, 20, 30 (1983) (attesting that the Community has a "surprisingly complete system" of environmental law while simultaneously complaining of lack of priorities and of depth of regulation and characterizing Community environmental law as "patchwork").

b. Multiplicity of Underlying Rationales

A second characteristic of Community environmental law is that selection of subjects for harmonization can not be explained by any single factor.

Many authors maintain that the primary rationale for Community environmental policy is the desire to eliminate obstacles to trade and distortions of competition. They argue that Community environmental policy can only be incidental to economic and competition policy.[2] This opinion derives from the economic foundation of Community legislative powers granted by Articles 100 and 235 of the EEC Treaty. But this argument overlooks the distinction between motivation and constraint.

The limitations of Articles 100 and 235 do indeed constrain environmental policymaking in the Community. Because the Commission must justify new policy proposals in the framework of the existing legal structure, it tends to address environmental problems that have some substantial economic impact. The emphasis of Community environmental law on pollution and the neglect of land use, natural resources, and protection of nature are a clear indication that, although environmental programs are more broadly conceived, Community environmental policy can not dissociate itself from the economic foundation of the legislative powers granted by Articles 100 and 235

However, it does not follow that Community environmental policy is motivated by trade and competition considerations. The thesis of the exclusively economic motivation of Community environmental law is wrong because it ignores the fact that environmental priorities for the common environmental policy are set by the Community environmental programs, which are not based on narrow trade-related economic concerns, but seek to promote environmental quality as an important goal in its own right. To be sure, economic considerations of a broader sort play a role in the impulse for harmonization, which often comes from "environmental" states that seek to achieve, by harmonization, a Europeanization of the economic burdens imposed on their industry by progressive environmental policy. The political bargaining within the Council over strategies and tools has often been marked by the attempt of "polluter" states to retain competitive advantages arising from the absorption capacity of a comparatively clean environment. A more differentiated analysis of the motivations for selection of topics for Community law is accordingly necessary.

Community regulation is strongest in the case of products associated with health or environmental hazards. According to the conventional wisdom, prod-

[2] H. BUNGARTEN, UMWELTPOLITIK IN WESTEUROPA 226 (Europa Union Verlag, Bonn 1978); WEIDNER & KNOEPFEL, *Implementation der EG-Richtlinie zur SO_2-Luftreinhaltepolitik*, 4 ZEITSCHRIFT FÜR UMWELTPOLITIK 27, 63 *et seq.* (1981). WEINSTOCK, *supra* note 1, at 7 *et seq.*, 13 *et seq.*, 42, 44 (stating that Community Environmental policy can only be conceived as competition policy, but at p. 20 saying that the regular foundation of environmental directives on both Articles 100 and 235 of the EEC Treaty underlines the double function of the policy). *See also* VON MOLTKE & HAIGH, *EC – Major Issues for 1981*, 7 ENVT'L POL'Y & L. 23 (1981).

uct regulation is the obvious candidate for harmonization on economic grounds, and the strength of Community measures in this area is therefore taken as evidence that economic considerations dictate Community policies. But the economic premise of the conventional wisdom is subject to serious question. It may well be that different product requirements distort competition less than different process requirements. Process requirements are limited to national manufacturers; they deteriorate their competitive conditions both on the national and foreign markets. By contrast product requirements are equal for all producers for a given national market.[3] Moreover, the cost of having different product requirements in different national markets is overestimated by neglecting their connection with other market factors, such as market phases and product innovation.[4] Finally, the degree of distortion depends on the size of the national market in which stricter standards are introduced.[5]

Nonetheless, different national requirements for products can not be tolerated in an integrated market because they are a direct threat to the functioning of the Common Market. The desire to eliminate obstacles to trade clearly constituted the rationale for early Community action in the environmental field. Indeed, most such action was called for by the general program of 1969 for the elimination of technical obstacles to trade.[6] Another motivation for the Community's legislative action has sometimes been, as in the case of toxic substances, the need to establish a common bargaining position towards third countries. However, even with respect to product regulation, Community environmental policy has largely been emancipated from exclusive emphasis on economic harmonization. The current emphasis is on progressive solutions for health and environmental protection.

Outside the area of product regulation, contrary to what an exclusively economic foundation for Community environmental policy would imply, there is no clear emphasis on pollution from large industrial sources. Some directives, such as those on the aquatic environment, nuclear safety standards, toxic waste, and chemical accidents, and the proposal on environmental impact assessment are conceptually or practically relevant only to large projects. Others, such as the SO_2 limit values and PCB waste directives, will be more relevant for large projects than for non-point pollution. However, there are many Community directives, such as those on water quality standards, waste disposal, and use of chemicals, that regulate pollution from small sources. The

[3] I. WALTER, INTERNATIONAL ECONOMICS OF POLLUTION 70, 71 (J. Wiley, New York, Toronto 1975).

[4] Gröner, *Umweltschutzbedingte Produktnormen als nichttarifäre Handelshemmnisse*, in UMWELTSCHUTZ UND WETTBEWERB 143, 156 *et seq.* (H. Gutzler ed., Nomos Verlag, Baden-Baden 1981).

[5] Gray, *Commercial Policy Implications of Environmental Controls*, in STUDIES IN INTERNATIONAL ENVIRONMENTAL ECONOMICS 159, at 172–173 (I. Walter ed., J. Wiley, New York, London, Sydney, Toronto 1976).

[6] Of 28 May 1969, JO No. C 76, 17 June 1969, p. 1, as updated by the Council Resolution of 17 Dec. 1973 on industrial policy, OJ No. C 117, 31 Dec. 1973, p. 1.

1980 progress report of the Commission even stresses the need for a still stronger Community commitment to regulating diffuse pollution from small sources.[7]

In many respects, process regulation reflects primarily health and environmental priorities rather than economic considerations. For example, directives such as those on waste disposal, SO_2, chemical accidents, and protection against radiation are clearly motivated by the perceived urgency of the health, safety, and environmental problems addressed. Moreover, empirical evidence does not support the view that industry in environmental states suffers substantial competitive injury from progressive national solutions and the lack of harmonization.[8] Some authors maintain that the emphasis of early Community environmental policy on water pollution was motivated by economic considerations. Since different national regulations for control of water and air pollution have a fairly equal cost incidence on the industry concerned, this reasoning can not explain the emphasis on control of water pollution. However, economic considerations did motivate extension of water pollution regulation for hazardous substances to all Community watercourses, and they also play an important role in selecting strategies and tools for addressing the relevant problem. The dearth of Community legislative activity relating to land use, natural resources, and protection of nature is also more easily explained by the lack of economic incentives for harmonization.

Some environmental problems, such as climatic impacts of air pollution, and protection of migratory or endangered species, are by their nature so international that harmonized action at the Community level was considered appropriate, even in the absence of strong trade and competition concerns. The need for Community intervention to remedy serious transboundary pollution problems is also an important motivating factor. The emphasis of post 1973 Community environmental policy on water pollution is clearly motivated by the fact that several member states are riverains of the Rhine and that the heavy pollution of this river is an urgent environmental problem. Marine pollution is another example of a common transboundary interest. Although transboundary pollution has thus at times been a strong argument in favor of Community legislation, it has recently hampered political bargaining on other initiatives because national claims of sovereignty were affected.[9]

There is accordingly no single rationale for Community legislation in the environmental area. The internationality of a problem, transboundary pollution (including marine pollution), the perceived seriousness of the environmental problem in the light of the inadequacy of most or even all national solu-

[7] Commission, Progress Made in Connection with the Environment Action Programme and Assessment of the Work Done to Implement It, Communication from the Commission to the Council, DOC COM(80)222 final, Annex I, at 8[hereinafter cited as Progress Report 1980].

[8] For an empirical research project in this field, *see* KNÖDGEN & SPRENGER, *Umweltschutz und internationaler Wettbewerb*, 1981 *IFO*-SCHNELLDIENST No. 1–2 at 43.

[9] *See supra* pp. 97–98, 99–100, and *infra* pp. 241–243.

tions, the greater environmental efficiency of centralized solutions, the objective of eliminating distortions of competition – they all may help to explain the identification and development of candidates for harmonization and/or the substantive solutions adopted. It is not easy to identify a primary rationale even for a single directive. Although the economic interest of environmental states in shifting the burden of progressive environmental policy to industry throughout the Community is an important impetus to Community environmental policy, it does not explain the consensus on a particular proposal.

The sequence and timing of legislative initiatives depends on the environmental programs' selection of candidates for harmonization and on unilateral national initiatives (proposals submitted to the Commission or drafts reported under the information/standstill agreement). Of course, the final adoption of Commission proposals is largely conditional on the speed of the political bargaining over a proposal. The rationale underlying the selection of candidates for harmonization in the environmental programs is not simply the urgency of environmental problems. It could hardly be maintained that in the Community the most serious environmental problems have been addressed first. The state of existing knowledge, preferences of member states, the prospective political chances of a proposal, and public awareness all play an important role in setting priorities.

For example, Community commitment in the field of radioactivity had long been limited to protecting workers and the general public by setting radiation safety standards. Serious problems such as the location and safe design of nuclear power plants were addressed by the Community only when they had become a political issue in several member states. Community regulation of toxic substances was originally limited to classification, packaging, and labeling requirements. The restructuring of this regulatory system by the sixth amendment to the directive of 1967 and the directive on major accidents was a response to the Seveso accident in Italy and the enactment of toxic substances legislation in the United States and Japan. Even the emphasis on water pollution control can not be entirely explained by the urgency of water pollution in the Community. The aquatic environment, drinking water, and source of drinking water directives are designed to address urgent pollution problems. But, directives such as the fish water, shellfish water, and bathing water directives seem to be more the result of political spillover effects from successful legislation in areas of urgency. Finally, the disequilibrium between water and air pollution control existing in Community environmental policy can hardly be explained by differences in the seriousness of the relevant environmental problems.

c. *Environmental Policy Diversity Along National Lines*

The third important characteristic of existing Community environmental law is its strong tendency to nationally non-uniform standards. The problem of uniformity of environmental protection standards is a sub-issue of the larger problem of federalism or, in the context of the European Community, supranationalism. The question is basically whether the member state or the Community is the optimal level of decisionmaking. An environmental problem may be addressed at the Community level with a uniform ("total harmonization") or a non-uniform solution including measures which provide for partial, optional, minimal or alternative harmonization.[10] The Community example shows that supranational environmental legislation need not necessarily require uniform standards and controls. The frequent use of non-uniform standards in the Community may be explained by the still embryonic stage of the Community, and the primary role that the member states, acting either through the Council or outside Community institutions, play in environmental policymaking. Seen in this perspective, non-uniform standards represent an inferior form of supranational decisionmaking. However, national non-uniform standards may also be seen as a necessary response to the diverse environmental and economic conditions, population densities, and values existing in member states. As such they can mitigate many of the shortcomings of supranational decisionmaking and even promote public acceptance of supranational policies.[11]

Given the tendency towards nationally non-uniform standards, there are still remarkable differences between product and process regulation. Optional harmonization of product regulation is an expression of a general policy shift in harmonization policy which started about 1969 and gained general recognition after the new member states joined the Community.[12] Prior to that time, harmonization had been used by the Community as a vehicle for aggressively promoting integration. Hence, the prevailing harmonization concept was unification of law ("total harmonization"). The new member states insisted upon a more pragmatic approach that enchroached as little as possible on the member states and left them the power to legislate for the domestic market. Thus, optional harmonization became the rule, and total harmonization required special justification. As will be discussed later, the choice between total and non-total harmonization of product requirements is to a certain extent predicated on environmental considerations. However, the choice also reflects the general change in harmonization concepts.

Total harmonization has never played an important role in process regulation. As early as the first environmental program, the Community established the rule that member states in principle are free to set standards stricter than those in a Community directive.

Harmonization strategies in product regulation. Many product directives, especially those regulating detergents and chemicals, set uniform requirements. Some of these directives are relatively old and have merely been adjusted to

[10] *See supra* pp. 7–9.

[11] *See* Weinstock, *supra* note 1, at 6, 25, 26, *et seq.* (viewing non-uniform standards as transitory).

[12] *See* Dashwood, *Hastening Slowly: The Community's Path Towards Harmonisation*, in Policymaking in the European Communities 273, 288 *et seq.* (H. Wallace, W. Wallace & C. Webb eds., John Wiley, New York 1977).

technical progress in recent years; in these cases, the continued use of total harmonization may reflect the inertial effects of traditional concerns with creation of a truly integrated market. However, this rationale does not explain why some recent and wholly new product directives choose total harmonization while others choose optional harmonization. Some authors[13] believe the perceived seriousness of the health or environmental hazards presented by a product explains the choice. But this argument is not very convincing if one compares, for example, detergents, which are subject to total harmonization, and motor vehicle emissions, which are subject to optional harmonization. In general, advocates for strong Community environmental policies favor total harmonization.

An alternative to total harmonization with no negative effects on economic integration is optional harmonization. The member states are obliged to grant products meeting the (generally stricter) Community requirements access to their market but may set other (more liberal) standards for the domestic market. Thus, the motor vehicle, tractor, motorcycle, and construction machinery directives set maximum standards whose observance guarantees the producer access to the whole common market. Each member state may retain or introduce less stringent national requirements, in which case it must allow use of a vehicle or machine that conforms merely with them. Optional harmonization may at first glance appear to confirm the prevalence of economic interests over environmental considerations in regulation of exhaust emissions and noise, because it allows lower national standards and leaves enterprises the choice of complying either with the stricter EEC or the more libral national standards. For these reasons, the European Parliament has denounced it on various occasions.[14]

However, the negative environmental impact of optional harmonization is tempered by economy of scale considerations. Insofar as an industry is export oriented, different standards for home and export production will frequently run counter to the requirements of mass production and economies of scale. Therefore, producers of cars, motorcycles, and tractors normally opt for the stricter EEC emission standards in order to have the advantages of a European production line. Thus in practice, optional harmonization often is but a means of flexible adjustment to new standards, i.e. it leaves industry time to adjust to new standards.[15]

[13] Dashwood, *supra* note 12, at 289; P. J. Slot, Technical and Administrative Obstacles to Trade in the EEC 83 (Sijthoff, Leyden 1975); E. Stein, P. Hay & M. Waelbroeck, European Community Law and Institutions in Perspective 416 (Bobbs-Merril Co., New York 1976).

[14] European Parliament Resolution of 10 Feb. 1972, JO No. C 19, 28 Feb. 1972, p. 29; EP Doc. 181/71, at No. 26 and 96.

[15] P. J. Slot, *supra* note 13, at 83; Henssler, *Einige Aspekte des Abbaus technischer Handelshemmnisse im Verkehr*, in Umweltschutz und internationale Wirtschaft 173, at 174 (V. Götz, D. Rauschning & G. Zieger, eds., Carl Heymanns Verlag, Köln 1975); E. Röhling, Überbetriebliche technische Normen als nichttarifäre Handelshemmnisse im Gemeinsamen Markt 142 (Carl Heymanns Verlag, Köln 1972);

Optional harmonization also enables member states and industry to experiment with progressive national solutions to the technical problems posed by exhaust emissions and noise. It does so by permitting a member state to set stricter domestic standards so long as it leaves industry the choice of whether to comply with them. Thus, the German car industry has voluntarily agreed to reduce car emissions considerably below the level established by the relevant Community directive. From an environmental point of view, optional harmonization could also be interpreted as an accommodation to divergent environmental conditions and divergent national policies on regulation of exhaust emissions and noise.[16] For example, in a member state with low car density and few urban areas, strict controls over automobile emissions may seem unwarranted.

Minimal harmonization of product requirements, which allows a member state to set stricter mandatory national standards, is at variance with the political idea of harmonization understood in the sense of creating a fully integrated market. Although this harmonization method is not forbidden by the prohibition on discrimination by nationality under Art. 7 of the EEC Treaty, it causes direct competitive disadvantages to the industry of the member state setting stricter standards as well as that of other member states. Where domestic producers export products meeting the stricter domestic requirements they will normally incur higher costs per unit and thus be at a competitive disadvantage as compared with their foreign competitors. Compliance with different standards for home and export production normally runs counter to the exigencies of mass production and economies of scale.

Nonetheless, the 1978 directive on lead content of gasoline adopted a minimum harmonization strategy. It establishes a harmonized minimum level of 0.40 g/l for lead in gasoline, but permits member states to set a stricter lead level as low as 0.15 g/l. This regulation clearly allows existence of technical obstacles to trade, whose elimination is the ultimate goal of harmonization. The lead directive is a compromise necessitated because West Germany considered its standard of 0.15 g/l as vital and was unwilling to sacrifice it to European harmonization, while the other states considered the West German standard as economically unacceptable. The directive illustrates the inherent limitations of Community environmental policy, but at the same time also demonstrates the degree of its emancipation from trade policy. In this case free trade was sacrificed to achieve a political compromise which, environmentally, is at least a second best solution. The example also shows that minimal harmonization is not simply a convenient way of escaping all responsibility since even the Community solution of 0.4 g/l represents progress over the levels previously allowed in member states. Moreover, as the recent Commission

W. Schmeder, Die Rechtsangleichung als Integrationsinstrument in der Europäischen Gemeinschaft 72, 268 (Carl Heymanns Verlag, Köln 1978).

[16] P. J. Slot, *supra* note 13, at 84.

proposals show, the optional level may ultimately become the Community solution.[17]

Sometimes it is possible to reconcile environmental concerns which militate in favor of minimal harmonization of product requirements with trade considerations which would require total or at least optional harmonization. This reconciliation can be achieved by resort to the concept of partial harmonization. The potential of this harmonization technique is evidenced by the directive on the quality of water intended for human consumption. Under this directive, member states are empowered to set stricter mandatory national quality standards for water intended for human consumption, especially for that used in the food industry. However, these stricter requirements may not be applied to foreign products; thus, the erection of technical obstacles to trade is avoided. However, for economic and environmental reasons this harmonization concept is not appropriate where foreign firms have a large share of the domestic market.[18]

Harmonization strategies in process regulation. With respect to process related requirements, there may be more latitude for environmental diversity because divergent national requirements have only indirect impact on competition within the Community. Therefore, process related directives almost invariably employ minimal harmonization, i.e. the Community sets minimum environmental standards and member states may establish more stringent requirements. Even directives without express powers of this kind are interpreted to intend only minimal harmonization, e.g. the SO_2 limit values directive and the waste directives. The motivation for minimum harmonization is that in the absence of a Community initiative some member states would not be sufficiently responsive to the common Community interest, such as the need to address an urgent environmental problem, cope with transboundary spillovers, or diminish the attractiveness of "pollution havens." On the other hand, there generally is no strong Community interest in preventing other member states from going beyond the minimum. Normally, only member states with strong environmental policies, a particularly clean environment, or access to more advanced control technologies are expected to make use of this option. If distortions of competition result from such measures, as would be expected when a member state sets stricter emission or specification standards although not necessarily in the case of stricter ambient quality standards, this will primarily disadvantage the member state concerned and can easily be remedied by it.[19]

[17] In this respect, the borderline between minimal and alternative harmonization is fluid. *See* WEINSTOCK, *supra* note 1, at 27, 29. *See also* Krämer, *Umweltpolitik*, in KOMMENTAR ZUM EWG-VERTRAG 1609 at No. 41 (H. VON DER GROEBEN, H. VON BOEKH, J. THIESING & C.-D. EHLERMANN eds., vol. 2, 3d ed., Nomos Verlag, Baden-Baden 1983).

[18] For criticism of partial harmonization as an integration mechanism *see* E. RÖHLING, *supra* note 15, at 140–141; W. SCHMEDER, *supra* note 15, at 72; Seidel, *Beseitigung der technischen Handelshemmnisse*, in DIE ANGLEICHUNG DES RECHTS DER WIRTSCHAFT IN EUROPA 733, 740 *et seq.* (Carl Heymanns Verlag, Köln 1971).

[19] H. BUNGARTEN, *supra* note 2, at 231. *See also* WEINSTOCK, *supra* note 1, at 26 *et seq.*,

Sometimes, environmental diversity is also achieved by allowing member states to choose between a common and an alternative strategy for the control of pollution (alternative harmonization). For example, the aquatic environment directive establishes a system of uniform effluent standards, but permits a member state to opt for water quality standards if it can prove to the Commission that the water quality standards can be met without applying the effluent standards. These two strategies will result in varying environmental quality because effluent standards, when used as the sole pollution control strategy, require unnecessary control in clean areas and insufficient control in polluted areas, while ambient standards tend to lead to uniformly polluted levels of environmental quality everywhere. The directive provides that the grant of the option is to be reviewed at a later date. Thus, alternative harmonization represents an unlimited, although not permanent exception in favor of states who wish to take advantage of environmental conditions that permit higher discharge levels. The advantage of this harmonization concept over minimal harmonization is that it contains a built-in mechanism for eventual total harmonization.[20] However, in the long run, minimal harmonization in the Community context may prove more dynamic.

The option accorded in the SO_2 limit values directive to utilize, in lieu of the common ambient air quality standard and associated measurement methods, a fixed alternative standard and associated measurement methods is not designed to protect national interests in environmental diversity. Rather, it is a concession to established monitoring practices in the member states.

Conflicts over industrial location play a prominent role in both minimal and alternative harmonization.[21] It is not so much the interest of polluter states in attracting new industries but, rather, the interest of polluter states in preserving competitive advantages for existing industries. These advantages may stem from inadequate regulation in a heavily polluted state or part of that state or from lenient regulation in a clean state. In the 1960s, Belgium was a pollution haven, in the sense that its lax environmental measures attracted new industry, but it has long since become a heavily polluted country and has been compelled to stiffen its environmental controls. Even Greece, a classic flag of convenience state for shipping, is now attempting to regulate its shipping industry in order to protect the marine environment of the Mediterranean Sea. That the typical pollution haven problem does not exist in Europe seems due to the fact that polluter states have other disadvantages which deter investors.[22]

42 *et seq.;* Krämer, *supra note 17. Contra* AMADUCCI, *Fresh and Sea Waters of the EEC: Common Solutions?,* 1975 DIRITTO COMUNITARIO E DEGLI SCAMBI INTERNAZIONALI 513, 526 (because of the impact on localization of industry).

[20] *See* WEINSTOCK, *supra* note 1, at 26 *et seq.*, 42 *et seq.* (calling this concept "two-tier harmonization").

[21] *See* WEINSTOCK, *supra* note 1, at 7 *et seq.*, 34 *et seq. See also* PRITZEL, *Die Umweltpolitik in den intereuropäischen und innerdeutschen Beziehungen,* 13 DEUTSCHLAND-ARCHIV 834, at 835 (1980).

[22] For Ireland *see* Conservation Foundation News Letter, August 1982, at 213. For developing countries, *see* KNÖDGEN & SPRENGER, *supra* note 8; KNÖDGEN, *Environment and Industrial Siting,* 2 ZEITSCHRIFT FÜR UMWELTPOLITIK 407 (1979).

d. Conservativism

It is a widely held opinion that Community environmental law is characterized by lowest common denominator solutions.[23] This view is correct only in a qualified form. "Environmental" states, i.e. member states which have developed a progressive solution for a particular environmental problem, do not sacrifice their solution to Community harmonization.[24] Very often the Council adopts the progressive solution for the whole Community. In a sense, Community environmental policy often represents the highest, although not necessarily optimum, common denominator. In cases of sharp conflicts of interest among member states, the common resort to vague compromise formulae, harmonization of environmental protection principles instead of standard setting, and minimal or alternative harmonization may be considered lowest common denominator harmonization. They are lowest common denominator in the sense that they allow "polluter" states to more or less have their own way or, in the case of minimal harmonization, bind them to a solution low enough that they can agree to it. Such a solution may still represent progress beyond existing law in many member states. In any event, changes in environmental directives are very difficult because member states defending the status quo have a stronger bargaining position than states who wish to change it.

Whether its lodestar is the policy of "environmental" or "polluter" states, Community environmental policy is generally more conservative than innovative.[25] The environmental programs in their programmatic parts sometimes proclaim wholly new solutions, but with respect to concrete actions they do not attempt to free Community policy from its linkage to member state policies.[26] The Community's role is to generalize and diffuse solutions adopted in one or more member states by introducing them throughout the Community. The solutions of these member states normally set the framework for the Community solution. The "outrider" role of environmental states is, therefore, an essential prerequisite to the success of progressive policy proposals.[27] In this

[23] In this sense *see* H. BUNGARTEN, *supra* note 2, at 126, 230 (policy of the weakest member state); F. BEHRENS, RECHTSGRUNDLAGEN DER UMWELTPOLITIK DER EUROPÄISCHEN GEMEINSCHAFTEN 254, 258 (Erich Schmidt Verlag, Berlin 1976); WEIDNER & KNOEPFEL, *supra* note 2, at 62; Krämer, *supra* note 17, at No. 48. *See also* Progress Report 1980, *supra* note 5, Annex I, at 11. *See generally* F. MARX, FUNKTION UND GRENZEN DER RECHTSANGLEICHUNG NACH ART. 100 EWG-VERTRAG 146 *et seq.* (Carl-Heymanns Verlag, Köln 1976) (because of the structural conservativism of harmonization and the lack of substantive criteria for positive policymaking).

[24] Institute for European Environmental Policy, ANNUAL REPORT 1981, at 2 (Bonn 1982).

[25] In this sense *see* F. BEHRENS, *supra* note 23, at 258; Krämer, *supra* note 17, at No. 49. *See generally* F. MARX, *supra* note 23, at 156.

[26] F. MARX, *supra* note 23, at 156.

[27] VON MOLTKE, *Europäische Umweltpolitik*, 2 ZEITSCHRIFT FÜR UMWELTPOLITIK 77, 82–83, 87 (1979); WEINSTOCK, *supra* note 1, at 12; Institute for European Environmental Policy, ANNUAL REPORT 1981, at 3 (Bonn 1982).

sense, national environmental policy always has a European dimension. At the Community level, on the other hand, attempts at new solutions are rarely made. An exception is perhaps the PCB directive, which had no parallel in existing member state regulation.

e. Conclusion

The deficiencies of Community environmental policy are obvious. Nevertheless, Community environmental policy may be called a success.[28] This is due not so much to the considerable quantity of directives and other legislative texts produced after adoption of the first environmental program; rather, it is because the Community has been able to adopt a number of quite important directives with major effects or implications. Examples are the sixth amendment to the hazardous substances directive of 1967, which introduces a screening procedure for new chemicals; the major accidents directive which addresses the problem of chemical accidents; the bird protection directive, which amounts to a fundamental departure from long established customs in some member states; the sulfur dioxide limit values directive establishing, on a Community-wide basis, ambient air quality standards, which most member states did not previously use as a control strategy; the aquatic environment directive which addresses the urgent problem of hazardous water pollutants; and perhaps even the amendments to the motor vehicles directive which shifted the emphasis from abolition of technical obstacles to trade to protection of health and environment. In the future, an environmental impact directive may have to be added to this list. On balance, the record is much better than many critics of Community environmental policy assert.

2. Strategies and Tools

Existing environmental directives use a variety of strategies and tools to implement the policy goals specified in the directives and the environmental programs. For water, air, and noise pollution and radioactivity, environmental quality and emission standards are the normal control strategy. Standards are designed to attain a level of pollution acceptable from a health or environmental perspective. In these areas no attempt is made to influence the structure of polluting activities and thereby prevent or limit pollution at its incipiency. Wastes are largely controlled by regulating their disposal. More recently, the Community has also tried to limit waste generation and to encourage re-use and recycling of waste. Chemicals are subject to screening procedures, both with respect to preventing accidents in their production and with respect to preventing health and environmental hazards from their marketing. Apart from the usual classification, packaging, and labeling requirements, direct regulation of chemicals by prohibitions and restrictions on their production, mar-

[28] VON MOLTKE, *supra* note 27, at 77, 78; Kupfer, *Einflüsse der EG auf die deutsche Umweltpolitik*, in IWL-FORUM 1981-II 57, 61–62 (Institut für gewerbliche Wasserwirtschaft und Luftreinhaltung, Köln 1981); Krämer, *supra* note 17, at No. 44.

keting, and use is infrequent. This may be explained by the need to first develop sufficient data to evaluate chemicals as well as by the reluctance of Community policymakers to encroach on the freedom of entrepreneurs and consumers.

These strategies are normally chosen on a case-by-case basis. The environmental programs do not discuss or establish general principles for selecting among alternative strategies and tools. The major single factor explaining the selection of a particular strategy or tool appears to be its previous utilization in the law of one or several member states. Community policymakers have as yet not shown much innovative capacity in the selection of strategies and tools. They prefer to rely on the experience of member states, primarily because the choice of alternative strategies would almost invariably disrupt established national practices and therefore endanger adoption of a particular proposal.

a. Technology Forcing

Community environmental law does not normally attempt to force or even encourage technological change. Instead, directives select a particular strategy when and insofar as it is technically feasible. Timetables are designed to give enterprises some latitude in adjusting to existing technology rather than forcing the development of new technology. The simplified decisionmaking procedure which many directives establish for amendments to adjust them to technical progress is also an expression of this passive approach. The procedure is necessary because directives are based on existing technology.

The motor vehicle directives are the most prominent example of this approach. Here, the Community expressly rejected the American approach of technology-forcing by statute. The relevant directives started at a relatively low level of control and were then upgraded several times and extended to other pollutants following technological progress.[29] Likewise, the product standards relating to biodegradability of the directive on detergents were considered to represent the present state of technological development and not to impose an undue burden on industry. Under the aquatic environment directive, the Council is to set effluent standards in implementing directives. Here, technological feasibility, in addition to environmental factors such as toxicity, persistence, and bio-accumulation of hazardous substances, is one of the factors to be considered in setting the standard. Finally, the passive approach to technology is also evidenced by the titanium dioxide directive. It subjects an authorization for a new source to the requirement that the applicant agree to use the commercially available materials, procedures, and techniques that are least harmful to the environment.

On the whole, it seems obvious that the Community has never seriously tried to force technological development of environmentally less harmful products and industrial processes. The reason seems to be that no member state has na-

[29] *See supra* pp. 74–78.

tional legislation employing a technology-forcing strategy. Given the inherent limitations of Community legislative powers under Art. 100 of the EEC Treaty, it would have been difficult to justify a departure from the regulatory strategies prevailing in the member states. Moreover, the American example is not considered encouraging. However, the regulatory passivity of the Community is somewhat compensated by the initiation and financing of research activities in areas where it is thought that technological progress should be fostered for the improvement of environmental conditions.

b. Standards

In the Community no limitation on total loadings of emissions has ever been attempted or even been discussed as a legal strategy for pollution control. Again, this may be explained by the total absense of such a strategy in member state law. Although several member states endeavor to stabilize or reduce total emissions as a matter of policy, none has adopted limits on total emissions as a legally binding strategy, and any Community commitment to this strategy, in view of the associated loss of flexibility for industrial development, would probably meet with much opposition. In the field of solid waste disposal, the relevant directives proclaim a vague principle to the effect that member states are to encourage prevention of waste. A recent Commission proposal would seek to regulate the volume of wastes in a particular area by giving priority to re-use rather than recycling or disposal. The strategy is to limit total loadings of an environmentally harmful substance. However, the policy implications of this strategy are still unclear because there is much disagreement on the environmental and economic merits of re-use as compared to recycling.

i. Ambient Quality v. Emission Standards

The political discussion on strategies for reducing water, air, and noise pollution has centered around the dichotomy of ambient/risk standards v. technology-based emission, performance, and specification standards. Both types of strategy are now used in Community environmental law, although seldom cumulatively as in some member states such as West Germany.

Technology-based emission, performance, and specification standards are the strategy chosen for control of vehicle exhaust emissions and noise emissions (motor vehicles, motorcycles, tractors, aircraft, and construction machinery). This choice reflects, in addition to the obvious trade considerations, the technical difficulties of controlling vehicle emissions (except for those attributable to gasoline additives) and noise in any other way than through product related requirements. The emphasis is clearly on performance standards rather than specification standards, thereby leaving producers enough flexibility to select a technically and economically optimal solution.

The most extensive discussion about source-related and ambient quality standards arose in the context of the aquatic environment directive relating to toxic and hazardous pollutants. The majority of member states favored uniform effluent standards at the Community level.[30] The effluent standards in question are not purely technology oriented; in setting the standards, toxicity, persistence, and bio-accumulation must be considered as well as available technology. The preference for effluent standards as a control technology was partly due to the fact that they were used under national law. Moreover, effluent standards were considered a simple and efficient method to eliminate water pollution by hazardous substances. Finally and perhaps most importantly, it was thought that only by establishing a system of uniform effluent standards could distortions of competition throughout the Community be avoided.

However, the United Kingdom insisted on a system of water quality standards.[31] The primary reason was that it considered uniform emission standards too expensive and wanted to preserve existing locational advantages for its industry, arguing that these advantages compensated its industry for various locational disadvantages, such as remoteness from major consumer centers. British industry benefits from the high volume of flow in the short British watercourses and the possibility of industrial discharges into estuaries. Especially with respect to discharges into estuaries it was argued that there was less need to establish costly treatment facilities. Probably for this reason the United Kingdom has long avoided putting into effect the parts of its 1974 Control of Pollution Act providing for regulation of all discharges into estuaries. Furthermore, the United Kingdom maintained that even for highly hazardous (list I) substances the effluent standards could be varied according to local circumstances and that uniform effluent standards were consequently unnecessary to maintain appropriate water quality in any river basin.

Since the divergent views could not be reconciled, a compromise was found. With respect to list I substances, effluent standards were the rule, but a member state could, under narrowly defined conditions and subject to later review, opt for the alternative of water quality standards.

[30] For the following section, *see generally* Brusasco-Mackenzie & Kiss, *Quelques réflexions sur l'action des Communautés Européennes en matière de protection d l'environnement*, 1978 Revue du Marché Commun 310, 312; Pleinevaux, *European Policy of Protection of Rivers and Waters Against Pollution*, in The European Alternatives 379, 398–399 (G. Ionescu ed., Sijthoff & Noordhoff, Alphen a. d. Rijn 1977); von Moltke & Haigh, *supra* note 2, at 27–28; Rat von Sachverständigen für Umweltfragen, Umweltgutachten 1978, at No. 1682 (Kohlhammer, Stuttgart 1978); Weinstock, *supra* note 1, at 24 *et seq.*, 28 *et seq.* For arguments against uniform effluent standards (because of the "overkill" effects) *see* Amaducci, *supra* note 19, at 534; Economic and Social Council, Resolution of 26–27 Feb. 1975, OJ No. C 108, 15 May 1975, p. 78.

[31] For the following section, *see generally* Pleinevaux, *supra* note 30, at 391; von Moltke & Haigh, *supra* note 30, at 27–28; Robertshaw, *Water Pollution Control: Problem of Harmonization in EEC States*, 1974 J. of Planning & Envt'l L. 642 *et seq.*; Weinstock, *supra* note 30; Booth & Green, *The European Community Environmental Programme and United Kingdom Law*, 1 European L. Rev. 535, 551–552 (1976); H. Bungarten, *supra* note 2, at 205 *et seq.*; P. Barella, Normes et objectifs de qualité de l'eau dans la Communauté économique européenne p. xiv *et seq.* (Unpublished Thesis, Université des sciences sociales, Toulouse 1980).

Furthermore, the directive tries to avoid exclusive reliance on uniform effluent standards in urban areas with many sources of pollution. Where needed to maintain water quality in a particular section of a watercourse or lake, member states must set more stringent requirements. To this extent, the directive combines effluent standards with use-related water quality standards. For less dangerous (list II) substances, the directive adopts the strategy of controlling pollution exclusively by water quality standards. Here, the member states are to establish water improvement plans which must contain differentiated water quality standards.

Generally speaking, uniform efffuent standards are easy to implement and enforce, but they impose costly burdens on parts of the Community where waters have a high absorptive capacity. In the absence of a preventive strategy, they may therefore be considered inequitable. The standard argument in favor of effluent standards is that they eliminate distortions of competition.[32] The argument assumes that uniform emission standards are mandated by the requirements of a common market, and that differentiation according to the state of the regional environment is inconsistent with the logic of Community law. The weakness of this argument is that Community law would then require more uniformity than even that of highly centralized countries. Normally, the use of the "natural" locational advantage of a clean environment only compensates local industry for other disadvantages, reflected in its low level of industrial development to date. Also, the quality standard system adopted by the directive for list II substances considerably weakens the argument that uniform effluent standards are absolutely necessary to avoid unjustified competitive advantages. However, the "overkill" effect of uniform effluent standards is less of a problem in the control of ultrahazardous pollutants.[33] It is noteworthy that during bargaining on the first mercury directive the United Kingdom for the first time conceded that all new sources of mercury pollution should comply with state-of-the-art treatment technology.

While a system of uniform effluent standards clearly seems environmentally warranted for all ultrahazardous pollutants, it remains to be seen whether this concept is politically viable within the Community's complex decisionmaking structure. The task of setting effluent standards for a large number of substances has proven to be almost insurmountable. It imposes a heavy burden on the Community's political system, and the compromise allowing coexistence of the effluent and water quality standards has not ended the controversy among the member states. Due to the difficulty of comparing the cost incidence of the two strategies, each side suspects that the other strategy as implemented by a particular standard would give the other's industry an undue competitive advantage.[34] That there was no clear decision on whether the water quality standards should be uniform or use oriented adds to these difficulties. Because of these difficulties with the aquatic environment directive, the family of direc-

[32] *See* in particular WEINSTOCK, *supra* note 1, at 6 *et seq.*, 24 *et seq.*, 42 *et seq.*

[33] Pleinevaux, *supra* note 30, at 391.

[34] Progress Report 1980, *supra* note 7, at 5.

tives providing for use-based water quality standards may ultimately emerge as more important than the aquatic environment directive.[35]

While use of both control strategies in combination is appropriate in heavily polluted sections of watercourses or lakes, the aquatic environment directive does not expressly provide for setting Community water quality standards to serve as a basis for control measures in these waters. The water quality standards to be established for list I substances are mandatory only for those countries which generally opt for the water quality strategy, i. e. only for the United Kingdom. Nonetheless, the combination of emission standards and ambient quality standards would avoid the disadvantages of reliance on a single strategy. It has rendered good results in air pollution control in West Germany. There is no reason why it should not also be used by the Community to control water pollution.[36]

Where the Community has regulated water pollution by water use, i. e. drinking water, water for human consumption, bathing water, and fish and shellfish waters, water quality standards are used rather than effluent standards. One explanation for this choice is the member states' desire to have more flexibility. There are also less likely to be competition impacts from controlling non-industrial water uses. Finally, in some cases water is used as a "raw material" for the production of foods and beverages, thus requiring ensurance of a specific level of water quality.

In the field of air pollution, the SO_2 limit values directive employs ambient quality standards. Ambient quality standards were selected as an approach suited for dealing with the problems of polluted urban areas as well as of areas of special protection whose superior air quality is to be maintained. However, given the substantial implementation problems involved in translating ambient air quality standards into individual emission limitations, the problems of Community/member state cooperation in establishing implementation programs, and the long deadline for attaining the standard (1993!), it is doubtful whether this strategy should have been used to the exclusion of other strategies such as emission standards, which can be more easily implemented. In addition, an extension of the input standard approach, which is as yet confined to light fuels, could have been envisaged. It has been maintained that adoption of the ambient control strategy represents a general tendency of Community environmental policy systematically to favor industrial interests at the expense of environmental concerns.[37] At any rate, it is remarkable that industry and member states, which argued so strongly their interest in equal competitive conditions as justifying use of effluent standards for water pollution, have until recently, when West Germany urged introduction of state-of-the-art technology as a cure for its forest problems, not been interested in uniform emission standards for air pollution. One reason may be that most member states already control air pollution by some form of emission limitation and that they

[35] *See* von Moltke & Haigh, *supra* note 2, at 28.

[36] In the same sense *see* H. Bungarten, *supra* note 2, at 208.

[37] Weidner & Knoepfel, *supra* note 2, at 56, 61 *et seq.*

consider the Community ambient quality standard as only a necessary supplement to existing national strategy. Another reason may be that polluter states among the member states wanted to retain flexibility and the ability to use the absorptive capacity of relatively clean airsheds.

ii. Input Standards

Finally, Community environmental law sometimes uses product related input standards rather than, or in addition to, technology-oriented emission or ambient quality standards. This is true for detergents, lead content of gasoline, and sulfur content of light fuels. The regulation of detergents and gasoline is an ecologically effective alternative to control at the source, e. g. treatment of sewage or exhaust filters. Regulation of the sulfur content of gas oil poses some problems, both for environmental and energy/economic reasons. Apparently, this approach was chosen because some member states had taken the initiative in adopting it and thereby endangered the functioning of the Common Market in fuel trade. From an environmental perspective input standards are easy to enforce and have proven potential for reducing air pollution. On the other hand, input standards may prevent the use of scarce low sulfur fuels in the heavily polluted areas where they are most needed. The directive tries to counteract this environmentally undesirable effect by allowing higher sulfur fuels in clean air areas. Input standards would also seem to hamper technological development towards more efficient control technologies. From an energy conservation point of view, input standards may lead to depletion of stocks of high quality low sulfur fuels and lack of demand for local, higher sulfur fuel alternatives. However, this effect may be offset by the development of fuel desulfurization techniques and by higher prices for low sulfur fuels.

That Community institutions are aware of these complex feedback effects is demonstrated by the controversial 1975 Commission proposal for a directive on the use of fuel oils whose aim was to decrease sulfur emissions.[38] The proposal would only be applicable to special protection zones. In these zones it would prohibit the use of heavy (residual) fuel oil with more than a certain sulfur content. However, exemptions would be allowed for heating installations which use processes that eliminate sulfur at the source, e. g. fuel gas desulfurization, fluidized bed combustion, or fuel gasification. Such processes are considered environmentally equivalent and perhaps less costly alternatives to fuel desulfurization. Nevertheless, because of its economic and energy implications the member states have not as yet adopted the proposal, and it has for practical purposes been superseded by adoption of the SO_2 limit values directive.

iii. Regionalization of Pollution Control

One issue in establishing pollution control standards is whether they should be geographically uniform or differentiated. National differentiation is

[38] *See supra* pp. 80–81.

achieved through strategies of optional, minimal, and alternative harmonization. The rationales for such differentiation have already been discussed. Regional differentiation of standards is based on somewhat different considerations. Although the interests in environmental diversity, development in "clean" areas, and economic efficiency may justify many kinds of differentiated standards, differentiation along regional rather than national lines has the advantage of in principle not threatening Community economic and political integration. Also, it is better suited to actual environmental conditions in member states than the somewhat crude classification into "environmental" and "polluter" states.[39] It is striking that the Community has not yet used the concept of regionally differentiated standards as a distinct harmonization strategy. A few environmental directives, however, allow member states to establish regionally differentiated standards in zones designated by them in accordance with broad Community guidelines. The rationales for allowing such differentiation are quite varied.

The SO_2 limit values directive allows for four types of zones: (1) areas where the harmonized mandatory ambient air quality standards are applicable; (2) nonattainment areas until 1993; (3) development areas, i. e. areas likely to experience increased pollution in the wake of development and therefore requiring special controls based on the more stringent guide standards rather than the mandatory standards; and (4) areas which should be afforded special environmental protection. It seems clear that it is not possible to develop a coherent explanation for this zoning scheme. The toleration of nonattainment zones for a limited period is a compromise between environmental and economic considerations, particularly with regard to existing sources. Similar regimes exist in the law or administrative practice of some member states. The establishment of development zones is clearly motivated by environmental concerns. However, it is not an expression of environmental diversity, but rather an application of the principle of prevention. It is designed to prevent the future deterioration of air quality down to the mandatory minimum standards in the face of continuing economic and industrial development. Special protection zones present a clear case of environmental diversity. A member state wishing to specifically protect a clean air area or a particularly sensitive environment can achieve this protection by making a political decision to designate the area a special protection zone. Since member states have some discretion in designating zones, the zoning concept is also a recognition of environmental diversity along national lines.[40] Similar considerations underlie the system

[39] *See* Institute for European Environmental Policy, ANNUAL REPORT 1982, at 12 (Bonn 1983) (calling for intensified pollution control in "action regions"); WEINSTOCK, *supra* note 1, 44 (pleading for "loosened, less stringent and regionally differentiated forms" of Community pollution control but seeming to favor "two-tier" (alternative) harmonization which perpetuates the division into "environmental" and "polluter states").

[40] The relationship between the designation of special protection zones and the directive's nondeterioration requirement is unclear, since special protection zones are by definition low pollution areas which should be protected by the nondeterioration re-

of use-oriented water quality standards for list-II substances under the aquatic environment directive.

The regionalization concepts of other directives have different rationales. The input standard of the SO_2 gas oil directive differentiates between heavily polluted areas and areas where SO_2 pollution is sufficiently low or where gas oil does not significantly contribute to air pollution. The rationale underlying this bilevel system of product standards is economic. Given the scarcity and high price of low sulfur fuel and the costs of desulfurization, it was considered necessary and environmentally justifiable to limit the mandatory use of low sulfur fuels to heavily polluted areas. The cleaner but economically weaker regions in the northwest and south of the Community are thereby accorded competitive advantages, but of course the concept also applies within a particular member state. However, some member states, such as West Germany, have applied the stricter input standard throughout the country.[41]

The drinking water directive provides for a Community system of geographically varied quality standards which correspond to different standard methods of obtaining drinking water. This system is motivated by economic concerns rather than by recognition of environmental diversity. In view of the poor overall water quality in major parts of the Community and the necessity of using surface water as a source of drinking water, it was considered necessary to allow the use of certain low quality surface water when special methods are employed.[42]

iv. Other Forms of Differentiation

Some directives also provide for or allow differentiation of standards by industry or product. Thus, the SO_2 gas oil directive exempts conventional power plants in heavily polluted areas from the requirement of using low sulfur fuel. This exemption is based both on energy considerations and on the availability of adequate technology for controlling SO_2 emissions at the source. The aquatic environment directive provides that the Community effluent standards relating to particular substances may be differentiated on an industry or product basis. Again the rationale is economic. Finally, there are directives or Commission proposals to set effluent standards confined to a particular industry or process (e.g. mercury, "drines").

c. Nondegradation Policies

The more recent pollution directives, particularly the SO_2 limit values directive and the water pollution directives, all prohibit degradation of existing ambient

quirement. The explanation lies in the "political" nature of the nondeterioration requirement; *see infra* pp. 224–225.

[41] *See supra* pp. 80–81, at note 93.

[42] Clearly, all environmental directives providing for emission standards will result in geographical variation in the quality of the relevant environmental medium. This is the necessary consequence of any system of pollution control exclusively based on emission standards.

quality. The role of nondegradation in Community environmental policy is not easy to assess. The costs and benefits of the Community nondegradation policy have never been discussed in public or even in the legal literature. Moreover, the prohibition on degradation is couched in vague language which gives rise to considerable problems of interpretation. In fact, the directives merely say that implementation of member state measures pursuant to the directive may not cause degradation of current ambient quality.

First, it is unclear how the linkage that the directives establish between their implementation and nondegradation operates to limit the scope of the nondegradation requirement. In some member states, such as West Germany, some authors take the view that the nondegradation requirement applies only to national legislation. Under this view, a member state, when incorporating the relevant directive into its national law, may not change other provisions of its national law where the effect of such change would be deterioration of existing ambient quality.[43] This narrow position is hardly tenable since the directives' prohibition of degradation of existing ambient quality is directed at measures taken pursuant to the directive in order to implement it, and not to collateral changes in national law.[44]

A second and greater problem is that the prohibition on degradation of ambient quality is apparently absolute. In the water quality directives, there is not even the qualification that the deterioration must be "significant." Therefore, pragmatic interpretations of the nondegradation requirement, such as those given by the US Environmental Protection Agency and the federal courts prior to the Clean Air Act Amendments of 1977,[45] might seem to be entirely ruled out. The consequence of a strict interpretation of nondegradation would be that industrial development in clean water areas within a particular member state and perhaps even in an entire "clean" member state such as Ireland or Denmark would be practically foreclosed. This heavy economic burden would be accompanied, in all but a few areas of exceptional scenic or ecological significance, by rather small environmental benefits.

A blanket nondegradation requirement is not economically efficient resource use,[46] given the preference for economic development and the power of member states to select more stringent ambient standards if they desire. Of course, the nondegradation policy contributes to a cleaner environment in the

[43] Several discussants at the 1979 Annual Meeting of the German Society for Environmental Law took positions in this sense. *See* GESELLSCHAFT FÜR UMWELTRECHT, DOKUMENTATION ZUR WISSENSCHAFTLICHEN FACHTAGUNG 1979, at 162 (Erich Schmidt Verlag, Berlin 1980).

[44] In the same sense *see* Pleinevaux, *supra* note 30, at 382. *See also* the clarification in one of the more recent directives, the directive on water intended for human consumption (art. 11), Directive 80/778/EEC of 15 July 1980, OJ No. L 229, 30 Aug. 1980, p. 11.

[45] Fri v. Sierra Club, 412 U. S. 541 (1973); Sierra Club v. EPA, 540 F. 2d 1114, at 1140 (D. C. Cir. 1976).

[46] *See* STEWART, *The Development of Administrative and Quasi-Constitutional Law in Judicial Review of Environmental Decision-Making: Lessons from the Clean Air Act*, 62 IOWA L. REV. 713, at 745 *et seq.* (1977).

whole Community; it may also be considered a policy of "mandatory" environmental diversity. The sacrifices associated with this policy are perhaps tolerable if it is applied moderately. Therefore, Community nondegradation policy must allow some flexibility, whose extent, however, can not be derived from the text of the relevant directives.

There seems to be a common understanding among member states that the nondegradation obligation is a soft, flexible one that does not require strict controls on industrial growth and location of new industries. It is more a political guideline than a legally binding obligation. Consequently, with the exception of West Germany, member states did not formally incorporate the nondegradation principle into their national laws. This is even true of the Netherlands which adjusted its Water Act to the Community directives in 1981. In the context of water pollution control, West Germany explicitly limits the prohibition to a "not insignificant deterioration" and provides for exceptions "if required by paramount considerations of public interest" (Art. 36b, Federal Water Resources Management Act). This provision reflects fairly well the common understanding of the member states. However, since experience with national implementation in general shows a gradual dilution of central policies from top to bottom, it is not very probable that the nondeterioration requirement will become an effective tool for pollution control. It is also probable that the powers granted to the Commission under some of the directives for coordinating member state implementation (including implementation of the nondegradation requirement) will also prove to be ineffective.[47]

The SO_2 limit values directive deviates from the earlier nondegradation requirements in that it contains two qualifications. The deterioration of ambient air quality must be "significant," and the requirement applies only to "clean" air areas where existing ambient air quality is superior to that required under the mandatory standards established by the directive. This limited nondegradation requirement, proposed by the Netherlands and Denmark, is more balanced because it retains some national or regional options for economic development at the expense of the environment, while preserving clean air areas in the interest of the Community. However, the vagueness of the requirement may lead to quite different interpretation and implementation throughout the Community. Under recent case law of the European Court of Justice, it is also unclear whether the nondegradation requirement would be interpreted by the Court so as to leave member states a margin of discretion, in which case only the limits of this discretion would be reviewable, or whether the requirement will be considered to be fully reviewable. The relevant Council protocol expressly states that there is no absolute prohibition on location of new industries in clean air areas but rather that member states have much flexibility in im-

[47] For criticism regarding the drinking water directive, *see* EUREAU, *Erfahrungen mit der EG-Richtlinie 75/440 über die Qualität von Oberflächenwasser für die Trinkwassergewinnung in den Mitgliedstaaten der Gemeinschaft*, 122 GAS- UND WASSERFACH – WASSER/ABWASSER 555, 559 (1981).

plementing the policy.[48] In any case member states will be able to avoid any challenge to their implementation policy by abstaining from establishing generalized implementing rules that could be reviewed as to conformity with the directive. Moreover, given the unclear relationship between the prohibition of significant deterioration of ambient air quality and the power accorded member states to designate clean air areas as special protection zones and to set special ambient air quality standards for these zones, it also is possible that a member state might simply evade the prohibition by designating special protection zones and setting standards that would permit substantial degradation of existing air quality.

d. Existing Sources

The treatment of existing sources of pollution raises difficult policy issues. On one hand, environmental considerations militate in favor of equal treatment for new and existing sources. On the other, the application of this postulate meets with economic and technological problems and may even raise constitutional questions. Community policy in this area is characterized by a pragmatic, flexible approach, in principle recognizing the vested interests of existing polluters, while varying the protection afforded these interests according to the circumstances.

Community directives containing product related requirements sometimes postpone (generally for a short time) their effective compliance date in order to allow producers time to adjust to the new requirements. The adjustment period is normally determined according to economic and technological feasibility. This is true, for example, of the motor vehicle directives and the gas oil directive. Other product related directives do not provide for any adjustment period and in principle call for immediate compliance. However, in these cases the time required for member states to incorporate the directive into national law and to promulgate implementing regulations has the practical effect of granting producers enough time for adjustment.

In contrast to the standard legislative technique of fixing adjustment periods, the toxic substances directive (sixth amendment) contains entirely different regimes for new and existing chemicals. Existing chemicals are subject only to the classification, packaging, and labeling requirements. Producers need not register them, and they are not required to perform tests for development of health and safety data. This differentiation between new and existing substances reflects considerations of administrative and economic feasibility. It was thought that the problems associated with testing and evaluation of chemicals could be reduced to manageable proportions only if regulation was targeted to new chemicals. Since the risks presented by chemicals may be the product of long-term exposure and it is hardly defensible to use people exposed to existing chemicals as guinea pigs, this policy decision is highly objectionable from a health and environmental point of view.

[48] *See* THE ENVIRONMENT IN EUROPE, BULLETIN OF THE INSTITUTE FOR EUROPEAN ENVIRONMENTAL POLICY No. 19, Supplement (Sept. 1982)

In the case of source related requirements, a differentiation between new and existing sources is frequently, although not always, made. Basically two legislative techniques have been used for protecting the interests of existing sources: deadlines for adjustment, and interim variances in substantive requirements.

The aquatic environment directive provides a typical example of an adjustment deadline for existing sources. For existing sources emiting list I substances, it provides that member state implementation programs must set adjustment deadlines whose maximum extent may be limited by implementing directives. The implementing directives are to take into account the features of the industrial sector and, where appropriate, the types of products. Improvement programs for emissions of list II substances must also contain adjustment deadlines whose length, however, is primarily at the member state's discretion although the Commission has some coordinating powers. Other examples are: the bathing water directive which provides a ten year deadline for adjustment of existing sources to ambient water quality standards; the waste oil directive which sets a four year timetable for existing enterprises; and the directive on major accidents which fixes a three year adjustment period for existing facilities.

The titanium dioxide directive represents a more flexible regulation of existing sources. New sources must obtain a prior authorization preceded by an environmental impact assessment and must also agree to use the best available technical means. Existing sources are subject to improvement programs to be established by the member states. These improvement programs are to set general and intermediate targets for gradually phasing out pollution by 1987 and are to specify the measures to be applied to each polluter. This flexible regime allows for individual requirements that take into consideration technical and economic feasibility as well as environmental needs.

The allocation of control burdens among new and existing sources may also be left to the member states' discretion. Thus, under the SO_2 limit values directive, the mandatory ambient air quality standards must be enforced in non-attainment areas by 1993. The required member state improvement plans will normally differentiate between new and existing sources. However, it is up to member states to decide what requirements are to be applied to existing sources.

e. Alternatives to Regulation

Community environmental legislation relies heavily on regulation. Non-regulatory alternatives, such as economic incentives or disincentives, are rare. This may be explained by the simple fact that member states do not widely use these alternatives. Since Community environmental policy ultimately depends on the political will of the member states, innovative solutions to environmental problems can not generally be expected of Community institutions.

i. Examples of Economic Instruments

An exception which confirms the rule just given is the waste oil directive. Relying largely on the West German model, the directive requires member states to organize collection of waste oil and allows them to subsidize its collection, regeneration, and combustion. The subsidy may be financed by levying a charge on waste oil, which may be imposed either on the waste oil itself, i. e. the user of oil, or on products eventually transformed into waste oil, i. e. the producer, who may shift the charge to the user. The German experience shows that such a multidimensional system of controls, charges, and subsidies functions well under the particular conditions affecting waste oil disposal.

There are also discussions within the Commission on a possible proposal for an effluent charge system for water pollutants.[49] In as much as France, the Netherlands, and West Germany already use effluent charge systems, such a proposal would not be too innovative. Because these charge systems are meant not only to attain national effluent or water quality standards – and, in the future, Community standards – but also to serve as an economic incentive for improvement of water quality beyond the standards, they impose a higher cost on national industry. Their harmonization would contribute to the elimination of distortions of competition and would be justified under Art. 100 of the EEC Treaty just as much as harmonization of regulatory standards. However, it will be difficult to actually make a proposal with a chance of being accepted. Since the existing effluent charge systems are complicated and very different conceptually, their harmonization is technically difficult. Even more importantly, the other member states do not seem much interested in the introduction of a Community effluent charge system.

ii. The Polluter-Pays Principle

The extensive discussion within Community institutions of the polluter-pays principle, which relies primarily on concepts developed in West German environmental policy, has had only limited relevance in the choice of alternative instruments. The polluter-pays principle is one of the basic principles established by the first environmental program of 1973. The Council Recommendation of 1975 and the annexed Commission Communication regarding cost allocation and action by public authorities on environmental matters[50] estab-

[49] *See* Third Environment Action Programme, OJ No. C 46, 17 Feb. 1983, p. 1, Annex No. 12. *See generally* HAAGSMA, *De milieuheffing in Europeesrechtlijk perspectief*, 28 SOCIAAL-ECONOMISCHE WETGEVING 512, 523 *et seq.* (1980).

[50] Council Recommendation (75/436/Euratom, ECSC, EEC) of 3 March 1975 regarding cost allocation and action by public authorities on environmental matters, OJ No. L 194, 25 July 1975, p. 1. The Commission Communication regarding cost allocation and action by public authorities on environmental matters is annexed to this recommendation and forms an integral part of it. *See also* Council Recommendation 79/3/EEC of 19 Dec. 1978 to the Member States regarding methods of evaluating the cost of pollution control to industry, OJ No. L 5, 5 Jan. 1979, p. 28. *See* BEHRENS, *Umweltschutzsubventionen, Verursacherprinzip und Europäisches Gemeinschaftsrecht*, 12 EUROPARECHT 240, 247 *et seq.* (1977); RAT VON SACHVERSTÄNDIGEN FÜR UMWELTFRAGEN, *supra* note 30, at No. 511–512; WEINSTOCK, *supra* note 1, at 13 *et seq.*

lish principles and detailed rules governing application of the polluter-pays principle and establish guidelines on possible exceptions to the principle. According to the Commission communication, the polluter-pays principle requires persons responsible for pollution to pay the costs of control measures necessary to eliminate the pollution or to reduce it so as to comply with standards or equivalent measures. The polluter-pays principle, as understood by the Community, is a pragmatic statement of a cost internalization goal – the polluter should not bear the total social costs imposed on the general public, but only the costs of compliance with environmental regulations.

Therefore, it would be wrong to conclude from the polluter-pays principle that the primary instruments for its enforcement are economic incentives and disincentives. Likewise, the polluter-pays principle does not require that Community standards disregard regional differences in the state of the environment. Hence, formal "competitive neutrality" is not inherent in the concept.[51] The Commission expressly states that under the polluter-pays principle, all kinds of standards, as well as charges and combinations of the two, are the major instruments available to public authorities.

iii. Subsidies

However, the polluter-pays principle, as understood by the Community, does imply that environmental policies should not, subject to some exceptions, depend on subsidies which place the burden of combatting pollution on the Community or member states.[52]

In the communication on the polluter-pays principle, the Commission has expressly stated that it would comply with the rules for application of the polluter-pays principle in the performance of its tasks. It is therefore not by chance that, with the exception of the waste oil directive, no directive or proposal for a directive calls for public subsidies to polluters. The Commission informally established a special environmental fund to finance public projects for environmental protection, but it was not funded until fiscal year 1982. In that year, roughly four million dollars were allocated for the development of clean technologies, protection of the natural environment in sensitive areas, implementation of anti-pollution measures and implementation of environmental measures to create new jobs. The sum for 1983 is even less.[53] This approach was formalized with the recent adoption of a Commission proposal for a regulation on common environmental action which appropriates, for the

[51] *Contra*, WEINSTOCK, *supra* note 1, at 13 *et seq.*, who, however, quite correctly points out that the conflicts inherent in the polluter-pays principle have never been politically discussed. Weinstock also admits that, as a practical matter, the principle excludes only state subsidies.

[52] *See* BEHRENS, *supra* note 50, at 248.

[53] *See* BULL. EC 7/8-1982, at p. 35, point 2. 1. 83; THE ENVIRONMENT IN EUROPE, BULLETIN OF THE INSTITUTE FOR EUROPEAN ENVIRONMENTAL POLICY No. 23 (April 1983).

next three years, roughly eleven million dollars for the development of clean technologies, monitoring techniques and procedures and the protection of endangered habitats.[53a] To a rather limited extent, the European Investment Bank and, within the framework of the common agricultural and regional policies, the agricultural and regional development funds grant funds for the active improvement of the environment, e. g. for the construction of sewage systems and water treatment plants.[54] A more active Community environmental policy would probably be greatly aided politically if more Community grants were available.

The recommendation on the polluter-pays principle provides for two groups of exceptions regarding subsidies by member states. First, some subsidies are not considered contrary to the polluter-pays principle. Examples are: financial contributions to public authorities for construction and operation of public facilities for the protection of the environment, the cost of which is not recoverable in the short run from user charges; financing designed to compensate for particularly heavy costs imposed on some polluters in order to achieve an exceptional degree of environmental quality; and contributions for research and development.

The second group consists of state subsidies where an exception to the polluter-pays principle may be justified only under certain conditions. For example, subsidies granted in the context of other policies, e. g. the regional, industrial, social, and agricultural policies, and intended to solve particular structural problems may also be granted for investments affecting environmental quality. Furthermore, subsidies may be granted during a transitional period for the adjustment of existing plants and products to new regulations if the immediate application of very stringent standards is likely to lead to serious economic disturbances. However, in both cases subsidies may be granted by member states only in accordance with the Treaty provisions on state aids, particularly Articles 92 through 94 of the EEC Treaty.

A Commission memorandum, the so-called Community framework for public aids for environmental protection,[55] attempts to clarify the recommendation on the polluter-pays principle in light of Articles 92 through 94 of the EEC Treaty. In substance, it attenuates the polluter-pays principle. It became necessary because member states made extensive use of subsidies and granted

[53a] Regulation (EEC) 1872/84 of 28 June 1984 on action by the Community relating to the environment, OJ No. L 176, 3 July 1984, p. 1. *See also* C. Levy, Towards a European Community Environment Fund (Institute for European Environmental Policy, London 1983).

[54] *See* P. Barella, *supra* note 31, at 308 *et seq.*

[55] Community framework of 6 Nov. 1974 for public aids for environmental protection, DOC SEC(74)4264, Appendix I. *See also* Bull. EC 11/1974, at pp. 41–42, point 2.1.1.5; Commission Communication concerning financial aids granted by Italy to cover investment by existing firms to combat water pollution, OJ No. C 180, 7 Aug. 1975, p. 2.

them in different forms and at different levels. The memorandum sets time limits and maximum levels for the continuation of national subsidies. It allows national subsidies to aid compliance with environmental requirements only until the end of 1980 and only for production facilities operating before 1975. The maximum level of subsidy starts with 45% of investment in 1975 and falls to 15% during the last two years that subsidies are allowed. Such subsidies are justified as aids to the promotion of important projects of common Community interest within the meaning of Art. 92(3)(b) of the EEC Treaty. The memorandum covers both direct subsidies and preferential tax treatment of environmental protection investments. In the Commission's opinion subsidies not meeting these requirements are consistent with the Treaty only when necessary in connection with particular regional or sectoral objectives. This means that investment for environmental protection may be subsidized in the framework of a member state's regional, industrial, social, agricultural, or research and development policy if necessary for solution of structural problems.

Pursuant to this memorandum, the Commission has on various occasions objected to proposed national acts providing state subsidies. Examples are: a Belgian draft regulation subsidizing water treatment investment beyond the maximum limit of the memorandum; a German tax bill granting accelerated depreciation to environmental protection investments after 1980; the German bill on water pollution charges; and the French industrial branch contracts.[56] Belgium adjusted its regulation, which had already become law, to the Commission demands. West Germany limited the operation of the tax law to 1980, while the Commission ultimately agreed that the effluent charge bill was consistent with Community law. The French branch contracts were eventually determined to be consistent with Art. 92(3)(c) of the EEC Treaty.

However, all member states felt that the ban on subsidies for environmental protection investments after 1980 was not consistent with sound environmental policy. The Commission was politically too weak to test its legal position in an infringement proceeding before the European Court of Justice. Therefore, the Commission acknowledged that, although considerable progress had been made in cleaning up the environment, the overall objectives of the environmental program had not been achieved because the economic recession starting at the beginning of the transitional period had reduced the financial resources available for environmental protection. Moreover, the Commission acknowledged that there was a backlog in adoption and implementation of environmental directives, that scientific and technological progress required new legislation, and that the public demanded greater improvement of the environment.[57] Thus, the Commission granted member states an additional transitional period for giving subsidies.

In a communication of 7 July 1980[58] the Commission prolonged the transitional period during which subsidies are allowed until 1986. During this peri-

[56] *See* Rat von Sachverständigen für Umweltfragen, *supra* note 30, at No. 1659.
[57] *See* Commission, Tenth Report on Competition Policy (Brussels 1981), No. 224–225.
[58] Commission, *supra* note 57, No. 226.

od subsidies for investments to comply with new environmental regulations are deemed within the exception of Art. 92(3)(b) of the EEC Treaty if the subsidy does not exceed 15% of the net investment and the enterprises entitled to receive the subsidy have production facilities that operated at least two years before the environmental regulation became effective. Member states must submit to the Commission an annual report on public subsidies for environmental investment to enable the Commission to oversee national practice and study the effectiveness of such subsidies.

The efficiency of subsidies as an incentive for environmental protection is not easy to assess. Although economists almost universally condemn them as inefficient, little empirical research has been done in Europe. Thus, the major factors explaining the continuation of state subsidies are that they are established practice in member states, that fundamental change would cause political problems, and that member states think that subsidies help support governmental regulation.

f. Impact of Monitoring Problems on the Selection of Strategies and Tools

Monitoring problems are particularly significant in setting and implementing ambient quality standards. The Community has developed the practice in directives of simultaneously setting both ambient quality standards and the associated measurement methods. This is necessary because the stringency of the relevant standards depends on the measurement methods. Since national measurement methods are quite different and since the imposition of new methods disrupts established national practices, there have sometimes been bitter controversies over the choice of measurement methods. In particular, progress on the proposal for the SO_2 limit values directive was delayed for years because West Germany and the other member states could not agree on common measurement methods. This problem was only solved by accepting both the majority and the German systems (which possibly amounts to national differentiation of ambient quality standards).

Except for political controversies of this kind, monitoring problems have not played an important role in the selection of strategies and tools. The difficulties in monitoring water quality for hazardous pollutants could be an explanation for the choice of a Community system of effluent rather than water quality standards under the surface water directive. Indeed, the advantage of effluent standards is that they are easy to implement and enforce. However, in the selection of strategies this consideration has been far less important than the distortion of competition rationale. Input standards also have clear advantages in implementation and enforcement. Nevertheless, they are rarely used, and in the case of SO_2 the recent trend for various reasons already discussed is to prefer ambient air quality standards to input standards.

3. Patterns of Implementation and Enforcement

The simple fact that an environmental directive is in force does not mean that member states are implementing it. Implementation and enforcement of environmental law typically falls short of stated legislative goals. This is especially true in federal systems which leave implementation and enforcement to the states or regions. However, in the Community this phenomenon has dimensions which probably do not exist in most developed federal systems.

First, the policy process in the Community has more levels of decisionmaking than in many federal states. Hence, there is not one, but rather two possible implementation gaps between agreement on an environmental directive and its application.[59] First, the directive must be incorporated into the national legal order by national legislative measures, and second, it must be implemented and enforced by the national administration through the establishment or designation of competent authorities, rulemaking, administrative guidelines, plans and programs, their application to individual cases, and enforcement in case of noncompliance (although both stages are not easy to distinguish where a particular directive also contains organizational or procedural obligations). In addition to the basic problem of two implementation gaps, the Community role in the process of incorporation, implementation, and enforcement is limited to supervision of member states as to Treaty violations. At best, the Community has weak coordination powers. The primary competences are vested in member states. The extent to which the states must act largely depends on the specificity of the directive, and the implementation problems associated with a particular directive vary accordingly. Another problem is that the political and administrative systems of member states are so diverse that great variations in the incorporation, implementation, and enforcement of environmental directives necessarily result. For example, central governments in federal states or states with a high degree of regionalization – such as West Germany, Italy, and recently Belgium – where the Länder or regions dispose of their own legislative and/or administrative competences, are not necessarily able to ensure complete incorporation, implementation, and enforcement of environmental directives. In centralized states, such problems do not normally arise, although this is not to say that there are no problems of incorporation, implementation, and enforcement in such states.

a. Incorporation

Incorporation is the first stage where harmonized environmental policies may become "diluted." Generally speaking, there are two ways to incorporate a directive: member states may enact new statutes, regulations, or administrative rules, or amend existing ones, or they may determine that the provisions and powers contained in – frequently rather scattered – existing statutes, regulations, or administrative rules are sufficient to comply with the directive. There is a marked tendency in the practice of member states to use the latter method of incorporation, if at all possible.[60] Data generated by infringement proceed-

[59] *See* von Moltke & Haigh, *supra* note 2, at 28.

[60] There is no comprehensive survey of the ways in which member states have incorporated environmental directives. For a thorough study of incorporation behavior with respect to environmental directives in the United Kingdom *see* N. Haigh, EEC Envi-

ings suggest that there is a relatively high degree of noncompliance with the obligation to incorporate directives into national law and to enact the necessary implementing provisions. There is even a pronounced unwillingness by member states to reach a settlement after informal infringement proceedings are instituted by the Commission under Art. 169 of the EEC Treaty.[61]

Between 1978 and the end of 1983 more than sixty informal infringement proceedings ending with a reasoned opinion were instituted.[62] The number of infringements may be even higher since until mid-1980 the available data relate only to the second, or conciliatory stage of the infringement procedure. This conciliatory stage of the procedure is that which, in the absence of a settlement, is concluded with a reasoned opinion. It is believed that only about one-third of all the infringement proceedings which are initiated result in a reasoned opinion.[63] It is not known how many of the environmental cases not concluded with a reasoned opinion have been settled. There are some estimates that all cases not concluded with a reasoned opinion are settled.[64] Therefore, the

RONMENTAL POLICY AND BRITAIN – AN ESSAY AND A HANDBOOK (Environmental Data Services Ltd., London 1984). For the incorporation of some water pollution directives *see* P. Barella, *supra* note 31, at 256 *et seq.* For the incorporation of the gas oil directive *see* P. KNOEPFEL & H. WEIDNER, HANDBUCH DER SO_2-LUFTREINHALTEPOLITIK, vol. 2, at 45, 192, 313, 379, 467, 515, 592, 682 (Erich Schmidt-Verlag, Berlin 1980). General information on the environmental law of member states is contained in ENVIRONMENTAL RESOURCES LTD., THE LAW AND PRACTICE RELATING TO POLLUTION CONTROL IN THE MEMBER STATES OF THE EUROPEAN COMMUNITIES, 10 volumes (Graham & Trotman for the Commission of the European Communities, London, 2d ed. 1982).

61 Progress Report 1980, *supra* note 7, Annex I, at 57; *but see* P. Barella, *supra* note 31, at 325 who speaks of a high compliance rate after institution of informal proceedings.

62 Figures according to the listing "infringement proceedings" in the BULLETIN OF THE EUROPEAN COMMUNITIES; *see also* P. Barella, *supra* note 31, at 324. The following proceedings were instituted: with respect to the gas oil directive against Italy and Luxembourg; with respect to the gasoline lead directive against Belgium and Italy; with respect to the aircraft noise directive against Italy, Ireland and Luxembourg; with respect to the drinking water directive against Belgium and the Netherlands; with respect to the bathing water directive against Belgium, Italy, the Netherlands, and the United Kingdom; with respect to the fish water directive against Belgium; with respect to the directive on detergents against Italy, France, and the United Kingdom; with respect to the aquatic environment directive against Italy, Belgium, the Netherlands, and the United Kingdom; with respect to the waste directive against Italy and Luxembourg; with respect to the toxic waste directive against Italy; with respect to the waste oil directive against Italy; with respect to the titanium dioxide directive against Belgium; with respect to the various toxic substances directives on several occasions against Belgium (6), France (3 and 2 cases not pursued), West Germany (2), Ireland (5), the Netherlands (6), Luxembourg (2), Italy (1), the United Kingdom (1) and Greece (1 and 1 case not pursued); with respect to the PCB and PCB waste directives against Luxembourg, Ireland, Italy, and the United Kingdom; with respect to the bird protection directive against Belgium and Italy; and with respect to the ground water directive against France and the Netherlands.

63 For the period until 1969 *see* H. A. H. AUDRETSCH, SUPERVISION IN EUROPEAN COMMUNITY LAW 161 (North Holland Publ. Co., Amsterdam 1978).

64 *Id.*

number of infringements in the case of environmental directives is probably much higher than the available data reveal.

There are a variety of political reasons why the Commission does not immediately institute formal infringement proceedings. The Commission prefers to negotiate with member states before instituting a formal infringement proceeding. Furthermore, when delay in incorporation is widespread, the Commission often concludes that the time limits granted by the relevant directive for incorporation are in fact too short, and does not institute infringement proceedings unless there are complaints by private parties or the European Parliament.

Also, when an infringement has no actual impact on Community environmental policy, the Commission may postpone any intervention; thus, the Commission has not yet challenged the lack of government powers in Italy and West Germany to implement effluent standards to be set under the aquatic environment directive.[65] Sometimes, as in the case of the chloride pollution of the Rhine, the decision whether to intervene may be purely political.[66]

Finally, the Commission is reluctant to prosecute in "gray areas," i. e. where the exact content of member states' obligation to incorporate an environmental directive is relatively uncertain. For example, the bathing water and drinking water directives raised the question whether the Dutch system of nonmandatory guidelines for the reduction of water pollution constitutes implementation of mandatory water quality standards.[67] Similar questions arose in connection with the French industrial branch contracts. There are or were also unsolved legal questions about whether discretionary powers constitute sufficient implementation of mandatory standards, whether simple administrative guidelines can be used to incorporate Community standards into national law, whether designation of areas of special protection such as under the bathing water and the SO_2 limit values directives is obligatory, and whether, in the absence of Community effluent standards for list I substances under the aquatic environment directive, member states must set national standards. Until such legal uncertainties are removed by judicial interpretation,[67a] the task of the Commission in reviewing the compliance behavior of member states is a delicate one. The result of such uncertainties may be that infringements are at least temporarily tolerated.

[65] *See also* SCHEUER, *Aktuelle Probleme der Durchführung der EG-Gewässerschutzrichtlinien in den Mitgliedstaaten der Gemeinschaft,* 5 ZEITSCHRIFT FÜR UMWELTPOLITIK 65, 76, 78 (1982).

[66] *See also* H. A. H. AUDRETSCH, *supra* note 63, at 190 *et seq.*

[67] European Court of Justice, case 96/81, Commission v. Netherlands, [1982] ECR 1791; case 97/81, Commission v. Netherlands, [1982] ECR 1819. The Court held the Netherlands to be in violation of the relevant directives.

[67a] The decision of the European Court of Justice, case 145/82, Commission v. Italy, [1984] ECR 711, suggests that the legal nature of the administrative provisions may be decisive.

There may also be many cases where the Commission does not detect nonincorporation. It is true that the problem of detecting infringements is somewhat less important for environmental directives than in other areas of common or harmonized policies. All recent environmental directives require member states to submit "compliance notices" to the Commission stating actual and planned measures for implementing the directive.[68] This procedure works well where clear or detailed directive provisions are to be incorporated into national law, e. g. permit requirements and emission standards. On the other hand, there are real problems in reviewing the incorporation of vague directive obligations into national law, especially where the systemic structure of national law differs from that of the relevant directive.[69] Much more personnel would be needed for a thorough review of national incorporation of directives. Complaints by member states, individuals, or associations are rare.[70] Questions from the European Parliament play some role, but do not offset the basic problems of detecting infringements.

While there is a relatively high degree of initial noncompliance with the obligation to incorporate environmental directives into national law, the informal infringement procedure usually results in member states ultimately performing their duty. It is relatively rare that the Commission has had to bring an infringement action before the European Court of Justice, although the number of such actions has increased in recent years.

As of the end of 1983, only thirty infringement actions for nonincorporation of environmental directives have been filed against member states. Most of these are against Italy and Belgium.[71] Since the Commission normally institutes infringement proceedings as a matter of routine in any case where it believes that an environmental directive has been clearly violated and the relevant state does not remedy the violation, it is safe to conclude from these figures that, at the level of incorporation, the real problem is less nonincorporation than belated or incomplete incorporation. The reasons for delay[72] may lie in constitutional and political difficulties, such as the constitutional reform in Belgium and in Italy the exclusive power of parliament to incorporate directives and the requirement for any new government to submit to parliament *de novo* the legislative proposals of the previous government. Given the rapid changes of government in Italy, it has been difficult to comply with the deadlines set in environmental directives. Italy is even in violation of quite a number of decisions by the European Court of Justice finding a violation of environmental di-

[68] *See also* Ayral, *La transposition des directives dans les droits nationaux*, 1977 Revue du Marché Commun 411, 417; J. Weiler, Supranationalism Revisited – Retrospective and Prospective, EUI Working Paper No. 2, 62 *et seq.*

[69] *See* P. Barella, *supra* note 31, at 172.

[70] Ayral, *supra* note 68, at 418; H. A. H. Audretsch, *supra* note 63, at 144 *et seq.* (more optimistic).

[71] Figures from the Bulletin of the European Communities.

[72] P. Barella, *supra* note 31, at 325, 329; *see also* Progress Report 1980, *supra* note 7, Annex I, at. 58.

rectives.[73] In other cases, member states do not meet the deadline for incorporation because they have not yet been able to effect a necessary change in their regulatory system, have not yet finalized implementing regulations or administrative guidelines, or simply want to give their industry additional time for adjustment. Inappropriate or incomplete incorporation may be due to divergent interpretation of a particular directive.

b. Ultimate Implementation and Enforcement

Even if member states incorporate environmental directives and enact the implementing provisions required by a particular environmental directive, the harmonized policies may not necessarily be effectively implemented and enforced. For effective implementation, a member state may need to adopt regulations and administrative policies; authorities must be set up or designated; the directive must be translated into individual decisions; and authorities must enforce the directive in case of noncompliance.[74] Beyond the level of incorporation, the Community has only a limited influence on the member state policy process. The one variable which it can deeply affect is the normative agenda.

By setting rather specific rules, such as emission or input standards, prohibitions, and labeling obligations, the danger of inadequate implementation can be considerably narrowed. However, as has been described, much of Community environmental law is rather unspecific, providing for ambient standards, mere environmental protection principles, or even relying on member states themselves to develop substantive environmental policies according to Community guidelines. The implementation of such directives is necessarily accompanied by severe slippages.

Moreover, many factors that determine the outcome of the policy process are not subject to harmonization. The organization and attitudes of the administration implementing the directive play an important role. For example, member states or agencies that place a low value on environmental protection will be less vigorous in implementing and enforcing directives than those which identify themselves with environmental policy goals. Thus, the implementation process will reflect the differing interests of environmental and polluter states even though Community authorities may have decided to ignore such differences in formulating a directive. Other factors influencing the timing and content of state action are the organization and access to the policy process of neighbors and environmental groups. The variety of dynamic factors that determine the outcome of the policy process are part of national political and ad-

[73] European Parliament, Written Question No. 388/82 by Mr. Purvis, OJ No. C 198, 2 Aug. 1982, p. 32. However, the Law of 9 Feb. 1982 (Gazz. Uff., 25 Feb., no. 55), No. 42, delegated to the Italian Government for a period of six months the power to incorporate these specific directives by decree (instead of parliamentary act).

[74] *See generally* H. W. Rengeling, Rechtsgrundsätze beim Verwaltungsvollzug des Europäischen Gemeinschaftsrechts 14 *et seq.* (Carl Heymanns Verlag, Köln 1977); W. Schmeder, *supra* note 15, at 35.

ministrative systems, and they are bound to be quite different in different member states. An empirical study of SO_2 policy in the EEC member states (and Switzerland)[75] shows that national patterns of implementation and enforcement are quite varied. The findings of this study can certainly be generalized. Another study concerning the effects of Community environmental policy in one member state, the United Kingdom, shows that the practical effects may vary from directive to directive.[76] Thus, a high degree of variation in the implementation of harmonized environmental policies is inherent in the legal and political system of the Community.[77]

Community involvement through monitoring and coordination of national implementation can only partially offset this structural deficiency. Theoretically it would be possible to require member states to make public registers of emissions and reports on improvements occurring after incorporation of a directive. However, given the preference of many member states for extensive secrecy about pollution data, a Community initiative for mandatory publicity of such data can not be expected.[78] The Community has made arrangements for the submission of national pollution data to the Commission in sensitive areas such as water pollution and SO_2/particulates.[79] This information is not public. The Commission can not generate information on its own, but rather must rely on and may at best refine and improve the quality of information made available by member states.[80] Even if such information exists, it is aggregate data which does not allow identification of specific deficiencies in implementation and enforcement.

More recent directives have attempted to establish a system of coordination of national implementation by the Community or joint Community/member state institutions. Although there has been little experience with such arrangements, they will probably not normally reach as far as individual implementation decisions and enforcement activities. At best they will affect the national

[75] P. KNOEPFEL & H. WEIDNER, *supra* note 60, vol. 2. *See also* WEIDNER & KNOEPFEL, *supra* note 2, at 57–58.

[76] N. HAIGH, *suprá* note 60.

[77] *See also* Pleinevaux, *supra* note 30, at 400; WEINSTOCK, *supra* note 1, at 21 *et seq.*; RAT VON SACHVERSTÄNDIGEN FÜR UMWELTFRAGEN, *supra* note 30, at No. 1651; H. W. RENGELING, *supra* note 74, at 297. Krislov, Ehlermann & Weiler, *Political Organs and the Decision-Making Process in the U. S. and the European Communities*, at VII.D.2, in INTEGRATION THROUGH LAW, Vol. 1, Book, 2, speak in this connection of Europe as a "weak confederation."

[78] In the same sense *see* VON MOLTKE & HAIGH, *supra* note 2, at 28.

[79] *See* Council Decision 77/795/EEC of 12 Dec. 1977 establishing a common procedure for the exchange of information on the quality of surface fresh water in the Community, OJ No. L 334, 24 Dec. 1977, p. 29; Council Decision 75/441/EEC of 24 June 1975 establishing a common procedure for the exchange of information between the surveillance and monitoring networks based on data relating to atmospheric pollution caused by certain compounds and suspended particulates, OJ No. L 194, 25 July 1975, p. 32.

[80] *See* Progress Report 1980, *supra* note 7, Annex I, at 56.

implementation process at some intermediate level, i. e. the level where policy decisions on implementation programs are made. For example, the Commission will be able to detect and challenge the failure of a member state to establish an improvement program for existing sources under the titanium dioxide directive,[81] to establish implementation plans under the drinking water directive,[82] or to set up programs for list II substances under the aquatic environment directive.[83] It is doubtful whether, beyond mere formal discharge of these obligations, the Commission can effectively probe into the substantive adequacy of these programs. As a practical matter, decisions about controls on particular sources are immune from Commission scrutiny. A notable exception is the Commission involvement in exempting a particular existing source from a member state improvement program under the titanium dioxide directive. Such involvement in decisions on particular cases, at least in the form of a Commission power to have a case referred to it, would seem necessary if uniform implementation and enforcement were to be ensured.

Finally, the infringement procedure is not a suitable instrument for supervising implementation and enforcement of harmonized environmental policies. Virtually all infringement proceedings have so far concerned failures of a member state to enact laws or amend existing law as required by a directive. The Commission has never tried to probe into the actual implementation and enforcement activities of member states.[84] One reason is that the Commission does not have sufficient personnel to monitor implementation and enforcement. Reporting by enterprises, affected citizens, and environmental associations through the informal complaint procedure has been of marginal importance.[85] Of course, to the extent that a directive mandates a particular administrative activity, such as organizing an administrative body or establishing an implementation plan, failure to formally comply can be easily detected and prosecuted. Inadequacy of an implementation plan or individual cases of misapplication of a directive are for practical reasons not amenable to prosecution.

Thus, the normal gap inherent in implementation of all environmental law is aggravated in the Community by the paramount role of the member states, the diversity of national political and administrative systems, and the lack of substantial Community involvement in the process of implementation and enforcement. This aggravated gap threatens environmental goals and, from the perspective of European integration, results in a lack of uniformity along national lines that severely limits substantive harmonization of environmetal poli-

[81] *See* 80 UMWELT, INFORMATIONEN DES BUNDESMINISTERS DES INNEREN 28 (16 Jan. 1981).

[82] *See* SCHEUER, *supra* note 65, at 76.

[83] *Id.* at 78. As for the control of chloride effluents, *see infra* pp. 242–243 and note 97.

[84] AYRAL, *supra* note 68, at 419. *Cf.* WEIDNER & KNOEPFEL, *supra* note 2, at 56–57 who state that there is no systematic "deterring" control over national implementation of environmental directives.

[85] AYRAL, *supra* note 68, at 418–419.

cies. The lack of uniformity among member states and the incompleteness of the integration process are distinctive features that represent a qualitative difference between the implementation and enforcement problems in developed federal systems and in the Community. This problem, however, has not yet been perceived as a fundamental political problem of Community environmental policy.[86]

c. *Role of Courts*

Whether state courts and the European Court of Justice will be able to meet these implementation gaps is at the present stage of development largely a matter of speculation. First, it should be noted that there are considerable variations among member states as to participation in administrative proceedings and the role administrative and judicial review play in controlling implementation and enforcement. These variations, which reflect the diversity of legal/administrative systems and political cultures existing in the Community, condition the exercise of the review powers of the European Court of Justice under Art. 177 of the EEC Treaty and of state courts.

The most important of these variables are the national rules regarding substantive questions such as the degree of discretion accorded to national agencies and those regarding procedural issues such as access to the court (especially standing to sue), the powers of the court, and scope of review,[87] national implementation and enforcement practices, frequency of litigation, and the behavior of private parties. The willingness, especially on the part of lower national courts, to refer questions to the European Court of Justice is an additional factor which expresses political preferences in the latent conflict between national sovereignty and supranationalism. This access to the indirect review of the European Court of Justice is neither *de jure* nor *de facto* uniform in all member states. The disproportion in frequency of references to the European Court of Justice from various member states is striking.[88]

There are fundamental differences in the roles played by, say, West German, Dutch, French, and British judges in controlling national implementation and enforcement. These differences reflect differences in access to the court, the number and kind of issues taken to the court, the politicization of review of politically controversial environmental decisions, the powers of the court with regard to the executive branch, and feedback effects to the political process. These differences must also necessarily affect the potential for indirect review by the European Court of Justice. For example, if in most member states third parties could not seek review of a violation of the nondegradation re-

[86] In the same sense *see* WEINSTOCK, *supra* note 1, at 22. The Third Environmental Program (*supra* note 49, Annex. No. 13) devotes two sentences to the problem.

[87] J. Weiler, *supra* note 68, at 66 speaks of "a disturbing inequality of remedies."

[88] *See* MORTELMANS, *Observations in the Cases Governed by Article 177 of the EEC Treaty: Procedure and Practice*, 16 COMMON MKT. L. REV. 557 (1979); EVERLING, *Die Mitgliedstaaten der Europäischen Gemeinschaft vor ihrem Gerichtshof*, 18 EUROPARECHT 101, 122 (1983).

quirement established by the SO_2 limit values directive, the chances that the European Court of Justice would ever decide on interpretation of the nondegradation requirement would be small.

In addition to national variability in access to the national courts and the European Court of Justice, it is probable that judicial procedures will be little used in environmental regulation. In a political society where bargaining rather than enforcement is the primary administrative device for seeking compliance with environmental law, the role of the courts and ultimately of the European Court of Justce is bound to be marginal. Comparative empirical research in the field of air pollution control[89] suggests that informal implementation and enforcement, although to varying degrees, are very important in all member states. Assuming this phenomenon applies generally to environmetal law, the future issues that ought to be clarified by the national courts and the European Court of Justice will largely remain under the control of the immediate partners in the "implementation game" in the member states, namely state agencies and regulated firms. This practical elimination of the national courts and especially of the European Court as the guardian of environmental supranationalism reinforces the already strong centrifugal forces existing in the implementation of environmental directives. A corollary is that it is also not possible to predict the environmental relevance of the preliminary ruling procedure based on past experience in other areas.

4. Transboundary Pollution

Global and regional pollution problems, such as marine pollution, transboundary pollution, appropriation of shared resources, and industrial location in border areas, are often given as the primary justification for transfer of legislative competences from member states to the Community. Since these problems surpass the ambit of any single member state, the Community is considered the appropriate decisionmaking level for addressing them.[90] And indeed, the Community has been quite active in negotiating a variety of international and regional conventions (or at least coordinating negotiations by the member states), especially for marine and international river pollution, global problems of protecting wildlife, and long range transport of air pollutants. The emphasis of Community environmental policy on water pollution clearly results from the obvious transboundary implications of pollution of European rivers and seas. The pollution of Western Europe's major river, the Rhine, to which three important member states are riverains, served as an impetus to the development of a general common environmental policy. Consultation and coordination clauses inserted in most water pollution directives as well as in

[89] *See supra* note 76.

[90] *See* Progress Report 1980, *supra* note 7, at 4; H. Bungarten, *supra* note 2, at 112, 115–116, 158, 228, 232, 287 *et seq.*; Riegel, *Notwendigkeiten und Probleme einer gemeinschaftrechtlichen Integration des Umweltschutzrechts unter besonderer Berücksichtigung des Wasserrechts*, 3 Natur und Recht 90 (1981); Rat von Sachverständigen für Umweltfragen, *supra* note 30, at No. 1647, 1649.

the SO_2 limit values and major accidents directives[91] demonstrate that this concern for transboundary pollution has generated common rules to which member states are bound.

It would certainly be premature to attempt at this time to fully evaluate the contribution of Community environmental policy to the control of transboundary pollution. Most of the conventions and directives have not yet matured to the point that they could be implemented or that their implementation could show clear results. But it is safe to assert that transboundary pollution would be worse or become worse in the future than it now is but for the effect of the many Community directives setting ambient quality, emission, and input standards for significant water and air pollutants.

On the other hand, the common environmental policy has suffered serious failures in the very field of transboundary pollution.[92] None of the most urgent problems of pollution of the Rhine have been solved. The failure of the Chloride Convention, negotiated under the auspices of the Community but not submitted by the French government to parliament for ratification, is perhaps the most serious setback. After the failure of this convention several years were necessary to negotiate a new agreement and to induce France to ratify the convention.

The convention for the prevention of chemical pollution of the Rhine has been ratified, but its implementation, especially the establishment of effluent standards for the most hazardous pollutants, has made as little progress as the parallel work within the framework of the aquatic directive. The existing water pollution directives, the SO_2 limit values directive, and the chemical accidents directive do not contain clear rules mandating consideration of out of state spillovers to the same extent as domestic effects.

Recently, transboundary pollution has even become a political threat to agreement on new proposals where vital national interests are involved. Thus, agreement on Commission proposals concerning the establishment of common substantive criteria and a common, Commission-based consultation procedure for locating power plants in border areas has long been stalled because France considers these proposals a challenge to its independent nuclear energy policy. Final adoption of the proposal on major accidents had to be postponed several times because there was disagreement on the proposed consultation procedure concerning the location of, and the handling of accidents caused by, chemical installations in border areas.[93] Similar problems occurred in negotiations on the Commission proposal for environmental impact assessment.[94]

The compromise finally agreed upon in negotiations on the major accidents directive – consultation in the framework of "bilateral" relations – is indeed considered a precedent for the future.[95] But, this compromise shows that national claims of sovereignty are still considered very vital. Some member states

[91] *See supra* Ch. VI, note 78.
[92] For the following section *see supra* at pp. 97–98, 99–100.
[93] *See supra* at p. 97.
[94] *See supra* at pp. 104–108.
[95] *See supra* at p. 98.

are stepping up their efforts to strengthen bilateral consultation and cooperation in exactly the areas covered by Commission proposals, thereby emphasizing the primary role of intergovernmental decisionmaking. Vital problems of global or regional pollution, such as acid rain and the potential destruction of the atmosphere's ozone layer, have at best been addressed with half-hearted measures. All told, transboundary pollution and the international character of pollution problems are no longer forces for further integration in the field of environmental protection.

A clear role for national courts and the European Court of Justice in the field of transboundary pollution has also not yet emerged, although there are remedies available. The infringement action is available both to the Commission and to a receptor member state when transboundary pollution violates an environmental directive. Similarly, a national of a receptor state could probably (subject of course to national rules concerning standing, justiciability, and scope of review) seek judicial review before the courts of the emitter state to challenge its authorization of the emitter's activities as inconsistent with a relevant environmental directive, and ultimately the case may be referred to the European Court of Justice for a preliminary ruling. Litigation among private parties may have a supplementary function in controlling the implementation and enforcement of directive obligations with respect to transboundary pollution.

However, the chances that these remedies will be effectively used are rather remote. As already noted, it is unclear to what extent, beyond coordination and consultation, the water pollution, SO_2 limit values, and major accidents directives oblige member states to consider transboundary spillovers on the same basis as domestic impacts. Hence, it will be difficult for the Commission to find a particular member state to be in violation of a directive and to take the case before the European Court of Justice, the more so since the infringement procedure is poorly adapted to deal with implementation in particular cases. The politicization of transboundary pollution conflicts as recently experienced may add further difficulties.

An example of the obstacles to be overcome in transboundary pollution conflicts was the controversy over chloride pollution of the Rhine between France and the other member states as well as the Commission. France had not ratified the chloride convention nor had it taken any measures under national law to limit the discharge of chloride into the Rhine. The Commission was not prepared to initiate infringement proceedings against France although the French salt discharges into the Rhine arguably violated the provisions of the drinking water directive. The sodium chloride value established by the directive is not a mandatory standard but, rather, a guide value which member states are obliged to try to attain. The Commission maintained that the failure of a member state to comply with a guide value was not an infringement of the directive.[96] This position is legally debatable and the issue ought to be settled

[96] Written Question No. 361/80 of 14 May 1980 by Mr. Muntingh, OJ No. C 236, 15 Sept. 1980, p. 15, at 16.

by the Court. However, it is obvious that the Commission preferred a political solution[97] through negotiation within the framework of the International Commission for the Protection of the Rhine against Pollution.

It is improbable that a member state would institute infringement proceedings under Art. 170 of the EEC Treaty when the Commission fails to do so. There is only one case of an infringement action instituted under Art. 170 by a member state against another member state, namely the litigation between France and the United Kingdom on access to fishing grounds off the British coast.[98] There are some other cases in the field of fisheries and internal trade where member states have recently threatened that they would institute court proceedings, but then have acquiesced in a settlement through the conciliatory services of the Commission. These cases could be taken as an indication that member state invocation of the infringement action has its potential in exactly those politicized conflicts where the Commission, in view of the overriding interests of the states concerned and the threat to Community stability involved in the Commission's choosing sides, is unable or unwilling to act as a mediator or bring the case before the Court. Pollution of the Rhine might seem to be such a conflict. However, given the need to continue negotiations over a variety of issues not yet covered by Community or convention rules, member states are reluctant to bring a particular conflict before the Court unless it can clearly be resolved by an existing, self-executing Community or convention regulation.

As for resolution of transboundary pollution issues by private litigation against neighboring member states, the dearth of such litigation in areas already covered by Community directives indicates that its present and medium-range role is modest at best. The normal barriers to access to the judiciary in environmental controversies, such as standing, cost, lack of scientific and technical information, and lack of discovery into the internal process of the agency concerned, are aggravated in litigation over transboundary pollution by the internationality of the conflict. However, the recent French *Rhinewater* case[99] shows that this kind of litigation has a certain potential.

Litigation among private parties has at best a supplementary function. It will be limited in most cases to suits demanding damages for transboundary pollution because the chances of obtaining injunctive relief are low; there is only one case, the *Zurich-Kloten airport* case,[100] where such relief was demanded (and partially granted). In some member states the private law of compensation for environmental harm is, at least for certain causes of action, disassociated from administrative regulation of the environment, so that damage actions can not be maintained on the basis of regulatory violations and are not barred

[97] MALANCZUK, *EC - Developments*, 6 ENVT'L POL'Y & L. 186, at 187 (1980).

[98] European Court of Justice, case 141/78, France v. United Kingdom, [1979] ECR 293.

[99] Tribunal administratif Strasbourg, 27 July 1983, 1983 REVUE JURIDIQUE DE L'ENVIRONNEMENT 343.

[100] Landgericht Waldshut-Tiengen, 11 Feb. 1982, 1983 UMWELT- UND PLANUNGSRECHT 14, which ordered an extension of the existing limitations on night flight.

by the fact that the polluter has been granted an authorization. In such cases, private damage suits can not directly serve as an instrument for implementation and enforcement of Community directives; however, they may be an indirect incentive for polluters to move in the direction of controls required by the directive. In other member states or in other cases private damage actions can be based on regulatory violations. In any event sporadic private litigation is not as a practical matter a very serious threat to polluters in violation of an environmental directive.

Besides the somewhat spectacular Dutch *Rhinewater* case,[101] there have been very few private court cases on transboundary pollution within the Community over the last three decades. Two early German holdings concerning water pollution in the Saar region[102] applied French substantive law because it was considered more favorable to the German victim than German law. The same is true of a more recent German case involving air pollution by toxic substances originating from a French pesticide plant.[103] The French titanium dioxide case applied French law as the law of the place of injury.[104] There are some other French/Belgian and Belgian/Dutch cases involving minor neighborhood conflicts.[105] There is not a single case where harmonized environmental law was involved. Given the dearth of case law and in particular the substantive and procedural problems arising in private transboundary pollution litigation, it does not seem very likely that this litigation will play a major role in the near future in aiding implementation and enforcement of harmonized environmental policies.[106] Although member states may be ready to consider out of state impacts of polluting facilities and are probably ready to

[101] *See supra* pp. 171–172, note 97.

[102] Oberlandesgericht Saarbrücken, 22 Oct. 1957, 11 NEUE JURISTISCHE WOCHENSCHRIFT 752 (1958), DIE DEUTSCHE RECHTSPRECHUNG AUF DEM GEBIET DES INTERNATIONALEN PRIVATRECHTS IN DEN JAHREN 1956 UND 1957, at No. 42 (Walter de Gruyter, Mohr Siebeck, Berlin, Tübingen 1962); Oberlandesgericht Saarbrücken, 5 March 1963, DIE DEUTSCHE RECHTSPRECHUNG AUF DEM GEBIET DES INTERNATIONALEN PRIVATRECHTS IN DEN JAHREN 1962 UND 1963, at No. 38 (Walter de Gruyter, Mohr Siebeck, Berlin, Tübingen 1969).

[103] Oberlandesgericht Karlsruhe, 4 Aug. 1977, 23 RECHT DER INTERNATIONALEN WIRTSCHAFT 718 (1977), DIE DEUTSCHE RECHTSPRECHUNG AUF DEM GEBIET DES INTERNATIONALEN PRIVATRECHTS IM JAHRE 1977, at No. 27 (Mohr Siebeck, Tübingen 1979).

[104] Tribunal grande instance Bastia, 6 Dec. 1976, 1977 DALLOZ-SIREY JURISPRUDENCE 427; *aff'd* Cour d'Appel Bastia, 28 Feb. 1977, 1980 FORO ITALIANO IV 406, at 408; *aff'd* Cour de Cassation Civile, 3 April 1978, 1978 DALLOZ-SIREY JURISPRUDENCE I 367.

[105] *See* SIEHR, *Grenzüberschreitender Umweltschutz*, 45 RABELS ZEITSCHRIFT FÜR AUSLÄNDISCHES UND INTERNATIONALES PRIVATRECHT 377, at 383, note 28 (1981); Jessurun d'Oliveira, *La pollution du Rhin et le droit international privé*, in RHINE POLLUTION/LA POLLUTION DU RHIN 81, 83–84 (Tjeenk Willink, Zwolle 1978).

[106] Jessurun d'Oliveira, *supra* note 105, at 83 *et seq.* SIEHR, *supra* note 105, at 382–383, 395 *et seq.* also agrees transboundary pollution litigation will have only limited importance.

recognize foreign permits, isolated private party litigation will remain secondary to political management of conflicts and to systematic administrative implementation and enforcement of environmental directives because the underlying problems are genuinely international.

If private litigation does not significantly contribute to implementation and enforcement of existing directives, one can ask whether it may at least contribute to development of common rules for transboundary pollution conflicts not yet covered by directives. Generally, court intervention is a poor way of addressing the highly complex problems associated with transboundary pollution. Resource management through the coordinated activities of state agencies is the real answer to transboundary pollution. Private litigation could perhaps stimulate central initiatives. Spectacular cases such as the Dutch *Rhinewater* and the titanium dioxide cases might arouse enough public concern about an environmental issue so that the Community would finally get involved. Excessive optimism, however, is not warranted. Private litigation in the *Rhinewater* case may have had some impact on the conclusion of the chloride convention of 1976, but the judgment requiring the French operator of the alkali factory to pay damages for the chloride pollution of the Rhine did not induce the French government to submit the chloride convention to parliament for ratification. In the titanium dioxide case, criminal proceedings instituted prior to the private litigation caused the Italian government to take the initiative for a Community solution to the dumping of titanium dioxide wastes,[107] although such a move could also have been induced by the private litigation. But such spectacular transboundary pollution conflicts are rare.

B. Major Influencing Factors

1. Legal and Institutional Constraints

a. Legal Constraints

i. Articles 100 and 235 of the EEC Treaty

Community environmental policy has developed under legal constraints because the Community was designed as an economic institution and environmental protection was not an original objective of the Treaties. As analyzed in Chapter II, Articles 100 and 235 of the EEC Treaty in conjunction with the preamble and Art. 2 of the EEC Treaty do not provide a secure legal basis for the development of environmental policy as a new common policy within the framework of the Treaty. Environmental policy goals can in principle be pursued only as incidental to harmonization measures motivated by trade or competition considerations. The assessment of many legal writers is that these deficiencies in Community legislative powers have played and will in the future

[107] *See* Kiss, *Un cas de pollution internationale – l'affaire des boues rouges*, 102 Journal du Droit International 207 (1975); Siehr, *supra* note 105, at 381–382.

play a significant role in impeding the development and implementation of Community environmental policy.[108] However, in practice these limitations, although not insignificant, have not proven very onerous. Thus, the Commission could state in 1980: "Recourse to Art. 235, either on its own or in conjunction with another Article of the Treaty, has not caused any particular difficulties."[109] The Community institutions have not had to make concessions on the substance of any new proposal in order to meet or quiet objections to their legislative competence. Using a pragmatic, incrementalist approach and concentrating on problems where the benefits of common action were evident, they have step by step established a network of over seventy legislative texts for the protection of the environment and thereby created a mosaic of precedents[110] as to the legislative competence of the Community which will be hard to overrule. The deficiencies in the legal basis for Community environmental policy were compensated by the political will of the member states.[111] This is all the more remarkable as the member states have had quite different views and priorities with respect to environmental issues.

Controversies between France, on one hand, and the other member states and the Commission, on the other, as to the Community competences for the protection of the environment marked the beginning of the common environmental policy in 1971.[112] Their result was that the several environmental programs were adopted only as a joint resolution of the Heads of State and Governments (now called the European Council) and of the Council of the Community. A further result was that the division of labor between the Community and member states was not clearly delimited. The development of a common environmental policy also aroused much criticism among legal writers.[113] However, there was no serious political challenge to Community competences for environmental matters in the early years following adoption of the first environmental program.[114] The German Bundesrat, originally very critical, accepted in 1975 that the Community had legislative powers over matters directly related to trade, industry, or economic affairs in general,[115] and that this provided a basis for a Community environmental program.

Due perhaps to the increasing density and scope of Community environmental legislation,[116] the situation has recently changed somewhat. In 1978,

[108] *See supra* pp. 18–19, especially at notes 12 & 13.

[109] Progress Report 1980, *supra* note 7, at 6.

[110] H. Bungarten, *supra* note 2, at 159, 175.

[111] Von Moltke, *supra* note 27, at 79.

[112] *See* Pleinevaux, *supra* note 30, at 394 *et seq.*

[113] *See supra* at p. 18 *et seq.*, especially at notes 12 & 13.

[114] H. Bungarten, *supra* note 2, at 228, in 1978 could still state that there was no serious attempt to challenge the legislative competence of the Community in environmental matters.

[115] *See* Bundesrats-Drucksache 142/75, 282/76.

[116] This is the interpretation of Kapteyn, *Annotation*, 16 Common Mkt. L. Rev. 703, 706 (1979). *See also* House of Lords, Select Committee on the European Communities, Session 1977–78, Approximation of Laws under Article 100 EEC Treaty, 22nd Re-

the British House of Lords published a report critical of the ever increasing extension of Community environmental law,[117] and other national parliaments have joined in this criticism.[118] In the West German Bundesrat, it has been suggested that the Länder should have the right to veto a Commission proposal.[119] It also is remarkable that Community officials who had cleared the way for recognition of Community environmental competences by publishing a series of articles in the early seventies,[120] but from then on had not bothered to discuss the question, have more recently felt compelled to defend once again the legal position of the Community.[121]

The real issue is not so much the superficial controversy over interpretation of legal notions, but rather the realization of politicians outside the governments of member states that every new piece of Community environmental legislation shifts legislative competence from member states to the Community and therefore erodes the power of national parliaments.[122] These reservations may cause some governments to be more prudent in agreeing to new directives. Legally, they will remain unimportant as long as private litigation concerning environmental directives does not increase. Member states which have participated in a directive's development will not normally challenge its conformity with the Treaty in infringement proceedings.[123]

The most visible practical result of the limitations inherent in Articles 100 and 235 is the emphasis of Community environmental policy on environmental problems related to trade and industry. The Community has concentrated on regulation of products, control of pollution from stationary sources, and waste disposal. Further substantive expansion into other areas of environmental policy, especially natural resources and land use, is improbable.[124] Denmark

PORT No. 22(5) (HMSO, London 1978), partially *reprinted in* 4 ENVT'L POL'Y & L. 193 (1978).

[117] House of Lords, Select Committee, 22ND REPORT, *supra* note 116. *Cf.* VON MOLTKE, *supra* note 27, at 82, who feels the House of Lords is the precursor of future political resistance to the expansion of the Community into environmental policy.

[118] *See* KAISER, *Grenzen der EG-Zuständigkeit*, 15 EUROPARECHT 97, 100, 102 (1980) (with further references). *See also* VON MOLTKE, *The Legal Basis for Environmental Policy*, 3 ENVT'L POL'Y & L. 136 (1977); VYGEN, *Ergänzung des EWG-Vertrages im Hinblick auf eine europäische Umweltpolitik*, 6 ZEITSCHRIFT FÜR RECHTSPOLITIK 58, 60 (1974).

[119] *See* KAISER, *supra* note 118.

[120] *See, e. g.*, CARPENTIER, *L'action de la Communauté en matière d'environnement*, 1972 REVUE DU MARCHÉ COMMUN 381; SCHEUER, *Aspects juridiques de la protection de l'environnement dans le Marché Commun*, 1975 REVUE DU MARCHÉ COMMUN 441.

[121] *See, e. g.*, BÉRAUD, *Fondements juridiques du droit de l'environnement dans le Traité de Rome*, 1979 REVUE DU MARCHÉ COMMUN 35; CLOSE, *Harmonisation of Law: Use or Abuse of the Powers under the EEC Treaty?*, 3 EUROPEAN L. REV. 461 (1978).

[122] House of Lords, Select Committee, 22ND REPORT, *supra* note 116, at No. 15, 16.

[123] *See also, e. g.*, European Court of Justice, case 91/79, Commission v. Italy, [1980] ECR 1099. J. Weiler, *supra* note 68, at note 84 quite correctly speaks here of "political estoppel."

[124] *See also* Progress Report 1980, *supra* note 7, Annex I, at 36, 37.

pointed out very early that it did not favor expansion of Community environmental policy into protection of nature beyond the directive concerning wild birds, the regulation on whales, and the accession of the Community to some treaties for protection of wild fauna. Denmark sees its traditional links with other Scandinavian countries threatened by the automatic transfer of foreign relations competences to the Community once a directive has been issued and a subject area is occupied by "internal" Community rules.[125] It therefore has general reservations against any further Community expansion. The majority of member states have also objected to any Community regulatory activities regarding land use planning.[126]

The reservation of particular areas of environmental policy to state legislation is a phenomenon that also exists in many federal states which grant the federal government broad legislative powers. Controversies over the exact scope of federal powers are also common and should not be interpreted as a special deficiency of the European Community. Especially in West Germany and Canada, controversies over the legislative competence of the federal government are or were part of the day to day business of environmental politics.

However, it must be noted that the refusal of member states to let the Community legislate in areas such as natural resources and land use has significant practical consequences. Specifically, the shift announced in the second environmental program from pollution control towards rational use of natural resources and from the remedial to the preventive approach can at best be only partially implemented. Any Community involvement in the solution of certain truly international matters, such as international protection of wildlife, is also put into question. This is an indication that there are definite limits to Community power to implement a coordinated concept of environmental policy. These limits are not so much legal as institutional and political. Their primary source is the decisionmaking procedure established by Articles 100 and 235, under which all member states must agree that a particular problem should be addressed at the Community level.[127]

[125] *See* Progress Report 1980, *supra* note 7, at 6; LACHMANN, *Some Danish Reflections on the Use of Article 235 of The Rome Treaty*, 18 COMMON MKT. L. REV. 447, 437-438, 459 (1981). The reason is the jurisprudence of the European Court of Justice to the effect that Europeanization of a particular area amounts to a transfer of foreign relations competences to the Community under Art. 113 of the EEC Treaty. *See* case 22/70, Re European Road Transport Agreement, [1971] ECR 263; cases 3, 4 and 6/76, Kramer (Biological Resources of the Sea), [1976] ECR 1279; opinion 1/76, Re The Draft Agreement Establishing a European Laying-Up Fund for Inland Waterway Vessels (Rhine case), [1977] ECR 741; opinion 1/78, Re International Rubber Agreement, [1979] ECR 2871; MASTELLONE, *The External Relations of the EEC in the Field of Environmental Protection*, 30 INT'L & COMP. L. Q. 104 (1981).

[126] *See* 78 UMWELT, INFORMATIONEN DES BUNDESMINISTERS DES INNEREN 44 (12 Sept. 1980).

[127] Wallace, *National Bulls in the Community China Shop: The Role of National Governments in Community Policy-Making*, in POLICY-MAKING IN THE EUROPEAN COMMUNITIES, *supra* note 12, at 33, 45.

A more interesting question is whether the insecurity of the legal basis for environmental policy has political consequences for proposals within the core area of Community environmental policy. More precisely, the question is whether the alleged absence of Community legislative competence is frequently and in some cases successfully used as an argument against adoption of a particular proposal. This is not the case. Although there are frequently controversies among member states and the Commission as to the Treaty provision on which to base a particular directive, the dispute is not whether the Community has competence in a particular matter but rather reflects different and broader considerations.[128]

Some member states, such as West Germany and the Netherlands, and also the Commission favor a liberal interpretation of Art. 100, while other member states prefer to rely on Art. 235 whenever the particular environmental problem is not directly related to trade or industry. One may interpret these divergencies as an expression of different approaches to legal integration. Art. 100 stands for a broad interpretation of Community powers with respect to expansion into new areas while recourse to Art. 235 is the expression of a narrow view of the Common Market and the normal powers granted to the Community. However, a member state may also have internal reasons for preferring a particular Treaty provision as the legal basis for Community action. For example, West Germany prefers Art. 100 and accepts Art. 235 as at most an additional basis because the Federal Government has only limited legislative competence.[129]

Although controversies of this kind may cause delay and absorb time of personnel which could be better devoted to policy formulation, they do not normally impede adoption of a proposal. Member state objections to Commission proposals normally do not contest the legislative powers of the Community, but instead are based on national interests such as different priorities, policies, strategies, or patterns of implementation in the particular field. Even where the need for harmonization is at issue, the issue is normally not interpretation of Articles 100 or 235. Normally the relevant member state merely has different priorities and does not want Community legislation for political reasons. The fate of the more controversial recent directives, such as the aquatic environment, SO_2 limit values, and toxic substances directives, clearly shows that the issues relate primarily to different policies and strategies.

When a member state considers its interest as paramount to the interest in harmonization, it may veto adoption of the directive or insist on major changes, such as resort to optional or alternative harmonization, national exceptions, or a shift from substantive regulation to mere coordination of

[128] *See* F. BEHRENS, *supra* note 23, at 259, 292–293; H. BUNGARTEN, *supra* note 2, at 181 *et seq.*; Pleinevaux, *supra* note 30, at 397; VIGNES, *43-100 et 100-235*, 1976 CAHIERS DE DROIT EUROP. 810; OFFERMANN-CLAS, *Die Kompetenzen der Europäischen Gemeinschaften im Umweltschutz*, 6 ZEITSCHRIFT FÜR UMWELTPOLITIK 47, 55 *et seq.* (1983).

[129] *See* Bundesrats-Drucksache 142/75.

member state implementation.[130] The lack of a secure legal basis for Community environmental legislation does not play a significant role in the decisionmaking process. Therefore, contrary to what has often been argued,[131] to the extent there is any danger of lowest common denominator Community solutions for environmental problems,[132] it has nothing to do with the limitations of Community legislative powers. It is instead an institutional and political problem.[133]

Finally, the narrow harmonization concept underlying Art. 100 does not seriously impede, as a legal matter, the Community's power to adopt innovative policies or strategies. It has been argued that the harmonization competence under Art. 100 is irreconcilable with a comprehensive, coordinated concept of environmental policy and that it prevents the Community from addressing environmental problems not yet regulated by at least one member state.[134] However, this argument ignores the instrumental function of the legal provisions which grant competences for development of a policy. The environmental programs of the Community clearly show a perspective that goes beyond eliminating obstacles to trade.[135] That they are unlawful has never been asserted. The political practice has largely been emancipated from a narrow concept of harmonization.[136]

It is recognized that harmonization has not only the function of abolishing barriers to trade and distortions of competition but also of implementing substantive policies.[137] And where Art. 100 fails, the member states have easily resorted to Art. 235, either in conjunction with Art. 100 or even as an exclusive basis for legislative competence. Also, given the rapid expansion of environmental law in all member states, the problem of finding regulation by at least one member state in order to establish a need for harmonization has lost much of its practical significance,[138] especially since it is sufficient that a particular environmental problem be covered by general regulations. This is demonstrated by the PCB waste directive which establishes a special regime of waste disposal for substances previously covered only by the general waste disposal laws of member states. Further, it has never been suggested that the Communi-

[130] VON MOLTKE, *supra* note 118, at 138, after having stated that the Treaty does not allow establishment of a comprehensive environmental policy, admits that the existence of a secure legal basis is no guarantee for such policy (*e. g.* European transport policy).

[131] *See supra* p. 213, note 23.

[132] *See supra* pp. 213–214.

[133] In this sense *see also* F. BEHRENS, *supra* note 23, at 254, 258; Krämer, *supra* note 17, at No. 48.

[134] H. BUNGARTEN, *supra* note 2, at 125; F. BEHRENS, *supra* note 23, at 295–296; F. MARX, *supra* note 23, at 155–156; VON MOLTKE, *supra* note 118, at 138.

[135] In the same sense *see* F. BEHRENS, *supra* note 23, at 295–296. *Contra* F. MARX, *supra* note 23, at 156.

[136] This is admitted by H. BUNGARTEN, *supra* note 2, at 227.

[137] *See supra* pp. 21–22.

[138] F. BEHRENS, *supra* note 23, at 258.

ty, when harmonization is justified, is legally barred from adopting regulatory techniques that have not previously been used in the relevant national laws. The relative conservativism of harmonization in the field of environmental protection[139] is an institutional and political rather than a legal problem.

ii. The Directive as a Legislative Instrument

The directive has proven to be a suitable instrument for implementing Community environmental policy.[140] Due to its enormous flexibility – ranging from mere coordination of member state policies to the setting of detailed standards and associated measurement methods – it has been possible, when the political will existed, to devise the kind, depth, and intensity of regulation appropriate to the kind of environmental problem to be addressed and to the particular conditions of the member states that had to incorporate the directive into their system of environmental law and implement it within their administrative organization. The European Court of Justice's recognition of the principles of direct effect and supremacy for directives has also blurred the distinction between regulation and directive and thus removed some of the directive's legal disadvantages.[141] Therefore, the kind, depth, and intensity of regulation via directive today largely depends on the political will of the member states; it is not a function of the availability of legislative instruments.[142] Commission proposals for detailed environmental regulation have sometimes been reduced by the Council to mere harmonization of environmental protection principles or coordination of member state policies. However, this has nothing to do with deficiencies of the directive as a legislative instrument, but was motivated by political considerations, such as the rejection of excessive harmonization.

iii. Legal Constraints in the Field of Implementation and Enforcement

A severe legal constraint on Community environmental policymaking is the lack of Community power to implement and enforce Community programs. State and local governments have the dominant, if not exclusive, role in implementation and enforcement. This extreme decentralization of authority, reinforced by the control of these governments over land use decisions and, with minor exceptions, regulation of individual activity, imposes significant limitations on the realization of the policy objectives of Community legislation. Apart from product regulation, where the regulated industry normally favors uniformity and where oversight of implementation is easy, many member states and the regulated industry have an interest in adjusting the implementation and enforcement of environmental directives to national conditions, such

[139] *See supra* pp. 213–214.

[140] W. SCHMEDER, *supra* note 15, at 53; F. BEHRENS, *supra* note 23, at 252, 258; H. P. IPSEN, EUROPÄISCHES GEMEINSCHAFTSRECHT 695 (Mohr Siebeck, Tübingen 1972). *Contra*, P. J. SLOT, *supra* note 13, at 89 *et seq.*

[141] *See supra* pp. 36–40.

[142] *See* the authors cited *supra* note 140.

as established administrative practices, regional or local development objectives, and labor market problems. This is normally done without industry threats to locate new or existing plant abroad because the interests of member states and industry largely converge. The gap between what is proclaimed in legislative texts and what happens in practice is a general phenomenon of environmental law, especially in federal states. However, in the Community it gains particular significance because it occurs in a political society in which the features separating its components are still much stronger than those uniting them. In short, this gap threatens the unfinished integration process.

b. Institutional Constraints

Institutional constraints are certainly more significant impediments to effective environmental regulation at the Community level than are legal constraints.

i. Lawmaking Procedure

The rather cumbersome constitutional structure of the Community and in particular of its lawmaking procedure does not work well when there are fundamental conflicts of interests on a proposal, which is often the case in environmental regulation. The frequently long delay, in cases of strong controversy, between an initial proposal and its final adoption as a directive indicates that Community lawmaking procedure is not well suited to the resolution of such conflicts. One reason why political decisionmaking in controversial fields takes so long is the multilevel organization of the political process. It reflects the involvement of multiple levels of government and the existence of complex networks of inter-governmental relations at the member state and Community levels.[143] Since there is at most only weak direct representation of national interests other than governmental ones at the Community level, member states must coordinate the various interests at the national level. Moreover, since the Commission has lost much of its political leadership as a driver of European integration and maker of substantive policies, there exists no open and ongoing forum for formulation of the Community interest.[144] Consequently, the struggle among competing interests is more complex than that normally existing in a nation state.

ii. Filtering of Interests

A second institutional constraint is the systematic filtering of interests in the Community policy process.[145] The environmental programs fix the scope of

[143] *See* Wallace, *supra* note 127, at 33–34; C. HULL & R. A. W. RHODES, INTERGOVERNMENTAL RELATIONS IN THE EUROPEAN COMMUNITY 72 (Gower Publ. Co., London 1976); Webb, *Variations on a Theoretical Theme*, in POLICY-MAKING IN THE EUROPEAN COMMUNITIES, *supra* note 12, at 1 *et seq.*

[144] *See also* Wallace, *supra* note 127, at 35 *et seq.*

[145] This thesis was developed by F. MARX, *supra* note 23 at 157, and expanded by WEIDNER & KNOEPFEL, *supra* note 2, at 61 *et seq. See also* Wallace, *supra* note 127, at 43.

Community lawmaking only to a limited extent. Other factors are who has the right of initiative, who in fact makes initiatives, and who ultimately has the power of decision. It is certainly not true, as maintained by some authors,[146] that the Commission's monopoly on proposing initiatives prevents development of policies that reflect and balance all interests concerned. The Commission, at least in the area of environmental policy, is not blindly committed to the idea of integration. It rather actively pursues substantive environmental policies. However, since the Community bureaucracy is insulated from the pressure of concrete social, economic, and environmental problems, its perception of the urgency of such problems does not necessarily reflect the weight of societal preferences.[147] Other factors equally important in filtering expression of environmental interests include the decisionmaking monopoly of the Council,[148] the principle of unanimity established by Articles 100 and 235 and by the Luxembourg compromise, and the virtual absence of open participation by parliaments, the media, and interested organizations.[149] As will be analyzed later in greater detail, all this has the result of shifting societal conflicts of interest to the level of national interests. Societal interests are thereby systematically filtered and distorted.

iii. Lack of Political Legitimacy

Because it is predicated on harmonization, Art. 100 does not in itself provide the means to devise long-term environmental policies. This feature does not, as a strictly legal matter, impose significant limits on Community's legislative competences for environmental protection.[150] But it does have political implications. Although the harmonization competence necessarily includes Community authority to establish substantive policies in the areas to be harmonized, neither Art. 100 nor the Treaty as a whole provide any guidance as to the content of these policies. This reflects the fact that harmonization is conceived as an expression of the "negative" state. Environmental policy, however, is an interventionist policy.[151] Under the logic of the Treaty regarding interventionist (common) policies, the Treaty must provide some normative direction as to their content in order to legitimize the transfer of powers from member states to the Community. But the Treaty provides no such direction in the case of environmental policy. In a democratic political system, democratic bargaining processes compensate for such a lack of substantive standards for legislation. However, in the present state of the Community's development, the lack of legitimating substantive standards can not be remedied by democratic decisionmaking.

[146] F. Marx, *supra* note 23, at 157.
[147] *Id.*
[148] In the same sense *see id.*
[149] *See infra* pp. 269–278.
[150] *See supra* pp. 21–26.
[151] *See* F. Marx, *supra* note 23, at 146 *et seq.;* H. von der Groeben & H. Möller, Möglichkeiten und Grenzen einer Europäischen Union, vol. I: Die Europäische Union als Prozess 391 (Nomos Verlag, Baden-Baden 1980).

iv. Organizational and Budgetary Constraints

Finally, there are institutional constraints stemming from the organizational structure and budget of the Commission itself. Like environmental administrations everywhere, the Commission's Environment and Consumer Protection Service (now Directorate-General for Environment, Consumer Protection, and Nuclear Safety) has been understaffed and underbudgeted in comparison to other departments.[152] Only about ninety people, out of which thirty-five are professionals, are employed in Directorate A (the division concerned with environment) and in the two general administrative units for the Directorate-General (legal and legislative aspects of program implementation; international affairs). Until 1982, the budget of the Service remained constant in real terms, with most of the money going towards the "basic studies" envisaged in the environmental programs. In 1982 it was increased by about 200%, due mainly to the pressure exercised by the Parliament during the budget procedure. However, more than 60% of the increase was allocated to the Environmental Fund so that the increase for "traditional" Community activities, such as basic studies and implementation of directives and decisions, is less dramatic. The budget for 1983 provides for a 26% increase, mainly allocated to basic studies and implementation. Over the last two years, apart from the Fund, funding for implementation has been considerably strengthened, mainly on account of new tasks related to the dangerous substances directive. Even considering that certain research activities are covered by another chapter of the budget, the 1983 environmental budget of 12.2 million European Account Units (roughly US $12 million) is extremely modest in absolute terms. It accounts for not more than 0.5% of the total Community budget.

Another weakness is the standing of the Service within the Commission. Since the Commission as a whole still reflects the primarily economic orientation which led to establishment of the Community, it has proven difficult for the Environment and Consumer Protection Service to obtain the necessary support from the Commission as a whole (or at least the eight Commissioners represented in the *ad hoc* group on Environment). On the other hand, the Environmental Council and even the Agricultural and Economic Council, the actual legislative bodies in the Community structure, have been relatively constructive and willing to continue with the environmental programs at a time when other policy areas clearly mandated by the Treaty have faced political problems.[153]

v. Consequences

These structural features of the Community policy process explain many of the deficiencies of environmental policy. The patchwork character of Com-

[152] *See* Third Environmental Program, *supra* note 49, Annex No. 5; Progress Report 1980, *supra* note 7, at 4, Annex I, at 7; von Moltke & Haigh, *supra* note 2, at 23; The Environment in Europe, Bulletin of the Institute for European Environmental Policy No. 23 (April 1983).

[153] Von Moltke & Haigh, *supra* note 2, at 23.

munity environmental law reflects the pragmatic approach of the Commission in making policy proposals. This approach is in turn explained by the unwillingness of member states to agree to comprehensive transfer of sovereignty as well as by technical and personnel problems. The lack of consensus among member states concerning priorities, a characteristic handicap for a new policy not explicitly mandated by the Treaty, also contributes to the importance of political expediency in the Commission's selection of proposals. In addition, the Commission is often forced to take priority action in response to national initiatives, about which the Commission is informed under the information/standstill agreement,[154] in order to avoid new obstacles to trade and preserve Community options for new environmental legislation.

Because of these structural factors, Community environmental policy has not been as truly innovative as might have been expected from the shifting of decisions to a higher decisionmaking level. The solutions of one or more member states normally set the framework for Community solutions.[155] Because there is no forum for the formulation of a Community interest and because societal interests are transformed – and distorted – into national interests, it is not possible to develop a Community environmental policy completely divorced from member state policies.

These structural factors also help account for the fact that the development of Community environmental policy often comes to a virtual standstill when the national policies are too far apart. Negotiations on a controversial proposal easily take several years. Resolution of the conflict is often possible only by resort to lowest common denominator politics. Such solutions involve a compromise formula vague enough for general agreement or expressly leaving member states substantial discretion.[156] Examples are the shift from substantive to procedural solutions or to simple coordination of member state policies, optional harmonization, minimal harmonization (priority for stricter national law), granting of options between two Community strategies, national exceptions, and use of a recommendation to encourage national measures rather than a binding directive. From the perspective of effective environmental regulation, these "escape" devices are not necessarily bad because they often favor innovating states.

However, concealing lack of true consensus by resort to vague formulae will almost invariably cause serious problems in the future. A prominent example is Article 6 of the aquatic environment directive which lists criteria for selecting "hazardous" substances and for setting effluent and quality standards for such substances. The directive does not indicate priority among these criteria (toxicity, biodegradability, bioaccumulation, technical and economic feasibility), nor does it establish qualitative and quantitative guidelines for their ap-

[154] H. Bungarten, *supra* note 2, at 174; Weidner & Knoepfel, *supra* note 2, at 63 *et seq.* *See generally* Wallace, *supra* note 127, at 39; F. Marx, *supra* note 23, at 157.

[155] *See* authors cited *supra* note 27.

[156] *See* authors cited *supra* note 1.

plication.[157] Moreover, these criteria are not exclusive. It has therefore been extremely difficult to establish the list of most harzadous substances and the associated effluent standards.

Also, compromises which grant member states a choice between two fundamentally different strategies (alternative harmonization) do not necessarily lead to final resolution of the conflict. The discussions on the implementing directives to be issued under Article 6 of the aquatic environment directive again provide a good example. These directives are to set effluent and water quality standards for the most hazardous pollutants (list I) identified under the directive. The controversy between the United Kingdom, on the one hand, and the Commission and the other member states, on the other, over the best strategy for control of water pollution by dangerous substances was seemingly resolved by allowing the two competing strategies – effluent and water quality standards – to coexist. However, this conflict still dominates the political bargaining over determination of standards for list I substances because each side suspects that the other side, by setting the relevant standards, will gain cost advantages for its industry. This conflict has as yet prevented agreement on more than three particular standards. On the other hand, it presents a chance for negotiating issues that have been resolved by a bad compromise.[158] Thus the United Kingdom, which used to stiffly oppose effluent standards, has now accepted the need for effluent standards for new sources of mercury. The need to issue implementing directives can also provide a useful opportunity for reconsideration of an initial compromise that tolerates measures since shown to be unwise. Thus, alternative harmonization may initiate a learning process that ultimately leads to a common and uniform solution.

vi. Reasons for the Relative Success of Community Environmental Policy

The relative success of Community environmental policy despite institutional constraints appears to have two reasons.

The most important is that there is often at least some common interest of all member states in harmonized environmental policies. Economic considerations may militate in favor of a common solution, especially in the area of product standards. The institutional mechanisms of the Community afford the member states a forum for exchanging innovations in environmental policy. Harmonization removes the economic disadvantages each member state would incur when introducing environmental controls individually because it imposes equal or at least similar economic burdens on industry throughout the

[157] *See* KEUNE, *Kollidierende rechtliche, politische und wirtschaftspsychologische Gesichtspunkte bei der Auswahl der Stoffe für die Liste I der EG-Gewässerschutz-Richtlinie*, 17 ZEITSCHRIFT FÜR WASSERRECHT 193 (1978); G. MALLE, EG-Gewässerschutz – Vorschriftenflut droht, 1978 UMWELT 422, 424–425 (Verein Deutscher Ingenieure, Düsseldorf 1978); THE ENVIRONMENT IN EUROPE, BULLETIN OF THE INSTITUTE FOR EUROPEAN ENVIRONMENTAL POLICY No. 19, Supplement (Sept. 1982).

[158] *See* VON MOLTKE & HAIGH, *supra* note 2, at 27–28; WEINSTOCK, *supra* note 1, at 29, 32, 45.

Common Market. Finally, where transboundary pollution is involved, the problem can, as a practical matter, be addressed only by the Community.

The other reason is that harmonization of environmental law is in some respect easier than harmonization of a more traditional body of law. In administrative law the formal, dogmatic, and systematic elements are less important than in private or criminal law. Since environmental law is mostly administrative law, the technical harmonization work is less difficult, and the role of conservative jurists who adhere to traditional solutions is less important.[159] What counts are substantive interests, protection levels, strategies, and implementation systems. Harmonization in the field of environmental law is normally confined to protection levels and strategies. It does not encroach on the traditional body of general administrative law or require administrative reorganization. Although in real terms substantive interests are much more significant than legal technicalities,[160] it appears that negotiation over substantive interests is easier than over legal technicalities or administrative reorganization. The difficulties with the proposal for environmental impact assessment are a good example. Finally, environmental law is relatively young in all member states. It has undergone considerable and rather frequent changes in a single decade. Therefore, there are less reservations against changes brought about by new Community environmental legislation, so long as they are not regressive.[161]

2. Actors and Interests

Environmental policymaking is influenced by the same institutional and political variables that characterize the general policy process of the Community. Although the development of environmental policy may be interpreted as a substantive deepening of European integration, environmental policymaking has not remained unaffected by the developments which have resulted in the destruction of the institutional balance and in the decline of the supranational decisionmaking procedure established by the Treaty. These developments include the following: the Commission has declined as a force of integration; the Council has emerged as the major political force in the Community; intergovernmental decisionmaking has taken priority over supranational decisionmaking; and institutional sub-systems, such as the Committee of Permanent Representatives and the various technical committees and working groups established at the Council level, have become an integral part of the Community decisionmaking system.[162]

[159] W. SCHMEDER, *supra* note 15, at 26.

[160] *Id.; but see* H. WALLACE, NATIONAL GOVERNMENT AND THE EUROPEAN COMMUNITIES 13 (Chatham House/IPEP, London 1973).

[161] *Contra*, F. MARX, *supra* note 23, at 156.

[162] *See* Krislov, Ehlermann & Weiler, *supra* note 77, at §§ V.B.1. & VII.D.3.

a. Commission, Council, and Member States

i. Making Proposals

Environmental policymaking nonetheless has some distinctive characteristics. For example, it appears that the Commission exercises more influence on the development of environmental programs than in other areas of Community policymaking.[163] It has often been emphasized that the political initiative to develop a Community environmental policy was taken not by the member states or the Council as representative of the member states, but rather by the Commission. And it was the Commission which drafted the first environmental program on the basis of objectives, priorities, and strategies it had basically devised on its own.

In interpreting these events, however, one must bear in mind that when the initial decision was made to develop a common environmental policy, the national governments had not yet adopted strong national policies of their own. There were not yet strong national interests which could be thwarted by development of a common policy.[164] Moreover, dynamic factors have facilitated the success of the Commission initiatives. Environmental protection had been discovered as a new policy area in all industrialized countries. It had suddenly attracted the attention of the mass media and general public, and it would not have been easy for national governments to object to giving the Community responsibility for the protection and enhancement of the environment in cases where Community-wide measures seemed most appropriate. Thus, it would be premature to draw from the initial development of Community environmental policy the conclusion that development of new policies in general or of environmental policy in particular is inherently more amenable to supranational decisionmaking.

The Commission has retained much of its role as an institution for initiating policy proposals in the area of environmental protection.[165] It was primarily responsible for both the first and second environmental programs. Proposals for environmental directives are mostly initiated by the Commission pursuant to the objectives and priorities set in the environmental program.

However, it is safe to say that member states are increasingly influencing both the identification and development of candidates for harmonization. The member states have exerted a much larger influence on the third environmental program. The change from a source oriented pollution control strategy in the first environmental program to a preventive and more resource oriented strat-

[163] *See generally* R. PRYCE, THE POLITICS OF THE EUROPEAN COMMUNITY 61 *et seq.* (Butterworths, London 1973); J. Weiler, *supra* note 68, at 28 *et seq.*; S. HENIG, POWER AND DECISION IN EUROPE (Europotentials Press, London 1980).

[164] In this light, France's resistance to formal recognition of Community competences and its insistence that the basic policy decisions be made outside the institutional framework of the Treaty – specifically, by the Heads of State and Representatives of Governments – may be understood as an attempt to retain the option for national environmental policymaking.

[165] H. BUNGARTEN, *supra* note 2, at 168.

egy in the second program was based on the Commission's political preferences. However, the member states have already expressed their objections to further extension of Community activities regarding natural resources and land use. Realization of the new policy approach is thereby impeded. Several larger member states and the Council have become involved in initiating environmental policy proposals. Normally, such a move does not involve submitting a fully formulated draft directive; rather, the relevant member states will call upon the Commission to make a proposal. Since Commission proposals are not made from scratch but normally lean on national models, it is difficult to determine who took the initiative.[166]

In the past member states have also been able to indirectly set the pace of environmental legislation by taking unilateral national initiatives which established the framework for future action by the Community. Under the information/standstill agreement of 1973[167] such initiatives mut be reported to the Commission. The Commission must then decide within the time limit established by the agreement[168] whether it wishes to make a Community proposal. The agreement is designed to serve as a mechanism for coordinating state and Community policy, but it has not functioned well. Since the member states normally report only advanced drafts, the agreement's deadline for initiating Community action has often proven too short for arriving at an acceptable Community solution. Thus, the relevant national government is able to go forward with its initiative. Sometimes the Community eventually makes a proposal for harmonization which is based on the national model. National initiatives thus create a fait accompli for later harmonization.[169] In any case, such national initiatives have absorbed much of the Commission's available personnel and have directed their efforts in line with priorities set by national governments rather than by the Community. However, in recent years the agreement has become less and less effective; the number of notifications dropped from forty-one in 1974 to two in the first half of 1981.[170] This may be a sign of the general slowdown of environmental policy, but probably also reflects increasing reluctance on the part of national authorities to involve the Community in national policy proposals.

166 Institute for European Environmental Policy, ANNUAL REPORT 1981, at 3 (Bonn 1982).

167 Agreement of the Representatives of the Governments of the Member States meeting in Council of 5 March 1973 on information for the Commission and for the Member States with a view to possible harmonization throughout the Communities of urgent measures concerning the protection of the environment, OJ No. C 9, 15 March 1973, p. 1, as amended by the agreement of 15 July 1974, OJ No. C 86, 20 July 1974, p. 2.

168 The Commission is allowed two months to notify the member state concerned of its intent to make a proposal and another three months to submit the proposal to the Council, which must then decide on the proposal within five months.

169 *See* VON MOLTKE, *supra* note 27, at 84–85; H. BUNGARTEN, *supra* note 2, at 186.

170 *See* Commission, Fifteenth General Report of the European Communities (Brussels 1981), No. 363; Third Environmental Program, *supra* note 49, Annex No. 13.

ii. Bargaining over a Proposal

The stage of the policy process where national interests of member states are most vigorously asserted is the bargaining within the Council over the contents of a Commission proposal. Before making a proposal, the Commission normally consults experts from national governments (who, however, do not formally represent the government), industrial experts, scientists, and formal representatives of governments.[171] There are also often formal working groups, consisting of a Commission representative as chairman and experts from national governments, which develop proposals.[172] Thus, in this consultative stage member states can already exercise some influence on new directives.[173] Discussions within the Committee of Permanent Representatives, its working groups on the environment, agriculture, transport, and economic matters, and the Council itself provide member states with ample opportunities to assert and bargain over their national interests on a particular proposal.[174] Here the conflicting interests of the national governments (and sometimes even conflicting interests within national governments) and the views of the Commission undergo a lengthy and complex process of mutual adjustment and accom-

[171] *See* H. Bungarten, *supra* note 2, at 167.

[172] The Community has established quite a number of consultative committees for environmental matters. Of particular importance are the committees for the adaptation of environmental directives to technical progress, which, in contrast to other consultative committees, are decisionmaking bodies. *See infra* at pp. 280–281. Consultative committees exist in the areas of waste (Council Decision (79/968/EEC) of 12 Nov. 1979, OJ No. L 293, 20 Nov. 1979, p. 19; Commission Decision (76/431/EEC) of 21 April 1979, OJ No. L 115, 1 May 1976, p. 73), oil pollution on the high sea (Commission Decision (80/686/EEC) of 25 June 1980, OJ No. L 188, 22 July 1980, p. 11), nuclear safety (Commission Decision (79/520/Euratom) of 16 May 1979, OJ No. L 141, 9 June 1979, p. 26), and for managing research programs in the area of nuclear energy (Council Resolution of 18 July 1977, OJ No. C 192, 11 Aug. 1977, p. 1). There are some scientific consultative committees in the area of chemical substances (pesticides: Commission Decision (78/436/EEC) of 21 April 1978, OJ No. L 124, 12 May 1978, p. 16; testing of chemical compounds: Commission Decision (78/618/EEC) of 28 June 1978, OJ No. L 198, 22 July 1978, p. 17, as amended OJ No. L 316, 25 Nov. 1980, p. 21).

The composition of the committees for adjustment to technical progress and of the other consultative committees follows the usual pattern of management committees.

[173] Henssler, *supra* note 15, at 173. *See generally* R. Pryce, *supra* note 163, at 73; D. Lasok & J. W. Bridge, An Introduction to the Law and Institutions of the European Communities 112 (Butterworths, London, 2d ed. 1976). The increasing role of joint Commission/member state programs and management committees may be interpreted as reflecting the increasing political weight of member states in both formulating and implementing Community policies. However, since under the procedural rules governing many of these committees decisions can be made by majority vote, this reinforcement of national interests is in a way offset by increased decisional supranationalism; *cf.* J. Weiler, *supra* note 68, at 41–42, 47.

[174] *See* H. Bungarten, *supra* note 2, at 174. *See generally* Wallace, *supra* note 127, at 59–60.

modation in which both strategies and tactics of the principal players exercise an important influence on the final outcome.

The environment and industry groups within the Committee of Permanent Representatives play a particularly important role in ensuring that the directive which finally emerges is compatible with the national interests affected. Issues that remain controversial within these groups are decided by the Council. There, the acting president and the Commission may act as mediators.[175]

The relative slowness in decisionmaking is an expression of the complexity of this political bargaining process which involves multiple levels of government.[176] Although the Working Group on the Environment works more extensively than other Council groups, the average time lag between submission of a proposal to the Council and its formal adoption is about two years. However, many noncontroversial directives are adopted within eighteen months, while more controversial directives may require more than four years before their formal adoption. To permit final adoption, proposals have sometimes been entirely restructured; the level of environmental protection afforded by a directive has sometimes been considerably weakened; and on still other occasions the Council has opted for techniques of optional harmonization, minimal harmonization, alternative harmonization, or national exemptions.

It would perhaps be an overstatement to identify the Commission as a pacemaker for progressive environmental policy and the Council as an institution more concerned with moderating the economic and administrative costs of environmental regulation. Sometimes, the Council adopts directives more stringent than the original Commission proposal. The Commission often makes strong proposals (for example, a proposal for total harmonization) to use as bargaining chips. Nevertheless, the Council normally does opt for solutions that temper the economic and administrative costs of environmental regulation and are less supranational than the Commission proposals. This division of roles is consistent with the Commission's view that, since it is not an executive authority and is, therefore, in principle not involved in the implementation and enforcement of environmental directives, its genuine task is in the field of legislation. The Commission's distance from the real problems of implementation may lead to some overproduction of legislative texts as well as inappropriate substantive solutions.[177]

Environmental policymaking is clearly a process of intergovernmental bargaining.[178] However, environment policy is, on the whole, still more supranational in its decisional patterns than other policy areas. This is evidenced by the virtual absence of package deals. Reasons may be the absence of strong politicization, the remoteness of the decisionmaking process from national atten-

[175] *See* R. Pryce, *supra* note 163, at 67.

[176] C. Hull & R. A. W. Rhodes, *supra* note 143, at 72.

[177] *See* Institute for European Environmental Policy, Annual Report 1982, at 9 (Bonn 1983); G. Malle, *supra* note 155, at 422. *See generally* C. Hull & R. A. W. Rhodes, *supra* note 143, at 23.

[178] *See generally* H. Wallace, *supra* note 160, at 83 *et seq.*

tion, its bureaucratization, and the lack of sufficient public pressure.[179] Although environmental policy, due to its interrelation with economic and social policy, is an important and controversial field of national politics,[180] a particular environmental directive is seldom a political issue in member states before its adoption by the Council. It may become such an issue after its adoption, but then it is normally too late. Recent exceptions to this pattern are the environmental impact assessment proposal and the baby fur seal directive.

iii. Interests and Attitudes of Member States

Controversies between member states relatively seldom concern the question of whether any common solution at all should be adopted. By adopting the environmental programs the member states have committed themselves to further development of Community environmental policy in the areas of pollution and product related requirements. Discussions on matters of principle are therefore unnecessary. Moreover, in these areas the Commission seldom makes proposals in which most member states are uninterested. There is also agreement in principle that protection of nature and regulation of land use should remain within the competence of member states.

The conflicting national interests that emerge in the Community policy-making process reflect a variety of factors, including different environmental protection philosophies, different priorities, different strategies of coping with environmental problems, different environmental conditions and geographic locations, different economic problems and conditions, and different administrative structures or monitoring systems.[181] Short term considerations often prevail over medium or long term considerations.[182] Member states that place low value on domestic environmental policy (polluter states) object to substantive increases in environmental protection. Conversely, member states with stricter national environmental policies (environmental states) try to achieve Europeanization of the burdens which they have imposed on their industry. Even if they do not achieve this goal, they are unwilling to lower domestic standards. Therefore, the principle that member states may retain and introduce stricter national standards has recently found wide acceptance as a means of achieving at least minimal harmonization and thereby narrowing both the environmental protection and industrial cost gaps existing among member states. With respect to products, optional harmonization may fulfill a similar function.

[179] C. Hull & R. A. W. Rhodes, *supra* note 143, at 7–8; H. Wallace, *supra* note 160, at 13.

[180] H. Bungarten, *supra* note 2, at 224; H. von der Groeben & H. Möller, *supra* note 151, at 383–384, 391.

[181] *See* Progress Report 1980, *supra* note 7, at 5–6, Annex I, at 7; Pleinevaux, *supra* note 30, at 400; H. von der Groeben & H. Möller, *supra* note 151, at 397–398; Kupfer, *supra* note 28, at 60.

[182] *See* Pleinevaux, *supra* note 30, at 400; Pritzel, *supra* note 21, at 835.

Divergent opinions on the methods for implementing common policies, especially on strategies and to a lesser extent tools, are another source of controversy. Member states are reluctant to give up established national patterns of implementation and enforcement and therefore seek the Community solutions most consistent with their national systems of environmental protection.[183]

There are some member states, such as the Netherlands, which have traditionally favored strong Community environmental measures. West Germany tends to advocate progressive Community solutions for economic reasons. In other member states, such as Italy and Belgium, there is a large implementation gap which allows them to agree to rather strict Community measures because they anticipate that they will not have to be fully implemented. Member states located at the margins of the Community, which have large underdeveloped, relatively clean regions for which expensive environmental controls are too costly in relation to the benefits derived from them, are often more reluctant to agree to a preventive environmental policy than the richer, more densely populated states in the center of the Community.[184] But generalizations are hardly possible. There are no permanent coalitions. Depending on its interests, any member state can be a positive or negative force with respect to a particular proposal.[185] A general classification of all states on the periphery of the Community (United Kingdom, Ireland, Italy, and Greece) as polluter states and of all central states (France, West Germany, Netherlands, Belgium, Luxembourg, and also Denmark) as environmental states is not supported by the past experience of Community environmental policy.

Given the predominance of national interests in the Community policy process, the formulation of these interests is of vital importance. It is clear that in all member states the national executive authorities are by far the most important single factor.[186] They all avoid public debate because they prefer bureaucratic bargaining and because public debates would foster interagency conflicts. Thus, only a limited elite participates in the formulation of the national interest.[187] Of course, the national bureaucracy is not a monolithic block with a single perspective, and coordination within national executive authorities in

[183] *See* Institute for European Environmental Policy, *supra* note 177; *see generally* H. WALLACE, *supra* note 160, at 13.

[184] *See* RAT VON SACHVERSTÄNDIGEN FÜR UMWELTFRAGEN, *supra* note 30, at No. 1667; WEINSTOCK, *supra* note 1, at 34 *et seq.*

[185] VON MOLTKE, *supra* note 27, at 83; Institute for European Environmental Policy, ANNUAL REPORT 1981, at 6–7 (Bonn 1982); for argument favoring the classification rejected in the text *see* WEINSTOCK, *supra* note 1, at 34 *et seq.*, who, however, admits that an empirical base for it does not exist. In particular, Weinstock concedes that the affinity of the central states is not particularly great.

[186] *See* Sasse, *Governments, Parliaments and the Community of Members*, in DECISION-MAKING IN THE EUROPEAN COMMUNITY 1, 7 *et seq.*, 68 (C. Sasse, E. Poullet, D. Coombes & G. Deprez, Praeger Publishers, New York, London, Sydney, Toronto 1977); H. WALLACE, *supra* note 160, at 39 *et seq.*

[187] H. WALLACE, *supra* note 127, at 47, 57.

the Community has proven to be a complex, time consuming, and only partially successful process.

Formulation of the national interest is also influenced by regional governments (within federal or decentralized member states) and local governments.[188] These sub-levels are important because they are normally responsible for the ultimate implementation of environmental directives. There may also be jurisdictional problems, such as in West Germany where the Federal Government does not have legislative competence in all of the areas covered by environmental directives. Formal information and consultation procedures normally afford regional and local governments less opportunity to participate than informal participation in the consultations between the Commission and member states prior to a formal proposal.[189]

The impact of national parliaments on the formulation of national policies regarding Community matters has remained weak. Recently, however, some parliaments, especially in the new member states, are trying to play a more active role.[190] National parliaments have had no noticeable direct effect on the institutional and economic development of the Community. In most old member states, there is at most formal participation by national parliaments. In the new member states, especially in Denmark and the United Kingdom, the parliaments try to exercise extensive control over formulation of national policies regarding environmental directives. However, even here the parliament remains an outsider to the political bargaining over a proposal, and it is the policy of the relevant executives to maintain their bargaining position within the Community by restricting the information given to the parliament.[191]

[188] *See* C. HULL & R. A. W. RHODES, *supra* note 143, at 25 *et seq.*; HRBEK, *Politikverflechtung macht an der Grenze nicht halt*, 1979 DER BÜRGER IM STAAT 38; Blumenwitz, *Europäische Gemeinschaft und Rechte der Länder*, in DAS EUROPA DER ZWEITEN GENERATION, GEDÄCHTNISSCHRIFT FÜR C. SASSE, vol. 1, at 215 *et seq.* (R. Bieber, A. Bleckmann & F. Capotorti eds., Nomos Verlag, Baden-Baden 1981).

[189] However, under the new § 85 a of the Rules of Procedure of the West German Federal Government (in force since 1 Sept. 1980) the Länder must already be given access to preliminary drafts and documents of the Community. This may improve their capacity to influence central decisions on Community policy proposals.

[190] *See* Sasse, *supra* note 186, at 72; *id., The Control of the National Parliaments of the Nine over European Affairs*, in PARLIAMENTARY CONTROL OVER FOREIGN POLICY 137 (A. Cassese ed., Sijthoff & Noordhoff, Alphen a. d. Rijn 1980); Wallace, *supra* note 127, at 47–48; FOYER, *Le contrôle des Parlements nationaux sur la fonction normative des institutions communautaires*, 1979 REVUE DU MARCHÉ COMMUN 161; C.-C. SCHWEITZER, DIE NATIONALEN PARLAMENTE IN DER GEMEINSCHAFT, IHR SCHWINDENDER EINFLUSS IN BONN UND WESTMINSTER AUF DIE EUROPAGESETZGEBUNG (Europa Union Verlag, Bonn 1978); DUTHEIL DE LA ROCHÈRE, *Le Parlement britannique et les Communautés européennes*, 1978 REVUE TRIMESTRIELLE DE DROIT EUROP. 595; GULMANN & CLAUSON-KAAS, *Control by the Danish Parliament of Community Legislation*, 16 COMMON MKT. L. REV. 227 (1979).

[191] For the United Kingdom *see* VON MOLTKE, *supra* note 27, at 80–81; DUTHEIL DE LA ROCHÈRE, *supra* note 190. For Denmark *see* GULMANN & CLAUSON-KAAS, *supra* note 190.

iv. Towards a Theory of Consensus Formation in Community Environmental Policy

It is rare in Community environmental policy for negotiations to fail. In most cases, a compromise on a particular policy proposal is ultimately reached, although its achievement may require years of negotiations in the sub-groups of the Committee of Permanent Representatives as well as in the Council. The price is often considerable attenuation of the original Commission proposal.[192] In the present state of knowledge, it is difficult to formulate a theory as to which factors lead to consensus. Of course, general negotiation theories can be applied to the Community decisionmaking process. An important factor seems to be the dynamics of long lasting negotiations, i. e. the "entanglement" of the negotiators which ultimately exerts such pressure on the representatives of dissenters (especially when there is only one dissenting state), that a compromise can be reached.[193] It appears that the new member states, especially the United Kingdom and Denmark, are tougher negotiators and risk blocking ongoing negotiations more often than the old member states. But on the whole, no member state is willing to assume the responsibility for causing the failure of negotiations that have lasted for years and in which mutual trust in the willingness of all negotiators to contribute to an agreement has been built up.

Interesting theories have been advanced by von Moltke[194] and Dashwood[195] to explain the dynamics of the Community negotiation game. Von Moltke, with his "consensus cycle" theory, specifically addresses environmental policymaking, while Dashwood's "radiator effects" theory is a general one also applicable to environmental policymaking. According to von Moltke, the impulse for a Community proposal regularly comes from existing or proposed national legislation. The Commission then makes its proposal which leans on the national model. The consequent bargaining process soon stagnates because the other member states are, at first, unwilling to accept the proposal. In the meantime, one or more other member states consider the proposal as the basis for new or modified national legislation, often without considering the Community source of the national debate. After closure of the national debate, the Community proposal is ultimately adopted, at least in modified form. Dashwood's ideas go in the same direction, although he is more cautious in generalizing. Dashwood states that if a member state unilaterally adopts or accepts the substance of a Commission proposal as the basis for na-

[192] *See supra* pp. 261–262; H. Bungarten, *supra* note 2, at 174.

[193] *Cf.* Krislov, Ehlermann & Weiler, *supra* note 77, at § V.B.1 (obstruction policy does not pay).

[194] K. von Moltke, Environmental Impact Assessment Procedures, at 4 *et seq.* (unpublished) paper given at the International Seminar on"Protection and Rational Management of the Environment and Natural Resources in Europe – The Key Role of Land Use Planning," Strasbourg 17–18 Dec. 1981), expanded in: Institute for European Environmental Policy, Annual Report 1981, at 4 *et seq.* (Bonn 1982).

[195] Dashwood, *supra* note 12, at 195–196.

tional reform, agreement on it at the Community level becomes possible. The Community proposal has a "radiator effect" on the national policy process which in turn "radiates" back to the Community process.

These theories, however interesting they may be, are too simplistic to explain the consensus shaping process within the Community political system. They do not explain what made the other, "uncommitted" member states ultimately agree to the possibly modified Commission proposal. To overcome this weakness, one could argue that whenever at least two member states favor a Commission proposal, it will be adopted because two out of the ten member states are by and large representative in their national debate, because they have anticipated the possible arguments for and against a regulation of the kind envisaged by the proposal, and because their endorsement gives it democratic legitimacy. However, given the marked differences among member states with respect to environmental policy priorities, environmental protection levels, economic conditions, strategies and implementation systems, such a hypothesis is implausible as long as the policy process in the "uncommitted" member states is not included in the analysis. It is more probable that the national debate leading to adoption of the substance of a Commission proposal in a particular member state is but a special form of the political process in all member states for formulating a national position on the proposal. In any event, the "uncommitted" member states must also be prepared to incorporate the proposal into national law after its adoption. Therefore, it would seem that the adoption of a proposal as a national measure is neither a necessary nor a sufficient condition for reaching agreement at the Community level.

Nevertheless, von Moltke and Dashwood may have developed at least the first part of a theory of consensus formation in Community environmental policy. It is clear that there are always member states that have no strong economic interest in the harmonization of environmental policy. With respect to processes, polluter states should normally oppose harmonization because their industry would lose cost advantages it previously enjoyed. With respect to products, the economic interest of polluter states in harmonization depends on the size of their own market and the export orientation of their industry. Indeed, if the *Cassis de Dijon* doctrine were expanded, their industry would in the future be entitled to free access to foreign markets having stricter requirements, although the incentive for polluter states to seek harmonization in order to ensure access to foreign markets on more favorable terms would remain.

Accordingly, the explanation for why consensus on environmental harmonization is reached within the Community must lie in factors other than a common economic interest. Implicit norms of reciprocity seem to be most important. When several member states are strongly interested in a particular policy proposal, the other member states may ultimately acquiesce because they need their support on other issues of harmonization. National officials may also support Community initiatives because they favor progressive environmental measures and believe that they can be more easily introduced domestically through a Commission directive than through the national legislative process. Finally, the Treaty norms calling for establishment of a Common Market and the abolition of barriers to trade seem to promote consensus on harmonization of product regulation. All told, there seems to be a common value system that allows for a fair amount of harmonization even in the presence of conflicting economic interests.

However, reciprocity has its limitations. There are policy proposals that have never been adopted by the Council despite support form some member states. Evidently, the reciprocity incentives for an "uncommitted" member state to accede to a proposal may be outweighed by other national interests generated by factors ranging from different environmental protection philosophies to administrative structures incompatible with the proposal. In order to have explanatory power, the consensus cycle theory must be able to measure and determine the vector of these various elements in order to determine when member states will ultimately acquiesce to a proposal despite lack of interest in it or even in the presence of a countervailing interest. This task appears to exceed the present state of knowledge. A further qualification of the consensus cycle theory is that it does not explain a policy's content, i. e. the substantive terms upon which an agreement is reached.

b. European Parliament

The European Parliament has generally favored strong Community environmental policy both with respect to the extent of harmonization as well as the level of substantive protection. As early as 1967 a parliamentary question addressed pollution problems. Before the development of a common environmental policy the European Parliament, in 1970, urged Community measures to control pollution of the Rhine and, in 1972, called for Community action to control air pollution.[196] Since then, the European Parliament has regularly favored far reaching Community involvement in environmental protection.[197] The only qualification is that, while the environmental and planning committees of the European Parliament are pro-environmentalist, the legal committee often objects to Commission proposals on the ground that they are not within the legislative competences established by the Treaty.

The European Parliament has devoted much time and energy to giving opinions on Commission proposals, and it has become a natural ally of the

[196] European Parliament Resolution of 19 Nov. 1970, JO No. C 143, 3 Dec. 1970, p. 30; EP Doc. 161/70.

[197] For the activities of the European Parliament up to 1978 *see* Küster, *European Policy of Protection of Rivers and Water Pollution*, in THE EUROPEAN ALTERNATIVES, *supra* note 30, at 403 *et seq.*; H. BUNGARTEN, *supra* note 2, at 161 *et seq.*; M. TAMBURINI, COMPETENZE COMUNITARIE IN MATERIA DI PROTEZIONE DELL'AMBIENTE ED INTERROGAZIONI SCRITTE DEL PARLAMENTO (Studi Parmensi vol. 23, Guiffrè, Milan 1978). For the activities of the European Parliament since 1981 *see* THE ENVIRONMENT IN EUROPE, BULLETIN OF THE INSTITUTE FOR EUROPEAN ENVIRONMENTAL POLICY No. 18 (April 1982), No. 25 (Oct. 1983), and especially No. 28 (June 1984).

Commission. However, its real influence has been relatively small.[198] Although its right of initiative is recognized in the Community's political practice,[199] its function has been more to reinforce existing policy proposals and to prevent stagnation and blockages in bargaining. Its ability to stimulate new initiatives has been weak. The Parliament is consulted only after a draft directive has been submitted to the Council. It therefore can not directly influence the preparation of proposals, and is confined to commenting on a proposal already finalized by the Commission. It is said that the Commission seriously considers, to the extent permitted by national interests, proposals and comments made by the European Parliament.[200] It is true that the Commission will readily amend a proposal pursuant to the Parliament's request, but it appears that the Commission does not strongly defend such a modification if it concludes that national governments oppose it. The Parliament's repeated rejection of optional harmonization has not prevented the Commisson from adopting this principle in various proposals for product related directives. The European Parliament did not influence the bargaining on highly controversial proposals such as the aquatic environment, toxic substances, and the SO_2 limit values directives.

However, two more recent events have strengthened the position of the European Parliament. One is the 1980 holding of the European Court of Justice that a Community regulation is void if the European Parliament has not been consulted.[201] This holding has strengthened the procedural role of the European Parliament in the Community policy process. It may also be the beginning of a greater substantive role for the European Parliament in the formulation of Community environmental policies. If the consultation required under Articles 100 and 235 of the EEC Treaty merely involves referral of an initial Commission proposal to Parliament, the requirement can become a mere formality. The real decision is often made later through bargaining within the Council. However, the Treaty might be interpreted to require that Parliament be consulted whenever the Commission agrees to a substantive change to its original proposal. Whether this would cause total blockage of Community lawmaking or be an improvement[202] is an open question. The second event is the direct election of the European Parliament since 1981 which tends to give it more weight in the Community policy process. The directly elected Parliament has become more self-conscious and is starting to make detailed counter-proposals to Commission proposals (such as to the draft directives on environmental impact assessment, major accidents hazards and transfrontier

[198] *See generally* Wallace, *supra* note 127, at 44 (with further references).

[199] H. BUNGARTEN, *supra* note 2, at 161.

[200] Küster, *supra* note 197, at 411.

[201] Case 138/79,SA Roquette Frères v. Council (Isoglucose), [1980] ECR 3333.

[202] Commission fears that the Court might take up this issue seem to be the reason why the two pending cases concerning the titanium dioxide directive (case 78/ 79, BTP Tioxide Ltd. v. Commission, case 79/79, Laporte Industries Ltd. v. Commission, OJ No. C 153, 20 June 1979, p. 5) are presently dormant.

transport of wastes, as well as the third environmental program). Parliamentary initiatives on the protection of baby seals, combat of acid rain and regulation of transfrontier transport of toxic wastes have substantially influenced the development of, or bargaining on, Commission proposals. In 1983, the European Parliament for the second time created a committee of enquiry, namely on the handling of wastes.[202a] A side effect of this development is some strain in its relationships with the Commission. Parliament is also using its rights to participate in the budgetary process to strengthen Community environmental policy. Nevertheless, the substantive impact of the Parliament is bound to remain insignificant as compared to developed federal systems so long as the Parliament is simply a consultative assembly.

c. Economic and Social Committee

The Economic and Social Committee, due to its composition and mandate, tends to stress the economic perspective with regard to environmental directives.[203] Environmental interests are not represented, and the influence of industry and agriculture is strong.[204] Like the European Parliament, it is consulted only after a draft directive has been submitted to the Council. It has nothing to do with the preparation of policy proposals, and its influence on the political bargaining concerning a particular proposal is small.

d. Participation of the General Public

The extent of public participation, particularly by industry and trade associations and environmental groups, varies considerably from case to case. Generally speaking, the influence of European groups on the Community policy process is considerably weaker than that of national groups on national processes. In the early years of the Community when political scientists discovered the emergence of European groups, they predicted that they could become an increasingly significant integration factor and ultimately replace national

[202a] *See* European Parliament Report 1-1376/83; Resolution of 11 Apr. 1984, OJ No. C 127, 14 May 1984, p. 67, at p. 68.

[203] *See* Colliard, *European Policy of Protection of Rivers and Water Against Pollution*, in THE EUROPEAN ALTERNATIVES, *supra* note 30, at 413. *See generally* R. PRYCE, *supra* note 160, at 84; Wallace, *supra* note 127, at 43; MCLAUGHLIN, *The Work and Aims of the Economic and Social Committee of EEC and Euratom*, 15 J. OF COMMON MKT. STUD. 3, at 9 (1976).

[204] *See* WIRTSCHAFTS- UND SOZIALAUSSCHUSS DER EUROPÄISCHEN GEMEINSCHAFTEN, DIE EUROPÄISCHEN INTERESSENVERBÄNDE UND IHRE BEZIEHUNGEN ZUM WIRTSCHAFTS- UND SOZIALAUSSCHUSS 30 (Nomos Verlag, Baden-Baden 1980); K. SCHWAIGER & E. KIRCHNER, DIE ROLLE DER EUROPÄISCHEN INTERESSENVERBÄNDE 86 (Nomos Verlag, Baden-Baden 1981). Recently, a representative of the Geman "Working Group for Environmental Affairs," a quasi-official association that includes members from governments, political parties, industry, trade-unions and environmental organizations, has been elected as a member.

groups.[205] In recent years this assumption has given way to a more sober assessment of the role of European groups in the integration process. One political scientist finds that the development of European groups is less an integration factor than a product of the state of integration. This observer also finds that they are often not independent of national membership organizations, that national client relations have been maintained, and that there is even a certain renationalization of European groups.[206] All this may explain their relatively limited influence on Community policy.

There are no formalized procedures at the Community level for participation in environmental policymaking. The extent of informal influence exerted before a proposal is made depends on the importance of the proposal and the public attention it has gained in the preparatory stage. National industrial associations as well as environmental groups may be consulted by the Commission, which may send out preliminary drafts for comments. After a proposal has been submitted to the Council, organizations are able to influence the discussion on the proposal in various informal ways. However, there are marked differences in access to these informal channels by industry and environmental groups.

i. Industry

There are many industry and trade associations organized at the Community level, including the European Federation of Enterprises (UNICE) and various European organizations of particular industries.

These groups are well organized, financed, and equipped. They are able to comment on and influence a variety of policy proposals. Despite lack of unanimity, they are more integrated than most other groups.[207] They all lobby the Commission to some degree regarding preparation of environmental policy proposals[208] without, however, exercising strong pressure.[209]

[205] E. B. HAAS, THE UNITING OF EUROPE 16 (Stanford Press, Palo Alto 1958); J. MEYNAUD & D. SIDJANSKI, L'EUROPE DES AFFAIRES: RÔLE ET STRUCTURE DES GROUPES 175 *et seq.* (Payot, Paris 1967); Wallace, *supra* note 127, at 65.

[206] J. Caporaso, The Emerging European Groups: The Problem of Interest Group Hedonism (unpublished paper delivered at the Joint Workshop Conference of the European Consortium for Political Research, Brussels 17–21 April 1979); *see also* K. SCHWAIGER & E. KIRCHNER, *supra* note 204, at 30 *et seq.*; Kirchner, *Interest Group Behavior at the Community Level,* in CONTEMPORARY PERSPECTIVES ON EUROPEAN INTEGRATION: ATTITUDES, NONGOVERNMENTAL BEHAVIOR AND COLLECTIVE DECISION MAKING 95 *passim* (L. Hurwitz ed., Aldwych Press, London 1980).

[207] *See* WIRTSCHAFTS- UND SOZIALAUSSCHUSS, *supra* note 204, at 19, 57 *et seq.*; K. SCHWAIGER & E. KIRCHNER, *supra* note 204, at 47 *et seq.*

[208] *See* WIRTSCHAFTS- UND SOZIALAUSSCHUSS, *supra* note 204, at 69 *et seq.*; K. SCHWAIGER & E. KIRCHNER, *supra* note 204, at 88 *et seq.*

[209] Würtenberger, *Die Verbandsproblematik aus europarechtlicher und integrationstheoretischer Sicht,* in VERBÄNDE UND EUROPÄISCHE INTEGRATION 29, 37–38 (K. M. Meessen ed., Nomos Verlag, Baden-Baden 1980).

These efforts are mostly directed at the Directorate-General III, which is responsible for internal market and industrial affairs and, parallel to the position of national ministries for economic affairs, is usually opposed to strong environmental measures. They are also directed to a lesser extent at the Environment and Consumer Protection Service (now Directorate-General XI). Formal, although weaker, contacts also exist with the Council, and industry is represented in various Council committees.[210]

However, industry influence tends to be directed to a larger extent towards influencing national governments, particularly the competent national ministries.[211] This behavior may be explained by the "logic of influence" since national governments are the most important factor in the Community policy process. The national industrial organizations have easier and earlier access to information from their national governments. The governments seek advice and information from industry about its interests in order to formulate a national policy towards a Community policy initiative. The "primary loyalty" of industry is to national governments, and the traditional client relations have been maintained.[212] The supranational level is only a supplementary level of interest representation.

According to official statements of UNICE, industry's primary goal regarding Community environmental policy is to maintain the functioning of the Common Market and ensure a "sound" balance between ecological needs and economic possibilities.[213] However, this statement implies a harmony of interests within European industry that does not exist. The economic interests of industry often vary depending upon the environmental status quo (including existing legislation) in a given country, the export orientation of the industry concerned, and the internationality of the market affected. All of the firms in a particular industrial sector of the Community do not necessarily uniformly favor elimination of distortions of competition or technical obstacles to trade caused by different national environmental laws; rather, a firm's position largely depends on the level of environmental protection in a particular member state.

Generally speaking, a higher national level of environmental protection implies greater interest by that country's industry in far-reaching harmonization through measures requiring a high level of protection throughout the Community. In member states that have a low level of environmental protection, there will normally not be much incentive for industry to favor harmonization

[210] *See* Wirtschafts- und Sozialausschuss, *supra* note 204, at 30; K. Schwaiger & E. Kirchner, *supra* note 204, at 78, 79, 83, 85 *et seq.*

[211] *See* K. Schwaiger & E. Kirchner, *supra* note 204, at 94 *et seq.*; Würtenberger, *supra* note 209, at 38; A. Leitolf, Das Einwirken der Wirtschaftsverbände auf die Agrarmarktordnung der EWG 117 *et seq.* (Nomos Verlag, Baden-Baden 1971).

[212] K. Schwaiger & E. Kirchner, *supra* note 204, at 32, 94 *et seq.*

[213] *See* UNICE Document on Environmental Policy, Nov. 1976, reprinted in Kabelitz, *Umweltstrategie der europäischen Industrie*, 7 Umwelt 172 (Verein Deutscher Ingenieure, Düsseldorf 1977). *See also* Weidner & Knoepfel, *supra* note 2, at 63; Wirtschafts- und Sozialausschuss, *supra* note 204, at 74.

at a higher level. Other things being equal, industry will favor uniform regulation for products and preemption of national legislation in order to avail itself of the advantages of a European product line. However, with respect to a particular product, there may still exist distinct national markets, and the maintenance of a national product line and hence of national regulation may be to the advantage of particular firms. In industries operating worldwide, the specific conditions prevailing in competing countries outside the Community, such as the United States and Japan, may affect the industry's approach to harmonization. (This is true, for example, in the case of the sixth amendment of the toxic substances directive).

At present, the supranational representation of European industry lacks sufficient independence from national membership organizations, and there is even a certain re-nationalization of industrial elites (parallel to the decline of political integration).[214] Therefore, also the "logic of membership" means that industrial influence is normally exerted on national governments. It is accordingly difficult to harmonize industrial interests at the European level when substantive questions are at issue. Often, agreement is only possible by descending to the lowest common denominator.[215]

ii. Environmental Organizations

There is one central European environmental organization, the European Environmental Bureau (EEB), which since December 1974 has tried to influence at the Community level the formulation of policy proposals and their implementation.[216] The EEB consists of fifty-seven national environmental organizations, including all of the more important organizations operating nationally.[217] It was originally built up by the Commission as part of its constituency[218] and receives financial contributions from the Commission as well as from some member states and foundations to organize conferences and projects.

The EEB has financial problems and its resources are extremely modest; however, to a certain extent this is compensated by the assistance of the membership organizations which, for example, organize seminars and write policy statements for the EEB.[219] The EEB possesses a low degree of decisional integration. It has no authority over its membership organizations, and the large

[214] K. Schwaiger & E. Kirchner, *supra* note 204, at 94 *et seq.*

[215] *See* Würtenberger, *supra* note 209, at 38 *et seq.*; von Voss, *Arbeitgeberverbände und europäische Integration*, in Verbände und europäische Integration, *supra* note 209, at 87, 97–98; Sasse, *supra* note 186, at 68; R. Pryce, *supra* note 163, at 88–89 (microcosm of the difficulties of the Community's own political system). The consensus problems of European industry groups are also admitted by Wirtschafts- und Sozialausschuss, *supra* note 204, at 66.

[216] *See* Wirtschafts- und Sozialausschuss, *supra* note 204, at 457 *et seq.*

[217] As of 1 Jan. 1984; *see* European Environmental Bureau, Annual Report 1983, at 11 *et seq.* (Brussels 1984).

[218] *See generally* R. Pryce, *supra* note 163, at 87 *et seq.*

[219] *See* Wirtschafts- und Sozialausschuss, *supra* note 204, at 462–463; K. Schwaiger & E. Kirchner, *supra* note 204, at 47 *et seq.*

number of membership organizations creates problems in making decisions which are only to some extent offset by a majority vote rule for EEB decisions.[220] Structural problems also result from considerable differences in the organization, finances, and political power of the national membership organizations. The members from the Netherlands and the United Kingdom are financially strong, well established, and powerful organizations. The Belgian members have the advantage of proximity to Community institutions. However, the German, French, and Italian members are financially weak, loosely organized, and not very powerful in domestic politics. Consequently, most initiatives within the EEB come from the Dutch, British, and Belgian membership organizations. The German and French members are more or less passive, but may disturb the work of the EEB by objecting to particular initiatives or by seeking direct access to the Commission in order to assert their own position. The EEB's structural problems also stem from the fact that it is only a bureaucratic organization of national groups. Although the leaders of national groups cooperate with it, it does not receive active support from the membership of these groups.

The EEB tries to exert influence on all European institutions. Its influence is strongest with the Commission. The EEB and the Commission's Environment and Consumer Protection Service regularly hold information meetings, and there are many informal contacts between Commission officials and representatives of the EEB. Even if the EEB does not always share the Commission's opinion on particular issues, e. g. the role of nuclear energy, the relationship between the EEB and the Commission has been good.[221] In 1979 the EEB strongly objected to plans to merge the Environment and Consumer Protection Service with the service on regional policy.[222] Recently, the EEB has also undertaken extensive lobbying with the European Parliament, an effort facilitated by the fact that some parliamentarians belong to the membership organizations of the EEB.[223] Since 1979 the EEB has also regularly held meetings with the acting President of the Environmental Council and is trying to exert stronger influence on the Council.[224] Besides directly lobbying Community institutions, the EEB tries to influence the formulation of national poli-

[220] *See* Wirtschafts- und Sozialausschuss, *supra* note 204, at 462–463.

[221] Wirtschafts- und Sozialausschuss, *supra* note 204, at 464, 470; K. Schwaiger & E. Kirchner, *supra* note 204, at 107.

[222] European Environmental Bureau, Annual Report 1979, at 6 (Brussels 1980).

[223] *See* K. Schwaiger & E. Kirchner, *supra* note 204, at 79, 90. *See also* European Environmental Bureau, Annual Report 1979, at 2 (Brussels 1980); *id.*, Annual Report 1980, at 4 (Brussels 1981); Wirtschafts- und Sozialausschuss, *supra* note 204, at 464.

[224] *See* European Environmental Bureau, Annual Report 1979, at 1 (Brussels 1980); *id.*, Annual Report 1980, at 4 (Brussels 1981); *id.*, Annual Report 1982, at 2, 3 (Brussels 1983); Wirtschafts- und Sozialausschuss, *supra* note 204, at 464, 465; K. Schwaiger & E. Kirchner, *supra* note 204, at 107. Whether these meetings have been continued in 1983 is unclear; the Annual Report 1983 (Brussels 1984) only refers to memoranda addressed to the acting Presidents of the Environmental Council.

cies regarding Community environmental policy by coordinating action of its membership organizations at the national level. However, in contrast to industry groups, environmental organizations operating at the national level are on the whole infrequently consulted by national bureaucracies, although the extent of effective participation varies from country to country (perhaps on a spectrum ranging from the Netherlands to Italy and Greece).

The EEB tends to support strong environmental policy proposals.[225] It comments on all the more important Commission proposals for environmental directives. It also tries to influence the common agricultural and transport policies with a view towards strengthening environmental considerations. It strongly objects to the expansion of nuclear energy and favors energy conservation as an alternative. In particular, it advocates new directions for environmental policy as well as innovative strategies and tools. Examples are the reorientation of Community agricultural policy, the adoption of nondegradation policies, introduction of environmental impact assessment, strict regulation of chemicals, control of acid rain and reorientation of development policy in developing countries.

The explanation for the integrationist role played by the EEB is that its membership organizations favor strong environmental policies. Although they have a primarily national perspective and try to press for national solutions, most of them seem to consider harmonization as a way to achieve appropriate environmental protection levels in environmentally less progressive member states or to overcome domestic political obstacles to desired environmental regulation.

The EEB exercises some influence on formulation of Community environmental policy. However, its overall influence seems to be much weaker than that of industry.[226] The influence of the EEB is mostly felt at the preparatory stage of policy proposals. It is relatively weak once a proposal has been submitted to the Council. Since Commission proposals are often changed substantially by the Council, the imbalance of effective participation at all levels of Community environmental policymaking is a major weakness not adequately compensated by the membership organizations' lobbying of national bureaucracies. From the Commission's perspective, the EEB is a useful organization with no risk of becoming "dangerous."

The reasons for the relative weakness of the EEB as the only supranational environmental organization are not easy to ascertain. Many authors believe that the primary incentive for development of European groups is the already developing Europeanization of the policy area in which the relevant group is

[225] The following text is based on various statements in the reports of the European Environmental Bureau on its acitivities since 1975: ANNUAL REPORT 1975/76 (Brussels 1977); ANNUAL REPORT 1979 (Brussels 1980); ANNUAL REPORT 1980 (Brussels 1981); ANNUAL REPORT 1981 (Brussels 1982); ANNUAL REPORT 1982 (Brussels 1983); ANNUAL REPORT 1983 (Brussels 1984).

[226] *Cf.* H. BUNGARTEN, *supra* note 2, at 217 (as of 1978).

interested.[227] In addition, the growth of a European group may also be a response to the challenge posed by the prior development of a competing group.[228] Finally, the strength of a European group presumably depends on the strength of its component national membership organizations, although the strength of this correlation has not yet been empirically researched.[229] These theories could explain the emergence of the EEB as a central organization at the Community level, exclusively concerned with Community environmental policy. The modest growth of the EEB since its foundation in 1974 can be related to the growth of Community environmental policy. The fact that the EEB is weaker than the industrial organizations could be explained by the relative weakness of its national membership organizations. However, all this gives only a rough picture. It does not explain why the EEB, in contrast to industry, has been unable to direct its lobbying efforts at those forces in the Community policy process which really matter. This is probably due to structural factors that invite the national membership organizations and their members to target their efforts on national environmental politics, an incentive that produces a national orientation in organizations and members. Thus, both the "logic of influence" and the "logic of membership" seem to play a role.

In the present state of European integration, environmental interest groups in most member states do not primarily seek Community solutions. Instead, they prefer to press their national governments for national solutions. Environmental groups have a comparatively greater impact on policy decisions at the national level for several reasons. Participation in the preparation of national legislative proposals involves less transaction costs to establish an adequate organization and to undertake effective interest representation. Environmental groups also have a comparatively greater impact on national policy decisions because national legislators and bureaucracies are more open to political pressure, and the national decisionmaking process is more political than the Community's.[230] National decisionmaking processes are influenced by under-represented interests, grass roots movements, and new values to a greater extent than the Community decisionmaking process because at the national level the distance to the decisionmaker is shorter. The Community policy process, although it is inextricably interwoven with the national policy processes, is far removed from the public political conflicts in member states. This insulation from public politics ordinarily extends to national participation in preparing Community policy proposals as well as the formulation of a national position on a particular Commission proposal. Such matters seldom leave the con-

[227] Sidjanski, *Pressure Groups and the European Communities*, in EUROPEAN INTEGRATION 401 (M. Hodges ed., Penguin Books, London 1972); Ionescu, *The European Social Partners*, in FEDERAL SOLUTIONS TO EUROPEAN ISSUES 71 *et seq.* (B. Burrows, G. Denton & G. Edwards eds., Macmillan Press, London 1977); K. SCHWAIGER & E. KIRCHNER, *supra* note 204, at 37–38, 72 *et seq.*

[228] K. SCHWAIGER & E. KIRCHNER, *supra* note 204, at 33, 37.

[229] *See* K. SCHWAIGER & E. KIRCHNER, *supra* note 204, at 28–29.

[230] *See* WEIDNER & KNOEPFEL, *supra* note 2, at 61 *et seq.*

trol of the national bureaucracies and their clients. National parliaments have no substantial impact on the final outcome of the proposal. The insulation between national politics and Community decisionmaking also inhibits effective national political responses to Community activities. What happens in Brussels very often becomes a political issue only when the national executive is to implement a particular directive. Exceptions such as the bird protection directive, the proposal for environmental impact assessment, and the directive on baby seal furs confirm the rule. This lack of politicization of the Community policy process impedes environmental organizations which, for structural reasons, require "visible" conflicts to thrive.

iii. Conclusions

The foregoing analysis shows that European industry and environmental groups are differently structured and exert very different degrees of influence on Community policy. Direct comparison of the two groups emphasizes this point. With respect to the structure of the two groups, the degree of a group's Europeanization can be determined by a set of criteria such as comprehensiveness of organizational objectives, finances, equipment, organizational strength, and integration of its decisionmaking process. Using this set of criteria, UNICE is a well structured European group far superior in nearly all respects to the EEB. In fact, the EEB possesses one of the lowest Europeanization rates of all European interest groups.[231] As for the political influence of the two groups, economic interests are, both at the national and Community levels, better organized and have better access than environmental interests to the most important channels of influence.

Industry has its main power base with national governments, which dominate the development of Community environmental policy. The EEB, on the one hand, is more oriented towards the Commission which, even in the field of environmental policy, has lost much of its central role as a policy body. On the other hand, most of its national membership organizations do not have a truly European perspective which would enable them to influence the formulation of national interests regarding Community policy. Thus, they concentrate their attention on national policy objectives. This imbalance in the leverage of industry and environmental groups on Community policymaking reinforces the existing disequilibrium between supranational and national forces in Community institutions. It also results in a systematic filtering of interests[232] which undermines the role of environmental interests in Community policymaking.[233]

[231] *See* K. Schwaiger & E. Kirchner, *supra* note 204, at 47 *et seq.*, in particular at 71–72.

[232] *See* authors cited *supra* note 145.

[233] There are two other European environmental organizations which exercise some influence on Community environmental policymaking, namely the Institute for European Environmental Policy and the European Council of Environmental Law.

The Institute for European Environmental Policy has its main office in Bonn and branch offices in Paris and London. It is financed by the European Cultural Foun-

e. Other Actors

Other actors are all relatively unimportant. The courts, the media, and the scientific community have as yet very limited impact on Community environmental decisionmaking.

Environmental litigation at the Community level is still rather limited. There are almost no state court decisions which have reviewed Community environmental law. The European Court of Justice has not yet become a major player in Community environmental policymaking. The few environmental decisions of the Court convey the impression that the Court is willing to support the common environmental policy by broadly interpreting the Community legislative powers granted under Articles 100 and 235 of the EEC Treaty. On the other hand, it is unlikely that the courts will assume a major role in implementation and enforcement of environmental directives.

The recent case law concerning the application of Articles 30 and 36 of the EEC Treaty to national regulation of products, particularly the relatively strict review of the justification for national regulation under the *Cassis de Dijon* doctrine,[234] is perhaps more important, although it is not easy to predict what its effects will be. Since there already is comprehensive Community regulation for most widely marketed products, as a practical matter the *Cassis de Dijon* doctrine would apply only to restrictions on existing products, especially chemicals, where Community regulation is still thin. Theoretically, an extension of the *Cassis de Dijon* doctrine and the ensuing dismantling of national regulation could foster further harmonization of national product requirements to protect human health and the environment. However, the reverse effect is more probable. Judicial invalidation of national regulation could lead to harmonization at the lowest common denominator without subsequent Community legislation because polluter states would be granted free access to foreign markets with stricter product controls. Hence, they would lose all incentive to agree to more stringent Community regulation.

dation. It undertakes applied policy studies relevant for the development of European environmental policy and tries to disseminate the results of these studies, especially to assist the European and national parliaments in their control function and in their ability to make policy initiatives. The Institute publishes a newsletter. It regularly meets with European and national parliamentarians and has been able to initiate a European consultative interparliamentary committee for the environment in which interested parliamentarians exchange information with a view to coordinating national and European action in environmental policy.

The European Council of Environmental Law is a group of law professors and practioners from the major EEC member states and Switzerland. It is financed by a German foundation. It meets several times during the year and discusses legal/political issues of European environmental policy with a view to influencing the discussion on Commission proposals and to initiating new proposals. *See* European Council of Environmental Law, Resolutions 1971–1981 (Erich Schmidt Verlag, Berlin 1981).

[234] European Court of Justice, case 120/78, Rewe-Zentral-AG v. Bundesmonopolverwaltung für Branntwein (*Cassis de Dijon*), [1979] ECR 649.

The primary reason for the relative weakness of the media is that there is no European daily or weekly newspaper that could shape a European public opinion. Furthermore, the Community bureaucracy is rather remote from actual environmental controversies and, unlike a national government, not truly accountable to public opinion.

The scientific community has some impact on the development of Community solutions to environmental problems in that the Commission often relies on experts commissioned to prepare a particular legislative proposal. However, the general opinion of the scientific community is far less relevant for identifying candidates for harmonization, and has little or no influence on the bargaining process following submission of a policy proposal to the Council. Scientists rarely call for or criticize Community action on an urgent environmental problem. Like environmental interest groups, they are normally oriented to their national governments and seek support for their views in a political environment with which they are more familiar.

3. Dynamic Factors

a. Changes in Knowledge and Technology

A sound environmental policy is unthinkable without adequate scientific and technical information concerning environmental problems. It is also necessary to accommodate changes in knowledge and the resulting changes in the perception and definition of environmental problems. The Community is not well equipped for these tasks.[235]

Subject to some qualification for nuclear energy, the Community has no research facilities of its own for developing or acquiring the scientific and technical information needed for sound regulation. It has to rely on information provided by experts from national governments, on the advice of consultants from universities and research institutes selected for the preparation of a particular proposal, and on research results generated through Community financed research programs by scientists from national governments (so-called concerted action programs) or from independent research institutions (so-called indirect action programs). The sectoral research and development program in the field of the environment, which runs from 1981 to 1985,[236] provides for an appropriation of 42 million European Account Units (about US $ 40 million) of which 33 million are appropriated to indirect action in the field of environmental protection. The research topics of the program include: sources, pathways, and effects of selected pollutants, such as heavy metals, organic micro-pollutants, asbestos, selected air and water pollutants, and noise pollution; reduction and prevention of pollution, such as by pollution abatement technologies and clean technologies; protection and management of natural environments, such as ecosystems conservation and bird protection; and

[235] *Cf.* Progress Report 1980, *supra* note 7, at 5 (where the Commission complains of the lack of available scientific information).

[236] Council Decision (81/213/EEC) of 3 March 1981, OJ No. L 101, 11 Apr. 1981, p. 1.

environmental information management. Besides the general research program, there are special programs, especially in the field of nuclear safety.

These procedures have several shortcomings. National government experts may be biased; the selection of consultants is not without risk; it is not easy to ensure that the research results are relevant to regulatory policy choices; and the Commission may even find it difficult to assess the research results and draw the necessary policy consequences. Also, the usual strategies and tools for implementing Community environmental objectives afford little flexibility for accommodating changes in knowledge.

Sometimes Community law uses broadly defined environmental regulatory principles, such as use of best practicable means of control, and leaves member states the task of making them operable. This allows speedy adaptation to new technological knowledge, but there is a lack of real harmonization and the danger of a severe implementation gap. Therefore, most commonly adopted strategies for addressing environmental problems in the Community involve the setting of standards, such as emission, specification, input, and ambient standards, or the establishment of lists of hazardous substances that must be controlled. Standard setting is not left to the discretion of the Commission; rather, the standards are set in the relevant directives themselves. The same is normally true of the establishment of lists of hazardous substances. The lengthy and cumbersome decisionmaking procedure for establishing environmental directives will often mean that by the time a directive is adopted, its scientific or technological basis is or will soon be outdated. Sometimes, the adoption of standards or the establishment of lists of substances may be delayed for years. The fate of the aquatic environment directive is a good example. In any case, it will be difficult to adjust directives to the requisites of new scientific or technical knowledge and a resulting change in the definition of the relevant environmental problem. This raises the question whether there are sufficient institutional guarantees to permit a flexible response to the danger of obsolescence of directives.

The problem of legal obsolescence has been aptly analyzed in the general context of Community legislation by Calabresi, Dashwood, and Marx.[237] Marx points out that the Spaak report, which elaborated the essential structures of the EEC Treaty, was based on an erroneous idea of stability and that therefore the concept underlying Art. 100 of the EEC treaty is a static one.[238] Since the functioning of the Common Market is affected by differences between national regulations independent of their content, the primary purpose of Art. 100 is harmonization. Article 100 provides no guidance as to the content of a directive harmonizing a particular area. Consequently, amendment of an existing directive can not be justified by the objective of ensuring the functioning of

[237] Calabresi, *Incentives, Regulation and the Problem of Legal Obsolescence*, in NEW PERSPECTIVES FOR A COMMON LAW OF EUROPE 291 *et seq.*, in particular at 297, 301 (M. Cappelletti ed., Sijthoff, Leyden, London, Boston 1978); Dashwood, *supra* note 12, at 295–296; F. MARX, *supra* note 23, at 144 *et seq.*

[238] F. MARX, *supra* note 23, at 144 *et seq.*

the Common Market. Therefore, strictly speaking, the Community has no legislative competence to modify a directive once issued under Art. 100. Practice and prevailing opinion has ignored this legal nicety,[239] and it is improbable that the European Court of Justice would deny that the Community has legislative powers to amend existing directives. Nonetheless, as has been described by Calabresi and Dashwood,[240] serious institutional problems of obsolescence remain, especially with respect to product regulation.

The initial adoption of a directive for harmonization of product requirements is probably much easier than agreement on its modernization. In the initial stage of Community lawmaking, all member states have some interest in adopting a directive because the differences between national provisions have substantial impacts on trade. This common incentive no longer exists once the area has been harmonized. Legal innovations in an area already harmonized can no longer be motivated by Community trade policy. Instead, they must be based exclusively on environmental policy objectives of the Community as to which the economic interests and opinions of the member states concerned may greatly diverge. Even if a member state proposes to amend an existing directive on the ground that it has not achieved its objectives – which is the argument of West Germany in proposing to stiffen the automobile emission standards, other member states may have other priorities, such as protection of the industry affected or of jobs, and, in the absence of countervailing common trade policy considerations, may object to any amendment.[241] On the other hand, unilateral innovation by a single member state is no longer possible because under the principle of supremacy, the harmonized law is paramount to national law and Art. 36 of the EEC Treaty does not justify a violation of this principle.[242] This is also true where a directive has become obsolete because it has failed to achieve its objectives, although this case is not yet covered by the supremacy jurisprudence of the European Court of Justice. In any case, a member state proposing new national legislation inconsistent with an existing directive would find it difficult to push this initiative through its own legislative bodies. Therefore, as a practical matter, it will have to seek the agreement of the other member states.

The problem of legal obsolescence in Community environmental law is somewhat mitigated by the establishment in most environmental directives of a special decisionmaking procedure for the adaptation of the directive to

[239] *See* F. BEHRENS, *supra* note 23, at 50, 253; F. MARX, *supra* note 23, at 47–48; W. SCHMEDER, *supra* note 15, at 10; Vignes, in LE DROIT DE LA COMMUNAUTÉ ÉCONOMIQUE EUROPÉENNE, vol. 5, at 154, Art. 100 annotation 4 (J. Mégret, J. Louis, D. Vignes & M. Waelbroeck, Presses Universitaires, Brussels 1973). *Contra,* House of Lords, Select Committee, 22ND REPORT, *supra* note 116, No. 13(4).

[240] *See* authors cited *supra* note 237.

[241] Here, the description of Community environmental policy as "lowest common denominator" policy certainly has some truth to it. *See* Dashwood, *supra* note 12, at 295–296. *See also* Progress Report 1980, *supra* note 7, Annex I, at 11; Kupfer, *supra* note 28, at 63 *et seq.*

[242] *See supra* pp. 39–41; Kupfer, *supra* note 28, at 63 *et seq.*

scientific progress. This procedure is established by the Council resolution of 1975 on the adaptation of environmental directives to technical progress,[243] but is often modified in particular respects in the relevant environmental directives. An environmental directive normally creates a Committee chaired by a representative of the Commission and composed of representatives of the member states. The Commission has the right of initiative. The Committee decides on the Commission's proposal by a qualified majority. If the Committee approves the proposal, it is adopted. If it rejects the proposal or no opinion is adopted, the matter must be brought before the Council, which is also to act by a qualified majority. If the Council has not acted on the proposal within three months after the proposal has been submitted to it, the measures proposed can be adopted by the Commission.

The adaptation procedure is designed to relieve the Council of the technical work involved in adjusting existing directives to technical progress. The procedure has been used to establish stricter standards when warranted by the improvement of scientific knowledge or technical progress.[244] The Commission is not allowed to use the procedure where important political or economic questions are involved.[245] In such a case, the Commission has to submit the proposal directly to the Council. However, the Council also acts on these proposals by a qualified majority rather than by unanimous vote.

The adaptation procedure shows that the Community is aware of the danger of legal obsolescence. The requirement of a qualified majority in an area in which the Community could initially legislate only by unanimous vote lowers the institutional barrier to adjustment of existing environmental directives. The structure of the procedure reflects a sense of need for more supranationalism in areas where the initial decision to establish harmonized policies has already been made.[246] That it does not solve all problems is evidenced by the fate of the German endeavors to stiffen the emission standards for motor vehicle noise and exhaust emissions.

It should be noted that the adaptation procedure is not applicable where a problem is not yet covered by a directive. Thus, broadening the scope of an existing directive in response to new scientific or technical knowledge requires

[243] Council Resolution of 15 July 1975 on the adaptation to technical progress of Directives or other Community rules on the protection and improvement of the environment, OJ No. C 168, 25 July 1975, p. 5. *See* F. BEHRENS, *supra* note 23, 60 *et seq.*, 255–256. *See generally* P. MATHIJSEN, A GUIDE TO EUROPEAN COMMUNITY LAW 61–62 (Sweet and Maxwell, London, New York, 3d ed. 1980).

[244] *Contra*, P. J. SLOT, *supra* note 13, at 107.

[245] This would be contrary to Art. 155 of the EEC Treaty. *See* European Court of Justice, case 25/70, Einfuhr- und Vorratsstelle v. Köster, [1970] ECR 1161, which, in principle, recognized that the adaptation procedure is in conformity with the Treaty provided the relevant committee is given clear direction as to the contents of the measures to be adopted. *See also* Jacobs & Karst, *The "Federal" Legal Order: The U. S. A. and Europe Compared – A Juridical Perspective,* at notes 74–79 & 103, in INTEGRATION THROUGH LAW, Vol. 1, Book 1.

[246] In the same sense *see* P. J. SLOT, *supra* note 13, at 107.

action similar to that for adoption of the original directive. In such cases, however, threatened unilateral action by a member state will exert leverage on the Community.[247] The Community may be compelled to broaden the scope of the directive or issue a new directive; otherwise, the member state can go forward with its national initiative. However, the jurisprudence of the European Court of Justice in *Cassis de Dijon* and in the line of cases following this decision[248] may impose some constraints on member state ability to unilaterally adjust national regulation of products to scientific progress.

b. Changes in Attitudes and Preferences

A number of factors retard the response of Community institutions to changing public opinion. They are: the complex structure of the Community policy system with its several levels of interest representation, interest accommodation, and decisionmaking; the weakness of the European Parliament which is not compensated by greater involvement of national parliaments in the process of formulating a national position towards Community environmental policy; the lack of a truly European public opinion; and the almost complete decentralization of implementation and enforcement of directives. These factors retard Community reaction to environmental preferences even more than for other issues, e. g. economic and energy issues. National governments in particular act to filter out the expression of new environmental preference, while economic interests find easier access to the policy process. The Environment and Consumer Protection Service of the Commission acts as an agency with an environmental mission, but it is politically too weak to prevail over the member states.

It is, therefore, not surprising that Community environmental policy began several years after most member state environmental policies. The initial decision to expand Community activities into the area of environmental protection as well as the first substantive proposals of the Commission occurred when the problems of environmental protection had been "discovered" by the mass media as well as the general public throughout all or most of the member states. The high measure of public awareness and at the same time the lack of experience with the political and economic constraints within which environmental policy must operate presumably contributed greatly to the initial success of Community expansion into this area. However, the two years following adoption of the first environmental program were marked by the reluctance of many member states to put the programmatic declarations of the environmental program into operation. All kinds of jurisdictional obstacles were erected and the willingness to compromise was small. By the time this learning period was over and Community environmental policy had gotten seriously underway, the initial enthusiasm for environmental protection had been replaced in member states by a more sober assessment of the costs and benefits associated with it. Most of the environmental directives were adopted during

[247] Dashwood, *supra* note 12, at 295–296.
[248] *See supra* note 234. *See also* the discussion in Ch. II, *supra* at pp. 29–31.

this later stage. The Commission, however, did not readily take into account these changes in attitudes and preferences towards the environment in the member states. It thus continued making strong proposals. The member states in turn resisted many Commission proposals in the interest of new economic and energy concerns. The new preference for ambient quality instead of emission standards, the reluctance to further modernize the motor vehicle directives, and the general slowdown in Community legislative activities since 1980 are all an expression of this resistance. However, the recent phenomenon of wide-spread forest damages in central Europe will probably lead to a certain revival of environmentalism in the Community.

By the same token, the understaffing and underbudgeting of the Environment and Consumer Protection Service must be seen as a deliberate effort by the member states to temper environmental initiatives. The budget of the Environment and Consumer Protection Service remained equal in real terms over many years. Given the ever increasing responsibility of the Service, this budgetary policy has meant that major programs provided in the environmental program could not be adequately implemented. An environmental fund has been established, but it has until recently not become operational for lack of budgetary appropriations. The recent increases in the budget of the Service are mainly due to the pressure of the European Parliament. Member states which place higher values on environmental quality will not always resist the tendency to underbudgeting because they can often protect their interests by building sufficient flexibility into a directive to enable them to independently pursue their own national policy goals. An example is the regionalization concept adopted for economic and energy reasons by the gas oil directive. The regionalization is optional so that some member states, such as West Germany, could apply the stricter of the two Community input standards throughout their territory.

IX. The Policy Process in the US

A. Political Choices in Environmental Protection

1. Kinds and Characteristics of Environmental Problems Addressed by the Federal Government

a. The Dual Sovereignty Model of Federalism

The traditional constitutional theory of state and federal lawmaking competence is one of dual sovereignty.[1] Persons, natural and corporate, are citizens both of states and of the United States. The states and the federal government may each regulate, within their respective spheres of competence, such persons' conduct. These spheres of competence are established: (a) by the selective and restricted grant in the Constitution of powers to the national government, residual powers remaining with the states; and (b) by the extent to which the national government exercises its lawmaking power and the extent to which it invokes the Supremacy Clause to preempt state law in the same field. The negative commerce clause doctrine adds a further qualification: in the case of interstate commerce, even where Congress has not exercised regulatory or taxing authority, state measures may be preempted if they impose a discriminatory or undue burden on interstate commerce.

Under this model, one might expect to encounter either a system of national regulation or a system of state regulation in a given field, except where Congress permits overlapping but independent systems of state and federal regulation or where Congress's failure to legislate and the negative commerce doctrine together result in a total absence of regulation. In the field of environmental measures, as elsewhere,[2] the actual distribution of the two alternative systems might be explained by reference to economic, political, and functional factors. The national integration of the economy would simultaneously expand the competence of the federal government and the potential reach of the negative commerce clause doctrine. It would also favor federal rather then state regulation because of economies of scale in centralized regulation of national product markets, disparities in resources between states and large industrial firms, and the vulnerability of states to the mobility of capital and the

[1] *See* L. Tribe, American Constitutional Law 300–318 (Foundation Press, Minneola, NY 1978).

[2] *See* Heller & Pelkmans, *The Federal Economy: Law and Economic Integration and the Positive State - The U. S. A. and Europe Compared*, at § I, in Integration Through Law, Vol. 1, Book 1.

threat of industrial relocation. On the other hand, diseconomies of scale and the variability of local conditions would limit the tendency to centralization.

These factors have explanatory power in accounting for the present distribution of lawmaking activity in the environmental field. But their force is limited because the dual sovereignty model is overly simplistic.

First, the dual sovereignty model ignores the possibility of joint regulatory schemes in which federal and state governments play a shared role. Such systems, while conceptually untidy, often represent a desirable compromise among the respective considerations arguing in favor of centralization or decentralization.

Second, the tremendous revenue raising powers of the federal government through the individual and corporate income tax have had a profound impact on federal/state relations. The development of federal conditional grants in aid has become an important method for inducing state regulation and planning in the service of national objectives, and represents another form of shared enterprise.

Third, the fact that the federal government owns one third of the nation's land and more of its valuable mineral resources has profound implications in the area of environmental and natural resource policy. The federal government can advance national policies in this area through internal management and planning without resort to direct regulation of private conduct. Many of the political and institutional obstacles to creation of a system of centralized regulation are absent in the case of management of resources already owned by the federal government. The control and management of federally-owned resources, however, becomes another point of interplay between federal and state governments. Through its resource policies, the federal government can profoundly affect the welfare of those states in which it owns large amounts of land and natural resources. On the other hand, legal and political traditions have dictated that federal lands and resources are ordinarily subject to control and regulation by the states unless precluded by statute. States accordingly have a means of promoting their interests in the context of federal resources management. Moreover, state interests are represented in the federal political process by virtue of the territorial system of representation in Congress.[3]

b. The Negative Commerce Clause as a Spur to Integration

An alternative model of integration would attribute the rise of federal environmental regulation to the negative commerce clause doctrine. If state environmental regulation is liable to be preempted by the commerce clause, then citizens' demand for environmental regulation must be met by the federal government. Even if state regulation is not directly preempted, a state which adopts such regulation is likely to lose industrial and commercial development

[3] *See* WECHSLER, *The Political Safeguards of Federalism: The Role of the States in the Competition and Selection of National Government*, 54 COLUM. L. REV. 543 (1954). *But see* KADEN, *Politics, Money, and State Sovereignty: The Judicial Role*, 79 COLUM. L. REV. 847 (1980).

to states with less stringent regulations because industry's costs of operation in those states will be less.[4] States adopting environmental regulations might attempt to protect themselves against this competitive disadvantage by imposing restrictions on the ability of industrial capital to "exit" to other states or taxing or limiting imports of goods from states with laxer environmental controls. But such measures would almost surely be preempted by the commerce clause. Hence, states that favor environmental protection will support at least uniform minimum regulation by the federal government.

The available evidence, however, indicates that this model has at best weak explanatory power in the environmental area. Under prevailing commerce clause doctrine, few state environmental regulatory measures are subject to preemption. For example, the Supreme Court recently sustained the validity of a Minnesota ban on nonrecycled plastic containers despite evidence that the burden would fall mainly on out of state manufacturers and would benefit Minnesota manufacturers of paperboard containers.[5] The Court has also upheld a stiff Montana severence tax on coal mined in the state; most of the coal was exported to out of state consumers.[6]

Although negative commerce clause doctrine probably would bar states from imposing a compensating tax on imports from states with laxer environmental controls[7] this circumstance fails to provide a strong explanation for federal regulation. For even if such a tax were permitted, it would only partially alleviate the competitive disadvantages involved in the unilateral imposition by a state of pollution controls. Imposing such a tax on imports would not eliminate the competitive disadvantage of the regulating state in all of the other

[4] In theory, if labor markets were perfect the environmental benefits to citizens of states that impose environmental regulations would be reflected in correspondingly lower wage rates in those states. However, stickiness and national uniformities in union wage rates, the fact that some of the benefits of regulation would accrue out of state, and other complexities make this point a largely theoretical one.

[5] Minnesota v. Clover Leaf Creamery Co., 449 U.S. 456 (1981).

[6] Commonwealth Edison Co. v. Montana, 453 U.S. 609 (1981).

[7] It is not altogether clear that a compensating tax on imports from states with laxer environmental controls would be preempted. The closest analogy in the decisional law is a tax on beverage containers imposed by the state of Oregon in order to encourage recycling. The Oregon courts sustained the measure against a commerce clause challenge based in part on the fact that the tax was applied to containers imported from out of state. *See* American Can Co. v. Oregon Liquor Control Commission, 517 P. 2d 691 (Ore. App. 1973). However, the tax in that case was applied to beverage containers within, as well as without, the state. A tax which, although framed in general terms, imposed taxes on products in proportion to the degree of pollution control on their manufacturing processes, and applied only to out of state products, would create a difference in the treatment of products manufactured within and without the state that might be difficult to sustain. ***But see*** Minnesota v. Clover Leaf Creamery Co., 449 U.S. 456 (1981) (upholding a ban on recycled containers that, in practice, applied exclusively to out of state manufacturers).

states where its product must compete with those of the laxly regulating state.[8] In some cases, the existence of regional markets or a large internal market within a state might enable an "environmental" state that adopted compensatory taxes to restore its competitive position in those markets. But for many products, the internal or regional market of a state is small relative to the national market. Since a compensatory tax on imports into an "environmental" state would not redress the competitive disadvantages suffered by an "environmental" state producer competing against "polluter" state producers in the national market, the fact that the commerce clause might preclude such a tax can not be a major factor behind federal regulation. The competitive disadvantage involved in adoption of environmental controls is primarily a function of the integration of the national economy and the relatively small size of states rather than legal doctrine.

c. The Tripartite Pattern of US Regulatory Integration

No single model can explain the pattern of integration in US environmental policy. As predicted by the hypotheses in Chapter I, federal regulation has been most complete in the case of national product markets, where all states have a long run interest in avoiding trade barriers. Unlike the case in the EC, however, federal environmental regulation of national product markets in the US arose after those national product markets were already well established and before any extensive state regulation had been adopted. Federal regulation accordingly can not in most instances be explained as a response to state regulation that had been found to be inadequate or a barrier to trade. When a need for regulation was perceived, resort was made in the first instance to the federal government. This pattern suggests that the dominant reason for federal, as opposed to state, regulation in this area is the regulatory economies of scale associated with national product markets. The imposition of trade barriers as a result of local or regional regulation has not been a substantial factor. Fear, however, of the possibility of multiple and inconsistent state regulation is reflected in the preemption provisions which are common in the federal statutes authorizing this form of regulation.

Direct federal regulation of nuclear energy, oil tankers, and offshore oil development must be explained on other grounds. Unlike national product markets, these are not fields in which considerations of uniformity and economy of scale are paramount. They involve industrial processes and transporta-

[8] We therefore disagree with the thesis, advanced by Heller and Pelkmans, that the inability of states to levy such a tax is a major factor explaining the rise of Federal/Community regulation. *See* Heller & Pelkmans, *supra* note 2.

Conceivably the regulating state could subsidize its exports to the remaining forty-nine states. However, the commerce clause might well bar such subsidies. *But cf.* Hughes v. Alexandria Scrap Corp., 426 U.S. 794 (1976) (upholding state bounty system for scrap processors that favors in-state processors). Even if it did not, it is politically unrealistic to suppose that the regulating states could secure the tax revenues needed for such a subsidy.

tion activities whose impacts vary widely depending on the area in which they are carried out. Moreover, implementation and enforcement involves a good deal of decentralized monitoring and adjustment. These areas of regulation are therefore functionally similar to those (such as air and water pollution and hazardous waste disposal) that have typically been addressed through a system of federal standards implemented and enforced by the states.

Direct federal regulation of nuclear energy, oil tankers, and offshore oil development must in large part be explained by a perceived national security interest in promoting these technologies and activities in order to ensure adequate energy supplies, and a fear that this interest would receive insufficient weight if parochially oriented states and localities had a major hand in their regulation. These considerations also explain the preemption of local or state regulation which is a characteristic feature of federal programs in this area. There are a number of subsidiary factors which also help to account for the choice of direct federal regulation in these fields, including economies of scale in regulating nuclear technologies, the federal ownership of outer continental shelf resources, and the traditional paramount federal interests in control of the marine environment.

Most federal programs for regulation of industrial processes were generally preceded by state regulatory efforts that were judged inadequate. Fear by states that they would incur competitive disadvantages and lose economic development if they adopted strong process regulations appears to have been an important reason for the inadequacy of state regulatory efforts and the adoption of federal regulatory programs. The extent to which differences in the stringency of environmental regulation in fact influences industrial locational decisions is a matter of doubt; traditional factors, such as access to markets or labor or raw materials, appear to be a far more important consideration.[9] Some environmentally minded states did adopt strong regulatory programs of their own, although they were often prosperous states, like California, with relatively large internal markets and obvious pollution problems. In any event, the objective facts are of far less significance politically than the apparent or declared fear on the part of state politicians and officials that unilateral adoption by a state of stringent environmental controls will lead to "industrial flight." The insistence upon uniformity in federal standards by states and industry reflects and is designed to meet this fear by eliminating the "competitive distortions" that might be generated by non-uniform standards. This record is broadly consistent with the hypothesis generated in Chapter I, which predicted environmental state support for federal regulation in order to eliminate the competitive advantages enjoyed by polluter states.

The negative commerce clause does not appear to have played any substantial role in the support for national legislation by states favoring stronger process regulation. Established commerce clause principles would not preempt

[9] *See* H. Leonard & C. Duerksen, *Environmental Regulations and the Location of Industry: An International Perspective*, Columbia J. World Bus. (Summer 1980) 52.

state regulation of an industrial process that generated substantial pollution within the state.[10]

Scale considerations with respect to regulation of industrial processes are mixed. On one hand, the effects of residuals from industrial processes vary a good deal depending on local conditions, and siting and land use considerations are an important factor in their regulation. Moreover, the sheer number of sources regulated – about 200 000 in the case of air and water pollution control – favors decentralization. On the other hand, there are considerable scale economies in research and analysis of the scientific and technological issues involved in industrial process pollution control.

The choice between direct federal regulation and state implementation of federal standards does not appear to reflect the perceived seriousness of the environmental problem in question. Many of the hazards dealt with under the latter strategy – including air and water pollution and toxic wastes – have been viewed as equally or more serious than many of the hazards subject to direct federal regulation.

The third strategy of federal integration in the regulatory context is federal encouragement of state regulation. Examples include the Coastal Zone Management Act, the solid waste provisions of the Resource Conservation and Recovery Act (RCRA), and the section 208 planning process under the Clean Water Act.

The environmental problems addressed through this mechanism share several characteristics. First, the environmental problems are generally regarded as less serious than those addressed through direct federal regulation or state implementation of federal standards. Second, solutions to these problems draw heavily on traditional local functions, such as land use control and municipal services. Third, state and local regulation of these problems poses little threat to integrated national markets. Accordingly, consistent with the hypotheses in Chapter I, the incentive for environmental states to support federal regulation in these areas is weak.

The distinction between state implementation of federal standards and federal encouragement of state regulation is not always a clear one. Federal financial assistance, provision of information, and the threat of more intrusive federal measures are also present in programs involving state implementation of federal standards. On the other hand, the federal standards governing the eligibility of state regulatory programs for financial assistance are often quite detailed, allowing federal administrators to exert considerable authority over state programs.

In the case of state implementation of federal standards, however, there is usually legal authority in the federal government to assume direct enforcement and implementation responsibility if state performance proves unsatisfactory.

[10] In a much more compelling case for commerce clause invalidation of a local regulation, the Supreme Court upheld local regulation of smoke pollution from a vessel licensed by the United States and engaged in interstate transportation. Huron Portland Cement Co. v. Detroit, 362 U.S. 440 (1960).

By revoking delegations or directly enforcing state regulations, the federal authority can effectively convert a system of state implementation of the federal standards into a system of direct federal regulation. This threat, and its attendant incentives for cooperation by state officials, is absent under the federal encouragement strategy. Moreover, a program of federal standards that can be coercively implemented through federal authority usually reflects greater political support for a program than one involving mere federal encouragement of state measures.[11]

d. Different Degrees of Harmonization

In most programs of direct federal regulation, state regulation is preempted or is not a major factor. By contrast most programs which follow the strategy of state implementation of federal standards do not preempt more stringent state and local regulatory controls. These programs use the technique of minimum harmonization, in which the federal government establishes nationwide minimum standards, leaving states free to impose more demanding requirements. This difference between the two categories of federal regulatory programs can be explained by several factors. First, these programs involve regulation of industrial processes, whose environmental impact is highly dependent on their geographical location, the size of exposed populations, the number of other sources in the same area, and so on. There is accordingly a stronger interest in local variation and flexibility than in the case of national product markets. Second, the threat to national economic integration from varying local regulation is less than in the case of nationally marketed products, while the special national security interests that explain other forms of direct federal regulation in fields such as nuclear electricity generation and petroleum transportation are also missing. A third consideration is that fear of competitive disadvantage will restrain states from imposing excessively stringent local controls. The importance of this last factor finds indirect confirmation in the preemption issues presented under RCRA. As previously noted,[12] EPA takes the position that the Act precludes federal certification of state implementation and enforcement programs which unduly restrict disposal of out of state

[11] The municipal waste treatment program under the Clean Water Act and CERCLA present mixed cases.

The Clean Water Act imposes direct regulatory requirements on municipal waste treatment systems – requirements that could in theory be coercively enforced. As a practical political matter, however, such enforcement is not a realistic possibility without substantial federal assistance. The very magnitude of this assistance (up to 90% of project costs), on the other hand, gives the federal government a dominant hand in dictating the conditions for project construction.

CERCLA involves a federal cleanup program that the federal government is legally empowered to carry out independently. But there are powerful administrative and political reasons to involve the states in the cleanup process. The 90% federal funding formula gives both a strong incentive for state participation and considerable power to the federal government to dictate the terms and conditions of cleanup.

[12] *See supra* p. 124.

wastes. The economic benefits to a state of operating a waste disposal dump are small relative to the perceived risk. Accordingly, the economic incentives that normally temper state regulation of industrial processes are quite weak in the case of toxic waste facilities, creating a need for some form of federal preemption or other incentives in order to maintain the integrity of the national market economy.

The circumstance that the national economy was highly integrated before environmental regulation of products arose may serve to explain why optional or partial harmonization strategies have not been adopted in the United States. Because the market within a given state is generally small relative to the national market and the national economy is integrated, most producers already sell a substantial portion of their product in interstate markets. Therefore, most producers would find little to gain under a system of either optional or partial harmonization. In most cases the gains from a system of different standards for intrastate and interstate transactions would apparently not be worth the costs of producing two types of products. Alternative harmonization also has never been seriously considered, probably because of the non-uniformity and federal administrative discretion involved in such a system.

e. The Evolution of Federal Environmental Policy

Federal environmental programs display no fixed evolutionary pattern in relation to the three integrative strategies. In some areas, such as nuclear power and automobile air pollution, federal measures took the form of direct federal regulation from or near the outset. Others, such as air and water pollution control, started off as programs to encourage state regulation and later became programs of federal standards with state implementation, subject to the threat of direct federal enforcement. There is no evidence to suggest that the most serious environmental problems were necessarily addressed first, or that the form of initial federal intervention was necessarily correlated with seriousness.

The evolutionary history of federal initiatives raises many questions. Why should pesticides have been regulated so much earlier than other hazardous chemicals? Why were air and water pollution regulated before toxic wastes? The sequence in some respects is explained by the state of knowledge about environmental problems. The Public Health Service in the late fifties and the sixties devoted major research efforts to the study of the health effects of air pollution, laying the groundwork for later federal regulatory initiatives. Hazardous chemicals received a lower research priority. Water pollution control regulation was initially the responsibility of the Interior Department, which was more concerned with the clearly identifiable effects of oxygen depletion upon fish life and aquatic vegetation than with the subtle, long term health effects associated with low level concentrations of toxic substances. The contingencies of political entrepreneurship among the congressional sponsors of legislation and the occurrence of dramatic "media events" also played a role. For example, the important legislative initiatives of Senator Muskie were directed at air and water pollution control, rather than alternatives such as chemicals manufacturing, in large part because of the happenstance of the Senate's committee structure and assignments.

The developing effort to induce federal agencies with developmental and resource management responsibilities to place more emphasis on environmental values proceeded independently of regulatory initiatives. Different agencies (Interior, Agriculture, Atomic Energy Commission, Federal Power Commission) were involved, each with a different set of congressional committees and interest group allies. The political and operational obstacles to federal initiation and implementation of new regulatory controls against private industry were largely absent. On the other hand, the self-defined mission and institutional incentives of most such agencies made them largely indifferent or even hostile to environmental goals. While a few federal agencies or bureaus (Park Service and Fish and Wildlife) welcomed the new emphasis on environmental values, most others resisted.

Federal environmental policies have generally imposed fewer restrictions on the managerial autonomy of public resource managers than on that of private resource managers. Statutory efforts to promote greater consideration of environmental values by federal land managers have generally taken the form of provisions enlarging the considerations to be appraised in decisionmaking, and procedural requirements (such as NEPA) to the same end. Regulatory measures sharply limiting federal resource management discretion are rare; the Endangered Species Act, the PSD provisions of the Clean Air Act, and the Surface Mining Control and Reclamation Act are notable exceptions. This difference is attributable to the political power of the states and private interest groups allied with activities such as federal water resource projects; the related political influence of development oriented federal agencies; the consequently greater difficulty of enforcing controls over public than private investment; and the inherent problems in framing precise standards for multiple use natural resource management.

Basic shifts over time in the political support for environmental protection must be noted. The late 1960s and early 1970s were the heyday for bold, often naive efforts to redirect public and private investment policies in favor of environmental concerns and, through "technology forcing" measures, to transform the existing industrial base. More recently, concern with the performance of the economy and with energy supplies and adverse reaction to the crude enthusiasms of "first generation" environmental regulatory measures have modified the national sense of priorities. This change is most manifest in the Reagan administration's conduct; the lack of new environmental initiatives, the reductions in the budgets and staff of environmental regulatory agencies, and the attempted adoption of a frankly pro-development policy for natural resources. Yet concern with environmental values in Congress and among the public remains high, producing something of a stalemate in public policy. The Reagan administration has been unsuccessful in its efforts to change statutes such as the Clean Air Act in order to relax regulatory measures and introduce more explicit consideration of economic costs in standard setting. Instead it has cut EPA's budget, and slowed the issuance of new regulations, and subjected them to more intensive review by the Office of Management and Budget under Executive Order 12, 291.

2. Strategies and Tools Employed

Federal programs that take the form of direct federal regulation or of state implementation of federal standards have placed overwhelming reliance on command and control measures. Even outside the environmental area, regulatory programs in the United States have generally relied on command and control techniques, and there has accordingly been little operating experience with alternatives. The perceived urgency of environmental problems and public moral indignation, politically cultivated in order to provide support for legislation, have reinforced the tendency to adopt regulatory prohibitions to alter conduct.

a. Varieties of Regulatory Tools

In federal product regulation, the preference has been for uniform technology-based performance standards in those cases where the environmental performance of the product regulated can be quantitatively defined and measured on a consistent basis (e. g., auto air pollution). Where such definition and measurement is not feasible, reliance is placed on case by case screening of individual products under general criteria (pesticides, toxic chemicals) to weed out those judged unreasonably risky. There is a tendency to impose more stringent controls on new than on existing products, which tends to discourage innovation and capital investment in such products.[13]

The regulation of industrial processes through state implementation of federal standards has been the subject of ongoing debate between champions of uniform technology-based standards and advocates of regulation based on environmental quality standards. Water pollution, air pollution, toxic waste, and stripmine regulation (as well as federal nuclear regulation) incorporate some elements of each strategy, although there are great differences in the dominant emphasis. Technology-based controls are generally easier to adopt, implement and enforce, and reduce competitive "distortions" by denying firms in unpolluted areas the cost advantage they would enjoy under a system of environmental quality standards. Environmental quality standards tailor control efforts to environmental quality objectives, but are more difficult to implement, may give a competitive advantage to industries in certain regions, and (if nondegradation principles are not included) induce industrial relocation.

The choice among strategies to some extent reflects historical and institutional happenstance. The strategy of ambient standards adopted in the Clean Air Act in 1970 reflected the traditional understanding of the occupational and health professionals in the Department of Health, Education and Welfare, which was heavily involved in the early development of the legislation, that

[13] For general discussion of these points, *see* STEWART, *Regulation, Innovation and Administrative Law: A Conceptual Framework*, 64 CALIF. L. REV. 1256 (1981).

"safe" threshold levels of pollution can be ascertained. The difficulties in actually implementing the environmental quality strategy of the Clean Air Act Amendments helped persuade Congress to adopt a technology-based approach in the 1972 Federal Water Pollution Control Act Amendments. The reliance on an environmental quality standard in the Clean Air Act was tempered by reliance on uniform technology-based controls for new sources in order to reduce incentives for industrial relocation. But fear of "competitive distortions" was more acute in the context of water pollution, perhaps because of the nature of the industries involved (there is likely to be more vigorous competition among paper mills than electric utilities, for example). This led Congress in the 1972 water pollution control legislation to adopt a system of uniform technology-based controls, established on an industry by industry basis, for existing as well as new sources. This system was, however, superimposed on a preexisting federal regulatory scheme that relied upon a strategy of ambient water quality standards established by the states. As a result water quality standards are also part of the federal water pollution regulatory system, and they will probably assume increasing importance in the future. This experience shows how federal regulatory programs are the result of an iterative incremental process of policy "exfoliation."[14]

The US experience also suggests that a combination of environmental quality standards and technology-based controls is often appropriate in the control of industrial processes. Sole or principal reliance on environmental quality standards places great strain on the technically complex process of modelling and allocation. Centralized federal implementation and enforcement of such a system involves overly rigid and time consuming review procedures. But delegation to states of such responsibilities runs the risk of a serious "implementation gap." Moreover, uniform environmental quality standards create strong, disruptive pressures for relocation of industry to presently clean areas. It is difficult to devise and adopt a system of non-uniform ambient quality standards in order to deal with this problem without creating a host of other problems, although it may be appropriate and feasible to create zones of special protection for pristine or exceptionally sensitive areas. On the other hand, uniform technology-based controls can lead to misallocation of control resources to areas where they are not needed, and to inadequate protection of sensitive areas. A mixed system which imposes a moderate level of technology-based controls on all sources, supplemented by ambient standards that will operate in polluted areas as longer term goals and in sensitive or pristine areas as a protection against significant degradation, is probably superior to either strategy alone. While both are mixed systems, the Clean Air Act and the Clean Water Act have probably given excessive weight to one or another of the two strategies.

[14] *See* J. KRIER & E. URSIN, POLLUTION AND POLICY 12, 289–95 (Univ. of Calif. Press, Berkeley, Calif. 1977); STEWART, *History and Policy Analysis,* 31 STANF. L. REV. 1159 (1979).

b. The Transformation of Regulatory Strategies Through the Implementation Process

Both environmental quality standards and technology-based standards in federal regulatory programs have often been based on a regulatory philosophy of "technology-forcing" designed to require industry to devise and adopt environmentally superior processes, products, and control technologies.[15] Environmental quality standards are designed to "force" technology by establishing control requirements solely on the basis of health and environmental considerations and threatening shutdown if these requirements are not met by stated deadlines. In the case of technology-based standards, regulatory agencies are supposed to force technology by requiring levels of control based on the future state of the technical art. In practice, neither approach has had much success in forcing technology. Instead, they have largely served to require firms to adopt existing control technologies. Where regulation is based on environmental quality standards, as in the Clean Air Act, sources have generally not been shut down when deadlines for achieving standards have passed. Deadlines are postponed and extensions are granted so long as a source is making reasonable progress in installing available control technology. In the case of technology-based standards, considerations of administrative practicality and the need to survive legal challenges have led agencies to base standards on the existing rather than on some projected future state of the technological art. Agencies with limited staff, resources and experience are ill equipped to identify the future state of the control technology in a given industry or to persuade reviewing courts that such technology will be workable and affordable. The practical realities of implementation have thus transformed the initial premises of the regulatory system.

Regulated firms have an incentive to develop new control technologies and processes that would enable them to meet existing regulatory requirements more cheaply. But they generally have strong disincentives to develop technologies and processes that would make more stringent requirements feasible. In such a case, innovation would be punished by agency adoption of the more stringent requirements, which would oblige the regulated firms to spend additional money to install the new technology. Firms that manufacture and supply pollutional control equipment to industries subject to regulation do have incentives to develop superior control technologies (although these are undermined by regulatory uncertainty). But such firms generally need the capital and the cooperation of regulated industry in developing new technologies to commercial scale, for the reasons already noted. Such cooperation is unlikely to be forthcoming. Federal research and development resources have been limited.[16]

[15] *See generally,* La Pierre, *Technology Forçing and Federal Environmental Protection Statutes*,.62 Iowa L. Rev. 771 (1977).

[16] For a general discussion of the problems of designing government programs that will encourage development of environmentally superior technologies, *see* Stewart, *supra* note 13; Henderson & Pearson, *Implementing Federal Environmental Policies: The Limits of Aspirational Commands,* 78 Colum. L. Rev. 1429 (1978).

The transformation of regulatory strategies in the course of implementation is also illustrated by the choice between performance, specification, and input standards. Performance standards impose specific limits on pollution or environmental degradation, but allow industry discretion in devising measures to meet that limit. A source must reduce emissions, for example, to a designated level, but has freedom to choose the cheapest and most convenient way to achieve that performance. Specification standards, in contrast, require the use of a particular control technology (such as flue gas "scrubbers"). Input standards limit the inputs to a process, requiring for example, that the sulfur content of fuel not exceed a given percentage amount. By limiting control options, specification and input standards reduce flexibility and increase control costs. On the other hand, specification and input standards are much easier to enforce than performance standards, which require regulators to monitor emissions. In many cases, monitoring technology is unreliable or very expensive, and requires considerable manpower.

Statutes generally provide that technology-based standards, such as the effluent limitations under the Clean Water Act, are to be performance standards. In actual practice, however, such standards strongly encourage use of particular control technologies. A variety of practical considerations lead regulators to set the performance levels required on the basis of what particular control technologies can achieve. This practice simplifies the process of adopting standards and persuading reviewing courts that the standards can be achieved. Firms have strong incentive to comply with the standards by installing the technology upon which the standards are based, because regulators will readily accept the use of such technology as establishing compliance. There are implications for federalism as well. If pure performance standards were adopted, federal regulators would either have to accept the adequacy of state implementation measures largely on faith or develop an elaborate federal inspection and monitoring system. When standards are based on known technologies, it is far easier for federal regulators to determine whether those technologies have been specified in state permits and installed by sources. Although they too may be framed in performance terms, the conditions and limitations contained in individual source permits are typically also based on the adoption of particular technologies or input limitations. In many cases, however, state permits and regulations adopted pursuant to federal programs often explicitly limit inputs or specify use of particular control technologies.

Another example of how federalism considerations have led to adoption of specification rather than performance standards is the New Source Performance Standard for coal-fired power plants. EPA originally adopted a pure performance standard (limiting SO_2 emissions in relation to heat value of fuel inputs), which gave low-sulfur western coal a competitive advantage over high-sulfur eastern coal because the latter would have had to have been washed before combustion or scrubbed after combustion in order to meet the standard. Congress, concerned about the resulting competitive impact on eastern coal interests, modified the Clean Air Act in 1977 to encourage, if not require, EPA to adopt a standard which required scrubbing regardless of the sulfur content of the fuel used.[17]

Whether they employ environmental quality standards or technology-based standards, federal regulatory statutes have as a general matter required that such standards be geographically uniform, a practice reflecting the political obstacles to agreement on non-uniform standards under a congressional form of government. In practice, however, implementation problems have resulted in a substantial degree of non-uniformity. In the Clean Air Act, for example, postponements of deadlines for achievement of national air quality standards in dirty air areas eventually resulted in a separate legal regime for nonattainment areas. On the other hand, litigation by environmental groups anxious to preserve existing air quality in clean air areas established the nondegradation principle. This principle was subsequently ratified by Congress, responding to environmental support for preservation of pristine regions and fear by industrialized areas of relocation of industry to clean air areas.[18] The inability of a congressional form of government to engage in geographically differentiated development planning is reflected in the blanket character of the PSD program. *All* existing clean air areas are subject to PSD increment controls regardless of whether they are ecologically sensitive or have special scenic or historic value. This fact, together with the burdensome character of new source review, has invited state and industry attacks on the PSD program.

This history again demonstrates the incremental, "exfoliating" character of environmental policy change. A system of uniform air quality standards has been transformed into a system of non-uniform standards because of the largely unanticipated problems and side effects of implementation; the change is not the product of conscious design. Even in the case of the Clean Water Act's technology-based effluent standards, a good deal of flexibility has been introduced into the system of uniform standards because EPA was led in the implementation process to multiply the industrial sub-categories for which standards are written in order to accommodate differences in industrial processes and control costs.

Because of the failure of technology-forcing strategies and the political reluctance to enforce measures that will have the effect of closing existing plants, new industrial facilities have generally been subject to more stringent regulation than existing ones. The level of pollution control which they must achieve is generally much greater than that required of existing sources; this

[17] *See* Clean Air Act § 111(a), (h), 42 U.S.C. § 7411(a), (h); Sierra Club v. Costle, 657 F.2d 298 (D.C. Cir. 1981) (upholding EPA regulations establishing new source performance standards for coal-fired power plants in a form that reduces but does not altogether eliminate the competitive advantages enjoyed by low sulfur coal in meeting pollution control requirements). For discussion strongly critical of the actions of Congress and EPA in this matter, *see* B. Ackerman & W. Hassler, Clean Coal/Dirty Air: Or How The Clean Air Act Became A Multibilllion-Dollar Bail-Out For High Sulfur Coal Producers And What Should Be Done About It (Yale University Press, New Haven 1981).

[18] *See supra* pp. 112–113.

difference is generally only partially justified by the lower costs of designing and building pollution control into a new facility. New facilities are also subject to extensive, time consuming licensing procedures that introduce considerable uncertainty and postpone returns from capital investment. These differences in the treatment of existing and new services have reduced the incentive to invest in new plant, hindering innovation and modernization of capital plant.[19]

c. Economic-Based Incentive Systems

The dominant federal reliance on command and control regulation has been supplemented by two forms of subsidies. First, federal grants for capital costs of municipal waste treatment have been provided in order to dissolve political opposition to federal regulatory requirements imposed on local public authorities.[20] Second, federal tax incentives have underwritten a modest portion of industrial compliance costs.[21] The municipal waste treatment program has been plagued by administrative red tape, capital intensive projects that are poorly maintained and operated, and emphasis on costly and sometimes environmentally inappropriate sewer systems with "end of pipe" controls. There is no evidence that the tax incentives are justified by economic efficiency.

Economists have long urged use of emission and noncompliance fees to bring about least cost allocation of abatement burdens and provide regulated firms with positive incentives to develop and adopt environmentally superior technologies.[22] However, these proposals have found little favor with federal legislators and administrators, despite growing public disenchantment with command and control regulation. Problems in implementing such proposals include determination of the appropriate fee level; uncertainty as to what level of control will be induced by any given fee level; the need to readjust fees to deal with inflation and industrial development; concern that firms with market power will simply pay for "a license to pollute"; inadequate monitoring technology; fear that a fee system would create local "hot spots" caused by geographical concentration of sources; political opposition to imposition of a new "tax" that might require greater total outlays by firms than command and control regulation; and jurisdictional disputes as to which congressional committees and executive agencies (environmental or tax) would be responsible for such measures. Taxes have been used to finance federal cleanup funds for oil

[19] *See* STEWART, *supra* note 13.

[20] *See* R. STEWART & J. KRIER, ENVIRONMENTAL LAW AND POLICY 507–508 (Michie Co. Bobbs-Merrill, Charlottesville, VA., 2d ed. 1978)

[21] *See* INTERNAL REVENUE CODE § 169, which provides that the investment in new qualifying air and water pollution abatement facilities constructed in connection with industrial plants in operation before 1 January 1976 may be amortized for purposes of federal income tax within 5 years. This accelerated tax write-off treatment is currently of only modest economic significance to firms because of other recent changes in corporate income tax law.

[22] *See* materials collected and discussed in R. STEWART & J. KRIER, *supra* note 20, ch. 6.

spills and toxic waste dumps, but the fees have been levied on production rather than pollution. Accordingly, they must be regarded as revenue raising devices rather than incentives to induce environmentally preferable conduct.

Congress has authorized a system of noncompliance penalties in the Clean Air Act to induce firms to comply with regulatory requirements by taxing away the economic gains of noncompliance.[23] However, these measures are designed to promote achievement of a specific regulatorily determined level of performance, and do not promote least cost allocation of abatement burdens or provide positive stimulus for development of environmentally superior technologies, as a fee system would do. Moreover, there has been enormous dispute and delay in determining the appropriate amount of the fees in relation to national variations in compliance costs. These difficulties were not encountered in the implementation of a similar program in Connecticut, which pioneered the noncompliance fee.[24] This experience illustrates some of the problems in centralizing regulatory programs. Perhaps the most serious such problem is that centralized federal regulation either precludes or discourages state experimentation with alternative regulatory techniques.

Another form of economic incentive is provided by transferable pollution rights systems.[25] In the pure form of such a system, a regulatory authority would establish a limit on pollution or other forms of environmental risk and allocate (by auction, grandfathering, etc.) pollution rights equal to the total permitted. Sources would have to own rights equal to the amount of their pollution; the government would police compliance with this requirement. Accordingly, the overall ceiling on total emissions would not be exceeded. These rights would be freely marketable and would acquire a positive price because of the limited number of rights and the increasing demand for them resulting from industrial development. The price commanded by rights would function like an emission fee from the perspective of an individual firm, promoting least cost abatement and stimulating innovation in processes and technologies that would reduce pollution, etc. Such a system would avoid most of the drawbacks of a fee system. For example, it would avoid the stigma of a new tax; provide a mechanism for financing environmental improvement by existing firms on a cost effective basis; and avoid the need for constant revision of fee levels or regulatory controls in the face of economic development. Problems include the initial allocation of rights and the danger of pollution "hot spots" caused by the "bunching" of pollution sources in a particular location.

A limited version of the marketable permit approach is found in the offset provisions of the Clean Air Act[26], which require new pollution sources in nonattainment regions to be offset by more than compensating reductions in exist-

[23] Clean Air Act § 120, 42 U.S.C. § 7420.

[24] *See* R. Stewart & J. Krier, *supra* note 20, at 600–602; U. S. Environmental Protection Agency, Connecticut Enforcement Project Report (1977).

[25] *See* J. Dales, Pollution, Property and Prices (University of Toronto Press, Toronto 1968). R. Stewart & J. Krier, *supra* note 20, at 587–599.

[26] *See* Clean Air Act § 173 (1)(A), 42 U.S.C. § 7503(1)(A).

ing sources. Other versions are found in EPA's "bubble" policies, which allow existing sources to reallocate pollution control burdens imposed by state SIPs and allow industrial complexes with new or expanded units in PSD areas to escape the full rigors of new source review and control if the increased emissions attributed to such units are offset by reductions from elsewhere in the complex.[27] These innovations originated with the staff of EPA as part of an effort to accommodate environmental goals with continued industrial development and concern over regulatory compliance costs. While the federal EPA has been primarily responsible for these initiatives, a few states (notably California, Connecticut, and New Jersey) are active as well.

Transferable permit systems, designed to efficiently allocate rights to a fixed quantity of emissions in a given region, represent a promising solution to problems of transboundary pollution spillovers, including acid rain and sulfate deposition and oxidants. If the total amount of permits and their allocation among states were determined by the federal government, while states were given the responsibility for allocating permits, such a system could ensure that national objectives were met while allowing a good deal of decentralized flexibility.

3. Patterns of Implementation and Enforcement

As a crude generalization, the rigor of environmental regulation of private conduct varies in proportion to the degree of federal responsibility for implementation and enforcement. This correlation reflects the greater leverage of industry over state and local decisionmakers; the more limited resources that states and localities devote to regulation; and the greater insulation of federal bureaucracies from local, short term political concerns.

But even in programs of direct federal regulation, implementation and enforcement typically fall far short of stated legislative goals. Such implementation gaps are even more serious in the case of federal programs that rely upon state implementation and enforcement of federal standards or on encouragement of state regulation. The occurrence of these gaps reflects several factors, including the non-parliamentary character of the federal government, the consequent divorce between political rewards for legislative initiatives and political accountability for implementation costs and failures, limitations on the staff and resources available to federal administrators (dramatized by recent budget and staff reductions at EPA), the failure of "technology forcing" regulatory strategies, the size and diversity of the nation, and the consequent need to decentralize implementation and enforcement to state and local authorities who place a lower priority on environmental objectives.

[27] *See* Del Calvo y Gonzales, *Markets in Air: Problems and Prospects in Controlled Trading*, 5 Harv. Envt'l L. Rev. 377 (1981); Landau, *Economic Dream or Environmental Nightmare? The Legality of the "Bubble Concept" in Air and Water Pollution Control*, 8 B. C. Envt'l Aff. L. Rev. 741 (1980); Note, *An Overview of the Bubble Concept*, 8 Colum. J. Envt'l L. 137 (1982).

The Congress has attempted to deal with the implementation gap problem by specifying control strategies in great detail, by imposing deadlines and other "action forcing" requirements, and by authorizing citizen suits to enforce these requirements against administrators. These measures as explained below, have created problems of undue rigidity and obsolescence in regulatory policy.

The federal courts have attempted to meet implementation gaps by expanding access of environmental groups to agency proceedings and judicial review, by expanding and enforcing with considerable rigor the procedural formalities that federal agencies must observe, by opening agency failure to implement and enforce environmentally protective measures to judicial review, and by instituting a "hard look" standard of review of discretion.

These steps have had an effect in stimulating initiatives to protect environmental values. On the other hand, they have added considerably to the cost and delay associated with regulatory decisionmaking. Federal courts have also been reluctant to overrule discretionary policy choices by agencies under statutes allowing them wide freedom of choice. Finally, the severe remedial problems faced by courts in correcting inadequate implementation and enforcement by uncooperative or inadequately funded federal or state agencies have become apparent in the past several years. Environmental groups have brought numerous deadline and other "action forcing" suits against the Reagan administration EPA, which has defended such suits on grounds of inadequate information or pending changes in underlying policies. Federal judges, particularly those in the District of Columbia, have become acutely aware of their limited powers in such cases.[28] A contempt citation for the EPA Administrator is hardly a realistic possibility. While orders to take action may have an effect, in part by mobilizing attention in Congress and the media, courts have repeatedly granted extensions in the face of EPA statements that deadlines can not be met.

In programs where states play a large implementation and enforcement role, federal courts have shied from remedies directed at state officials.[29] Instead, environmental advocates must generally seek judicial relief directed at federal agencies' failure to ensure more effective enforcement by the states. This is an inherently clumsy way of ensuring such enforcement.

Federal courts have been as concerned with excessively burdensome or ill founded regulatory impositions as they have been with implementation failures. The same procedural controls and "hard look" standard of review enforced in suits brought by environmental groups is also applied in industry suits complaining that particular regulatory controls are not authorized by statute,

[28] *See supra* Ch. VII, note 39.

[29] *See, e. g.*, Brown v. EPA, 521 F.2d 827 (9th Cir. 1975) (refusing to construe Clean Air Act as granting EPA authority to impose sanctions on state for failure to enforce control measures adopted by EPA), *vacated* (as not ripe for decision and possibly moot) 431 U.S. 99 (1977). *But cf.* Friends of the Earth v. Carey, 535 F.2d 165 (2d Cir. 1976), *cert. denied*, 434 U.S. 902 (1977) (EPA may require New York to enforce SIP controls adopted by New York.)

are not based on sound or adequate scientific, engineering, or economic data and analysis, or are otherwise unreasonable.[30] Industry frequently succeeds in having regulations set aside and remanded for further administrative proceedings. Since industry has more resources to devote to litigation than environmental groups, industry probably on balance benefits more than environmental groups from the courts' active development of administrative law to control agency discretion.

The requirement by courts and, more recently, by Congress,[31] of considerable formality in agency decisional procedures tends to prolong regulatory decisionmaking, promote adversary tactics and attitudes, and impede negotiated compromises. Despite frequently voiced complaints, there is little incentive to change the present system because both industry and environmental groups greatly distrust agency discretion and would be unwilling to relinquish the controls which the federal legal system gives them over the decisions of federal and (indirectly) state administrators.

Concern over regulatory costs and burdens, particularly in the field of environmental, health, and safety regulation, is also reflected in another new element in the federal administrative system: regulatory analysis review by the Office of Management and Budget (OMB). Regulatory analysis review, initiated as early as the Nixon administration, has been given considerable impetus by President Reagan's Executive Order 12,291, requiring federal regulatory agencies to conduct a cost-benefit analysis of regulatory proposals and adopt (unless precluded by statute) the most economically efficient or cost effective alternative. Compliance with these requirements is policed by OMB rather than the courts. Congress may ratify this effort to control regulatory costs through "regulatory reform" legislation that mandates a form of cost-benefit analysis by OMB of major new regulations.[32] As might be expected, industry generally applauds this effort while environmental groups oppose it. However, industry has found that efforts by the current administration to relax or streamline existing regulations have been hindered by the necessity of regulatory analysis review. Moreover, the guidelines for cost benefit analysis and decision are sufficiently general that a regulation-minded agency can largely have its way if it has sufficient political support.[33]

[30] *See* Stewart, *The Development of Administrative and Quasi-Constitutional Law in Judicial Review of Environmental Decisionmaking: Lessons from the Clean Air Act*, Iowa L. Rev. 713, 740–758 (1977).

[31] *See, e. g.*, Clean Air Act § 307(d), 42 U.S.C. § 7607(d) (providing for rulemaking procedures in which all relevant data and analysis must be incorporated in a documentary record serving as the evidentiary basis for agency decision and judicial review.)

[32] *See* S. 1080, 97th Cong., 2d Sess., 127 Cong. Rec. S2713 (1982).

[33] *See id.* § 4(a) (adding § 621(5), (6) and § 622(c)(2)(A), (B), (F) to 6 U.S.C.).

Another possible technique for controlling excessively costly or burdensome new regulations is the legislative veto procedure, by which a statute may authorize both houses of Congress, or in some versions one house, to set aside by majority vote, without the concurrence of the President, an agency's promulgation of a particular

The patchwork and often inconsistent or uncoordinated nature of federal environmental legislation, the fragmentation of environmental regulation and resource management responsibilities among various federal agencies and between federal and state authorities, the heavy reliance on litigation and formal procedures to control administrative decision, and the limited integrative capacities of the American political system (stemming from the use of congressional and federal forms of government and the accompanying weaknesses of political parties), have resulted in a pronounced lack of coordination and integrated planning in the management of environmental and other natural resources.

Partial efforts to correct this lack – for example, by merging the Interior Department, EPA, and resource related responsibilities of the Energy Department – have met with stiff opposition from environmental and industry groups and their constituencies who fear that reorganization would generate policies less favorable to their interests. Even within EPA, whose creation by reorganization was promised as the answer to the need to coordinate controls on air and water pollution and solid wastes as part of an integrated program of residuals management, there has been relatively little coordination among different bureaus. This lack is in part attributable to wide differences among the relevant authorizing statutes.

It remains to be seen whether a stronger system of central control and coordination by the Executive, building on the present system of OMB review, will eventually emerge and supplant to some degree the current system of judicial and informal congressional controls. While such a system of central control runs against the grain of US political traditions, there are many observors who believe that it may be necessary to ensure the productivity and international competitiveness of the US economy.

4. Transboundary Spillovers

Although touted as a major rationale for federal regulatory initiatives, transboundary spillover problems have not been solved by current programs; indeed, in some cases (such as acid rain and deposition) federal regulatory programs may have made the problem worse. No doubt in many instances transboundary spillovers would be more serious than they are but for federal regulatory programs. But existing programs suffer from serious gaps, including disregard of local or regional ambient effects under technology-based control systems; a focus on local effects in ambient strategies, which thus fail to effectively address region-wide problems like acid rain and ozone transport; and reliance on state by state implementation and enforcement. In addition, federal administrators are reluctant to take on politically sensitive interstate spillover controversies.

regulation. The legislative veto (at least in the traditional form described above) was, however, declared unconstitutional by the Supreme Court in Immigration & Naturalization Service v. Chadha, 103 S.Ct. 2764 (1983).

The Supreme Court has cut short judicial efforts to respond to some of these problems by developing a federal common law of interstate pollution.[34] Episodic litigation is concededly a poor way to deal with widespread spillover problems caused by multiple sources, a circumstance that led the Supreme Court to channel interstate spillover controversies toward legislative and administrative solutions. There are, however, serious structural political barriers to adoption of such solutions. These barriers are illustrated by the continuing stalemate within Congress and the administration over proposals for legislation that would require air pollution emissions reductions from midwest sources in order to reduce the acid rain and deposition problem in the northeast. Greater efforts may be made to obtain remedies through litigation in state court based on state law, but many problems limit the efficacy of this alternative.

B. Influencing Factors

1. Legal and Institutional Constraints

Legal constraints have not played a significant role in impeding the development and implementation of federal environmental policy. Courts have given an extremely broad contruction to the commerce and property powers of the Congress and its authority to preempt contrary state regulation. While there may be some constitutional limits on Congress's power to coerce states into implementing federal policy,[35] the practical significance of this limitation is doubtful. On the one hand, other methods to induce state cooperation, including conditional grants and the threat of a federal ban on private development, are available to induce state cooperation. On the other, there are definite political limits to the power of Congress, in which the states are effectively represented, to enact coercive measures.

More significant factors are the federal political structure and traditions of the United States and the non-parliamentary character of the federal government. State and local governments maintain a dominant role in land use decisions and regulation of individual activity, such as motor vehicle use. This decentralization of authority imposes pervasive limits on the centralization and rigor of environmental policy. The federal government, particularly in areas that do not involve regulation of national product markets or the management of federal lands, is heavily dependent on state and local cooperation. Industrial and developmental interests often exercise relatively greater power at the state and local level, and state and local authorities often lack adequate resources to engage in effective regulation and tend to take a more short term view of environmental issues.[36] These factors limit the degree of cooperation forthcoming.

[34] *See supra* pp. 197–199.

[35] *See supra* pp. 192–193.

[36] *See* STEWART, *Pyramids of Sacrifice? Problems of Federalism in Mandating State Implementation of National Environmental Policy*, 86 YALE L. J. 1196, 1213–15 (1977).

Variations in local conditions and the need to integrate environmental measures with other local functions introduce significant diseconomies of scale in centralized decisionmaking, and reinforce local opposition to dictation from Washington. These factors reinforce the institutional power of state and local government. The threat of industry to locate new or existing plants elsewhere if a locality or state insists on stringent environmental protection policies apparently has sufficient credibility to act as a substantial restraint on state and local environmental initiatives. While this constraint can to some extent be circumvented by shifting environmental policymaking to the national level, the need for state and local cooperation in implementation and enforcement of numerous programs gives that constraint continuing force.

One aspect of geographic and economic diversity has favored strong national environmental policies. That diversity has fostered the maintenance of national areas of great scenic beauty, particularly in the west. These special areas have accordingly become viewed as resources to be preserved and protected for the nation as a whole.[37] This attitude has supported strong federal measures to protect such areas from state and local development pressures.

Local and state authorities are not, however, inevitably less solicitous of environmental concerns than their federal counterparts. In many areas enthusiasm for industrial and commercial development has waned, and some forms of development (such as nuclear power plants and toxic waste depositories) are actively opposed because they are viewed as imposing serious local risks while their benefits accrue largely to others. Preemptive federal statutes and regulations in areas such as nuclear energy, tanker vessel regulation, and hazardous waste disposal attest to the significance of this perception. The balance of local and national interests in such situations is accordingly quite different than in many pollution control situations, such as that exemplified by the acid rain problem where midwest states are asked to bear the costs of controlling pollution in order to provide benefits for persons residing elsewhere.

As the Reagan administration has pursued relatively unrestrained pro-development policies, state and local governments have often become relatively more supportive of environmental and conservation values, and environmental groups have formed hitherto unlikely alliances with "sagebrush rebellion" interests in the West opposed to federal direction and control. Generalizations on this subject are, however, hazardous; an issue by issue, often state by state analysis is required.

2. Actors and Interests

Congressional entrepreneurship has been a major factor in the emergence of federal environmental policies. The decentralized committee structure of

[37] *See supra* pp. 132–133.

Congress permits and encourages politically ambitious members to enhance their power and reputation by sponsoring, obtaining passage, and overseeing the implementation of new legislation. As general public concern with environmental degradation has grown, congressmen have sought to capitalize on this concern through legislative initiatives in the environmental area.

The media have played an important role in this process by dramatizing environmental problems. The national television networks, nationally oriented newspapers such as the New York Times, Washington Post, and Los Angeles Times, and national news magazines have been important in developing public awareness of environmental problems throughout the nation and generating support for national legislation to deal with them.

There are fewer political rewards for careful and constructive legislative oversight and correction of ongoing administrative implementation and enforcement than there are for initiating new legislation.[38] This fact, combined with the "issue cycle" generated by the shift of media and public attention to new subjects, and the power of inertia, industry influence, and local interests in the implementation stage, results in a policy process that operates to some extent as a "filter," responding to public concerns with administrative programs that are not fully implemented and are in some measure symbolic. Enactment of ambitious federal programs and of adoption by federal agencies of implementing regulations are merely the beginnings of a long process of negotiation, accommodation, and compromise that yields results far short of what was nominally sought. Moreover, the budgets for federal environmental regulatory activities are often inadequate to carry out statutory programs in full. This "filter" process tends to discredit regulation, not only because results fall short of promise, but also because congressmen and regulators, anticipating this shortfall, adopt initial measures and goals that are extreme and unrealistic. Notorious examples of the practice are the 1985 "zero discharge" goal proclaimed in the 1972 Federal Water Pollution Control Amendments, and the 1970 Clean Air Act's goal of achieving federal air quality standards everywhere in the US within $4^1/_2$ years. Such goals are characteristic of the very ambitious "first generation" of major federal regulatory statutes enacted between 1969 and 1972, which reflect something of a national moral crusade that may be psychologically connected with the US experience in civil rights and Vietnam.

[38] A leading political scientist, Morris Fiorina, has observed that:

> In the end, the majority of our bureaucratic failures seem to have a large element of congressional failure underlying them. Wasteful, deceptive, disingenuous, paternalistic, and captive bureaucrats work in harmony with wasteful, deceptive, disingenuous, paternalistic and captive congressmen. ... The bureaucrats catch a disproportionate share of the public relations flak, while the congressmen appropriate a disproportionate share of the political credit, in return for which they shelter the bureaucrats.

Quoted in Weingast & Moran, *The Myth of Runaway Bureaucracy: The Case of the FTC*, Regulation (May/June 1982) 33, 38.

The President wields substantial political power, but during the past fifteen years presidents have been less significant as policy initiators in the environmental area than Congress. The juxtaposition of Republican presidents and Democratic Congresses during much of the period provides a partial explanation for this pattern. Presidents and their staff have been more concerned with moderating the industrial and economic costs of environmental regulation and promoting energy development. There are important exceptions to this generalization, such as President Carter's strong support of Alaskan wilderness preservation, but presidents have more often applied the brake to federal environmental initiatives. The brake is being applied with repeated force by the current administration.

Federal administrators are important actors because of the legal powers and resources which they command and the considerable statutory and political discretion which they exercise. Attitudes toward environmental protection vary widely depending upon the mission, political environment, sociology, and history of an institution. Environmental protection agencies will tend to take a quite different view than agencies with a development mission. Agencies with similar missions may show marked differences because of professional and bureaucratic traditions. The attitude of the Forest Service towards resource development is often different than that of the Bureau of Land Management. Such differences exist even within the same agency. The environmental zeal of the pesticides division of EPA, which was inherited from the Agriculture Department when EPA was formed through reorganization, has been far less marked than that in other divisions, which were inherited from the Interior and Health, Education and Welfare Departments. In addition to exercising discretion in administration, the federal agencies play a substantial role in the legislative process. They have in the past sometimes had an important indirect effect by stimulating public concern over environmental issues through research and publicity. The attention devoted by the Public Health Service to the health effects of air pollution is a notable example.

In recent years OMB has played an increasingly powerful role as concern over regulatory compliance costs and burdens has mounted. Its responsibility for implementing Executive Order 12,291 has made this power explicit.

The federal Council on Environmental Quality is a small organization within the Executive Office of the President. In the past it has done useful service in collecting and publishing, on a consistent basis, information about environmental conditions and government responses to environmental problems; identifying longer run problems and priorities; and serving as something of a watchdog on government environmental policies.[39] Its resources and functions have been drastically curtailed by the current administration.

The federal courts have assumed an important role in implementation and enforcement of environmental programs, and have generally been more active in this area than in most other areas of administrative law. They have sought to counteract the systematic institutional "filters" to effective implementation

[39] *See* the annual reports of the CEQ, entitled "Environmental Quality – [year]."

by expanding the access of environmental groups to administrative procedures and judicial review. They have also acted to curb the institutional biases of both development and environmental regulatory agencies by developing additional procedural requirements and imposing hard look review.

State and local authorities have had a limited role in the congressional legislation process, but they are generally not major players. They have played a larger role in implementation and enforcement of federal environmental protection regulations and in influencing federal resource management and development policies. Governors and other state officials often act simultaneously as advocates for and brokers among environmental and development interests in the complex policy implementation process.

Industrial firms, development interests, and their trade associations currently play a powerful role in federal environmental policy. Although industry influence was attenuated in the heyday of environmentalism in the early 1970s, it has grown as the problems in implementing ambitious environmental programs have become apparent and as concern with the economy and resistance to "overregulation" by Washington has mounted. Large industrial firms, trade associations, and inter-industry groups such as the Business Roundtable and Chamber of Commerce maintain Washington offices staffed by full-time professionals. In addition, business firms retain Washington lawyers or lobbyists to represent them before Congress, agencies, and courts. Substantial resources are devoted to administrative proceedings and federal court litigation in order to prevent, influence, or set aside unfavorable agency regulatory decisions. Industrial interests are also effectively organized to exert influence on states and local governments, stressing the need for economic development and jobs. Among the notable innovations in the industry effort in recent years are the formation of broad coalitions, such as the Business Roundtable, to coordinate business activities against government regulation; the emergence of trade associations as "repeat player" litigators pursuing coordinated strategies to weaken regulation; and the use of institutional and issue advertising designed to influence public opinion in favor of the business position.

The position of environmental advocacy groups in the US presents an even sharper contrast with the EC.[40] National groups that seek to influence federal policy are far better funded and organized than local groups. The local groups generally have very limited resources. Although they have sometimes succeeded in blocking or delaying development projects through a combination of litigation, administrative and legislative lobbying, and efforts to arouse public opinion, they have generally not played a substantial role in regulatory implementation and enforcement.

There are about a dozen leading national environmental advocacy groups. Most have annual budgets substantially in excess of $1 million. These groups

[40] For general discussion of "public interest" advocacy groups in the US, *see* B. Weisbrod, J. Handler & N. Komesar, Public Interest Law (University of California Press, Berkeley, Calif. 1978). Legal advocacy by environmental groups is examined in *id.* chs. 7–8.

have large full-time professional staffs that typically include lawyers, scientists, and sometimes economists. They usually have offices in several cities such as Washington, New York, Denver, and San Francisco. They rely for funding on mass mail solicitations and donations from foundations and wealthy individuals. The staff generates information and analysis in order to lobby administrators; litigates in order to challenge agency implementation failures or defend against industry attacks on environmental policies; and engages in legislative lobbying and efforts to influence public opinion. More of these efforts are directed at federal than at state and local officials.

Although the resources at the disposal of environmental groups are only a fraction of those commanded by industry, these groups have enjoyed considerable success in offsetting industry influence with administrators, securing court judgments requiring that administrative decisions be reconsidered, and identifying and publicizing new problems that require governmental action. They have played only a minor role in enforcing controls against particular sources. The political influence of environmental groups in Congress is due primarily to general public support for environmental values rather than such groups' ability to deliver large numbers of votes or campaign contributions, although some groups have enjoyed success in concerted efforts to elect or defeat particular members of Congress.

In the past few years "public interest" law firms supported by business interests have arisen to challenge governmental regulatory policies as excessively burdensome and unduly restrictive of economic development.

Finally, the press and broadcast media have played a quite important role in dramatizing environmental problems and persuading citizens that they represent an important national priority. By documenting the persistence of unresolved problems and publicizing the health and environmental hazards associated with pollution and toxic chemicals, the media have functioned as a watchdog of implementation failure, and strengthened political support for national regulation. On the other hand, the journalistic penchant for the dramatic and the episodic may foster a "pollutant of the month" approach which neglects the role of systemic factors, the need for systemic reductions, and the importance of setting priorities. A serious problem in a relatively open, pluralistic political process is educating the public, where attitudes have substantial importance, about the complexities and uncertainties in risk management and assessment. Despite progress in scientific, economic, administrative understanding of risk and its management, public debate often proceeds on the premise that exposure is either "safe" or "unsafe" and that achieving zero risk is feasible and desirable.

The responsibility for environmental and natural resource policy and management in the US is divided vertically among different levels of government (federal, state, and local) and horizontally among different authorities at the same level. For example, in the federal government, authority is horizontally divided among the two Houses of Congress and their respective committees; the White House and OMB; the various administrative departments, agencies and bureaus; and the courts. Integrative mechanisms, including the political parties, are relatively weak. As a crude generalization, Democrats are more sympathetic to environmental regulation than Republicans, but each party contains within it virtually the entire spectrum of views. Moreover, party affiliation primarily has significance in connection with presidental elections; environmental concerns played only a limited role in the 1976 presidental election and almost none in 1980. Environmental issues were quite significant in a number of congressional races, but were largely a function of the particular candidates involved and local constituency issues.

The multiplicity of decision centers has important implications for the policy process. There is a relatively low level of consistency and coordination among policies. Economists, for example, have delighted in documenting the enormous ranges in cost per death avoided among different environmental health and safety regulatory programs.[41] Actors and interests tend to focus energies on those fora which are most likely to be favorable to their respective interests. The identity of those fora will shift over time. For example, during the 1970s, environmental groups had considerable influence within the federal EPA. Industry devoted resources to federal court litigation and efforts to influence state-level authorities in order to blunt or defeat administrative initiatives by EPA. In the current administration, industry enjoys relatively greater influence within EPA. Environmental groups have been forced to devote more of their efforts to litigation and to state political activities in order to offset this shift. In actuality, environmental policies in the US are the product of a highly complex pattern of interaction among these multiple centers of decision and the various actors and interests.

Because changes in policy require the concurrence of many fora to be implemented, this structure tends to produce a high degree of inertia. It severely restricts the opportunities for coordinated or integrated planning of environmental and natural resource management. Although the legislative process of the US is based upon (concurrent) majority rule, in contrast to the rule of unanimity followed in the Council of the EC, the US system as a whole appears to be not much more able than that of the EC to make timely decisions when there are deep conflicts of views and interests.

3. Dynamic Factors

a. Changes in Knowledge and Technology

The history of US environmental policy over the past 15 years demonstrates the critical importance of adequate data and analytical methods; the need to establish and modify priorities; and the necessity of flexibility in responding to advances in economic and environmental science and to operating experience with various government regulatory strategies. Media attention, the legal leverage given to environmental groups in determining enforcement priorities, the vagaries of congressional entrepreneurship, and the weakness of integrative forces have often led to misdirection of energies. Congress, in its ef-

[41] *See* Benefit-Cost Analyses of Social Regulation (J. Miller & B. Yandle eds., American Enterprise Institute for Public Policy Research, Washington, D.C. 1979).

fort to control agency discretion, has often established detailed statutory requirements that prevent necessary adjustment to new knowledge and implementation experience. For example, the 1970 Clean Air Act strategy of basing air pollution controls on local ambient air pollution concentrations and state implementation plans has prevented effective response to the interstate acid rain and deposition problem. The specification of detailed command and control regulatory strategies in the Act has hindered administrative development of innovative economic incentive systems, such as "bubble" tradeoffs.[42]

While the federal government enjoys large advantages over state governments in developing the scientific and technical information needed for sound regulatory policy, the federal performance has often been disappointing. It has proven difficult to do scientific work that is both of high quality and relevant to the timely selection of environmental policies.[43] Scientists within regulatory agencies are hampered by low scientific status and limited resources. Scientists also fear that research priorities and implementing measures are set by political and legal considerations. Securing research by universities and national laboratories that is relevant to regulatory policy choices is difficult. Moreover, the current administration has drastically reduced the funds available for environmental research. There has, however, been a growing awareness of the need to bring good science to bear on regulatory decisions. The EPA has a Science Advisory Board and has established scientific advisory committees in particular areas (air quality standards, pollution control technologies, etc.). The Science Advisory Board in particular has played a useful role in bringing scientific understanding to bear on the framing and making of regulatory choices. Specific issues of major importance, such as acid rain, have been referred to the National Academy of Sciences for study and report by an Academy committee. Although the public still seems to believe that there are scientifically "correct" answers to tasks such as standard setting, administrators, lawyers, and judges involved in the policy process are coming to appreciate that there are large areas of scientific uncertainty about key issues, but that science can set bounds on uncertainty, help set priorities, and identify those issues on which additional research and information are likely to be most helpful to regulatory decisionmakers.

In addition to better and more relevant research, there is a need for selection of priorities and for flexibility in the design of strategies and tools employed to advance government environmental objectives. These goals imply greater administrative discretion, which is distrusted by Congress, environmentalists, and industry alike. Alternative tools, such as economic-based incentives, might in many instances represent a more appropriate response to uncertainty and the need for flexibility than command and control regulation. But the incre-

[42] NRDC v. Gorsuch, 685 F.2d 718 (D.C. Cir. 1982) (invalidating application of "tradeoff" concept to new sources in non-attainment areas), *cert. granted,* 103 S.Ct. 2427 (1983).

[43] *See* Committee on Environmental Decision-Making, National Research Council, II Decision-Making in the Environmental Protection Agency 45–67 (National Academy of Sciences, Washington, D.C. 1977).

mental "exfoliating" process of policy development that has followed the initial legislative breakthroughs in enacting new statutes has impeded basic changes in tools and strategies.

Over the long run it will be necessary continually to develop and adopt environmentally superior products and processes in order to maintain, much less improve, environmental quality in the face of continued economic growth. Regulatory approaches, even those aimed at "technology forcing," have resulted in diffusion and incremental development of state-of-the-art technologies but have not provided an adequate incentive for the development of fundamentally new technologies. Given constraints on the availability of funds for federal research and development, much greater use of economic-based incentives is the most promising way of stimulating the development of environmentally superior technologies.

The current administration has shown a disappointing lack of interest in such innovations, and until recently has instead devoted its principal efforts to cutting back on the vigor and enforcement of existing command and control regulation. This effort reflects the common perception in the US of a basic conflict between economic and environmental goals. This perception of conflict, fostered by some environmental groups as well as industry, is not shared by some other industrial nations, such as Japan, which see a long term community of interest between environmental and economic objectives. Better integration of these objectives in the United States will depend on wider adoption of decentralized, economic-type incentives, or upon adoption of some form of industrial and resource planning. Adoption of these alternatives is, however, remote at best.

In retrospect, it appears that the centralization of industrial process regulation at the federal level has in some respects had a deleterious impact on policy innovation. The highly detailed and complex provisions in the federal statutes have been difficult to change, creating serious problems of obsolescence. Centralization has also discouraged innovation by the states. Considerable experimentation in the states, including, for example, proposals to adopt pollution taxes, were cut short by the centralization accomplished by the Clean Air Act and the Clean Water Act. Given the current retrenchment in environmental policy in Washington, the states may play a larger role in developing new strategies for environmental programs if the commitment to environmental goals is not eroded by "competition in laxity" among states who fear that stringent controls will lead industry to invest elsewhere. States have, for example, pioneered measures such as bottle deposit schemes. The current efforts by some states, in cooperation with EPA, to promote "bubble" and transferable permit systems illustrate how innovative state programs might be accommodated within a system of federal standard setting.

b. Changes in Attitudes and Preferences

The federal structure of the governmental system in the US, the separation of powers at each level, the importance of large administrative bureaucracies, and the weakness of integrative forces all introduce strong inertial tendencies that diffuse and retard governmental responses to changes in public attitudes towards the environment. While the dramatic upsurge of public interest in environmental problems around 1970 produced a flurry of legislative and judicial initiatives, problems of administrative implementation and enforcement, the need for state and local cooperation, and the considerable autonomy enjoyed by development-minded federal agencies have delayed and diminished the realization of those initiatives. Indeed, anticipation of these problems helps explain many of the crude and very rigid "action forcing" measures in statutes such as the Clean Air Act and Clean Water Act. On the other hand, recent efforts by the administration to cut back on environmental protection policies have been resisted by the staffs of agencies with environmental protection missions, by state and local governments which place a high value on environmental quality, and by the federal courts. The multiplicity of fora with decisional responsibility affords the various actors and interests ample opportunity to block or slow changes in policy. In recent years the system as a whole has registered growing public concern with the performance of the economy. But this response has been much more marked in some parts of the system – such as the White House and OMB – than others, which maintain a steady commitment to environmental objectives. This tends to reinforce the perceived conflict between economic and environmental objectives and prevent coordinated solutions that would minimize that conflict.

X. Conclusion: Integration of Community Environmental Policy and Implications of the US Experience

A. The Integration Process in Federal Systems

1. Models of Regulation in a Federal System: Testing the Hypotheses

In Chapter I, we presented a model of regulation in a federal system and generated a number of hypotheses. The evidence examined in the intervening chapters broadly supports these hypotheses. But the evidence also shows that the model's assumptions are crude and that important qualifications are required.

The history and structure of regulation in the US and EC provide empirical support for the basic hypotheses. In both systems, centralized product regulation is more pervasive and intrusive than process regulation, which in turn is more fully established than regulation of land use and natural resources (putting to one side federal management of federally owned lands and natural resources in the US). As predicted, the degree of centralization in product regulation is comparable in the two systems (ignoring the lack of direct Community enforcement power), whereas process regulation is substantially more centralized and intrusive in the US than in the EC. Preclusion of more stringent state measures is not uncommon for product regulation, but is quite rare for process regulation.

The model's biggest defect is its failure to predict the patchy but substantial amount of process regulation in the EC. The model predicted that no such regulation would occur in a system requiring unanimous consent of member states, because those states with relatively low process standards (polluter states) would find it against their economic self-interest to agree to higher Community standards. At best, Community standards would be set at the lowest common denominator level of standards in the laxest polluter state.

This variance between prediction and experience is due to the fact that the actual process of decision in the EC is more complex than a model of economically calculating unitary actors allows. Environmental ministers and officials play a substantial role in representing member states in Community decision-making, and are likely to emphasize environmental goals even if they conflict with strictly economic calculations. Unless the matter becomes one of "high politics,"[1] their influence may be substantial. Even political leaders of "pollut-

[1] *See infra* at pp. 317–318.

er" states may personally believe that more vigorous environmental policies are socially desirable in the long term, and may therefore acquiesce in Community initiatives. The lack of direct domestic political accountability for Community decisions enlarges their freedom of action in this respect. In addition, the leading role of the Commission's environmental Directorate-General in formulating and shepherding proposed environmental directives through the policy process can not be ignored. Perhaps most important are the complex norms of reciprocity and consensus that appear to characterize relations among member states in the decisional process. These norms and associated practices may often lead a member state to acquiesce in a proposal that it would not otherwise affirmatively embrace.

On the other hand, the implementation gap that exists in the EEC may mean that agreement upon process regulation directives may be more apparent than real. To some degree, polluter states may acquiesce in environmental initiatives, giving ritual due to norms of reciprocity and consensus while foreseeing that implementation shortfalls will enable them to follow a lowest common denominator approach with relatively minor adverse domestic economic impact.

The evidence in other respects also shows a more complex pattern of motivation and interaction than the model allows. Rivalry among "polluter" and "environmental" states is an important political reality, as the PSD and nonattainment controversies in the US and the controversy over toxic water pollutants in the EC illustrate. But the distinction between "polluter" and "environmental" states is ambiguous. For example, California has some high pollution levels but generally supports stringent federal controls, particularly on automobiles. Utah has quite clean air, but in order to develop industry, it wishes to allow pollution increases beyond those permitted by the PSD increments while stopping well short of the ambient concentration levels in heavily polluted states such as California. In the Community the same kind of comparison can be made, for example, between West Germany and Ireland. Which is the "polluter" state and which the "environmental" state? Perhaps all that can be said is that economic rivalry among states is an important factor in the evolution of environmental regulation in a federal system, and that its general tendency is to shape regulation in the pattern predicted. But it may assume quite a variety of forms, as exemplified in the US struggle between eastern and western coal producing states over the extent of mandatory scrubbing of emissions from new coal-fired power plants.

In some cases, moreover, states as such do not play any active role in the integration process. For example, in the United States, federal laws preempting state regulation of automobile air pollution and certain state measures relating to toxic wastes were secured entirely by industry, although industry in this case might be viewed as a surrogate for the interests of many states.

As regards importing states, there is some evidence to support the hypothesis that such states, unconstrained by effects on industrial development and employment, will seek to impose strong product regulations in order to protect their consumers. The controls imposed by Denmark on chemicals are an example. On the other hand, in the case of automobiles there is no evidence that importing states such as Ireland or Greece are eager to impose additional controls. This circumstance probably reflects relatively low concern for environmental values and a greater concern for cost effects on consumers in such states.

In short, while the model and its hypotheses are helpful in understanding the process of regulatory integration in the US and EC, modifications in the model's assumptions are needed to approximate the actual complexity of the decisional processes and their results. At this point, however, it does not seem feasible to develop a more complex model that would generate empirically testable hypotheses.

It is also submitted that the integration theories developed by political scientists do not provide further insight into the process of regulation in federal systems, in particular in the European Community.

The neofunctionalist integration theories claim that the increasing entanglement of nation states in a network of international dependencies and institutions impairs their capability to act independently. They also claim that these entanglements – at least under certain further conditions and not necessarily in a continuous process – create a need for further cooperation and, ultimately, for supranational institutions and supranational decisionmaking.[2] In this perspective, the growth of integration is explained as an endogenous ("spillover") effect of previous steps of integration.

The critics of neofunctionalist theories maintain that the political independence of nation states is unbroken and that international systems such as the Community exercise only a loose coordination function. Integration is, in their view, confined to peripheral policy areas. Areas of "high politics," i.e. those policy areas which are considered by central policymakers as vital to the maintenance and adaptation of the national political system, to the allegiance of its citizen, and to its visibility to other nations, remain in the domain of the nation state.[3]

[2] *See* E. B. Hass, The Uniting of Europe 291 *et seq.* (Stanford Press, Palo Alto 1958); *id., The Study of Regional Integration: Reflections on the Joy and Anguish of Pretheorizing*, 24 International Organization 607 (No. 4, autumn 1970: special issue on "Regional Integration – Theory and Research," L. Lindberg & S. Scheingold eds.); L. Lindberg, The Political Dynamics of European Economic Integration (Stanford Press, Palo Alto 1963); L. Lindberg & S. Scheingold, Europe's Would-Be Polity: Patterns of Change in the European Community 117 *et seq.*, 141 *et seq.* (Prentice Hall, Englewood Cliffs 1970); Schmitter, *Three Neofunctional Hypotheses about International Integration*, 23 International Organization 161 (1969); *id., A Revised Theory of Regional Integration*, 24 International Organization 836 *et seq.* (1970); J. Nye, Comparing Integration Processes (Carnegie Paper, Geneva 1969); A. Etzioni, Political Unification 102 (Holt, Rinehart &Winston, New York 1965).

[3] S. Hoffmann, Gulliver's Troubles or the Setting of American Foreign Policy (McGraw-Hill Book Co., New York 1969) [cited following the German translation: Die Zukunft des internationalen Systems 376 *et seq.* (Bertelsmann Universitätsverlag, Bielefeld 1970)]; G. Zellentin, Intersystemare Beziehungen in Europa 183 *et seq.* (Sijthoff, Leyden 1970); J. Galtung, The European Community: A Superpower in the Making (Universitesforlaget, Oslo 1972).

It has been argued that the Community's development as a whole provides examples to support both theories,[4] and that this is also true of Community environmental policy.[5] From the perspective of the neofunctionalist integration theories, the development of a Community environmental policy could be interpreted as a function of the interrelation between already existing economic integration and the emergence of a new problem closely related to the economy. Since environmental problems arise to a large degree as a side effect of economic activities – if understood in the broad sense of including consumption activities – the existing economic integration required a concomitant integration of environmental policy in order to avoid the establishment of new barriers to trade or new distortions of competition. However, the fact that Community environmental policy, through an incremental process of extending the scope and objectives of directives, has been largely emancipated from constraints of trade and competition policy and has developed as a separate policy in its own right indicates that environmental policies are not simply a function of preexisting integration. They themselves represent a new form of integration, which can not be fully explained by the economic logic of previous integrative steps. Accordingly, neofunctionalist theories, at least in their present form, can not adequately explain the history of Community integration in the environmental area.

Arguing from the perspective of the critics of the neofunctionalist theories and using the distinction between high and low politics, environmental policymaking would normally belong to low rather than high politics. While complete transfer of competences for environmental policymaking from member states to the Community would be considered a severe encroachment on the central policy functions of the national policy system, the transfer of more or less isolated, narrowly defined competences in the field of the environment does not normally meet with much objection, although it is associated with some loss of democratic legitimacy. It is only in rare cases that environmental issues become so highly politicized that supranational decisionmaking, even in the attenuated form practiced within the Community, is not accepted by one or more member states. This politicization may reflect the reservation of a functionally related policy area to national decisionmaking (such as energy policy), a strong sense for the preservation of national sovereignty (such as in the case of transboundary pollution or accidents), or day to day politics (a single issue becoming so controversial that a transfer of decisionmaking competences is unacceptable).[6]

[4] Häckel, *Theoretische Aspekte der regionalen Verflechtung*, in Regionale Verflechtung der Bundesrepublik Deutschland, Schriften des Forschungsinstituts der Deutschen Gesellschaft für Politik, vol. 33, at 15 *et seq.* (Springer Verlag, München, Wien 1973).

[5] H. Bungarten, Umweltpolitik in Westeuropa 157 *et seq.* (Europa Union Verlag, Bonn 1978).

[6] H. von der Groeben & H. Möller, Möglichkeiten und Grenzen einer Europäischen Union, Volume I: Die Europäische Union als Prozess 392–393 (Nomos Verlag, Baden-Baden 1980).

The siting of nuclear power plants and major chemical plants in border areas and the salinity of the Rhine are or were such politicized issues, and it is not surprising that these issues have seriously impeded further progress of the integration process in environmental policy. However, these issues are not typical of Community environmental policy and, with the exception of siting nuclear power plants, agreement on them has ultimately been reached.

Nevertheless, the distinction between high and low politics appears to have little predictive or analytical value. Environmental policy is intimately related to competition, distribution, economic, and labor market policies. Its character as positive rather than negative intervention[7] moves it into the center of political and societal controversies over fundamental issues of economic and social policy in many member states.[8] Issues such as SO_2 control, toxic water pollution, and automobile emissions are of great economic and political significance. But this has not precluded agreement within the Community.
There is a tendency to retrospectively label issues on which Community agreement is not reached as "high politics," and label issues on which there is agreement as "low politics." This approach, of course, robs the distinction of all explanatory power.

2. Common Institutional Factors in the EC and the US

The model developed in Chapter I also fails to adequately incorporate some common institutional factors which experience shows have shaped environmental policy in the EC and the US.

In both systems, the nature of environmental problems is such as to make court litigation, whether privately or publicly initiated, relatively ineffective and inappropriate as a "front line" response. The limited capacities of courts in dealing with technical issues; the expense of litigation and the fact that environmental quality is a collective good; and the need for ongoing monitoring and supervision all dictate that environmental problems must largely be addressed through administrative systems of regulation or resource management. Thus, measures to harmonize private or public tort law, nuisance, and so on have little to contribute to effective integration of environmental policy.

In both systems, the type of environmental problem to be controlled determines, to a large extent, the type of regulatory approach that must be employed.

Where products, such as automobiles, are sold in integrated markets, uniform regulation is most feasible, and manufacturers have substantial incentives to favor such regulation. Where the environmental significance of a product, such as automobile air pollution, can be expressed in consistent, quantitative terms (such as emissions per mile of operation), uniform standards are

[7] H. von der Groeben & H. Möller, *supra* note 6, at 383–384, 391; H. Bungarten, *supra* note 5, at 224; Krämer & Rummel, *Hindernisse und Voraussetzungen für die Europäische Union*, in 1976 Aus Politik und Zeitgeschichte (Supplement B3 to Das Parlament) at 10 *et seq.*

[8] *See* the authors cited *supra* note 7.

feasible. Where consistent, quantitative measures of environmental significance are not feasible, e. g. pesticides, case by case screening of products will be necessary, but such screening can be performed centrally for all products.

Uniform regulation is less feasible for industrial processes. Uniform technology-based controls may be economically inappropriate in light of varying natural conditions because they require excessive controls in relation to environmental benefits in some areas, e. g. ocean outfalls in the US and UK, and inadequate controls in others. Uniform environmental standards may be inappropriate because of wide regional variations in the cost of achieving such standards, the desirability of maintaining some areas of exceptionally high environmental quality, and fear of "competitive distortions." On the other hand, it is very difficult to reach agreement on a system of non-uniform environmental quality standards. Some combination of the two approaches is often preferable to either alone.

Uniform measures are least feasible in natural resource management (including land use planning, and protection of wilderness and wildlife) and where it is necessary to regulate the activities of large numbers of individuals. Such regulation involves government functions that are strongly localized in response to variations in local conditions and traditions. Centralized or integrated uniform regulation would involve substantial diseconomies of scale.

3. Basic Institutional Differences

The only institutional difference between the EC and US recognized in the model developed in Chapter I is that Community legislation requires unanimous consent (a premise which, as we have seen, requires qualification), whereas the US employs a form of majority rule. While this difference has been important, experience shows that there are additional basic differences in institutional arrangements and history in the Community and the US which have powerfully shaped the evolution of environmental policy in the two systems.

Federal environmental policies in the US arose after far-reaching economic and political integration had already occurred. Economic integration made central product regulation efficient, and created a demand by environmental states and some industries for central regulation in order to prevent economic rivalry, "competitive distortions," and weak state standards as a result of state by state regulation. Political integration provided the foundation for federal implementation and enforcement of environmental policies through federal administrative agencies and courts. The federal lawmaking structure, which includes a nationally elected President, direct representation in Congress, an expansive legislative authority over commerce, a fully developed federal court system, and a federal bureaucracy with direct enforcement powers, has facilitated centralization of environmental policy in the US. (The principle of state representation in Congress and functional constraints on implementation and enforcement by central authorities have, however, limited centralization.) Because far-reaching economic and political integration had already occurred by the time environmental issues became important, the dominant motivation of federal environmental initiatives has been to correct weak, inadequate state regulation resulting from economic rivalry and inability to realize scale economies rather than to remove barriers to trade or promote integration.

Environmental policy in the US is more extensive than in the EC because the US federal government enjoys important resources and powers which the EC lacks. These include the federal government's ownership of one third of the nation's land and an even larger share of its important natural resources; its formidable taxing and spending powers; and its licensing authority over major industrial facilities. EC authorities do not exercise comparable powers.

In the EC,[9] the development and implementation of a common environmental policy has been constrained by the Community's origin as an economic institution, the differences in language and culture among member states, the politically insecure and limited definition of the Community's legislative powers, the lawmaking structure dominated by the Council and representatives of member states rather than the European interest, the lack of a fully developed Community court system, and the lack of a bureaucracy with direct implementation and enforcement authority. The development of common environmental policy is also constrained by the stagnation and even decline of integration in other areas, and especially by the decline of decisional supranationalism.[10] On the other hand, environmental policy is itself a factor of "substantive integration," influencing the direction and strength of the integration process. It has given European integration a new impulse,[11] although simple expansion of Community policy into a new area such as environmental protection does not fully compensate for the lack of overall substantive and institutional deepening of integration.[12]

These differences between the US and the EC may influence the evolution of particular policy issues. Consider, for example, the issue of environmental diversity. From an environmental point of view, it may sometimes be desirable to balance environmental and economic goals ensuring exceptionally high environmental quality in pristine or scenic areas and accepting lower quality in other areas. In other instances (for example, when protection of public health is the dominant concern) it may be appropriate to have a uniform level of environmental quality, which implies sharply different levels of source control in different regions, depending on natural factors and the existing degree of economic development. But integration is viewed by many in the EC as synonymous with uniformity in control requirements in order to eliminate barriers to

[9] For the following section *see generally* P. J. SLOT, TECHNICAL AND ADMINISTRATIVE OBSTACLES TO TRADE IN THE EEC 153 (Sijthoff, Leyden 1975); H. W. ROTH, FREIER WARENVERKEHR UND STAATLICHE REGELUNGSGEWALT IN EINEM GEMEINSAMEN MARKT 337 (C. H. Beck,München 1977).

[10] *Contra*, KAISER, *Grenzen der EG-Zuständigkeit*, 15 EUROPARECHT 97 *et seq.* (1980) (in this connection speaking of expansion and restriction of integration).

[11] H. BUNGARTEN, *supra* note 5, at 175.

[12] *Cf.* KAISER, *supra* note 10

trade and "competitive distortions." The question then arises whether the US can tolerate and achieve greater diversity in environmental standards and controls than the EC because its environmental policy is not linked with the process of political and economic integration.[13]

Due to the enormous differences in language, culture, and attitudes, there may be a greater need for harmonization in Europe.[14] However, harmonization measures tend to be centralist in character, such as the expansion of the "negative commerce clause" doctrine following the *Cassis de Dijon* decision. This tendency may reflect the lack of a federal tradition in most member states. Since the majority of member states are highly centralized, it may well be that Community policymakers coming from these states simply transpose centralist policy concepts to the higher unity and disregard the great potential for diversity existing in developed federal systems for shaping the division of powers between the Community and its member states.[15]

B. Environmental Policy and the Integration Process in the EC

1. The Degree of Integration Achieved by EC Environmental Policy

The European Community's environmental policy has been more successful than one would have expected at its beginning in 1973. Since adoption of the first environmental program, the network of Community environmental law has steadily expanded so that by now more than forty directives or amendments have been adopted, and twenty-five other regulatory texts, including recommendations, resolutions and decisions, have been issued. Many of the directives adopted by the Council, and in some cases by the Commission, cover a very narrow field of environmental protection or are of a technical nature. However, the Community has also adopted a number of quite important directives, e. g. the 1973 amendment to the motor vehicle emissions directive, the framework directive of 1976 on the aquatic environment, the bird protection directive of 1978, the sixth amendment of 1979 to the hazardous substances directive, the SO_2 limit values directive of 1980, the major accidents directive of 1982, and the industrial installations directive of 1984.

Some environmental policy issues, such as regulation of widely marketed products, are particularly closely linked to economic policy and interstate commerce. In these cases, the Community is almost invariably considered the appropriate forum for development of a policy, although these problems often transcend the geographical scope of the Community. However, it is remark-

[13] H. W. Roth, *supra* note 9, at 339.

[14] Slot, *Handelsbarrières, Nationaal recht en Europees recht*, 28 Sociaal-Economische Wetgeving 233, 262 (1980); Krislov, Ehlermann & Weiler, *Political Organs and the Decision-Making Process in the U.S. and the European Communities*, at § VII.D.4, in Integration Through Law, Vol. 1, Book 2, at n. 103 ("the rigidities of harmonization appear almost monomaniacal").

[15] This is the interpretation by Slot, *supra* note 14, at 261, of *Cassis de Dijon*.

able that the original preoccupation of Community environmental policy with the elimination of barriers to trade and hence with product related requirements has largely been replaced by the development of environmental policy in its own right. The most important reason for addressing environmental problems in a common or harmonized fashion is no longer that differing national regulations compromise the Community policy of eliminating technical obstacles to trade; rather, it is the interest of member states in an environmental problem as such (although this interest is not necessarily directed at the environmentally most serious problems). This does not mean that economic considerations such as the elimination of technical barriers to trade or distortions of competition have become irrelevant. They are an important factor limiting the scope and direction of Community activities. They also determine the acceptance of a proposal by member states, the length of a particular decision-making process, and the willingness of member states to implement the directive.

Within these limits, it is now accepted throughout the Community that there is a need for public intervention to protect the environment and that for a number of environmental problems the Community is the most appropriate decisionmaking level. There is no fundamental divergence of opinion as to the basic strategies to be employed in controlling pollution. There is common agreement on the use of regulatory controls rather than litigation or the wide use of charges or other economic incentives. Furthermore, critics of particular measures, such as some industrial associations, are convinced of the general need for Community environmental policy.[16]

In important respects, however, environmental policy has fallen well short of complete integration. First, the pragmatic approach used by the Commission in making policy proposals has given Community environmental law a patchwork character. Apart from a framework directive on wastes, which covers the whole area of wastes but whose provisions are rather vague, no single environmental sector is comprehensively regulated by the Community. The predominant emphasis is on water pollution and toxic substances. The important field of air pollution has been neglected, although the health and environmental effects of inadequate regulation as well as the impacts of divergent national regulation on competition are no less than in the case of water pollution. The piecemeal procedure of the Commission for proposing new legislation has resulted in directives in areas where harmonization is a low priority, while neglecting other areas which need a considerable amount of harmonization. Some water quality measures, especially the bathing, fish, and shellfish water directives, were not really mandated by urgent needs for a harmonized solution, whereas too little work has been done in other areas, especially air pollution. With respect to product regulation, regulation of new products is relatively comprehensive, but major gaps exist in the regulation of existing products.

[16] *Cf.* von Moltke & Haigh, *EC – Major Issues for 1981*, 7 Envt'l Pol'y & L. 23 (1980).

Second, there is a considerable political and regulatory implementation gap in Community environmental policy. The deadlines set for compliance in the environmental programs and the deadlines in framework directives for the adoption of new policy proposals are almost invariably exceeded. Because of the complexity of the Community decisionmaking process as well as budgetary constraints, these deadlines have proven totally unrealistic. As a result, the third environmental program to a great extent represents the continuation of work already begun or envisaged by the previous environmental programs.

In 1980, the Commission issued a comprehensive and remarkably frank document on the present state of work on environmental affairs.[17] In this report the Commission admits that it has been much more successful in controlling water pollution than air pollution. It stresses the principle of prevention and defines a number of tools for implementing a preventive policy. The Commission makes it clear that, apart from the pre-market testing of new chemicals, the preventive policy is still in its incipiency. It is characteristic of the low degree of public attention given to the development of Community environmental policy that this document has received little notice.[18]

Third, with the exception of some directives such as the sixth amendment of the toxic substances directive and the PCB directive, Community environmental policy tends to follow protection levels already existing in several member states and does not generate innovative strategies for implementing harmonized policy objectives. On the other hand, the common assertion that Community environmental policy is confined to lowest common denominator solutions is not entirely justified. Environmental states do not sacrifice their national solutions to Community harmonization. In case of sharply conflicting views among member states, agreement is often made possible by resort to vague compromise formulae, simple harmonization of principles of pollution control, or the technique of minimum harmonization. This allows environmental states to retain progressive solutions, while polluter states may have to stiffen their environmental controls, but not necessarily to the degree existing in environmental states.

This process of compromise, however, is threatened when an existing Community product directive needs to be modernized. In such a situation, polluter states have a stronger bargaining position than in the initial adoption of a product directive. In the absence of a preexisting directive, polluter states

[17] Commission of the European Communities, Progress Made in Connection with the Environment Action Programme and Assessment of the Work Done to Implement It, Communication from the Commission to the Council, DOC COM(80)222 final (7 May 1980) [hereinafter cited as Progress Report 1980].

[18] Besides the European Parliament, which has passed a resolution on the progress report (Resolution of 20 Nov. 1981 on the state of the Community's environment, OJ No. C 327, 14 Dec. 1981, p. 83; EP Doc. 1-276/81), only the subcommittee on environmental affairs of the British House of Lords' Select Committee on the European Community has conducted a general inquiry to evaluate the state of Community environmental policy and contribute to the formulation of a national position on its future direction. *See* von Moltke & Haigh, *supra* note 16, at 27.

have an incentive to agree to harmonized initiatives in order to preclude enforcement by environmental states of stiff standards to exclude imports from polluter states. Once a directive is adopted, however, environmental states are barred from unilateral introduction of stiffer controls. Accordingly, polluter states have no economic incentive to agree to modernization of the relevant directive, and only when there are paramount environmental reasons are they likely to agree to an amendment. Legal obsolescence of existing directives may occur for various reasons, e. g. new scientific knowledge as to health and environmental hazards associated with a particular pollutant, development of new technology, failure of a particular strategy to achieve its objectives, or simply the emergence of new preferences and values. In most of these cases, the necessary adjustment of the directive must be sought within the same cumbersome process required for adoption of new Community directives, although qualified majority vote is substituted for unanimity in the case of adaptation of existing environmental directives to technical progress. But even this short-cut procedure, which is limited to technical adjustments, does not effectively compensate for a deficiency inherent in the Community decisionmaking process, namely that there are fewer incentives for amending an existing product directive than for adopting a new product directive.

Fourth, the linkage of environmental policy with other areas of Community policy has as yet been relatively weak.[19] The report of 1980 on the progress made in implementing the environmental program and the third environmental program now identify this as a priority area.[20] The enormous task of ensuring consistency between agricultural and environmental policy, which has proven difficult even at the national level, is still in its incipiency in the Community.[21] There is also little integration between environmental policy and transport policy. The Commission's green paper on transport infrastructure[22] mentions environmental concerns in its programmatic part but ignores the subject entirely when it comes to concrete measures. In both policy areas the Commission's Directorate-General on Environment, Consumer Protection, and Nuclear Safety suffers the further handicap that there is no explicit authority in the Treaties to compel other Directorates-General to consider environmental effects.[23] It is remarkable that the Commission proposal on environmental impact assessment for national projects does not provide an equivalent procedure for assessing the environmental effects of Community projects and pro-

19 *See* von Moltke & Haigh, *supra* note 16, at 29; Institute for European Environmental Policy, Annual Report 1982, at 5 *et seq.* (Bonn 1983); P. Kromarek, New Trends in Community Environmental Policy, European Parliament, PE 74.086/Ann. I, p. 14 *et seq.* (1981).

20 Progress Report 1980, *supra* note 17, at 8; Third Environmental Program, OJ No. C 46, 17 Feb. 1983, p 1.

21 Within the purely national context, a major difficulty stems from the fact that agriculture is the responsibility of a separate, "mission-oriented" administration, and the environmental administration normally has at best a right of consultation.

22 DOC COM(79)550.

23 Von Moltke & Haigh, *supra* note 16, at 29.

grams. It remains to be seen whether, once the directive is adopted, it will lead to pressure on the Commission to assess the environmental effects of its own programs,[24] at least in areas where Community legislation mandates consideration of environmental effects, such as under the bird directive and the directive on farming in mountainous and other less favored areas.

Finally, Community environmental policy has failed to achieve full integration because of national differences in the effectiveness of implementation of environmental directives and because of the lack of effective Community control over such national implementation.

2. Legal and Institutional Constraints to Environmental Integration

The failure of the Community to achieve full integration in the area of environmental policy is due to a number of legal and institutional constraints. Contrary to what legal writers have often argued, in practice legal constraints are much less important than institutional ones. The narrow scope of legislative powers granted under Articles 100 and 235 of the EEC Treaty has not severely impeded the development of Community environmental policy. There has been little controversy raised by member state executive branches over problems of legislative competence and only relatively weak resistance by national parliaments to the expansion of the Community into environmental policy. In the long run, the interpretation of Art. 100 may parallel that of the US commerce clause.

It may be true that Art. 100 alone does not allow development of a comprehensive, long term Community environmental policy because under this Treaty provision environmental protection is authorized only incidentally to harmonization designed to abolish barriers to trade or distortions of competition. However, Art. 235 has been extensively used to remedy this shortcoming. The fact that Community directives have emphasized environmental problems related to economic activities, and that the preventive approach stressed in the second and third environmental programs has not been sufficiently implemented, can not clearly be attributed to legal constraints.

From an academic point of view the legal situation of Community environmental policy is, nevertheless, unsatisfactory. A "clean" solution is to amend Art. 2 of the Treaty to include environmental protection as a Community objective. Proposals of this kind were made as early as 1972.[25]

[24] In this sense *see id.*

[25] *See* European Parliament, Legal Committee, EP Doc. 9/72, at 104–114; E. Grabitz & C. Sasse, Competence of the European Communities for Environmental Policy (Erich Schmidt Verlag, Berlin 1977); H. Steiger, Competence of the European Parliament for Environmental Policy (Erich Schmidt Verlag, Berlin, 1977); F. Behrens, Rechtsgrundlagen der Umweltpolitik der Europäischen Gemeinschaften 298 *et seq.* (Erich Schmidt Verlag, Berlin 1976); H. von der Groeben & E. J. Mestmäcker, Verfassung oder Technokratie für Europa 115 (Scriptor Verlag, Kronberg 1974); European Parliament Resolution of 14 Feb. 1984 on a draft Treaty for a European Union, Art. 9 § 1, Art. 59, OJ No. C 77, 19 March 1984, p. 27.

The prospects for adoption of these proposals are not good. Any amendment of the Treaty would raise fundamental problems concerning the structure of Community institutions, and in particular the role of the European Parliament.[26] The Community and the member states are not at present in a position to take on such decisions. They prefer to "muddle through" and hope to achieve in that way further growth of the Community. Seen in this context, the development of common environmental policy is typical of the Community's institutional development. It is also doubtful whether the objectives of a common environmental policy could be fixed in the Treaty in such a way that the ensuing loss of national competences could be calculated and legitimized.

Even if the Treaty were amended, it is unlikely that Community environmental policy would develop differently. As long as the institutional framework of the Community remains unchanged, as long as there is no real forum for the formulation of the European interest, and as long as national interests prevail in identifying and developing candidates for harmonization, Community environmental law is bound to reflect member state preferences and their perception of the utility of common solutions as compared to national ones. Therefore, changes in the institutional structure of the Community more fundamental than the simple insertion of environmental policy as a Community objective are necessary.[27]

The directive has proven to be a suitable legislative instrument for implementing Community environmental policy. It has enormous flexibility ranging from mere coordination of member state policies via harmonization of environmental protection objectives and principles to the setting of standards and associated measurement methods. Given this flexibility and the extension of the direct effect doctrine to directives, there is no reason to believe that the availability of regulations as a legislative technique for Community environmental policy would result in a higher degree of harmonization. In the political practice of the Community, Commission proposals for detailed regulation have sometimes been rejected by the Council in favor of lowest common denominator harmonization of environmental protection principles or coordina-

[26] Therefore the Commission has always declared that the existing competences were sufficient. *See* Written question of 17 April 1973 by Mr. Jahn, OJ No. C 89, 25 Oct. 1973, p. 5; of 27 September 1977 by Mr. Jahn, OJ No. C 311, 27 Dez. 1977, p. 8. *See also* H. BUNGARTEN, *supra* note 5, at 229.

[27] For proposals *see* Report of the Working Party Examining the Problem of the Enlargement of the Powers of the European Parliament (Vedel Report), BULL. EC Suppl. 4-1972; The European Union, Report by L. Tindemans to the European Communities, BULL. EC Suppl. 1-1976; REPORT ON EUROPEAN INSTITUTIONS: PRESENTED BY THE COMMITTEE OF THREE TO THE EUROPEAN COUNCIL, OCT. 1979 (B. BIESHEUVEL, E. DELL & R. MARJOLIN, Council of the European Communities, Brussels 1980); H. VON DER GROEBEN & H. MÖLLER, *supra* note 6, at 209 *et seq.*; The Institutional System of the Community: Restoring the Balance (Commission of the European Communities), BULL. EC Suppl. 3-1982; European Union, Report of the Commission to the European Council, DOC COM (83) 723 final; Draft Treaty for a European Union, *supra* note 25.

tion of member state policies. However, there is nothing in the history of Community environmental policy that supports the view of critics that such phenomena reflect deficiencies of the directive as a legislative instrument for environmental policymaking. Rather, they reflect the fact that for political reasons the member states often can not agree on more extensive harmonization. Availability of the regulation as a legislative instrument would not change the political outcome.

The real causes of the bottleneck in Community environmental policy are several. They are: the complexity and slowness of the decisionmaking process, with its many levels of interest presentation, interest accommodation, and decisionmaking; the systematic filtering and distortion of interests in formulation of national positions with respect to policy initiatives; the predominance of national interest; the lack of a forum to formulate a European interest; and the importance of intergovernmental decisionmaking.

An additional disincentive for harmonization may be the European Court of Justice's intervention in national regulation through enforcement of "negative commerce clause" principles. Theoretically, extension of the approach taken in the *Cassis de Dijon* decision[28] could promote integration of environmental product regulation because free access of products from polluter states to the markets of environmental states gives environmental states a strong incentive to urge harmonized solutions. But the *Cassis de Dijon* approach simultaneously removes the incentive of polluter states to agree to such solutions. The political experience of the Community shows that progressive national solutions often set the pace for the Community solution. National diversity can accordingly be a force for integration. Compelling negative uniformity by dismantling national controls may therefore have a counter-productive effect with regard to environmental protection.[29] In evaluating the potential impact of *Cassis de Dijon*, however, it must be considered that the Community had already reached a high degree of harmonization for products before that decision was issued. As a practical matter, therefore, the impact of *Cassis de Dijon* will be limited to existing chemicals, the one area where Community regulation is still rather patchy, and even there member states may be able to justify restrictive national policies on health and safety grounds.

3. Environmental Policy and Substantive Approfondissement[30]

The expansion of the Community into environmental protection represents development of a kind of common policy not provided for by the Treaty. Al-

[28] European Court of Justice, case 120/78, Rewe-Zentrale-AG v. Bundesmonopolverwaltung für Branntwein (*Cassis de Dijon*), [1979] ECR 649.

[29] In this sense *see* VON MOLTKE, ***Europäische Umweltpolitik***, 2 ZEITSCHRIFT FÜR UMWELTPOLITIK 77, 82 *et seq.* (1979); WEIDNER & KNOEPFEL, ***Implementationschancen der EG-Richtlinie zur SO_2-Luftreinhaltepolitik***, 4 ZEITSCHRIFT FÜR UMWELTPOLITIK 27, 64 (1981). H. W. ROTH, ***supra*** note 9, at 327 also objects to complete elimination of technical barriers to trade because of the loss of innovative capacity.

[30] *Approfondissement* is the French word for deepening. The expression "substantive ap-

though Community environmental policy can arguably be based on a "dynamic" interpretation of the Preamble and Articles 2, 100, and 235 of the EEC Treaty, it is clear that the framers of the Treaty had a rather narrow vision of a common market as a primarily economic institution and never anticipated that the Community could become involved in environmental protection as such. The Community's initial decision to expand its activities into environmental protection therefore has a constitutional character.

The further development of Community environmental policy following adoption of the first environmental program shows that, despite divergences of opinion as to the exact scope of Community powers, there has been no serious challenge to the new common policy. Of course, as compared with agriculture, the degree of Europeanization of environmental policy is still relatively low. Using the scale of one to seven developed by Lindberg and Scheingold to measure the degree of substantive Europeanization of a policy,[31] before adoption of the first environmental program Community environmental policy could be rated at two, meaning the very beginning of Community involvement. At present a three rating would seem appropriate: there is substantial Community involvement, but national regulation still clearly dominates. On the other hand, more progress has been made in environmental policy than in other areas where the Community has a clear Treaty mandate to act – such as transportation and the free movement of capital, or where the Community has for many years been attempting to develop or implement a common policy – such as monetary union, regional policy, and consumer policy.

On the whole, the development of common environmental policy has become an important contribution to the overall integration process.[32] This contribution is mainly one of substantive approfondissement. The expansion of the Community into a new policy area not covered by the Treaty and the continuous growth of Community environmental law have given new impulses to the integration process. Development of the Community environmental policy does not fully compensate for the stagnation or even decline in older policy areas for which a clear Treaty mandate exists. However, it evidences the vitality of the Community as a forum for addressing novel problems for which common solutions are needed.

The contribution of Community environmental policy towards strengthening Community institutions and decisional supranationalism is less. Although in the field of environmental policy the Commission has retained much of its

profondissement" is used by J. Weiler, Supranationalism Revisited – Retrospective and Prospective, EUI Working Paper No. 2, at 27, to refer to expansion of Community activity into new areas and to the expansion of supranational decisionmaking.

[31] L. Lindberg & S. Scheingold, *supra* note 2, at 71.

[32] H. Bungarten, *supra* note 5, at 175; von Moltke & Haigh, *supra* note 16, at 23. The statement by H. von der Groeben & H. Möller, *supra* note 6, at 384, that Community environmental policy did not contribute to growth of the system is obviously untenable if one defines, as the authors do (at 345), this notion to encompass both institutional growth and extension of the scope of the Community.

original function of initiating new policy proposals, the overall decline of decisional supranationalism and the return to intergovernmental decisionmaking have also left their marks on environmental policymaking. As elsewhere, the Council, as representative of member state interests, is the Community's central decisionmaking body. It offers a forum for member state bureaucracies and also indirectly for some interest groups to bargain over a particular proposal in order to adjust it to national interests.

It has been suggested that the high degree of legal integration achieved by the jurisprudence of the European Court of Justice through the principles of direct effect, supremacy, and preemption may have dysfunctional effects on decisional supranationalism.[33] Experience with environmental policy does not support this hypothesis. The growing role of the member states in Community decisionmaking is reflected in the Council, the Committee of Permanent Representatives, and joint Commission/member state committees such as the waste management committee and the various committees for adjusting directives to technical progress. But this development is not primarily a response to the form of directives' legal effect (direct effect/supremacy or simple state obligation). It is rather a response to the economic and political importance and complexity of the substantive policies and strategies at issue. It is not so much legal integration, but rather the substantive integration of highly complex interventionist policies, such as environmental policy, that has brought with it a diminution of decisional supranationalism.[34]

The increasing specificity of many environmental directives has also stimulated a greater national role. To the extent that the margin of discretion normally granted member states in implementing a directive is shrinking towards zero, member states have a vital interest in influencing relevant policy proposals as early as possible. This factor may also explain the dislike of the British House of Lords for Community environmental law.

4. Effects of Community Environmental Policy on Economic Integration

The emergence of national environmental policies in the seventies threatened the progress towards economic integration achieved in the Community. National environmental regulation erected new barriers to intra-Community trade in widely marketed products, sometimes without real environmental justification or at least without due consideration of the European interest.[35] The intervention of the European Court of Justice in *Cassis de Dijon* and the line of cases following this landmark decision illustrates how seriously the challenge of the new interventionism is seen.[36] "Positive" harmonization of product related national environmental regulations through Community directives is an alternative response to this new challenge. Arguably, it is better suit-

[33] In this sense *see* the suggestion of J. Weiler, *supra* note 30, at 44–45.
[34] In the same sense *see id.* at 43.
[35] H. W. Roth, *supra* note 9, at 337 *et seq.*
[36] *See supra* note 28.

ed to the exigencies of environmental policy than the simple ("negative") abolition of national regulation by judicial intervention.

5. Effects of Community Environmental Policy on National Policies

The most obvious impact of Community environmental policy on national policies is that every new environmental directive amounts to a transfer of legislative competence to the Community from member states because the principle of supremacy of Community law bars them from making or at least applying new national law inconsistent with the relevant directive. The European Court of Justice has not yet held that a Community directive, by virtue of occupying a whole area of environmental policy, preempts national legislation not in direct conflict with the directive. But the Court has given the principle of supremacy a broad interpretation. As a result, a directive regulating the production and sale of a product might be held to limit member states' power to legislate with respect to the use of that product.

The reach of the supremacy principle has been extended by the commitment of the member states under the information/standstill agreement of 1973 to inform the Commission of any draft legislative, regulatory, or administrative measures of a binding nature. Although, as past experience shows, member states can frustrate the objectives of this agreement by reporting only drafts in a very advanced form and by flooding the Commission with a huge workload, the process has generated a number of directives and may therefore rightly be called an expression of "anticipatory" supremacy. That opponents of initiated national regulation invoke the threat of Community directives as an argument against speedy implementation of the relevant proposals has tended to compensate for the short time limits of the information/standstill agreement.[37]

Some effects of environmental directives on national environmental policy are subtle and difficult to assess. For example, some member states have found Community proposals not yet adopted by the Council useful as levers to push through a policy proposal which, because of internal political pressures, might have been difficult to implement in a purely national context.[38] The confrontation of national policymakers with new regulatory initiatives at the Community level may also have the effect of reorienting the national thinking on environmental priorities and regulating strategies and influencing national policies in areas not covered by those initiatives.[39] On the other hand, the Com-

[37] RAT VON SACHVERSTÄNDIGEN FÜR UMWELTFRAGEN, UMWELTGUTACHTEN 1978, at No. 1665 (Kohlhammer, Stuttgart 1978).

[38] VON MOLTKE & HAIGH, *supra* note 16, at 23, 24.

[39] This is the conclusion of a study on the impact of EEC environmental policy on the United Kingdom by N. HAIGH, EEC ENVIRONMENTAL POLICY AND BRITAIN — AN ESSAY AND A HANDBOOK (Environmental Data Services Ltd., London 1984). The study found, for example, that although only twenty-seven beaches in the UK were officially designated under the bathing water directive, the standards of the directive are used by local authorities as guide standards in framing measures with respect to beaches not designated.

munity can provide a "back door" method for adopting measures that would not be adopted by national parliaments. A good example is the SO_2 limit values directive which contains quite a number of structural elements, in particular the concept of regionalizing air pollution control policy, which had been proposed for national adoption in 1977 by the Federal Government of West Germany,[40] but then withdrawn due to stiff opposition by the Länder and most interest groups.

C. Assessment of Community Environmental Policy, Opportunities for Improvement, and Implications of the US Experience

1. Normative Assessment of Community Environmental Policy and Desirability of Further Integration

The establishment of Community environmental policy as a kind of common policy is in itself an important contribution to the European integration process. The emergence of Community environmental policy is in marked contrast to the Community's overall development. At a time when the Community has experienced a considerable decline in decisional supranationalism and stagnation in the development of other common policies, environmental policy has found a niche in the institutional structure of the Community where it is developing to an extent never expected when the first environmental program was adopted. Nevertheless, the contribution of the common environmental policy to European integration must also be evaluated in light of its substantive contribution to environmental protection. Whatever the intrinsic value of integration in its present inchoate state, the price paid for European integration may be too high if it is associated with unsatisfactory substantive solutions.

In this regard the tendency of Community environmental policy toward conservative solutions can not be ignored. Another serious problem, at least with respect to product regulation, is the lack of incentives for amending a directive in case of obsolescence. However, Community environmental policy can not be realistically assessed from the perspective of a hypothetical legislature that generates optimal solutions. The thrust of Community environmental policy is not to create entirely new solutions, but rather to generalize existing national solutions by expanding their application from one or several to all member states. For polluter states, Community environmental policy often means progress of a kind that either they would never have achieved by acting independently or would not have achieved as quickly. Also, environmental states do not normally sacrifice their solutions to European integration. To overcome sharp conflicts of interest among member states, the principle that stricter national law is not preempted by a directive has been adopted in the

[40] Bundestags-Drucksache 8/2751 (11 April 1979); *see* Soell, *Aktuelle Probleme und Tendenzen im Immissionsschutzrecht*, 13 Zeitschrift für Rechtspolitik 105 (1980).

case of process regulation. This principle is expressly stated in many process oriented directives and implicitly underlies many others. This approach establishes a Community "floor" while permitting member states with strong environmental preferences, special problems, or innovative solutions to go further.

However, this strategy of minimum harmonization has its limitations. The first environmental program states that environmental progress at the national level must be realized in a form which does not compromise the functioning of the Common Market. Stricter national law for products is inconsistent with this principle. Although sometimes allowed, as in the lead directive, it is contrary to the traditional idea of harmonization underlying Art. 100 of the EEC Treaty. In the case of process requirements, stricter national law does not so clearly endanger the functioning of the Common Market. However, there are often serious political obstacles to the adoption of more stringent national environmental measures. Such measures are likely to be opposed both by the industry concerned, which anticipates a loss of competitive position, and by national executive authorities, for whom employment and economic growth have gained higher priority. Thus the freedom of member states to go beyond Community minimums may be sharply constrained by economic factors. However, minimal harmonization at least allows environmental states to agree to a directive while retaining existing progressive solutions. All in all, Community environmental policy has meant at least relative progress in addressing environmental problems.

Since each member state can be a "polluter" or an "environmental" state with respect to a particular environmental problem, involvement in the process of Community environmental policymaking means a continuous cross fertilization of European policymakers with progressive national solutions. Furthermore, Community environmental policy is also a learning process in that solutions either rejected or not seriously considered by a particular member state may cause it to rethink its position when the same solutions are proposed as part of a future directive or an amendment to an existing directive. This process of reconsideration is inherent in the technique of alternative harmonization because a member state is continually confronted with the experience of other member states under an alternative available strategy, especially under directives that call for a periodic review of the equivalence of the Community solution and the alternative. In view of these advantages, the fact that Community environmental policy has not provided novel solutions and often lags behind the expectations of environmental interest groups should not be overemphasized.

Further development of Community environmental policy is desirable. This is especially true for problems which member states acting individually can not hope to adequately address, e. g. acid rain, ozone transport, fluorocarbons, carbon dioxide, migratory species, and toxic substances. For some of these problems even the Community is in some respects too small a decisionmaking unit. Further integration is also appropriate in many other areas of industrial process regulation. Harmonized solutions for industrial process regulation would not only remove considerable distortions of competition within the Common Market but would also afford polluter states the opportunity and incentive to introduce progressive solutions that they can not realistically be expected to introduce independently.

2. Institutional Structures and Procedures

As argued in Chapter VIII and developed elsewhere in this chapter, Community environmental policy suffers from the same institutional deficiencies that dominate the Community political process as a whole. The non-public process of Community decisionmaking is dominated by member state ministers and bureaucrats. Outside access to this process is generally limited to well organized industry interests. This process is deficient in political legitimacy, and fails to generate a European constituency of broad public support for the initiatives that are adopted. To the extent that they attract attention, Community initiatives may be regarded as a circumvention of established democratic decisionmaking procedures in member states. In addition, the "filter" effect of Community decisionmaking processes and the requirement of unanimity hinder the adoption of effective progressive Community environmental initiatives. Even if such initiatives are adopted, there is little Commission authority or Community law that ensures their effective implementation once they have been incorporated into national law.

By contrast, federal initiatives in the United States must be adopted through the normal processes of representative democracy. Administrative implementation is subject to procedural rules designed to ensure access by environmental and community groups as well as by industry. Implementation gaps, while persistent, are addressed through administrative monitoring of performance and judicial remedies.

Most of the institutional problems of Community environmental policy are, however, a reflection of historical and political factors that are unlikely to change substantially in the foreseeable future. Therefore, it is highly unrealistic to propose changes in the system focusing solely on environmental policy. This is true of the proposal to grant the European Parliament legislative powers for environmental matters.[41] It would also be unrealistic to expect the member states to agree to an amendment of Articles 100 and 235 of the EEC Treaty substituting majority rule for unanimity in environmental matters.

This does not imply that marginal changes addressed to specific problems of environmental policymaking do not merit attention. For example, the lengthy and cumbersome process for implementing framework directives, such as standard setting under the surface water directive, could be ameliorated by introducing an abbreviated procedure based on the regulatory agency model. Under this approach, which is already followed in adapting environ-

[41] *But see* E. FAURE, POUR UNE POLITIQUE EUROPÉENNE DE L'ENVIRONNEMENT (Fonds européen de coopération, Brussels 1977); F. BEHRENS, *supra* note 25, at 298 *et seq.*; H. STEIGER, *supra* note 25. *See also* VON MOLTKE, *The Legal Basis for Environmental Policy*, 3 ENVT'L POL'Y & L. 136, 138 (1976).

mental directives to technical progress, the Commission, a Council working committee, or a joint body would give detailed content to framework directives. If the framework directive fixes clear general standards, the requirements of Art. 155(4) of the EEC Treaty are arguably met.[42] It is doubtful, however, whether member states would agree to such a waiver of their powers.[43] As a matter of policy, an abbreviated procedure may also be questioned as a further depoliticization of Community decisionmaking.

Another potential marginal change would be to improve the procedure established by the information/standstill agreement of 1973 for the coordination of member state and Community environmental initiatives. This procedure does not function well because the deadlines set by the agreement are too short to allow the Community to prepare legislative proposals. It has been proposed that member states be obliged to report drafts which are still in a preparatory stage so as to afford the Commission more time for formulating its own position on the draft.[44] However, this proposal ignores the realities of national political processes. National parliaments can not be barred from changing tabled legislative drafts.[45] Also, given the slow pace of Community decisionmaking, any extension of the deadline for Community reaction to a national legislative initiative will undermine the ability of member states to implement innovative environmental policies. All in all, this is probably too high a price to pay for the "intrinsic value" of integration. The marked reluctance of member states in the recent past to report drafts shows that they are not prepared to pay this price.

Procedures to mandate assessment of the environmental impacts of policy proposals made by the "mission oriented" Directorates-General of the Commission in fields such as agriculture and transport[46] could improve Community policymaking by integrating the preventive approach to environmental policy with sectoral economic policies, although the experience in the US under NEPA suggests that the effective degree of integration likely to result would be modest. A necessary requirement for making such an impact assessment effective would be to institutionalize an internal review procedure whereby the Directorate-General for Environment, Consumer Protection, and Nuclear

[42] *See* F. Behrens, *supra* note 25, at 62; P. J. Slot, *supra* note 9, at 162; Economic and Social Council, OJ No. C 131, 13 Dec. 1972, p. 29, 30 (Oct. 1972); European Parliament Resolution of 16 Oct. 1981, OJ No. C 287, 9 Sept. 1981, p. 137.

[43] For example, it is not realistic to expect member states to leave the task of setting effluent standards under the framework directive on the aquatic environment to a management committee. This is because the fundamental disagreement over effluent and water quality standards has not been overcome by letting the two strategies coexist (*see supra* at pp. 216–219) but, rather, continues to dominate the ongoing bargaining over particular standards.

[44] In this sense *see* Rat von Sachverständigen für Umweltfragen, *supra* note 37, at No. 1663.

[45] Von Moltke, *supra* note 29, at 86.

[46] As has been proposed by the European Parliament Resolution of 18 Feb. 1982, OJ No. C 66, 15 March 1982, p. 87.

Safety would comment on program proposals made by the other Commission Directorates-General. In the US, the federal EPA has similar authority to comment on the Environmental Impact Statements prepared by other federal agencies although EPA has not in recent years made much use of this authority, in part because of its extensive other responsibilities and limited resources. If an environmental assessment directive is adopted for projects initiated by member states, it may eventually be extended to Community initiatives.

Several steps might be taken to ensure better implementation and enforcement. The US Council on Environmental Quality has in the past played a very useful educational and catalytic role in promoting federal environmental initiatives by collecting and disseminating information on the implementation of existing measures and identifying priority areas where new or strengthened measures were needed. Establishment of an EC institution with this responsibility, perhaps as an independent arm of the Commission or Parliament, or by giving the responsibility to a private institute, should be explored.[47] In addition, new law could be created to guarantee environmental and neighborhood groups procedural rights to obtain judicial review of administrative decisions in member states implementing, or failing to implement, Community directives. This alternative is discussed below.

3. Strategies and Tools

The Community has emphasized "traditional" command and control regulatory strategies. Most of the strategies selected had been previously used in all or at least several member states, at least in other regulatory contexts.

There are three major deficiencies in the Community choice of strategies. First, the Community almost invariably relies on a single strategy rather than combining, in an appropriate case, two different strategies (such as ambient standards and technology-based emission standards) that would together result in more effective protection. The combination of ambient standards and nondegradation policies in pollution control represents something of an apparent exception to this generalization. However, due to the vagueness of the nondegradation principle and the lack of experience in implementing it, it has not yet matured to the point where it could be called a real strategy. Second, there is a lack of innovative strategies. Normally, the Community adopts a strategy which has been extensively used by member states. There is a marked dislike of strategies relying on economic incentives and disincentives. This lack of innovative approaches does not result from limitations inherent in the legislative powers of the Community. It arises rather from the political linkage of Community policy to national policies and the problems of implementation that would arise when introducing a novel strategy. Third, with the exception of screening of new chemicals and recent, albeit timid, attempts to limit the amount of wastes, the Community has focused on ex post facto control of pollution and neglected preventive strategies. This may once again be explained

[47] In the same sense *see* von Moltke & Haigh, *supra* note 16, at 30.

by the linkage of Community environmental policy to that of the member states, but also by the lack of Community powers over land use and natural resources.

There appears to be little in the US experience with command and control regulatory strategies that suggests ways of strengthing EC environmental policy. The choices between uniform standards and case by case screening and (within a standards approach) between ambient standards and technology based source or product controls have been played out in the EC as they have in the US. US experience might suggest the desirability of a strengthened nondegradation principle in EC air and water pollution control. However, regional competition for development; the absence of a Community system of parks or wilderness areas; and the institutional obstacles to ensuring effective implementation and enforcement through review of new sources are potential obstacles to a Community nondegradation policy. US experience also suggests that the EC should be careful not to make nondegradation requirements unrealistically stringent or excessively broad in application.

Although the high degree of centralization in US regulatory policy retards experimentation, it has recently developed "offset" and "bubble" strategies for pollution control that make promising use of economic incentives by creating transferable rights to pollute. Systems of effluent charges or pollution fees have been used by some EC member states in the context of air and water pollution, but their rejection by most states and their entanglement in fiscal policy makes their adoption by the Community unlikely. However, the US experience suggests that it might be feasible in many areas to make the transition from the existing EC regulatory system to a system of transferable pollution rights. Such a system could have a number of advantages:

- In conjunction with limits on total loadings established by reference to ambient concentrations, it provides a cost effective way to secure achievement of ambient standards or to deal with widespread transboundary spillovers.
- It provides for member state flexibility in the allocation of permits, but also provides a clear benchmark for gauging compliance and provides regulated firms with strong economic incentives to police cheating by others.
- It provides substantial incentives for the development of environmentally superior technologies. Firms that develop new, cost effective ways to reduce pollution further can profit by selling off some of their existing pollution rights.

There are a number of untested problems in implementation, but they do not appear insurmountable. Application would be limited to air and water pollution, at least at first. Broader use of the charge system now permitted by the EC waste oil directive also seems warranted. This approach could, for example, be employed for hazardous wastes.

4. Implementation and Enforcement

Community environmental policy is confronted with two major implementation and enforcement problems. Despite considerable delays, incorporation of environmental directives into national law is largely satisfactory; the infringement procedure together with the reporting obligations of member states under environmental directives affords the Commission the necessary means to control the incorporation behavior of member states. However, member states have almost exclusive control over ultimate implementation and enforcement. Except for product regulation, which is easy to enforce and where the economic interests of competitors play a major role, the normal problems of implementing environmental policies in federal states are considerably aggravated by the great diversity of national legal and administrative systems and political cultures in the Community. Member states would probably be more cautious in agreeing to new policy proposals if they could not mitigate their ultimate effects through control over the implementation and enforcement process. Nonetheless, this diversity in implementation and enforcement is a direct threat to the harmonization of environmental policies.

Implementation problems in the Community are serious. Environmental groups and the courts – national courts as well as the European Court of Justice – have so far played a negligible role in supervising implementation and enforcement of environmental directives. In contrast, environmental advocates in the US have played an important role by initiating or participating in administrative proceedings and seeking judicial review of deficient implementation and enforcement. The courts have encouraged these efforts through expanded doctrines of standing and reviewability, by giving environmental advocates procedural rights before administrative agencies, and by taking steps to remedy deficient agency performance.

Development of an integrated administrative law that would provide similar access and encouragement for environmental advocates in the EC should be undertaken. The serious nature of implementation and enforcement problems in the EC justifies such a step despite the obstacles to it.[48] An active, legally recognized role for environmental advocates will not only directly promote implementation and enforcement, but should also be important in calling public attention to unresolved environmental problems and marshalling support for corrective efforts.[49]

[48] The European Parliament has on various occasions demanded that the European Court of Justice be accorded competence as a Community court of appeal for the review of member state implementation of the Treaty and directives. *See* Resolution of 27 April 1979, OJ No. C 127, 21 May 1979, p. 69; Resolution of 14 Oct. 1981, OJ No. C 287, 9 Nov. 1981, p. 47, EP Doc 1-414/81. *See also* P. Kromarek, *supra* note 19, at 14.

[49] *See* Stein & Vining, *Citizen Access to Judicial Review of Administrative Action in a Transnational and Federal Context,* 70 Am. J. of Int'l L. 219, 241 (1976) ("... where law is made by national and transnational executives through processes shielded from the glare of publicity, the judicial role is if anything even more essential than in a mature federation. ... But as the scope of the Community regulatory powers broadens to include other fields and affect other values, economic and non-economic – health and safety, environment, consumer protection, energy conservation – the Court may well feel called upon to broaden direct access by private complainants. If it does, we

In the US, expanded rights of access and participation for environmental and other public interest advocates were largely created by federal courts, but only after an integrated federal administrative law had already developed through statutes and judicial decisions concerning the powers of federal administrative agencies directly responsible for implementation and enforcement. Moreover federal courts had already created – principally in fields other than environmental law – federal remedial law which state courts and administrative agencies are obliged to use when dealing with federal substantive law. This latter precedent suggests that the European Court of Justice might create a Community remedial law allowing litigants to challenge deficient implementation and enforcement by member states of Community directives.

However, it is not very probable that this will happen in the foreseeable future. The European Court of Justice has on various occasions held that judicial review of administrative decisions applying Community law is, in the Community's present state of development, essentially within the responsibility of member states. The principles of nondiscrimination and reasonableness and the requirement that judicial review may not be entirely excluded[50] do not exercise a substantive corrective function.

It would probably be more realistic to create a body of Community administrative law by using the normal harmonization procedure of a directive. It is clear that Art. 100 of the EEC Treaty in principle allows harmonization of national procedural law.[51] However, there is likely to be strong opposition to any such initiative. The Commission proposal for environmental impact assessment is a first step in the direction of creating an integrated body of environmental administrative law. The final Commission draft is cautious, avoiding excessive encroachment on member state law. For example, public participation is required, but its extent is left to the discretion of member states. There has nonetheless been much opposition, precisely on the ground that the proposal threatens established national practices. Procedural harmonization would have to be far reaching if the Community were to create effective transnational private rights for controlling the implementation and enforcement of

suggest that it will act not only to protect private interests but also to advance the common interest in effective enforcement of Community legality and broader participation of citizens in Community administration."). Similarly, M. Cappelletti and D. Golay consider direct judicial review as a necessary corollary to the ever increasing power of the Community towards the citizen. *See* Cappelletti & Golay, *The Judicial Branch in the Federal and Transnational Union: The Impact on Integration*, at § VI, in INTEGRATION THROUGH LAW, Vol. 1, Book 2.

[50] *See supra* at p. 158.

[51] European Court of Justice, case 33/76, Rewe-Zentralfinanz v. Landwirtschaftskammer für das Saarland, [1976] ECR 1989, 1998; E. RÖHLING, ÜBERBETRIEBLICHE TECHNISCHE NORMEN ALS NICHTTARIFÄRE HANDELSHEMMNISSE IM GEMEINSAMEN MARKT 158 (Carl Heymanns Verlag, Köln 1972); W. SCHMEDER, DIE RECHTSANGLEICHUNG ALS INTEGRATIONSINSTRUMENT IN DER EUROPÄISCHEN GEMEINSCHAFT 178–179 (Carl Heymanns Verlag, Köln 1978); SEIDEL, *Aktuelle Probleme der Rechtsangleichung gemäß Art. 100 EWG-Vertrag*, 2 EUROPARECHT 202, 208 (1967).

environmental directives. It would not be sufficient to limit harmonization to judicial review, because administrative review is much more significant in several member states. Nor would it be sufficient to simply harmonize the national law governing access to administrative and court proceedings,[52] because the problem of access to justice is closely interrelated with the powers of the agency or court, especially with respect to the scope of review. The distribution of these powers is in turn a reflection of values concerning the relationship between citizen and administration, the privileges of the executive, and the general balance of private and public interests.[53] The problem can not adequately be understood solely from the perspective of environmental or even Community law.[54] Realistically, the most that could be achieved would be a general directive granting associations standing and prescribing certain types of remedies,[55] while leaving member states a broad margin of discretion in implementing the directive. The Commission proposal for public participation in the framework of the environmental impact assessment procedure is an example of the type of general directive that could realistically by expected. Its acceptance by the Council improves the chances of future harmonization in this field.

Given the difficulties in creating transnational rights of action, it would be premature to claim that creation of new types of legal services is the solution to the problem of implementing environmental rights in the Community.[56] As long as the more modest "first generation" objective of creating transnational rights of action is not achieved and could most probably be achieved only through a directive, "second generation" problems of access to justice can not realistically be discussed.

Independent of creating transnational private rights, EC financial support for environmental groups through grants for research or preparation of handbooks on environmental problems could be undertaken.

The importance in US environmental policy of implementation and enforcement by environmentally minded federal agencies indicates that further steps to increase the Commission's role in implementation and enforcement could promote integration of environmental policy in the EC. Perhaps the closest parallel is the work of the US Environmental Protection Agency in review of state implementation plans under the Clean Air Act. Although primary implementation and enforcement responsibility was given to the states, compliance with federal requirements was regularly reviewed and certified by a federal agency.

Given the precedents set in some recent directives that accord the Commission a substantial role in supervising member state setting of standards or

[52] The Commission once considered the introduction of association standing. *See* Commission, State of the Community Environment, Second Report (1979), at 74.

[53] *See supra* at p. 157.

[54] W. SCHMEDER, *supra* note 51, at 36.

[55] *Id.* at 175 *et seq.*, in particular at 178–179.

[56] *Contra*, ECONOMIDES & WEILER, *Accession of the European Communities to the European Convention on Human Rights*, 42 MODERN L. REV. 683, 694 (1979).

establishment of improvement plans, it would seem that there are no insurmountable obstacles to generally increasing the role of the Commission in implementation and enforcement. However, such a new role would necessarily require some departure by the Commission from its mission as initiator of policy proposals and legislation – a mission which in the past has perhaps misled the Commission into overproduction of proposals for new directives and neglect of the problems of implementation and enforcement.

5. Transboundary Pollution

In the Community, transboundary water pollution was a primary rationale for initial Community involvement in environmental protection. However, with the gradual development of environmental policy as a separate common policy, this rationale has lost much of its significance as a force for integration. The Community has not been able to develop clear substantive rules governing transboundary pollution conflicts. The trend has been toward Community controlled or encouraged cooperation among states. Many directives contain consultation obligations in case of transboundary spillovers. There is also a growing number of new or amended conventions providing for practical cooperation of the parties concerned, especially in the case of marine and international river pollution, to which member states and sometimes also the Community are parties. However, there remain politically sensitive transboundary spillover problems, especially those associated with the siting of nuclear power plants, major chemical plants (chemical accidents), and larger polluting installations (forest damage), where not all member states were or are willing to accept commitments for supranational conflict resolution.

In the US, the problem of transboundary spillovers has been a major proclaimed rationale for adoption of environmental measures by the federal government. However, federal statutes and administrative regulations tend to adopt uniform solutions for pollution problems which may not be responsive to particular transboundary spillover problems. Moreover, broad scale spillover problems, such as acid rain, can not be adequately dealt with under existing regulatory strategies. Congress and federal administrators have been reluctant to address politically charged interstate or inter-region controversies directly.

It appeared for a while that the federal courts would take a leading role in dealing with transboundary spillovers through a federal common law of interstate pollution. These judicial initiatives could be expected to stimulate legislative and administrative response to transboundary problems. But the Supreme Court has recently signalled retreat from such initiatives by indicating great willingness to find judge-made federal common law preempted by federal regulatory statutes.[57]

The US experience is not encouraging for the proposition that transboundary problems will stimulate development of an integrated environmental law. There are, however, two factors that might justify a somewhat more hopeful

[57] City of Milwaukee v. Illinois, 451 U.S. 304 (1981).

prognosis in the EC. First, with the adoption of additional directives – particularly those, like the SO_2 limit values directive, framed in sweeping yet vague terms – there will be more grounds for the claim by a receptor member state or the Commission against an originating member state that the spillover results from infringement of a directive. Such claims will ultimately be determined by the European Court of Justice, which has proven anxious to further integration, rather than by administrative officials shy of sharp controversy among member states. Second, there has been more use of compacts among EC member states to deal with problems such as interstate water pollution than in the US. These may be regarded as a step toward integration, and EC environmental initiatives must be harmonized with them. In the past, however, member states have carefully avoided suit against each other for infringement of directives. The need to continue cooperation and negotiation on a variety of issues within the framework of existing compacts has spawned a reluctance to institute court proceedings. It is also doubtful whether the Commission can be expected to institute infringement proceedings in highly politicized conflicts of transboundary pollution. Thus, there is arguably greater opportunity to deal with transboundary pollution conflicts through interstate consultation and cooperation than through supranational decisionmaking and an active judicial role.

6. Outlook

During the debate in 1980 on the West German toxic substances bill, the government sought to claim political credit for several provisions in a proposed regulation on chemicals without making it clear that it was just incorporating the sixth amendment of the EC directive on toxic substances into national law. Opponents of the bill called for stiffer controls, which in some respects were clearly inconsistent with the directive, and in other respects were arguably preempted because the directive might be considered to have occupied the field of chemicals regulation.[58] Nothing could show more clearly that Community environmental policy has no true constituency among, and no symbolic value for, the peoples of Europe. This represents a sharp contrast with the US, where national environmental issues often generate strong views among citizens; this phenomenon ultimately reflects a sense of nationhood in which all share a common destiny and choice.

The formulation of the European interest that justifies shifting a regulatory problem from the national to the supranational level is based on utilitarian considerations rather than on any idealistic commitment to an "intrinsic

[58] *See* Hartkopf, *Chemikaliengesetz vom Deutschen Bundestag verabschiedet*, 78 Umwelt, Mitteilungen des Bundesministers des Inneren 10 (12 Sept. 1980); Deutscher Bundestag, 8. Wahlperiode, Unterausschuß "Chemikaliengesetz" des Ausschusses für Jugend, Familie und Gesundheit, Protokoll über die öffentliche Anhörung, 3–4 March 1980 (Protokoll Nr. 4); *but see* Deutscher Bundestag, 8. Wahlperiode, 225. Sitzung (25 June 1980), at 18173, 18175, 18179, 18185 where several speakers stress the limitations originating from Community law.

value" of integration. It is only when member state governments and societal groups influencing their decisions consider the Community as the better decisionmaking level – because new barriers to trade or distortions of competition are to be avoided, because a genuine international problem is to be tackled, or because a progressive state solution embodied in a Commission proposal suggests a departure from normal domestic legislative procedures – that the governments agree to a transfer of national competences and accept a supranational solution.[59]

Unless in a particular case a member state has paramount countervailing interests, this approach allows for some further development of Community environmental law – if not an expansion into entirely new areas, then at least a certain *approfondissement* of existing legislation along the lines devised by the environmental program. The marked retardation of Community legislation since 1980 indicates that this progress will be slower than in previous years. As long as the contents of the supranational solutions are on average not greatly superior to national ones[60] and as long as the lack of political participation of the electorate and societal groups concerned about the environment in the Community decisionmaking process perpetuates a "democracy deficit," there is a real danger that further development of Community environmental law will be regarded as illegitimate. Such illegitimacy will ultimately strengthen disintegrative forces. Such forces already threaten economic integration in areas mandated by clear Treaty provisions, such as elimination of trade barriers.[61]

Environmental policy stands in even greater need of political legitimacy than trade and commercial policies forming the "classic" field of European integration.[62] This is so because environmental policy is not explicitly legitimized by the Treaty and, due to lack of suitable decision criteria, can not ultimately be legitimized by resort to legal rules alone. Further, the contents of environmental policy can not be derived by recourse to the market process.

This assessment shows that European integration can not easily be separated into several independent elements such as decisional (institutional), legal, and substantive integration. Without decisional legitimacy, the process of substantive *approfondissement*, to which Community environmental law has contributed so much, may ultimately be threatened.[63] Without substantive legitimacy based on superiority of solutions, the effects of continuing legal integration in the field of environmental protection may be increasingly resented. If this as-

[59] *See* H. BUNGARTEN, *supra* note 5, at 111 *et seq.*

[60] *Cf.* Krislov, Ehlermann & Weiler, *supra* note 14, at note 46 ("In the Community... [the principle of subsidiarity] has been said to operate in the negative sense: The Community should not have competence unless it can be demonstrated that exercise at Community level will be better").

[61] *E. g.*, unilateral restrictions of trade recently introduced by some member states; *see* DERINGER & SEDEMUND, *Europäisches Gemeinschaftsrecht*, 35 NEUE JURISTISCHE WOCHENSCHRIFT 1189–1190 (1981).

[62] J. Weiler, *supra* note 30, at 43–44.

[63] *See* H. BUNGARTEN, *supra* note 5, at 157 *et seq.*

sessment is correct, we should be cautious in advocating more harmonization in the field of environmental protection as long as the basic process of Community decisionmaking remains unchanged. As stated earlier, there are important areas of environmental policy where further harmonization is desirable in principle. These include international problems that can only be addressed transnationally, although even the Community is sometimes too small a decisionmaking unit. There are other environmental problems where divergent national measures leading to interference with the Common Market or the delay of some member states in addressing these problems justify Community commitment. Further attention to implementation and enforcement of existing directives is needed. But steps to accomplish these objectives must be tempered by an awareness of the fragile legitimacy of existing Community institutions and of the potential negative effects of harmonization on initiatives by member states.[64] In some cases, coordination and encouragement of national measures may be sufficient.[65] In other cases, concentration of pollution control measures on densely populated and highly polluted "action regions"[66] may be worth trying. This form of regionalization of pollution control is preferable to any kind of regionalization along national boundaries because it does not compromise political and economic integration, while taking into account environmental diversity. On the other hand, any concept of a "two tier" environmental policy that separates member states into "environmental" and "polluter" states according to their geographical closeness to the center of the Community[67] should be rejected. Its simplicity conceals that the state of the environment and even environmental values are not congruent with national territories. Besides such reorientation of harmonization policy, efforts to open the existing process of Community decision and to develop a European constituency must also continue.

[64] WEIDNER & KNOEPFEL, *supra* note 29, at 63 *et seq. See generally* H. W. ROTH, *supra* note 9, at 327.

[65] *See* Bungarten, *Umweltpolitische Aspekte einer europäischen Integration*, in MÖGLICHKEITEN UND GRENZEN EINER EUROPÄISCHEN UNION, vol. 2, at 165 *et seq.* (H. von der Groeben & H. Möller eds., Nomos Verlag, Baden-Baden 1976).

[66] P. Kromarek, *supra* note 19, at 12.

[67] *Contra*, WEINSTOCK, *Nur eine europäische Umwelt? Europäische Umweltpolitik im Spannungsverhältnis zwischen ökologischer Vielfalt und ökonomischer Einheit*, 6 ZEITSCHRIFT FÜR UMWELTPOLITIK 1, at 34 *et seq.* (1983).

Index

Integration Through Law

Europe and the American Federal Experience

A Series under the General Editorship of

Mauro Cappelletti · Monica Seccombe · Joseph Weiler

Part One

Volume 1

Methods, Tools and Institutions

edited by Mauro Cappelletti, Monica Seccombe & Joseph Weiler

Book 1: A Political, Legal and Economic Overview
Book 2: Political Organs, Integration Techniques and Judicial Process
Book 3: Forces and Potential for a European Identity

Part Two

Integration Policies in Selected Areas

Volumes 2—6

Volume 2: Environmental Protection Policy
by
Eckard Rehbinder & Richard Stewart

Volume 3: Consumer Law, Common Markets and Federalism in Europe and the United States
by
Thierry Bourgoignie & David Trubek (with Louise Trubek & Denis Stingl)

Volume 4: Legal Harmonization and the Business Enterprise: Corporate Law and Capital Market Harmonization Policy in Europe and the U.S.A.
by
Richard Buxbaum & Klaus J. Hopt

Volume 5: The Legal Integration of Energy Markets
by
Terence Daintith & Stephen Williams

Volume 6: Regionalism and Federalism: The Challenge of Regions in National and Transnational Polities
by
Yves Mény, Bruno De Witte & Jerry Webman

www.ingramcontent.com/pod-product-compliance
Lightning Source LLC
LaVergne TN
LVHW091042021026
849161LV00002BA/279